Forty Years Against the Tide

CONGRESS AND THE WELFARE STATE

by Carl T. Curtis
and Regis Courtemanche

REGNERY GATEWAY

Regnery Books is an imprint of Regnery Gateway, Inc. All inquiries concerning this book should be directed to Regnery Gateway, Inc., 950 North Shore Drive, Lake Bluff, IL 60044.

Library of Congress Cataloging-in Publication Data

Curtis, Carl T. (Carl Thomas), 1905-
    40 years against the tide.

    Bibliography: p.
    Includes index.
    1. Curtis, Carl T. (Carl Thomas), 1905- .
2. Legislators—United States—Biography. 3. United
States. Congress—Biography. 4. United States—Foreign
relations—1933-1945. 5. United States—Politics and
government—1945- . I. Courtemanche, Regis A.
II. Title. III. Title: Forty years against the tide.
E748.C9815A34 1986   328.73'092'4 [B]   85-14500
ISBN 0-89526-590-7

2

ACKNOWLEDGEMENTS

The authors thank those who have helped in bringing this book to completion. Without the help of Mildred Curtis, this book could not have appeared. To the law firm of Nelson and Harding, with its secretarial staff, Carl Curtis is much indebted. Senator Curtis and Dr. Courtemanche are grateful to The Educational Reviewer, Inc., for its sponsorship of the research and writing necessary for this historical study; and to the foundations, corporations, and friends that helped to supply funding for the project.

DEDICATION

This book is dedicated to the memory of the founders of our Republic, and to all those who, down through the years, have sought valiantly to keep our republican form of government.

CONTENTS

FOREWORD

by Russell Kirk

Nothing is deader than dead politics, we are told. Certainly this aphorism is true of the memoirs of most public men. For that matter, books about the political experiences of members of the Congress of the United States have been curiously, yet perhaps mercifully, few, considering that some eleven thousand persons have sat in Senate or House since the Constitution was ratified.

Of such memoirs, chiefly two are still consulted by historians: Thomas Hart Benton' s *Thirty Years' View* (two massive volumes, double columns, small print, 365 chapters, 1854) and James G. Blaine's *Twenty Years of Congress* (two volumes, 1884-86). Now we are presented with this political history by Carl Curtis and Regis Courtemanche, in a single volume, covering forty years of congressional activity during a period even more eventful, for good or ill, than the ages of Benton and Blaine. Senator Curtis has not been so picturesque a figure as either Benton or Blaine; but Curtis' well-written account of four decades in Congress surely will endure as a perceptive work of high value to readers seriously interested in the course of the Republic.

Carl Curtis was a member of House or Senate from the administration of President Franklin Roosevelt through the middle of President Carter's administration, never losing an election during that whole period. In foreign affairs, he held office from the approach of the Second World War to the captivity of American hostages in Iran; in domestic affairs, from the controversies of the New Deal to the revival of America's conservative character. As Mr. Curtis puts it, he contended against the tide of events all those decades. And he knew everybody of influence in national politics.

In this book, Curtis and Courtemanche emphasize certain grand issues and struggles of the age, particularly the coming of America's welfare state. They take up successively the attempt to maintain America's neutrality during the Second

9

World War and the government's neutrality in economic disputes; flood control and irrigation in mid-America; feeding a proletariat; growth of federal housing programs; deficit financing; the investigations of labor rackets, Billie Sol Estes, and Bobby Baker; the Goldwater campaign; Medicare; Social Security and the IRA (this latter the creation of Senator Curtis); the fall of President Nixon; political parties and principles in our day. In all of these measures and controversies, Carl Curtis was a principal participant.

In part, this vigorous piece of political history is an account of resistance to what Alexis de Tocqueville called "democratic despotism." Curtis was a determined and informed opponent, on conservative grounds, of the New Deal, the Fair Deal, the New Frontier, and the Great Society. He set his face against expansion of government's activities in many fields, and against the overwhelming increase of the national debt, deficit financing, inflation of the currency, and the centralization of power. A chief value of this book is its detailed examination of the Congress' gradual creation or acceptance of an American welfare state.

Carl Curtis did more than oppose the seeming wave of the future. During these four stormy decades he was a successful advocate of economic and technological measures that would permanently increase the nation's prosperity. And he was the principal architect of the Individual Retirement Act, a measure to preserve independent savings and private enterprise.

In the Senate, Carl Curtis was the ranking minority member of four major committees: rules and administration, aeronautic and space sciences, agriculture and forestry, and finance. For four years he served as chairman of the Senate Republican Conference. He directed the fight to nominate Barry Goldwater for the presidency at the Republican National Convention of 1964. He led the resistance in the Senate to the harassing of President Nixon. The stocky figure of Carl Curtis—called "the little tiger" by Senator Goldwater—was highly important in Republican councils, a stable power in unstable times. Unassuming, good-natured, and accustomed to endless labors as a public man, Curtis has been a pillar, rather than a Corinthian ornament, of the American Republic.

When one talks about Carl Curtis with people who have known him, in Washington or in Nebraska, the term that recurs is "integrity." Leaders of both parties testify heartily to Curtis' honesty and consistency throughout his eight terms in the House and four terms in the Senate. In a scandalous time, not one scandal touched him. Curtis entered Congress a man of modest means and departed a man of modest means, taking advantage of none of the numerous opportunities to profit through political influence that are offered even to inconspicuous members of Senate and House. He lived in what is said to have been the smallest Washington house inhabited by any senator in this century, entertaining friends in homely fashion in a little quondam recreation-room. Washington was a huge pool of money entirely surrounded by people who desired some of it, and who were not overly scrupulous as to means for acquiring it. In such concerns, too, Carl Curtis strove against the tide. He has much to say in this book about corruption; were he not a kindly man, he might say more.

Curtis did what he could to restrain governmental profligacy. When he first went to Washington, the federal budget amounted to less than twelve billion dollars; when he retired from public life, that budget was approaching four hundred billion dollars. In his efforts to make the federal government responsibly frugal, he often spoke to deaf ears. In 1949, for instance, Curtis warned Congress that unless reforms were adopted in the Social Security programs, Social Security payments would soon total thirty billion dollars annually. By 1984, Social Security expenditures totaled $227.6 billion for the year, more than one-fourth of all the taxes collected by the federal Treasury that year.

For thirty-six of his forty years in the Congress, Curtis was a member of the minority in either House or Senate. Thus he did not become the chairman of committees; but he was the ranking minority member of powerful committees in both houses and so was able to offer opposition, often effectual, to many of the political illusions and blunders of the era.

Yes, Carl Curtis' political years were years of personal integrity. In 1982, retired, Curtis published *To Remind*, a daily devotional for the entire year. (He is an earnest Presbyterian.)

His entry for February 13 is "A Good Name":

> A good name is a valuable asset. A business con-
> cern which has earned a good name through quality
> merchandise, dependable service, and honest deal-
> ings enjoys a good business and the respect of all who
> know of them. A good name for a boy or a girl, a young
> man or a young woman, a mature adult or someone
> in his closing years is indeed a treasure. It takes one
> a lifetime to acquire a good name, but one decision
> resulting in one act can lose it.
>
> Parents and grandparents who build a life which
> earns a good name pass on a valuable inheritance to
> their children. Neighbors, farmers, townspeople,
> teachers, and students, and all are given the oppor-
> tunity to earn a good name. The voters consider a good
> name as the first essential for holding a public trust.
> Our Book of Rules instructs us to acquire a good name.
> In Proverbs we read, "A good name is rather to be cho-
> sen than great riches." And, "The memory of the just
> is blessed." In Ecclesiastes we read, "A good name
> is better than precious ointment; and the day of death
> than the day of one's birth."
>
> Prayer: Our Father, may we as followers honor
> Thee by striving for a good name. In Jesus' name.
> Amen.

As all Christians should, Carl Curtis calls himself a sin-
ner. Yet surely he has been one of the least sinful public men
of our time; he has deserved his good name.

And this book, the joint production of a good politician
and an experienced historian, deserves the attention of everyone who endeavors to understand the events and the arguments
of American politics for four decades. To see that period
through the eyes of Carl Curtis is to employ the vision of an
honest man, regardless of whether one assents to his conclusions.

Mr. Curtis is no sanctimonious "political Christian." In

his devotion for June 26, "For Politicians Only", he touches on political humility:

> The politician knows that if he prays or makes a contribution or utters a religious statement to be seen and heard of men that he will attract many more votes than he will alienate. In order for a candidate to be elected, he may well be tempted to adroitly do some bragging. After he is elected, those who wish to impress him may use the weapon of flattery. All of which may cause him to be proud, vain, and egotistical. There is help, however, for the politician and all others who are tempted. "For I say . . . to every man . . . not to think more highly of himself than he ought to think." "All of you . . . be clothed with humility, for God resisteth the proud, and giveth grace to the humble." "There hath no temptation taken you but such as is common to man, but God is faithful, who will not permit you to be tempted above that ye are able . . . but will make the way of escape that ye may be able to bear it.'''

In this book, as in his congressional service, Curtis puts down vanity. He and Dr. Courtemanche have not space enough to tell us everything about the pomps and vanities, the successes and failures, of national politics from 1939 to 1979; but they do inform us most helpfully about those large questions and controversies of which Carl Curtis had close acquaintance. This is no exercise in dead politics: the issues discussed in this book will be quick the rest of this century and well beyond that. Curtis was on the losing side in many important decisions made by the Senate or House. Yet as he writes in his little devotion "Who Is in Charge?" (almost as T. S. Eliot put the same thought), "What seems to be a lost cause may have been a temporary defeat. The losers may influence the future more than they realize . . . Our God is still the God of history, and He can fashion both men and events to His will."

Curtis could no more turn back the tide than could King

Canute. Yet this book remains a hopeful political history, addressed not to what Santayana called "the running tide of our prosperity and triviality," but rather to the chastened and thoughtful America that today seems to be taking shape.

Chapter 1

The Road To Washington

THE EVE OF
AN EXPLOSION

In Nebraska's primary of August 8, 1938, a young country lawyer named Carl T. Curtis won the Republican nomination to the House of Representatives from the Fourth Congressional District. It was his first step toward four decades in the Congress of the United States.

We need first to paint the background of this picture: in the world, in the United States, and in Curtis' hometown of Minden, Nebraska.

Wars and rumors of wars, remote from Minden and insufficiently understood by most Americans, afflicted the world in that last year before a general catastrophe which would shake every continent from 1939 to 1945. The fierce fighting in China, Spain, and Ethiopia, during 1938, was merely a prelude.

In 1938, dictators and military juntas seemed to be sweeping everything before them. French governments were formed, and then fell, with monotonous feebleness. In Britain, Chamberlain's policy of appeasement, approved by most British subjects, was faltering toward disaster.

In February, 1938, the foreign secretary, Anthony Eden, resigned in protest against the policy of appeasement. "I must confess that my heart sank," Winston Churchill wrote of Eden's resignation, "and for a while the dark waters of despair overwhelmed me."

In the Third Reich, Hitler's new public buildings, strength-through-joy style, were rising near the burnt shell of the Reichstag; his Chancellery was the jewel. Before reaching the Fuehrer, one had to walk the length of a gallery four hundred and eighty feet long—twice the length of Versailles' Hall of Mirrors, Hitler boasted.

That March, Hitler brushed aside his generals' warning against a seizure of Austria. Kurt von Schuschnigg, the Austrian chancellor, courageously resisted through diplomacy, so long as possible, even scheduling a plebiscite to determine whether Austrians desired union with Germany. Only the menace of immediate invasion caused Schuschnigg to cancel the plebiscite. He would spend the next six years in a concentration camp as punishment for his audacity.

In the spring Hitler entered Vienna, the city of his youthful failures. His reoccupation of the Rhineland had occurred two years earlier. In March, the Archbishop of Canterbury had told the House of Lords, "The Treaty of Versailles was vindictive and arbitrary and could not possibly be permanent. The union of Germany and Austria was inevitable. I think it is plain that the union does receive the support of the great majority of the Austrian people."

Among appeasement's other supporters were the editor of the London *Times*; the economist John Maynard Keynes; and many other leaders of opinion in the British dominions. They accepted Germany as the natural dominating power in central Europe. Hitler was visited by the Duke of Windsor, Herbert Hoover, and other notables.

Yet somewhere in the background a bell tolled. The world waited for Adolf Hitler's next move, as if anticipating a boxer's blow. The Nazis' treatment of the Jews—although the extermination camps for Jews had not yet been constructed—roused American feeling against Hitler; and as the British historian A.J.P. Taylor remarks, the Nazi persecution of the Jews did more than anything else to turn English feeling against Germany.

In the Soviet Union, the purge-trials of the Old Bolsheviks dragged on. In his paranoia, Josef Stalin was decimating the army and the navy, executing senior officers in batches. Admiral Orloff, once commander of the Red Navy, was shot in August. The charge against him: planning for a defensive war, rather than an offensive one. The consequence of this, when Germany invaded Russia in 1941, would be a German advance of hundreds of miles within a few weeks.

Many intellectuals in Europe and America were proud, in 1938, to follow the Communist Party line. They took the Red dictatorship to be the champion of the working classes. The inverted religion of Communism, with its record of oppression and slaughter, was veiled by a propaganda effort that deceived both the worldly and the gullible. As Lincoln Steffens said of Marxist Russia, "I have seen the future and it works."

Spain was a test. There the American volunteers of the Abraham Lincoln Brigade fought and died for a utopian vision of a workers' state. In February, twenty-six United States senators and thirty-four representatives sent greetings to the Loyalist government of Spain. Yet General Franco, with his German and Italian allies, would crush the Reds in 1939.

In May , 1938, Hitler traveled through the Brenner Pass to Rome and Naples, cementing his alliance with Benito Mussolini, whom he called "the last Roman." The Duce had held power for sixteen years. "He made the trains run on time" and drained the Pontine marshes; he had crushed all opposition within Italy. By the time of Hitler's visit, the Italians had taken Addis Ababa, and the Emperor of Ethiopia had been carried to Palestine on a British cruiser. The future, it seemed, belonged to the Axis Powers.

Late that spring, the Czechoslovakian government, calling up armed reserves, sent nearly four hundred thousand troops to the German border. The Sudeten Germans, three and a half million of them, were seeking union with the Third Reich.

Yet life proceeded placidly enough in western Europe and in America. George VI of England and his Queen, visiting Versailles in the summer of 1938, lunched in seventeenth-century fashion in the Hall of Mirrors. The waiters wore appropriate costumes, and President Lebrun escorted king and queen about the park, where they "discovered nymphs and shepherds dancing in Apollo's Grove with white sheep as a chorus."

President Roosevelt sailed on a fishing expedition that July, landing at the Galapagos Islands, made famous by Charles Darwin. At Henry Ford's celebration of his seventy-fifth birthday, eight thousand children sang "Happy Birthday"; and Hitler sent Ford the Grand Cross of the German Eagle. In the autumn, the same distinction would be bestowed upon Charles Lindbergh, to his later regret.

In the course of these pleasantries, German shipyards launched their first battleship since 1918, the *Gneisenau*; also the new cruiser *Prinz Eugen*. War games and maneuvers occurred during 1938, Germany, Belgium, France, Britain, and the United States holding such exercises. In September, the French government confidently announced that their defenses in these games had held against a conceivable German invasion through Switzerland. That autumn, at Munich, Hitler would obtain from Britain and France their assent to his annexation of the Sudetenland.

On the other side of the world, Japan was triumphant. Since the summer of 1937, Japan had enlarged military operations in China: now there was a full-scale war with millions of men fighting. The famous photograph of a Chinese baby crying in the ruins of a railway station epitomized this suffering. The United States protested Japan's ignoring of the Open Door policy, but did nothing. Japan's imperial forces learned how to campaign on a grand scale.

Few Americans shared the antipathy toward Japan that animated Secretary of State Hull. Ten days distant from San Francisco by liner, Japan seemed no menace. Still, in the summer of 1938, the American League of Women Shoppers demanded a boycott of Japanese silk goods because of atrocities in China. At once they were opposed by the American Federation of Hosiery Workers, hundreds of the Federation's members marching with placards that proclaimed "Wear Silk Stockings, Save Our Jobs." Nylon, destined to supplant silk hose, appeared on the market for the first time that year, as toothbrush bristles.

The Japanese military government was not wholly unmindful of growing American unease. In 1938, Japan paid the United States government two million dollars, reparation for Japanese destruction of the American gunboat *Panay*, sunk in Chinese waters by naval bombers in 1937. American naval exercises in the Pacific during 1938 included a "game" attack on Pearl Harbor, launched by Admiral King's carrier *Saratoga* and supporting vessels; the direction and the tactics would be employed from the northwest by Admiral Yamamoto in 1941.

Although most Americans disliked the Nazis and the Japanese militarists, an overwhelming majority wished to stay out of European and Asiatic conflicts. A Gallup poll in 1938 showed that ninety-four percent of its sample held this conviction. The American public would be much relieved by the news of the Munich settlement with Hitler at the end of September.

In America, regional sentiments strongly influenced attitudes toward international affairs. Much of the Northeast and the Southeast, with strong British sympathies, grew alarmed at the successes of the Axis Powers. Much of the Middle West and the Far West was mindful of George Washington's warning against foreign entanglements.

People of Germanic ancestry were numerous in America's heartland, including Nebraska; and the prevalent feeling there was that the United States had been lured into the First World War by eastern bankers and industrialists, perhaps by eastern munitions-makers, Taylor Caldwell's "merchants of death." Then there was the question of European states' debts to America: this stuck in the craw. Children learned from their parents that Europeans seemed to be welchers generally: "only the Finns pay their debts."

Such was the condition of the world on the eve of a general explosion, when Carl Curtis defeated two other candidates for the Fourth District's Republican nomination to Congress.

THE UNITED STATES AND MINDEN, 1938

It was a year of deprivation and discontent in the American Republic, coast to coast—and in Nebraska especially. Washington seemed incapable of setting things aright.

The Great Depression, more than eight years old, grew worse in 1938: the pump-priming endeavors of the early New Deal had not reinvigorated the national economy. In April, President Franklin Roosevelt sent a special message to Congress, requesting enough funds to double the Works Progress Administration (intended to create temporary, if unproductive, employment) and more money for the Farm Security Administration, the National Youth Administration, and the Civilian Conservation Corps. Earlier in 1938, at a Jackson Day dinner, Roosevelt had denounced "the mere handful of businessmen, industrialists, and bankers who are contending to the last ditch to retain autocratic control of the industry and finances of the country."

These were times of prolonged, ruinous drought in the Plains States. It was not merely that farmers raised only poor crops or short crops: for several years there were next to no crops in large regions. Nebraska lay in the Dust Bowl. The state had been tormented by flood as well as by drought: the terrible Republican River disaster in the spring of 1935, which had drowned more than a hundred people and had devastated the Republican Valley, a hundred miles of it. (Flood control and irrigation became primary concerns of Curtis when he was sent to Congress.)

Like other states of the Great Plains, Nebraska had been smitten sorely by crop failures, year after year, for lack of rain, causing migration out of the state. Some Nebraskan counties had lost as much as a quarter of their population. The Great Depression merely added to the afflictions of farmers, merchants, and the whole population of an agricultural state.

For the Republican Party, too, times were hard. Nationally, Republicans endured their own political drought. Of the ninety-six United States senators in 1938, only seventeen were Republicans. In the House of Representatives, of 435 members, only eighty-nine were Republicans. Two years earlier, in the presidential election, Roosevelt had carried forty-six of the forty-eight states, with 29,757,300 votes to Alf Landon's 16,884,231. The editorial writers of leading newspapers suggested that the Republican Party might dissolve altogether, for lack of leadership and a coherent program. Roosevelt's "Brains Trust" at the White House, on the other hand, was fertile in new ideas, even if many of their proposals were wondrously impractical.

Nothing succeeds like success: popular support flocked to the winning party. Democratic men and measures dominated the news, the Chambers of Commerce, the farm organizations, the whole political tone and temper of the year. It seemed as if the only money available flowed out of Washington— spending, giving, loaning, hiring. In a Fireside Chat on June 24, 1938, Roosevelt made clear his plan to support only liberal Democrats, purging the Democratic Party of the conservatives he called "yes-but fellows."

It was the sixth year of the New Deal. FDR, fifty-six years old in 1938, might be adored or reviled, but never ignored. The Agricultural Adjustment Act; the Federal Securities Act; the Public Utility Holding Company Act; the Tennessee Valley Authority; the Home Owners Loan Corporation; the National Industrial Recovery Act; the Public Works Administration; the Social Security Act—some of these programs required public expenditure on a scale previously inconceivable.

The national debt, $22.5 billion in 1933, would rise by 1940 to nearly $43 billion. Soon there would be more than a million federal civil servants. The Social Security Act, the federal insuring of bank deposits, and various other New Deal measures were undoubtedly popular in 1939. In Roosevelt's phrase, "We will spend and spend, elect and elect."

Yet in 1938, shrewd observers might have detected a widespread uneasiness with the New Deal. Thereafter President Roosevelt's proposals did not enjoy smooth sailing. As Vice-

President Garner had said to FDR, "You know, you've got to let the cattle graze." The President had not been able to persuade Congress, in 1937, to approve his design for enlarging the Supreme Court—those obdurate "nine old men"—by appointing more justices who would favor New Deal measures.

Economically, 1938 was the Roosevelt Recession. Unemployment averaged eleven million; half a million more people would find themselves unemployed by 1939. In those years, an unemployed person was usually the sole breadwinner of the family. Employment of married women was discouraged, supposing their husbands to be employed. And it should be remembered that in 1938 the American population had reached only a hundred and twenty million; therefore eleven million unemployed in 1939 loomed up more grimly than would the same number of unemployed in 1985, with a present population of two hundred thirty million. Besides, in 1985 it is not uncommon to find two to four wage earners in the same household, so that today, when one individual falls out of employment, this may not dismay a household as much as it did in the 1930s.

Business failures were increasing very rapidly during 1938. The issuance of securities, which had attained a monthly average of almost a hundred million dollars in 1937, abruptly dropped to a monthly average of less than forty-one million dollars in 1938. Only the beginning of the Second World War in Europe, with its huge orders from belligerents for everything America could produce, would revive the prosperity of the United States and rescue the New Dealers from their economic perplexities.

Nevertheless, neither troubles abroad nor political and economic disputes within the United States obsessed the minds of most Americans in 1938. That was the year when Thornton Wilder's play *Our Town* was produced and published. America, in large part, still resembled the town of Grover's Corners created by Wilder's moral imagination. Not until World War II was won did there come to pass the domination of America by sprawling suburbs.

Carl Curtis grew up in a town not unlike Grover's Corners. Minden, the seat of Kearney County, in south-central

Nebraska's tremendous windswept prairie, had grown in population by merely five hundred since Curtis had been born near there in 1905. Two simple, pleasant dwellings of the Curtis family—one of them Carl Curtis' residence during his congressional decades—still stand on the very edge of the little town. A one-room schoolhouse, very like the school Carl attended, can be seen in Minden's "Pioneer Village" created by Curtis' friend Harold Warp; also a "kitchen of 1910" strongly resembling the kitchen of the elder Curtises.

The small town of Minden, characteristic of county seats across the face of rural America, centers on its courthouse square. In front of the courthouse stands the Civil War monument, flanked by gatling guns. As Kearney County's attorney, Carl Curtis first made a name for himself in the courthouse. Minden suited Carl Curtis, and he suited Minden. "He did everything for everybody," both Republicans and Democrats in Minden still say of Curtis.

The town is dependent upon agriculture. Now, as then, grain elevators tower above the place. The American Legion Hall is the great center for gatherings, with lunches and dinners of Swedish meatballs, corn, and potatoes. Despite the smallness of the town, somehow Minden has been a nursery and a stamping-ground of Nebraska politicians, both Republican and Democratic.

The newest thing in Minden, about 1938, was heating by natural gas, piped from Kansas; the coal dealers resisted this innovation as best they could. Minden was a conservative county seat; Roosevelt's New Deal was suspect.

Like most county towns, Minden was not prosperous in 1938. The Omaha livestock market was paying $12.00 to $13.50 per hundredweight for corn-fed steers; hogs brought $6.15 to $6.30 per hundredweight. Yet if commodity prices were low, so were prices at the shops. About the time Minden saw Carl Curtis off to Washington, sliced bacon cost 19¢ a pound; if one bought the whole slab, the price fell to 16¢ a pound. Pork chops were 19¢ a pound; a pork roast, 17¢ a pound.

One pound of wieners cost 19¢; a peck of potatoes, 30¢; two pounds of cheese, 46¢; two pounds of peanut butter, 24¢; two pounds of raisins, 15¢; two pounds of prunes, 15¢; fifteen cans of fancy corn, a dollar; peas, 10¢ a can; fresh strawberries, 15¢ a pint; a dozen cookies, 10¢; twenty-five pounds of sugar, $1.25; flour, twenty-four pounds for 63¢.

Carl Curtis kept a keen eye on commodity prices and retail prices, then and later. Butternut Coffee was sold for 28¢ a pound, but one could buy other good coffee for as little as 16¢. Crisco was 51¢ a can; Proctor and Gamble soap, ten bars for 33¢; Oxydol soap powder, two boxes for 39¢; Crackerjack, 3¢ a box. Small Babe Ruth and O'Henry candy bars cost a penny apiece.

Or consider the prices in a men's clothing store: suits, $13.88 to $22.50; a dress shirt, 98¢; three work shirts, a dollar; overalls, a dollar.

A new Ford coupe was $584, plus freight and taxes. Tires cost $9.12 apiece. During price wars between filling stations, in some towns the price of gasoline sank as low as ten gallons for a dollar. On Main Street, a twenty-dollar bill would stretch a long way.

But then, the minimum wage, set by federal statute, was thirty uninflated cents per hour, in 1938.

The Minden Courier, a weekly paper, ran an advertisement promoting its own circulation. The Courier offered a year's subscription—fifty-two issues—and as a bonus, the subscriber's choice, at no added cost, of any three magazines selected from a long list of publications, among them The American Boy, The American Girl, McCall's, Better Homes and Gardens, True Confessions. Total price, for a year of the Courier and any three monthlies, was $2.70.

Newspapers and magazines still were strong influences on the typical family of Minden or Grover's Corners. But in Minden, as elsewhere, the radio broadcasters increasingly formed public taste and opinion: less at Minden than elsewhere, perhaps, there being a single radio station in the Fourth Congressional District in 1938. The movies loomed large for most folk. At the Gem Theater, Minden, an especially popular film that year was Sweethearts, with Jeanette McDonald and Nelson Eddy. Demon TV had yet to rear its awesome head. A few people may have squinted at the tiny image flickering on the miniature screen of a primitive television set owned by some radio-shop proprietor.

The newspapers and the radio news broadcasts had a good deal to say, in 1938, about developments in aviation. Five Flying Fortresses, B-17s, flew from Miami to Argentina, peacefully. But even as they flew, other planes were bombing cities in Spain and China. A Lufthansa Condor flew nonstop from Berlin to New York in less than twenty-five hours. There had been made ready the technology that would enable Britain and Germany to obliterate one another's ancient towns:

> *Ash on an old man's sleeve*
> *Is all the ash the burnt roses leave.*
> *Dust in the air suspended*
> *Marks the place where a story ended.*
> *Dust inbreathed was a house—*
> *The wall, the wainscot and the mouse.*
> *The death of hope and despair,*
> *   This is the death of air.*

So Eliot, in "Little Gidding", would express the terror of incendiary bombing. Perhaps no one in Minden, during 1938, had much notion of the pulverization that was to come, beginning with Rotterdam and ending with Hiroshima and Nagasaki.

Some people in Minden intended to go to the New York World's Fair, a celebration of technology and science, in 1939. In the summer of 1938, while Carl Curtis was campaigning for the Republican nomination, a preview of the Fair's "World of Tomorrow" was offered at Flushing Meadow, Long Island. (The "tomorrow" predicted was the distant year 1960.) The trylon and the perisphere loomed over the Fair. Within the perisphere was exhibited the model "City of Tomorrow."

This utopian complex was styled Democracity. "No one lives in the city itself. Residents are housed in a rim of garden apartments in suburban developments and satellite towns."

> Bright daylight floods the model for two minutes, then evening falls and lights appear in the city. Stars come out, and suddenly a chorus of a thousand voices is heard in the distance, singing a march. High in the

heavens, ten marching columns are seen to converge on the city. As they approach, increasing in size, they are recognized as the various groups in modern society—farmers, laborers, machinists, artisans, bankers, miners, architects, engineers, educators—the various elements which must work together to make possible the city lying below. Arms upraised, the men and women sing the song of tomorrow.

Yet quite different tunes, as events came to pass, would be sung for the following six years. And the City of Tomorrow, in much of the world, would be a heap of blasted ruins.

CARL CURTIS
STANDS FOR CONGRESS

The huge prairie state of Nebraska, dusty and distressed in 1938, had a million inhabitants, widely dispersed, who sent five representatives to the House of Representatives in Washington. The Fourth Congressional District sprawled over two hundred miles; its largest town was Grand Island, with a population of less than twenty thousand souls. This was the district whose Republican voters, early in August 1938, chose Carl Curtis as their candidate for the House.

Curtis was a country lawyer, thirty-three years old, short, burly, and remarkably healthy. "I always wanted to be a congressman," he said years later, confessing that as a small boy he had practiced his oratory on the barnyard's pigs and calves. In 1930, standing as a Democrat, he had been elected county attorney. "I wasn't a good Democrat," Curtis later reflected. "I admired the intellectual integrity and the principles of Herbert Hoover. I believed then, and I believe now, that under a second Hoover administration, the Depression would have run its course and better times would have returned." In 1936, he had changed parties, ridden with Alf Landon on his special presidential-campaign train, and proclaimed himself a Republican by choice and by conviction.

Curtis had acquaintances in most of the twenty-five rural counties that made up the Fourth Congressional District. Otherwise, this unassuming Minden lawyer seemed to many people an unlikely Republican candidate for either primary or general election. He had no rich friends, no private fortune, and no political organization. "All I had upon which to build a campaign," he said in later years, "was a deep conviction that the course charted for our country by the New Deal was basically wrong, and that it would lead to dire consequences—plus the belief that I could win." At any rate, he had the endorsement of his wife, Lois, and considerable energy and enthusiasm for the fight.

Curtis' grandfather was a Swedish immigrant, Carl Swenson, who had run away from home. Aboard ship he had met a Swedish girl, Mary Johnson, and had followed her to Illinois, where they were married. To mark his parting from his parents, the young man had determined to change his name; his bride suggested "Curtis" as the new surname, so he became Charles Curtis. For half a century he was a blacksmith, not leaving the anvil until he had reached the age of seventy-six.

In Kearney County, Carl Curtis' father, Frank O. Curtis, was a small farmer and later custodian of the county courthouse. For a time he was a member of the county board of supervisors; and he never failed to vote in any election. The elder Curtis built the farmhouse in which Carl was born and where he lived with seven other Curtis children. Frank Curtis was also the principal builder of the country schoolhouse that Carl and his brothers and sisters attended.

The Curtis children took work for granted. At first light, every day, the boy Carl fed corn to the hogs, later reclaiming the corncobs for burning in the stove. He slept in an unheated bedroom upstairs. Some years later, while preparing for the bar examination, he lodged in a well-heated hotel in Lincoln. Finding his room too warm, he opened both the window and the transom above the hall door to induce a draft of cold air. Early in the morning there came a pounding at his door. "I wish you would shut this transom," a voice shouted. "If the snow doesn't bother you, it does us out here."

Carl's first school was the familiar one-room building in which the pupils—twenty-two of them—varied widely in age. The boy found it an advantage to overhear what was being taught to the older children. He took to reading history.

And the Chatauqua movement, that self-improvement program so strong at the turn of the century and not yet wholly extinguished, instructed the boy. His parents believed in Chatauqua; they bought season tickets. "Serious speakers" on politics, history, literature, and science were featured in the series. The Curtis family would go into town to hear them, fetching with themselves food and enthusiasm.

Upon completing high school at Minden, Carl enrolled for a short time at Nebraska Wesleyan University (long later to award him one of his honorary doctorates). One of his professors there, F.M. Gregg, would ask students, "What is the greatest cause of worry?" The correct answer? "The greatest cause of worry is unfinished tasks." It was an admonition Carl Curtis did not forget.

Curtis left the university when his mother, Alberta Mae, in her middle fifties suffered a paralytic stroke. For nearly a quarter of a century she would be wheeled about in a chair. Carl never once heard her complain.

Otherwise the Curtises were a hale family: His father lived to the age of sixty-nine; and throughout his long public career Carl would suffer scarcely a day's illness. Once, young Carl watched a mastoid operation on a member of the household: to relieve the pressure, "they actually cut through the bone with hammer and chisel" (the latter sterilized).

The profession of the law always had appealed to Carl, and it seemed to him the most promising way to advancement. In those days it was possible in Nebraska for applicants to take the state bar examination, and, if successful, to be admitted to the bar without having been graduated from a law school. Carl studied privately with a practicing lawyer for three years. In addition, he bought the fourteen volumes of the La Salle Extension Law Course and set himself to master fifty pages daily. Reading in the kitchen, he rested his stockinged feet in the mouth of the oven for warmth. When sufficiently prepared, he took a two-day examination at Lincoln, and was admitted to the bar in January, 1930.

While studying law, Curtis had taught history and mathematics at the public school, serving as its principal. He had married another teacher, Lois Wylie Atwater, a girl he had known since childhood. At the age of twenty-five Curtis was a Minden lawyer in the courthouse where his father had been custodian. (The name of Frank Curtis is cut into the cornerstone of that Kearney Courthouse, built in the year Carl was born.) He became involved in national political questions somewhat abruptly. This interest was to lead him out of Minden all the way to Washington, and to keep him there for more than four decades.

Curtis' talent for the law had a great deal to do with his winning the Republican congressional nomination that hot and dry August of 1938; in particular, his successful defense of a man named Lew Hawkes, charged with a felony in the district court of Frontier County. This incident deserves setting down here because it suggests the amusing intricacies of rural courthouse politics with which a good many important political careers still begin.

One night Curtis returned home late from a trip to Lincoln. His wife told him that Charlie Samuelson, of the Bank of Hildreth, had telephoned several times in his absence, and that he must see him no matter how late he returned to Minden. Tired as he was, Curtis drove the fifteen miles to Hildreth. There, Samuelson introduced Curtis to Lew Hawkes, who had been arrested for writing seven hundred dollars in "no funds" checks to the livestock auction barn at Eustis. Samuelson persuaded Curtis to undertake Hawkes' defense because Samuelson thought well of Mrs. Hawkes, and feared that if Hawkes were sent to the penitentiary, the disgrace would kill Mrs. Hawkes' parents.

Curtis proceeded to investigate. He interviewed the cashier at the Eustis bank, who had been clerk at the sale when Hawkes had paid with bad checks. "That man is a crook," the cashier told Curtis. "He beat us out of seven hundred dollars. If we don't get that money, the auction barn will have to close."

Curtis asked more questions; the cashier replied frankly. "I asked Hawkes," the cashier said, "after he had loaded up the two trucks of hogs he had purchased, if he would pay for a long-distance phone call to the bank on which the checks were written to see if the checks were good."

"What did Hawkes say?" Curtis inquired.

"Hawkes told me he would pay for the call, but he could tell me now that the checks weren't good, but that the checks would be good when he got to Omaha and sold the hogs."

It was clear to Curtis, on hearing this, that Hawkes was not guilty of defrauding the auction barn by deceiving them about his checks. Through its clerk, in effect, the auction barn had extended credit to Hawkes. Truck expenses, a drop in hog prices, and other factors had prevented Hawkes from depositing enough money to cover his checks.

Hawkes' case was tried in a packed courtroom at Stockville. Hawkes and his lawyer, Curtis, were desperately unpopular with that crowd, for Hawkes had struck a sorry blow to the auction barn, the chief hope of Eustis in those hard times.

The Eustis cashier, an honest man, told the same story on the witness stand that he had related to Curtis earlier. When the prosecution rested its case, Curtis moved for a directed verdict. The motion being denied, the case went to the jury.

"I gave the argument before the jury everything I had in behalf of unpopular Hawkes, whom I believed to be innocent of the felony for which he had been arrested, and who was being tried before a hostile crowd," Curtis reminisces. "The depression-ridden jury must have been impressed by my argument that a man should not be convicted of a crime merely because he could not pay his debts; and that Hawkes had committed no fraud or deceit. They quickly returned a verdict of not guilty. Hawkes, his wife, and I left the courthouse as swiftly as we could, got into my car, and started our seventy-five-mile journey home."

Three weeks after this trial, Curtis announced his candidacy for the Republican nomination for Congress. He started on a speaking tour that would carry him to every one of the twenty-five counties in the Fourth District. On a very hot day, he drove into Eustis, the town of the auction barn that had taken Hawkes' check. Looking at his list of men in the local Republican Party, he promptly recognized most of the names: these Eustis Republicans had been either officers and shareholders in the auction barn, or else witnesses in the case of *Nebraska* v. *Hawkes*.

A small crowd was seated on the benches in front of the village stores. The men were not rude, but he could extract no response from them. The silence seemed as intense as the day's heat. Without success, Curtis tried in every way to engage them in conversation.

At last a man spoke up: "Curtis, we're all for you up here."

Astonished, Curtis exclaimed, "What?"

"Yes, we are for you. You gave us a beating, and we want to beat Binderup [the incumbent Democratic congressman]. We think you can do it."

Those were joyous words. This Eustis auction barn affair, incidentally, had curious connections with Curtis' subsequent political fortunes. The prosecutor in *Nebraska* v. *Hawkes* was Frank Morrison, later governor of Nebraska. Curtis was to defeat Morrison in their contest for the House of Representatives in 1948, and to defeat him again in Curtis' race for reelection to the Senate in 1966. More significant, an observer of the Hawkes trial had been Frank Butler, brother of Hugh Butler, Republican national committeeman for Nebraska and later a United States senator. Carl Curtis' conduct and success during the Hawkes trial won for him the support of the Butlers, a very important cause of his success in the Republican primary of August 8.

Sixteen years later, when Curtis was campaigning for the nomination for the Senate, he met a man in the dusty livestock pens at the stockyards in south Omaha. This man said, "Curtis, I am doing all I can for you, and I am getting you some votes every day, because you saved me from the penitentiary." It was Lew Hawkes.

Campaigning for that first Republican nomination for the

House of Representatives against two other candidates, a banker and a farmer (the latter supported by the Townsend Clubs, then a political power in the land), Curtis twice toured all the counties in the Fourth District. On his second round, he mounted a loudspeaker atop his Chrysler, and spoke in every village or hamlet where two or more people were gathered. He played a record over the loudspeaker: "O give me some men who are stouthearted men, and I'll soon give you ten thousand more," his theme song. His voice carried into the open windows, for air conditioning had not yet arrived. When the record ceased, Curtis would introduce himself—and proceed to a public dissection of the New Deal.

On the recommendation of his supporter Jay Bracken, the two of them went to visit Congressman Frank Carlson at Concordia, Kansas. The congressman was in his wheatfields, driving a combine. Sitting in the shade of his machine, Representative Carlson emphasized to his two visitors the importance to a candidate of making as many calls as possible on individuals throughout the disputed district.

The price of wheat was low in the summer of 1938. Carlson told Curtis about the slowness of Henry Wallace, then Secretary of Agriculture, in giving effect to the recent act establishing a support-loan system for wheat. By the time support loans would be made available, most of the farmers would have sold their wheat, and the grain would be in the hands of the traders.

Seizing upon this issue, Curtis went up and down the Fourth District, reminding his audiences of the miserable price for wheat and telling them of Wallace's reluctance to commence the support-loan program. The storekeepers and the townspeople were generally as interested as the farmers, for all depended on farm income. The Nebraska farmers already resented the controls imposed on them by the New Deal; the wheat-loan affair helped to bring about the first rural revolt against the New Deal, discernible in the election of 1938.

Curtis' zeal carried the day: on August 8, he won the Republican primary. Now he had to campaign against Congressman Charles G. Binderup, another native of Minden (population 1,848), a gentleman with a radio voice as good as

FDR's. Both Binderup and Curtis attended the First Presbyterian Church, and voted in the same precinct.

Binderup, a friendly man who took a genuine interest in people's problems, had been a diligent member of the House of Representatives, a crusader for the New Deal. He was a monetary reformer: his addresses were reminiscent of the free-silver speeches of William Jennings Bryan, flaying Wall Street and the financial establishment.

In most of the United States, even Nebraska, experienced political observers thought in the summer of 1938 that Roosevelt and his New Deal remained so well established that Republican candidates had dim prospects. Curtis nevertheless expected to win the Fourth District seat. He went the rounds indefatigably—picnics, Old Settlers' days, county fairs, public auctions at livestock barns—over the hundreds of miles of "improved" gravel roads and dirt roads of his parched district.

"My advisers taught me early," he commented later, "that individuals should be asked for their vote. This never should be done in a way that calls for an embarrassing answer; a candidate should look each person in the eye and tell him that his vote means a great deal and that you will appreciate his support."

In his radio talks and speeches to rallies, Curtis discussed the balancing of the federal budget, the growing national debt; he condemned new massive federal programs that would lead one day to more than taxpayers could bear. He pointed out that local self-government had been weakened, and that welfare-dependency and the pseudo-employment of the Works Progress Administration were becoming ways of life. He argued that Roosevelt's concentration of power in the federal government and his attempt to undermine the independence of the Supreme Court were grave challenges to constitutional liberty.

When he visited Saline County, the most Democratic county in Nebraska, he was advised by a friend to tone down his attacks on the New Deal. He replied that he could not change. Two years earlier, in the presidential election, Roosevelt had carried Saline by 2,843 votes. But on his swing through the county, Curtis found the voters interested in what he had to say. At the November election, it would turn out that Curtis would carry Saline by seven votes—3,230 to Binderup's 3,223.

Campaigning for the general election was easier than the primary contest had been, for Curtis now had the support of the local Republican organizations and the knowledge that state and national Republican leaders were interested in his election. Many friends helped him heartily, notable among them Hal Lainson in Adams County and John Riddell in York County.

As the campaign approached its final weeks, Curtis' supporters, the press, and the opposition all grasped that Curtis was making headway, though he was still not expected to win. Congressman Binderup, disturbed, rented a circus tent to hold a huge rally, with white horses, bands, flags, and marchers. This exhibition became an object of ridicule by the press.

At the close of his campaign in Hamilton County, Curtis was taken aside by the county Republican chairman, Cecil Fraizer, who gave him a fatherly talk as preparation for defeat. Curtis appreciated Fraizer's concern; but in his heart he still thought he could win.

On election day, a candidate restlessly waits for the returns, thinking of the blunders he wishes he had not made and of what he would have done had he been permitted more time. On election day, November, 1938, two hours after the polls had closed, Curtis was telephoned by Harold Hamil, editor of the Hastings *Daily Tribune*. "Carl, you are going to be elected," he said. "We just got a partial unofficial report from one of our wards which usually runs heavily Democratic, and you are running very close. This tells us something."

By midnight, Curtis was running ahead of Binderup; by morning, he had won. The final vote was Curtis, 59,794; Binderup, 42,957—a turnover of 32,076 votes. (Two years earlier, Binderup had won by 15,239 votes.) The courthouse custodian's son had unseated a strong Democratic incumbent. Carl Curtis cried happily.

On January 3, 1939, he took his oath of office in Washington. At the Capitol, William Bankhead was then speaker of the House of Representatives, and Sam Rayburn, the Democrats' floor leader. The minority leader was Joseph W. Martin, Jr. Charles Halleck of Indiana, aged thirty-nine, was then beginning his fifth year in the House. Everett McKinley Dirksen, forty-three years old, was commencing his seventh term in the House.

In the Senate chamber, one saw and heard Vice-President John Nance Garner, Carter Glass, James F. Byrnes, George W. Norris, Arthur Capper, William E. Borah, Robert M. LaFollette, J. Ham Lewis, Burton K. Wheeler, Hiram Johnson, and Alben W. Barkley. Carl Curtis did not then anticipate that some years in the future he would become one of the better-known senators.

Washington, in 1939, was still a small city, elegant and distinctly an outpost of the South, a far cry from Minden. Its population was friendly and well-mannered. Streetcars crisscrossed it, tracks running directly in front of the White House, not then crammed with the offices of the grander members of the Executive Force. (For a dime, one could ride anywhere in the District of Columbia.) The Mall was encumbered, then and for years later, by "temporary" governmental structures erected during the First World War; and the gigantic expansion of massive new governmental buildings, the stone mushrooms of the New Deal, had begun. The Willard Hotel and the Occidental Restaurant flourished on Pennsylvania Avenue. As yet there was no Jefferson Memorial, nor a Pentagon. Into the magnificent distances created by L'Enfant stretched the neat and charming streets of small townhouses of a century earlier; Henry Adams and John Hay would have found the capital little altered outwardly.

In this city, contending against the tide of political events, Carl Curtis would spend forty years.

Chapter 2

The Defense
Of Neutrality

THE STRUGGLE AGAINST
MILITARY INTERVENTION

The Seventy-Sixth Congress was convened on January 3, 1939, and Representative Carl T. Curtis took his oath of office. He had closed his law office in Minden and had moved to Washington with his wife and small daughter. As a fledgling Congressman, Curtis had three principal objectives in mind: to resist enlargement of Roosevelt's New Deal; to work for flood control and irrigation in Nebraska; and to help keep the United States out of war.

His first day in Congress was not without its measure of embarrassment, for in his excitement he voted twice. Roll was being called for the election of a speaker. All the Democrats were responding with the name of their candidate, "Bankhead," and all the Republicans with the name of their candidate, "Martin." On that day Representative Edward Walter Curley, of New York (whose name stood just before Curtis' on the roster) happened to be absent. In his eagerness, when Curley's name was called and a pause occurred, Curtis shouted "Martin!" The next name called being his own, Curtis again shouted "Martin!" Understanding the blunder, the House reading clerk adjusted the vote in the record.

The next day, President Franklin Delano Roosevelt appeared before a joint session of the Congress to deliver his State of the Union Message. Roosevelt was an attractive-looking man, a New York squire, pince-nez and all. He had a way of holding his head that seemed—even to his best friends—cocky and full of self-importance. In the House chamber he did not display that long cigarette-holder which seemed as much a part of him as his pince-nez. Roosevelt's voice seemed to have been created for a radio audience. The President was endowed with aristocratic qualities of leadership and a sense of the dramatic.

On January 5, Roosevelt sent his budget message to Congress, asking that for every five dollars raised in taxes, the federal government enter into debt for three more dollars to finance his programs. This budget called for receipts of 5.6 billion dollars, expenditures of 8.9 billion—and a deficit of 3.3 billion dollars. The general economic recovery promised by Roosevelt when he had taken office six years earlier was nowhere to be discerned.

The congressional elections of 1938 had mightily strengthened the Republicans, although leaving their party still in a minority in both the Senate and the House. The new House consisted of 262 Democrats and 170 Republicans: a gain of 81 seats for the Republican Party in contrast with the previous Congress. All committee chairmanships, of course, remained in the hands of the Democratic majority; yet the Republican minority, on occasions when allied with anti-administration Democrats, had now gained enough strength to impede New Deal proposals. There arose Republican hopes for winning the presidency, and perhaps control of Congress, in 1940's elections.

Just that might have come to pass—had it not been for the eruption of war in Europe in 1939—for the economic programs of the New Deal were in serious difficulty.

Roosevelt's chief new economic proposal for 1939 was the Self-Liquidating Projects Bill, styled by its opponents and by most of the press the Spend-Lend Bill. This plan would have authorized federal special bonds totaling $1.85 billion (some fourteen billion in terms of 1985 dollars), the funds so raised to be expended by the Department of Agriculture, the Public Works Administration, the Public Roads Administration, the Rural Electrification Administration—or to be retained, in part, by the Reconstruction Finance Corporation for lending to public agencies and foreign governments. This was a fresh pump-priming measure—when the efficacy of pump-priming for getting out of the Depression had become suspect.

The Spend-Lend Bill was passed by the Senate; but in the House, the Republicans resisted it strenuously. The eighty-odd freshmen among the Republican representatives were especially vigorous in their opposition. To Roosevelt's chagrin, the Spend-Lend Bill was defeated in the House, despite the large Democratic majority there: the first time a Roosevelt spending proposal had been rejected. This was Curtis' first experience of a major congressional debate—and of victory over the Executive Force.

Despite his keen interest in such fiscal policies, Congressman Curtis soon found himself, along with Congress and the American public, drawn urgently into discussion of international affairs. British and French endeavors to appease Hitler and Mussolini had failed; it was sufficiently obvious that the European powers would soon come to blows. Could the United States avoid sharing in that imminent war?

Some influential voices had already declared that America should take her stand by the side of Britain and France—irresolute though those powers had been. But throughout the United States, public opinion in general remained powerfully opposed to involvement, in the winter and spring of 1939.

This opposition was particularly strong in such states as Nebraska, Wisconsin, and Missouri. The Plains States and the Mountain States generally were strongholds of what the interventionists soon would denounce as "isolationism." Europe and China were remote; suspicion of entangling alliances was undiminished. Some members of Congress became spokesmen for continued neutrality; in the Senate, Nye of North Dakota, Borah of Idaho, Wheeler of Montana, Brooks of Illinois; in the

House, Hamilton Fish, Karl Mundt, and others.

In Nebraska, as in many other states, public meetings in the cause of neutrality were frequent in 1939; newspaper editorials generally advocated neutrality; the papers were full of letters from citizens opposing involvement, and Congress was deluged with such letters. American veterans' organizations took their stand against entering a second world war.

At Minden, the American Legion post resolved "That we are opposed to any armament or preparation for any war except what may be reasonably necessary for defense, and that we are opposed to any interference by our Government in any controversy between foreign nations, and that we are opposed to any public statement being made by any official of our Government which might involve us in any foreign entanglements . . . We intend to hold our Congress and the officials of our Government strictly accountable for any action they may take or any public utterance they may make which may involve our country in a quarrel between other nations or which may result in a war except a defensive war."

The Minden post so resolved on February 2, 1939. Like most other Middlewesterners, Carl Curtis concurred with these sentiments; he would do everything he could to preserve America's peace. On March 2, in a short speech, he asked for continued neutrality in the contest of the European powers.

Curtis warned the House against war hysteria. What had happened in the preceding few months, he asked, that could imperil the security of the United States? What power was about to invade America? What foreign nation had issued menacing declarations against our country? A poll of newspaper editors, he remarked, showed how the vast majority of them feared that by degrees the United States was being inclined toward war. He concluded by saying that if indeed the country stood in peril of war, the Congress and the public should be presented with the facts; and that if such a danger were real, we ought to put our financial house in order.

Congress had passed the Neutrality Act in 1935, meaning to avert American involvement in European conflicts: its principal provision was a virtual prohibition of shipment of munitions to belligerent powers. The Roosevelt administration, early in 1939, had begun to move toward assistance to Britain, then rearming out of dread of Hitler. In April, President Roosevelt demanded that Germany give guarantees of nonaggression to thirty-one countries, an utterance that the British historian Paul Johnson calls "absurd" and "worse than useless." In an address to the Reichstag, Hitler contemptuously rejected this odd proposal. Roosevelt proceeded to ask Congress to amend the Neutrality Act, repealing the arms embargo.

To Carl Curtis, as to many others, this was America's first step toward war. To the members of the Seventy-Sixth Congress who opposed the lifting of the embargo, it appeared unnecessary that the United States take sides. If neutral, America might be able to maintain the international balance of power, thus exerting a moderating influence on both of the opposing forces in Europe. The American aim in foreign policy, this peace faction maintained, should be the protection of America's national interest. Were that principle abandoned, along with neutrality—why, just that had happened to the United States in the First World War. For every young American who had died on the field of battle in 1917 and 1918, many more might be sacrificed in a second world war. If this was "isolationism," make the most of it.

In the national dispute over the proposed repeal of the arms embargo, division of opinion did not occur strictly along predictable lines. Curtis' colleague Bruce Barton, a publicist, then a congressman from New York, reported that two gentlemen had called on him to discuss this burning issue. One caller was a distinguished clergyman: he urged Representative Barton to support measures that would result in American intervention in Europe. The United States had an obligation to become involved, this clergyman argued. The other caller was the head of a company that manufactured munitions: he urged Barton to vote against repeal of the embargo, for repeal would have permitted sale of munitions to the Allies. The manufacturer believed that this would be a stride toward American participation in the approaching war, and he did not wish to be charged with favoring involvement for the sake of material gain.

Curtis spoke to the House against repeal of the embargo, charging that the Roosevelt administration's pretended amendment of the Neutrality Act was in reality no neutrality bill. On the contrary, the bill embodied two adverse principles. First, it would repeal the embargo on military shipments to belligerents, which in fact would aid one power, Britain; second, the bill was a vast unwarranted delegation of powers to the President.

The administration's bill contained some twenty-nine phrases enlarging presidential powers, Curtis pointed out. Clearly the purpose of the measure was to enable the President to depart, when he chose, from the Congress' intended policy of neutrality. But the bill was passed in November, 1939, with long-run consequences of which we have not yet seen the end.

The events leading to hostilities in Europe need not be traced in detail here. Next Hitler demanded return of Danzig and the Polish Corridor to Germany; in August, Germany and the Soviet Union concluded their nonaggression pact, in effect working Poland's ruin. On September 1, 1939, the German assault on Poland commenced. Britain and France declared war on Germany. Poland promptly was overrun by Germans and Russians. But in western Europe, the "twilight war" lingered, for some chilling winter months neither side adventuring much. Then in April, 1940, the Germans seized Norway and Denmark; in May, the German army overran the Low Countries, broke the French forces, swept to the English Channel, and nearly succeeded in preventing evacuation of the British army from Dunkirk. Italy declared war on June 10; France surrendered to Hitler on June 22.

German bombing of Britain began. The war spread to North Africa. The Axis Powers proceeded to conquer Greece, and then the Balkans.

Would Britain fall? By the middle of September, 1940, the *New York Times* was declaring that "It may be that the coming weeks will be the most critical in the history of the British Empire." By October, it was widely predicted (erroneously) that the Germans would invade England very soon.

Yet during 1940, the greater the successes of the Axis Powers, the less the Roosevelt administration said about possible intervention in the European war. Why? Because a presidential election was approaching.

In a speech at Philadelphia on October 23, President Roosevelt promised that "We will not participate in foreign wars; we will not send our army, naval, or air forces to fight in foreign lands outside of the Americas except in case of attack." He repeated these words from the platform of the Democratic Party, adopted the preceding summer. Also he promised the Mothers of America that fateful autumn, "Your boys are not going to be sent into any foreign wars."

The peace plank in the Democrats' platform suggested that the strategists of the New Deal knew they could not win November's elections unless Roosevelt solemnly promised to keep out of war. Republicans recalled similar promises from President Wilson on the eve of America's intervention in the First World War.

At the time of his nomination for a third term, Roosevelt had insisted that his presidential duties would keep him from participating actively in the campaign. The growing strength of his Republican opponent, Wendell Willkie, made him change his mind. He spoke, still promising nonintervention, in New York, Boston, Brooklyn, and Cleveland, between October 28 and November 2; he carried the day.

On election day, November 5, 1940, President Roosevelt received twenty-seven million votes to Willkie's twenty-two million. The Democratic presidential ticket won thirty-eight states with a total of 449 electoral votes. Willkie and his running mate carried ten states with eighty-two electoral votes. In the Seventy-Seventh Congress there would be sixty-six Democrats in the Senate, twenty-eight Republicans, one Progressive, one Independent. The new House of Representatives would consist of 266 Democrats, 161 Republicans, three Progressives, one Farmer Laborite, one American-Laborite—plus three vacancies.

Curtis was returned to Washington by Nebraska's Fourth District. Approving his stand on nonintervention in Europe and his part in the spend-lend struggle, the Republicans had renominated him thumpingly: they had given him nearly twenty-four thousand votes, to six thousand for one of his opponents in the primary and little more than four thousand for his other opponent. In the general election, Curtis won easily: nearly sixty-seven thousand votes, to twenty-nine thousand for the Democratic candidate, R. O. Canady, and less than twenty thousand for Charles Binderup, the former congressman (running as a petition candidate).

His election won, President Roosevelt had resolved to aid Britain, by this time shorn of all effective allies on the Continent. In his Fireside Chat of December 29, 1940, concerning national security, Roosevelt said that "there can be no appeasement with ruthlessness, and the United States must be the great arsenal of democracy"—this merely two months after his Philadelphia election-pledge not to intervene abroad.

On January 6, 1941, Roosevelt presented his eighth State of the Union Message to Congress, outlining his intended lend-lease program for aid to the Allies. He emphasized his Four Freedoms: freedom of speech and expression, freedom of worship, freedom from want, and freedom from fear. (The latter two are liberties that no people ever have succeeded in guaranteeing.)

Like many phrases employed during World War II, the term "lend-lease" was never fully explained. It was understood to be a plan by which the United States would produce guns, planes, tanks, and other implements of war to provide to Britain and what remained of the forces of the other allies. In common usage, the term "lease" implies the renting of property, with the promise of the return of that property within a stipulated period of time. Just how weapons and munitions might be leased and then returned to their owners was never elucidated.

Carl Curtis was skeptical about the claim that Britain could defeat Hitler without the help of an American expeditionary force. In January, 1941, he spoke to the House against the lend-lease proposal.

"We are approaching a sad epoch in American history," he said. "It is a sad state of affairs when free Americans, who cling to the ideal of peace or who express their desire that the nations of the world make peace, are branded as pro-Nazi. Those of us who have been opposed to a program of intervention do not charge any honest Americans with being warmongers. We do not charge that their love of some other country exceeds their love of America.''

This was one more stride toward military participation by the United States, Curtis went on. ''Some months ago, the Chief Executive requested Congress to repeal the arms embargo. Many of you gentlemen in this Chamber had a high resolve that if you took that step, you would do it in the interest of building up America's defense industries, and that you would never, at a later time, extend credit in any form to a warring foreign nation. . . . Perhaps many members of this body now have a high resolve that they will never send an expeditionary force of American boys to Europe, even though they take this additional step of further participating in this war by the enactment of the pending Lend-Lease Bill.''

Such opposition by Curtis and more senior members of the House and Senate was overridden: the Lend-Lease Bill having been passed by both houses on March 11, 1941, President Roosevelt signed it.

President Roosevelt pressed on with his design for greater intervention. On April 11, he informed Winston Churchill that the maritime frontier of the United States would be extended to cover the western North Atlantic to west longitude 27°, so making it possible for the American navy to patrol much of the Atlantic against German submarines and surface vessels. The lend-lease proposal had been submitted to Congress with the understanding that implements of war would be transported in foreign ships; that the United States would not deliver such arms and munitions; nor use the American navy to escort merchant vessels containing arms manufactured in the United States.

Early in April, newspaper accounts appeared that American naval vessels already were convoying British merchant ships laden with munitions out of the ports of Baltimore, Philadelphia, and New York. Although the veracity of these reports was disputed, Representative Curtis tried to persuade Congress to prohibit any possible convoying, with its peril of naval engagements with German craft. His House bill to this effect got nowhere. In Curtis' speech on this subject, he reminded the House that President Roosevelt had admitted, in effect, that convoying meant shooting, and shooting meant war. Curtis tried to extract his Joint Resolution 152 from committee by petition (for 218 members could bring a proposal to the floor, without committee assent, by that tactic); he failed. The noninterventionists in Congress lost more ground.

When the fighting had begun in Europe, Nazi-dominated Germany and the Soviet Union had joined in the partition of Poland. During those months, the official Communist line had been that Britain and her allies were the imperialist powers. Then came an abrupt change: on June 22, 1941, Germany invaded Russia. Two days later, Roosevelt promised aid to the Soviets.*

A conspicuous member of the Left in the House of Representatives was Vito Marcantonio, from New York. That congressman's public statements had invariably coincided with the official line of the Communist Party of the United States. Previously, Representative Marcantonio, condemning the war, had spoken harshly of the Allies. When Hitler invaded the Soviet Union, Marcantonio changed his position 180 degrees.

"The war has been transformed from a war which is imperialistic in character," Marcantonio told the House, "into a war of national defense." America must aid the Soviet Union, he argued, to defend the United States. "I honestly believe," he continued, "that what is therefore essential in order to defend the United States is for the United States of America to

---

* In 1941, with forty or fifty other congressmen, Curtis had organized a study club, meeting weekly; they invited speakers to inform them about current issues. Shortly after Britain had become allied with Russia, Lord Halifax, the British ambassador to Washington, addressed the club. He was asked whether he thought it safe for Britain to lock arms with the Soviet Union. "If you were down in a pit," Halifax replied, "and could not get out, and a gorilla extended his hairy arm down to you, and you could grab that arm and get out of the pit, wouldn't you grab it—and then settle with the gorilla afterward?"

do everything possible to bring about the opening of a Western front and thereby prevent the triumph of Hitler..."

At this point in the debate, Congressman Karl Mundt, from South Dakota, asked Marcantonio whether he would favor sending an American expeditionary force to open this proposed Western front. "I will be honest with you," Marcantonio replied, "I am absolutely in favor of it, and I am not going to dodge any questions on this issue."

From that time forward, the Communist line in the United States unflinchingly supported the Roosevelt administration's program to aid the Allies against Hitler. Sentiment in other quarters for more aid to the Allies, and indeed for American participation in the war, grew through 1941. An American merchant vessel, the *Robin Moor,* was sunk in the South Atlantic by a German submarine early in June—the first American ship so lost. The attention of the White House, Congress, and the press was directed toward Europe; small attention was paid during most of 1941 to the Japanese menace in the Pacific.

Curtis carried on the struggle against military involvement. On August 6, 1941, he spoke nationwide over the Columbia radio network on the burning subject "Can We Follow the War Crowd?"

"The bitter controversy today," he said, "is whether or not the United States shall become a shooting participant in the wars now going on in Europe, Africa, and Asia.

"In the first place, I do not approve of any dictatorship anywhere, anytime, or under any circumstances. I am convinced the great majority of the American people as a whole are loyal to the United States of America.

"I believe the defense program in America should be carried forward as rapidly as possible; that nothing should be done to hamper or interfere with the fastest possible attainment of a completely adequate national preparedness. . . . The question before us is, shall we become enmeshed in the European, Asiatic, and African wars? The great majority of American people have expressed their desire that we do not enter these conflicts. A small but very militant minority are attempting to drive the United States into these wars."

Curtis quoted from an editorial in the New York *Herald-*

Tribune of June 27, declaring that "It is imperatively the hour to release our Navy—to win the Battle of the Atlantic." Frank Knox, Secretary of the Navy, had used almost the language of that editorial when addressing the Conference of Governors a few days later.

"These men surely know the United States Navy could not be used to clear the Atlantic and then call the job completed," Curtis declared in his radio speech. "It would mean only the beginning for us; we would become a full-fledged shooting participant in these foreign wars."

Not long before, he continued, the "war crowd" had been urging that the United States should "help brave little Finland in her struggle against the wanton and brutal aggression of the bloody hand of Dictator Joe Stalin. Today this war crowd wants us to assist godless communistic Russia. These wars make strange bedfellows from day to day. I believe I express the hope in the heart of every true American when I say that I hope that both the dictatorship of Hitler and the dictatorship of Stalin will wreck themselves completely and beyond repair in their battle with each other.

"On February 7, 1940, Representative John McCormack, now House majority floor leader, offered an amendment that would have removed our ambassador from Russia. Less than one year later, he introduced the Lend-Lease Bill, by which military aid is now being given to Russia."

Curtis then quoted Frank Kent, the influential syndicated columnist, a strong advocate of the Roosevelt foreign policy. On July 23, Kent had written of the Lend-Lease Bill, "Opponents of that measure were right in regarding it as a bill to take us into war; its proponents were wrong in saying that it would keep us out. That was a piece of false pretense, justified only by the necessity of getting it through."

Curtis' radio talk represented the convictions of most American citizens that August. But the Roosevelt administration was moving swiftly in the opposite direction. The Selective Service Act had been signed by Roosevelt on September 16, 1940, requiring one year's military training and service for all inductees: the first peacetime conscription in the history of the United States. With the minority in both House and Senate, Curtis had voted against it.

The early calls under this Selective Service program were small, many draft boards filling their quotas through volunteers. Young men, informed that they must serve for one year, volunteered for induction to get the requirement out of the way; they relied on the government's promise that at a year's end they could return to civilian pursuits.

In August, 1941, a measure to extend the required training-and-service period from one year to eighteen months was passed by the House, a vote of 203 to 201. It was not that the House came within one vote of ending the draft; rather, the issue before the House was this: should those men who relied on the government's promise of release within a year be compelled to serve another six months? Curtis and others who voted against the extension believed that this would be breaking faith with the volunteers. As matters turned out, those volunteers would have been recalled anyway, after the Japanese attack on Pearl Harbor and America's declaration of war.

The American public always has been reluctant to declare war. President Roosevelt could not have induced the public to enter the war against the Axis Powers directly, short of a German attack, which Hitler did not intend: the American people approve only those military operations they take to be defensive. There remained for President Roosevelt, now thoroughly convinced that the United States should intervene with full strength, only what the historian Charles Callan Tansill later called America's "back door to war."

The Japanese military clique, busy conquering China and Indochina and menacing the Dutch East Indies, did not understand either the reluctance of the American people to go to war anywhere, or the American constitutional restraints upon the executive branch of government. They seem to have fancied that the White House and the State Department were free to act internationally as they might choose. And they knew that President Roosevelt detested them.

Roosevelt outwitted them. Cordell Hull, Secretary of State, sent to bellicose Japan demands amounting, seemingly, to an ultimatum: Hull told them that Japan must withdraw from China and from France's Indochinese colonies, and resign ambitions to acquire the oil of the Dutch East Indies. As Albert Jay Nock was to write with only modest hyperbole a few years later, on receiving such an ultimatum as Hull sent to Tokyo, the principality of Monaco or the grand duchy of Luxembourg might have declared war upon the United States.

The Japanese cabinet did not apprehend that if Japan had ignored Hull, Washington would have ventured nothing in the way of military action. American public opinion, and Congress, would not have tolerated forcible intervention in the Orient. What Americans yearned to fight to preserve Dutch rule over the East Indies? To declare an oil embargo against Japan and to freeze Japanese assets in the United States, the public could assent; but not to shooting. The most that President Roosevelt and Secretary Hull really then thought of initiating against Japan was an oil embargo, which would have interfered, if enforceable, with Japan's military operations. On June 23, 1941, Harold Ickes, Secretary of the Interior, had written to President Roosevelt, "To embargo oil to Japan would be as popular a move in all parts of the country as you could make. There might develop from the embargoing of oil to Japan such a situation as would make it not only possible but easy to get into this war in an effective way. And if we should thus be indirectly brought in, we would avoid the criticism that we had gone in as an ally of communistic Russia."

Roosevelt, Hull, Ickes, and their close colleagues indeed desired a back door to the European war, through provoking Japan; but the White House could not strike first. The American public must be convinced that a *defensive* war could not be avoided. As the "revisionist" historians insist, Roosevelt and his intimates were groping for a "situation" that would make entry into the European fight—and incidentally, the Oriental fight—quite easy. Roosevelt even seems to have expected a Japanese blow at Pearl Harbor, by way of response to Hull's ultimatum. What he did not anticipate, presumably, was the successful magnitude of that attack, temporarily paralyzing in the Pacific.

If there is to be war, the power striking the first blow gains an advantage. Such had been Hitler's method. In their ignorance, fancying that American military action against Japan would come within three years if not sooner, the Japanese government struck hard at Pearl Harbor and the Philippines.

On the afternoon of Sunday, December 7, 1941, Carl Curtis was listening to the radio downstairs in his Washington house. His wife had taken the children upstairs for their naps. Like millions of other Americans, Curtis was astounded by the news of the Japanese bombing of Pearl Harbor that began just before eight o'clock in the morning. Japanese forces also struck at the Philippines, Guam, Midway, Hong Kong, and the Malay peninsula. Carl Curtis knew at once that all resistance to American participation in the Second World War was over.

Hitler foolishly and promptly declared war against the United States; so did Mussolini. Thus they fulfilled President Roosevelt's hopes, and were thereby ruined. After terrible sacrifices, American soldiers and American resources would break the Axis Powers.

On December 8, Congress assembled in joint session to hear President Roosevelt ask for a declaration of war against Japan—something he could not have hoped to obtain but for the miscalculations of the Japanese cabinet. The House of Representatives moved swiftly: thirty-three minutes sufficed for the House to consider the language of the declaration and vote for war. All members of the House approved the declaration except Representative Jeanette Rankin, from Montana, who had been a member of the House in 1917, then voting against entry into the First World War.

Before the tally was closed and announced, Curtis watched several members plead with Miss Rankin to make the declaration unanimous by changing her vote; among them was Harold Knutson, of Minnesota, who also had voted in 1917 against war. She refused. A few days later, when Congress at Roosevelt's request declared war on Germany and Italy, Miss Rankin voted "Present."

The thing was done; Americans must unite to win the war. The House, on December 22, voted to make men from the age of twenty to the age of forty-four subject to conscription, and to require all men from eighteen to sixty-four to register for the draft.

When the second session of the Seventy-Seventh Congress

was convened on January 5, 1942, Curtis published in *The Congressional Record* a statement about the war:

"America is going to win this war. There is no other answer to that deep-rooted determination that is found in the breasts of a hundred and twenty million American people. We are going to stand with our Commander in Chief and see this thing through.

"No one contends that the task that lies ahead is an easy one. It is one of toil, sweat, hardship, heartaches, disappointments, and bloodshed."

In retrospect, had the stand of the congressional noninterventionists or isolationists been untenable from the first? That question is complex. Until Hitler's conquest of Czechoslovakia, the Nazi power might have been restrained, conceivably, by Britain and France, without American assistance; but Britain and France were indecisive. Even later, after victories in western Europe, the Germans might have found themselves baffled by the immensity and the stubbornness of Russia; indeed, they were in such a plight by late summer, 1941. Similarly, the Japanese were unable to break Chinese resistance. It is improbable that Hitler ever could have occupied Britain; that was not his own expectation. In short, a military stalemate might have come about even if no American troops had gone overseas.

Britain and her Commonwealth might have found it necessary—American military intervention lacking—to come to a compromise peace with the Axis Powers; such a thing had happened before in British history. Hitler might have worn out his men and resources swiftly in the Soviet Union, and so have been content to grant easy terms to Britain; or, blamed for the Russian disaster to the German army, he might have fallen by one of those conspiracies repeatedly formed against him in Germany. Stalin's dictatorship might have collapsed before German persistence, even though the Russians, under one regime or another, would have continued to resist the Germans. (The American noninterventionists hoped that the two totalist powers would pound one another to pieces.) Had something of that sort actually come to pass, the history of the United States during the past four decades would have been interestingly different.

Even had Germany and Japan succeeded in retaining their conquests, neither of those powers ever seriously contemplated the possibility of invading the United States. It would have become necessary, in such circumstances, for America to co-exist with the expanded Third Reich and the triumphant Japanese empire; but such co-existence scarcely would have been so difficult and perilous as the present actual co-existence with the Soviet Union.

And the plight of the European Jews? American participation in the war did not save them: it hastened their destruction. For the Nazis' systematic slaughter of Jews in concentration camps did not begin until March 1942, months after the United States had declared war. (True, the SS, by the end of 1941, had shot a half-million Jews in occupied Russia, together with many other Russians.) So long as America remained even nominally neutral, Hitler put off his extirpation of Jews (with some 8.7 million of them in territories controlled by him in December, 1941), lest he outrage American public opinion. Once America had declared war, Hitler had nothing to lose by murder. Continued American neutrality might have averted or postponed the Holocaust.

Such a hypothetical case may be made for the congressional champions of a continued neutrality. Had the Japanese not been so imprudent as to undertake their "anticipatory" blows at American territory, just possibly a measure of neutrality might have been preserved. No war in which the United States has engaged since 1787, it may be argued, was a *necessary* war. But—

What might have been is an abstraction
Remaining a perpetual possibility
Only in a world of speculation.

After the war would follow victory. But the war would also bring what the advocates of neutrality had dreaded and foretold: more than a million American casualties, a huge national debt, complex social disruptions, economic dislocations, moral hardness or indifference, increased centralization of power. Out of the war came an American political habit of intervening, often rashly, in many quarters of the world; that trail would lead to Vietnam. And victory over the Axis Powers would leave America confronting, decade after decade, the grisly might of the Soviet Union, the other chief victor. Over both the superpowers would hang the ultimate weapon that America had employed against Japan in the war's last days.

Curtis and his House colleagues of the neutrality bloc would find, then, that the War produced many of the consequences they had predicted. Yet there was no turning back. The next best thing to preventing a war is winning it.

"The blood of man should be shed but to redeem the blood of man," Edmund Burke wrote of war. "The rest is vanity; the rest is crime." It could be said for the American people that they sent their armies abroad, in 1942, to redeem nations from servitude or the prospect of servitude; it was not for dollars that America went to war. War orders for goods of every sort, from every continent, nevertheless revived the American economy that the New Deal had failed to reinvigorate through pump-priming and regulation; and once Americans were fighting, all of America's productive capacity was required to support those troops. Efficiency of production would become a principal concern of Carl Curtis until the summer of 1945.

At the beginning of the fight, the news came to the American people that their armies and their allies' armies were losing in West and East. Singapore surrendered to the Japanese on February 15, 1942; Japanese forces completed their conquest of the Dutch East Indies on March 8; they took the Philippines on April 9, and Mandalay, in Burma, at the end of that month; the garrison of Corregidor surrendered to them on May 6.

As for the Germans, Hitler's Russian invasion had already failed before his divisions penetrated Stalingrad on August 23, 1942. But the world did not know the extent of that Pyrrhic victory, nor did Hitler confess it. Almost all Europe was his, or at his mercy; from Libya he threatened Egypt. There were plans for German and Japanese forces to meet in India.

Not until more than a year after the bombing of Pearl Harbor would American forces be able to compel the Japanese to evacuate Guadalcanal, or would American bombers appear over Germany. Senator Claude Pepper, just after the sinking of much of America's Pacific fleet at Pearl Harbor, proclaimed that Japan would be defeated in a matter of weeks. It was to be otherwise in the islands of the Pacific.

GOVERNMENTAL NEUTRALITY IN ECONOMIC CONTESTS

The coming of the war abolished unemployment for anybody in any way employable, set in motion once more the machines of every idle factory, and mightily stimulated agricultural production. But wartime conditions also brought on domestic economic clashes and abuses.

"We are faced with a battle of production, and in America's hands rests the fate of civilization. We must not fail." So Carl Curtis told the House of Representatives on March 13, 1942. To diminish obstacles to efficient production: that effort occupied much of Carl Curtis' time throughout the Second World War.

"Union shop" and "closed shop" were conspicuous among those obstacles. A closed shop is a labor arrangement by which only members of a particular union may be hired by the contracting employer—and must be hired through that union's own "hiring hall." A union shop, somewhat less exacting, requires that all employees must be members of a union (or at least pay union fees); but the union agrees to admit to its membership any person hired by the employer.

Such union exclusiveness was turning away from employment many qualified people who were not union members,

Curtis pointed out—and proportionately reducing war production.

Unjustifiable industrial strikes, interrupting production, also endangered the effort to win the war, he argued. In a House speech on February 2, 1942, he put this point strongly: "I challenge anyone to justify before the court of public opinion the right to strike against the public safety. If workmen in defense industries have a right to stop production when we need tanks, guns, ships, airplanes, and other equipment with which to save human life, then the fire department on its way to a burning school building filled with children also has a right to strike."

In April, Curtis introduced a bill to provide "that no person should be required to be a member of any religious, civic, political, fraternal, or labor organization in order to obtain employment resulting from expenditures made from his government." This measure, in effect, was meant to establish a right to work, regardless of union membership, in any industry or occupation connected with the war effort. On April 27, he told the House this:

"The evidence as to the need for this legislation is voluminous. I have in my possession many letters telling of individuals who have gone to seek jobs in defense plants, but who were first directed to see the union official to make a payment. They were required to put the cash on the barrelhead in order to get a job. Many times they were unable to raise the cash, and they had to go jobless. I have the written report of a plumber in a small county-seat town, in what used to be the drought area, where jobs have been very scarce, who sought a job in a Nebraska defense plant, but was told that he must raise two hundred dollars cash as an initiation fee for the union before he could work for his own government."

Curtis went on to cite a number of similar cases of unions' exclusiveness and restrictive practices, amounting in the case of "racketeering unions" to shameless extortion. On this issue Congressman Curtis received support in some quarters usually unfriendly to him. James Lawrence, editor of the Lincoln *Daily Star*, had been one of Curtis' more severe and consistent critics. But of the Curtis' right-to-work bill, Lawrence wrote:

"There is merit to it. Although frequently it is possible to disagree with Mr. Curtis, his proposal directs attention to a situation which never should have developed, and which cannot be tolerated indefinitely.

"If a man cannot work without paying tribute, it is a hell of a state of affairs. There is no quarrel with organized labor. It will find the public friendly, sympathetic, and generally inclined to support its legitimate aims. Through the years its fights have been won only because the public believed that the aims it sought to achieve were decent and just. The road divides when labor itself undertakes policies irritating to the public, contrary to national welfare, and in practice productive of hardships and unnecessary burdens."

The Denver *Post*, on April 18, heartily endorsed the Curtis bill, saying editorially that it "would outlaw the most despicable form of racketeering now prevalent in this country—the practice of forcing American citizens to buy work permits from labor unions before they can get jobs on government war-construction projects."

Despite widespread support of this sort, the Curtis Bill was not enacted by Congress. The Democratic majorities in both houses made that impossible. President Roosevelt's alliance with the big labor unions was a principal prop of his administration, not to be tampered with. What Carl Curtis' right-to-work proposal did accomplish was to draw public attention to this problem and to induce the unions and the Roosevelt administration to tread warily.

If enacted, the Curtis right-to-work proposal would have amended the National Labor Relations Act (the Wagner Act), passed in 1935. That piece of legislation had guaranteed workers the right to organize and join unions, to bargain collectively with their employers, and to strike. But the Wagner Act made no provision for restraining unfair practices by unions, nor for governmental intervention in an immense strike or lockout injurious to the public interest.

The National Labor Relations Board, created by the Wagner Act, distinctly had favored the unions in most of its decisions in industrial disputes. The Supreme Court had allowed the NLRB a high degree of freedom from judicial restraint. The

Department of Labor, throughout the Roosevelt years, was militantly on the side of the unions. After passage of the Wagner Act, unions gigantically increased in numbers, particularly "industrial unions" of the type of the United Automobile Workers. The financial resources and political influence of the unions had grown proportionately.

In advocating right-to-work policies in defense plants, then, Carl Curtis seemed to be contending against the stars in their courses. Not until passage of the Taft-Hartley Act, in 1947, would there be major alterations in the Wagner Act's provisions, and major remedying of the Wagner Act's deficiencies. But the Curtis Bill pointed the way.

Curtis' endeavor to devise restraints on strikes affecting the national interest encountered the same obstacles. Nevertheless, Curtis did not cease to demand such reform throughout the war and the years immediately following America's military victory. Disruptive strikes persisted throughout World War II: the Roosevelt administration, despite its concentration on the war, was reluctant to vex the unions. On July 3, 1945, Curtis demanded on the House floor, "Why can we not get on with the war? We on the home front must not desert our brave men in the Pacific. No one has a right to stop production in wartime."

The surrender of Japan on September 1, 1945, was followed by an increase in the number and scope of strikes, at a time when demand for goods was high, after wartime austerities. On December 11, 1945, Curtis took up this subject:

"The administration, with its sizable majority in both houses of Congress, has a tremendous responsibility in this strike situation. It is interesting to observe that all of the leaders who are playing such an important part in work stoppages today are the very same men who, by their own words, claimed credit for the election of the Roosevelt-Truman ticket in 1944. I call your attention to the activities of such men as R. J. Thomas, Walter Reuther, Phil Murray, August Scholle and Harry Bridges. . . .

"It is very significant to note that the vast majority of old-time labor leaders and heads of unions, who throughout the years have brought great gains to our working people, are conspicuously absent from these striking activities."

Curtis' stern criticism of many unions, and his crusade for right-to-work provisions and statutory restraints on strikes contrary to the public interest, did him no mischief with the voters of Nebraska. By 1942, in the Republican primary of August 11, because of congressional redistricting, he was cast into a contest with another incumbent, Congressman Oren Copeland; Curtis won by a margin of more than three to two. In the general election of November 3, 1942, he received nearly seventy thousand votes, about twice the combined total for his two opponents. (Curtis now sat for the First Congressional District of Nebraska, what with the reapportionment that had followed the census of 1940.)

In the 1944 primary and election, Curtis loomed even larger. He was unopposed (for the first time) in the Republican primary; in the election of November 7, he won more than one hundred thousand votes to his Democratic opponent's forty-three thousand. It had become clear to the Democratic leadership in the House of Representatives, and to the White House, that this Nebraskan thorn in their flesh, this conservative Republican lawyer whom they had reproached as "isolationist" and "anti-labor," was not to be dislodged from Capitol Hill.

Curtis' bluntness about abuse of power by many labor unions indeed strengthened his political base. The public throughout the country was waking to this problem, and was beginning to resent the ready acquiescence of the Roosevelt and Truman administrations to many union demands. (President Truman fell into a rage at the threat of a great railway strike, but in general he courted union support.) So public vexation at unions' demands and ambitions had much to do with the Republicans' congressional victories in the election of 1946, when the Democrats lost their majorities in both houses of Congress. (Curtis himself won greater majorities in both primary and election than ever before.)

Only months later, this Republican congressional triumph would lead to passage of the Taft-Hartley Act; to President Truman's veto of Taft-Hartley; and to the tremendous overriding of that veto by Congress, late in June, 1947. (The House voted three hundred and thirty-one to override, against eighty-three; the Senate voted seventy-eight to override, against twenty-five.) During the war years, Carl Curtis and some colleagues of the Republican minority in House and Senate had broken trail for this large and lasting labor reform.

It needs to be emphasized that in labor concerns, as in international affairs, Congressman Curtis stood for a policy of neutrality. Quite as the preservation and advancement of the national interest is the first principle of diplomacy, so the maintenance of the general economic interest should be the first principle of relations in industry and commerce. Federal and state governments necessarily are interested in the relationships between labor and management, that the public prosperity may not diminish. In time of war especially, the government must endeavor to make sure that economic productivity is vigorous.

The primary function of government is to keep the peace, which includes economic peace. A successful peacekeeper must be impartial, neutral. In the disputes between labor and management, government should not convert itself into the advocate of one side against the other. Blessed are the peacemakers—the neutralists, if you will.

Carl Curtis' strong objection to the labor policies of the Roosevelt administration was that the President, the Department of Labor, the Department of Commerce, the National Labor Relations Board, the War Labor Board, and even the federal judiciary appointed by President Roosevelt had become in some degree partisans of the great labor unions. It was his endeavor during the war years to remedy this imbalance, through legislation, in the national military and economic interest.

As he would tell the House in his speech of December 11, 1945: "I have faith in the integrity, honesty, and patriotism of the workers of America. They are suffering from a situation that is not of their own making. The longer the delay is in meeting the present situation, the greater the danger is that some unwise action will be taken." President Truman's attempt (in May, 1946) to persuade Congress to conscript striking railwaymen into the army, and to provide criminal penalties against recalcitrant Railway Brotherhood leaders, grimly fulfilled Curtis' prediction of unwise action.

The government, benevolently neutral—so, in effect, Carl

Curtis reasoned—had the responsibility of establishing rules, especially in time of war, for maintaining peaceful relationships between labor and management. Those rules, primarily statutes, should be determined by the Congress, not by the Executive Force acting unilaterally. But the government should never turn militantly partisan in favor of one side or the other in the contests of economic interests. The government's concern is not the triumph of this or that economic interest or class, but instead the preservation of the general public interest. When the government finds it necessary to intervene in economic disputes, that intervention should be temperate, impartial, persuasive rather than forcible in most cases, and conducted in obedience to constitution, statute, and established rules of procedure.

THE HEROIC STORMING OF FORTRESS MONTGOMERY WARD

All these principles of neutrality by government in the disputes between labor and management were violated in the notorious case of the federal government's seizure of the properties of Montgomery Ward and Company, in April, 1944. Carl Curtis took a large part in the congressional investigation of that affair, an abuse of the emergency powers of the Roosevelt administration. The Montgomery Ward case deserves its own section of this chapter.

The great mail-order firm of Montgomery Ward and Company had its headquarters in Chicago. It had no manufacturing facilities in that city in 1944, and indeed had only three small factories anywhere in the world. Of Montgomery Ward's abundant goods offered for sale, some 98.3 per cent were purchased from other concerns for retail distribution through ten mail-order centers and 637 retail stores scattered across the several states of the Union. One scarcely thought of Montgomery Ward, distributing corsets, overalls, dresses, shirts, toys, and assorted gewgaws to individual customers, as engaged in producing materials for the war effort—and therefore answerable to the National War Labor Board.

But in Chicago, Montgomery Ward had temporary labor troubles, allegedly involving an interruption of production. On that pretext, the government of the United States seized possession of the Chicago properties of Montgomery Ward on April 26, 1944. An assistant secretary of the Department of Commerce, accompanied and advised by an assistant attorney general from the Department of Justice, arrived at the offices of Montgomery Ward and took possession.

The next day there arrived at those offices Mr. Sewell L. Avery, chairman of the board of directors of Montgomery Ward and Company, a rather crusty old gentleman, outspokenly opposed to the unionizing of his firm. Avery declined to recognize the purported authority of the assistant secretary of the Department of Commerce to take control over the affairs of Montgomery Ward.

The assistant secretary, nevertheless, proceeded to issue orders to Avery. Moreover, the assistant secretary summoned into the office a number of soldiers in battle dress, equipped with helmets, rifles, and bayonets. Next there arrived at the offices no less a dignitary than Mr. Francis Biddle, Attorney General of the United States, to take personal charge of this civil and military expedition. When the obdurate Mr. Avery still refused to turn over his company's property to the management of the armed soldiery, Attorney General Biddle said to his troops, "Throw him out! What are you waiting for?"

Sewell Avery refused to rise from his chair. The soldiers picked up that chair, Avery still in it, and carried the chairman of the board out to the street. A photograph of the old man being borne away was published in nearly every newspaper in the United States. It looked curiously like a scene from that other war-effort country the Third Reich.

Perhaps Roosevelt and Biddle had expected the seizure and the expulsion to be popularly applauded, as exemplary treatment of one of Roosevelt's "malefactors of great wealth" who had failed to obey enthusiastically a directive of the National War Labor Board. But Mr. Sewell L. Avery, however crusty an old merchant he may have been, was no evildoer to anyone's knowledge; and after all, Montgomery Ward belonged to him and many other stockholders, not to Mr. Francis Biddle.

The American sense of property is strongly developed; so is the American sense of fair play. Had it been necessary to send helmeted riflemen to eject an old man from his own office, when the ordinary civil processes presumably were available? In some newspapers, the word "stormtroopers" was employed editorially. The memory of what had been done to Sewell Avery lingered in a good many voters' minds as a conspicuous instance of the New Dealers' arrogance of power; it would not be forgotten in the elections of November, 1946, that gave both houses of Congress to the Republicans.

Alarm and resentment were great in Congress, too. In the Senate, Robert Taft, at the time the War Labor Disputes Bill had been debated, had suggested that the seizure provisions of the proposal might lead to a general assault on property. Now Senator Stiles Bridges told the Senate, most emphatically: "While American soldiers and marines were dying in Italy and in the South Pacific, while airmen were being shot down over Germany, while navy officers and bluejackets were suffering exposure on the high seas in carrying the battle to the Japs, other soldiers were humiliated by obeying orders to rush the Montgomery Ward office in Chicago on order of the attorney general and forcibly ejecting the aged president from the plant."

On May 2, 1944, the House of Representatives passed House Resolution 521, providing that a select committee be appointed to investigate this seizure of the property of Montgomery Ward. The committee consisted of four Democrats and three Republicans. Robert Ramspeck, of Georgia, became chairman; the other Democratic members were J. Bayard Clark, of

North Carolina; William T. Byrne, of New York; and A. S. Mike Monroney, of Oklahoma. The Republicans on this select committee were Charles S. Dewey, of Illinois; Charles H. Elston, of Ohio; and Carl T. Curtis.

Testimony in Washington before this committee disclosed that the following events led to the seizure of Montgomery Ward.

This act followed from an order issued by the War Labor Board on November 5, 1942, directing Montgomery Ward to enter into a contract with the United Retail and Wholesale and Department Store Employees of America, affiliated with the Congress of Industrial Organizations. This National War Labor Board originally was a creation by executive order. The Board's original function was to promote the war effort. But the Board originally had no authority to issue orders and compel obedience; it was an advisory body, in essence. Later, in June, 1943, Congress passed the War Labor Disputes Act (the Smith-Connally Act), incidentally conferring greater powers upon the War Labor Board. So at the time of the Board's original directive to Montgomery Ward, in November, 1942, the War Labor Board had no lawful means of enforcement. Under the later War Labor Disputes Act, however, the President was given power to seize "any plant, mine, or facility equipped for the manufacture, production, or mining of any articles or materials which may be required for the war effort or which may be used in connection therewith."

The Board's original order to Montgomery Ward was intended presumably to forestall any interruption of "production" in the great retailing firm by giving the United Retail and Wholesale Employees Union what they desired, a union-shop contract with Montgomery Ward. War production, as far as Montgomery Ward was engaged in any activity of that sort, would be maintained uninterrupted through yielding to one party (the union) to a labor dispute precisely what the other party (the management) did not wish to yield. So much for governmental neutrality in labor relations.

The Board's directive to Montgomery Ward required, among other matters, that all employees be union members and that the company must withhold union dues from the pay of the employees, remitting these dues to the union: what was called "maintenance of union membership" and the "check-off system."

Montgomery Ward's management promptly sent to the War Labor Board a letter expressing opposition to the "maintenance of membership" provision. If the company were to sign such a contract with the union, it would be necessary to discharge those employees who had resigned from the union or who had never joined. This arrangement would be more nearly a closed shop than a union shop. Montgomery Ward pointed out that the previous November President Roosevelt had said, "The government of the United States will not order, nor will Congress pass, legislation ordering the so-called closed shop." The company's letter concluded, "If the President of the United States, as commander-in-chief in time of war, directs that Ward accept the Board's rulings, which we earnestly believe are illegal and uneconomic, we will respectfully obey."

Thereupon President Roosevelt sent a letter to Montgomery Ward ordering the firm to comply with the Board's order. On December 18, 1942, Montgomery Ward signed the required contract with the union.

But the matter did not end there. The contract with the union expired on November 8, 1943. On November 2, Montgomery Ward served notice as provided in the contract that it would not renew the agreement upon its expiration. Negotiations began between the company and the union for a new contract. Once the contract had expired, most of Ward's employees quit the union, no longer being under compulsion to pay dues or to belong to the union as a condition of employment.

So Montgomery Ward asked the union to supply evidence that it still represented a sufficient number of Ward's employees to be accepted as the employees' bargaining agent. The company requested this evidence because a recent check-off of union dues had shown that less than twenty per cent of the employees then at work were having union dues deducted from wages. This the union would not do; it refused to submit its membership cards to the company.

On December 16, 1943, the president of the union requested of the War Labor Board that Ward's property be seized by the federal government on the charge of the company's having violated a directive of the board.

About the middle of January, 1944, the Board issued an order extending the term of the old union-company contract that had expired. The company replied that if Ward were to obey, the firm must discharge all employees who had resigned from the union after expiration of the contract in November.

Montgomery Ward then proceeded to file suit in the federal district court, the District of Columbia, asking that the Board's order be declared in violation of law. (This suit was still pending when the Chicago properties of Montgomery Ward were seized.) There followed complexities with the National Labor Relations Board. Next, the War Labor Board relieved the union from any obligation to obtain the certification from the National Labor Relations Board that the company had requested.

At this stage of the proceedings, the union called a strike at Chicago on April 12, 1944. The strike was ineffectual. Not a single unit of Ward's operation was closed, and the large majority of Ward's employees crossed union picket lines on their way to work.

Montgomery Ward's operation at Chicago consisted of a retail business, the administrative offices, and a mail-order department. The day after the strike was called, the United States Post Office withdrew seventy of its seventy-five employees from the office it maintained on Ward's premises to handle outgoing parcel-post shipments. The Post Office declared that its employees would have nothing to do; Montgomery Ward declared that the government was using the Post Office Department to make the strike effective. Six days later, the Post Office refused to deliver first class mail to Ward in Chicago, although the company requested the Post Office to do so.

The unsuccessful strike ended on April 24; all interruption of Ward's business ceased. The union announced to the press that the strike had been terminated.

But about April 19, Samuel Wolchak, the union's president, had again demanded that the government seize Ward's property on the ground of violation of the War Labor Board's order.

In response to that insistence, two days after the strike had ceased and at a time when the Montgomery Ward business was operating fully, the Department of Commerce sought possession of Ward's properties. There followed Sewell Avery's defiance, and his forcible removal by soldiers.

So much for the general background of this controversy. The House's select committee was not charged with the responsibility of deciding how management and labor should behave toward each other, nor was the committee expected to decide which party was at fault in this dispute. The committee's duty was to determine whether the seizure of Ward's property had been lawful. Had Congress delegated to the President such authority? Did the President, under the Constitution, possess general aggregate powers including the authority to seize a private business?

Now the War Labor Disputes Act did confer authority upon the President, under certain conditions, to seize plants, mines, and manufacturing operations, for preventing the stoppage of war production. But testimony at the hearings of the select committee showed that no work-stoppage had occurred at Montgomery Ward at the time of the seizure. Besides, the Ward operation clearly was not within the categories of war production specified in the War Labor Disputes Act.

In the course of the hearings, Representative Curtis inquired of one sworn witness, a Ward executive, "Now, assuming for the purpose of this question that the federal government may have had a right to take possession of the plant because it was not in operation, that cause was removed two days before the exercise of that right?"

Mr. Barr: "The plant was in full operation prior to the seizure of the plant."

Despite such evidence, the Democratic majority members of the select committee filed a report generally supporting the action of the government in seizing Montgomery Ward. The Republican minority came to very different conclusions. Such divisions along partisan lines, of course, are frequent enough in congressional investigations.

The minority members contended in their report that the

War Labor Board, established by executive order, had no powers to enforce its orders; certainly no power of seizure. The War Labor Disputes Act, passed later, did grant power to the President, in limited circumstances, to seize property. But the retailing and mail-order business of Montgomery Ward did not fall within the categories of manufacture, production, and mining specified in the War Labor Disputes Act.

Moreover, the minority report continued, the President did not possess under the Constitution general or aggregate powers authorizing such seizure: such power was in the Congress, and the President could exercise only such power as might be delegated to him by the Congress. In the opinion of the attorney general addressed to President Roosevelt on April 22, 1944, and in the executive order of the President that authorized the seizure by the War Labor Board, it was contended that the President, as commander in chief, possessed an "aggregate of power" that permitted such seizures by armed force. But the Department of Justice was unable to cite a single court decision in support of this argument. The authorities, the minority of the select committee found, refuted such a claim.

Of several precedents in such questions examined by members of the select committee, one must suffice here. It was the opinion of Justice Brandeis in *Whitney* v. *California* (274 U.S. 357):

"While this Court sits, it has the inescapable duty of seeing that the mandates of the Constitution are obeyed. That duty exists in time of war as well as time of peace, and in its performance we must not forget that few indeed have been the invasions upon essential liberties which have not been accompanied by pleas of urgent necessity advanced in good faith by responsible men."

Even had the operation of Montgomery Ward been such that it was involved in the war effort, the minority's report additionally pointed out, there could have been no just power of seizure because at the time of the seizure, no work stoppage was occurring.

The House's select committee was not meant to judge the motives of the various parties in this controversy. But the minority did state that in its belief, the great power of the United

States government had been used on behalf of the union and not as an impartial referee.

The House took no action on the select committee's reports. Litigation about the dispute continued for several months in federal courts. The district court, Northern District of Illinois, ruled in favor of Montgomery Ward. In the words of Judge Sullivan:

"The Constitutional guaranties that protect the sacred rights, liberties, and property of American citizens, from the humblest to the most exalted, still remain inviolate. These rights may not be transgressed with impunity nor be disregarded because of expediency; neither may they be abridged or suspended, even for a single moment, except in the manner and under the circumstances specifically provided by law . . . I am of the opinion that the President was without authority, either under Section 3 of the War Labor Disputes Act, or under the war powers conferred upon him by the Constitution as commander in chief of the army and navy, to take possession of the plants and facilities of Montgomery Ward and Company."

This case was appealed to the Circuit Court of Appeals and then to the Supreme Court, which in effect dismissed the case as moot. Whether the case was declared moot because the strike had ended before the seizure, or because the war had ended, or for some other reason, remained unclear.

We have discussed the Montgomery Ward seizure at some length because that case illustrates all too well what may occur when government, abandoning neutrality in disputes between labor and management, becomes a partisan for one side or the other. It also suggests the corrupting influence of emergency powers assumed by executive authorities in time of war. The CIO, with which the union at Montgomery Ward was affiliated, had been indebted to President Roosevelt for much; and for much was President Roosevelt indebted to the Congress of Industrial Organizations. Yet honest government is not an instrument for repaying favors.

CHAINS
UPON POWER

Among the many lessons that may be learned from the history of the Second World War is one about the arrogance of concentrated political power—even in constitutional democracies that can boast of their large measure of order, justice, and freedom. In matters of power, said Jefferson, put no trust in men, but bind them down with the chains of the Constitution.

From 1941 to 1945, the advocates of neutrality were trampled on in more ways than one. Blessed are the peacemakers, we are instructed in the Beatitudes; yet often those peacemakers are blessed in the realm of spirit, but reviled here below. The Constitution of the United States was designed to keep the peace and to put chains upon arrogant and arbitrary power. Despite the Second World War and the vast centralizing programs that began with the New Deal, the Constitution endures as an instrument for a government of laws, not of men. It even shelters peacemakers.

During those war years, Carl Curtis did achieve one considerable success in Congress: the Flood Control Act of 1944. We pass with some relief from the fierce events of the war to an enduring internal improvement.

Chapter 3

Developing a Sixth of the United States

WHAT CAME OF THE REPUBLICAN VALLEY FLOOD

Nebraskans heard alarming news over their radios, early one spring morning in 1935. A severe flood had occurred on the Republican River in southwestern Nebraska. The broadcasters gave few details, but seemingly the flood was a disaster. Telephone and telegraph lines were out. Highways were flooded and railroad tracks impassable. Amateur radio operators soon told the state more of the grim circumstances in the Republican Valley.

On hearing the news, Carl Curtis drove from Minden directly south for some thirty miles to the Republican Valley. He did not forget the sight he encountered there. A wall of water, some ten or twelve feet high and four or five miles wide, coming from the west, had roared down the Republican Valley. Farm tractors, hurried along by the flood waters, were battered like tin cans that boys had used for hockey pucks. One

71

could hear the bellowing of cattle carried along by the flood.

Some people had clung to a treetop or to the roof of a building all night; snakes washed out of the hills came floating toward them. The highways had been destroyed, the railroads washed out: no transportation survived, and no means of communication.

Farmland near the river was terribly eroded. When the water subsided, the fields were filled with silt and debris. Livestock had vanished; devastation was general.

The Republican River enters Nebraska near the corner where Nebraska, Colorado, and Kansas meet; it flows eastward a distance of perhaps a hundred and forty miles before it turns south into Kansas. This is a rural region with no very populous centers. The flood had struck western Nebraska during the night, so that many folk had no warning or opportunity to escape.

More than a hundred people perished. Loss of life occurred chiefly along the first hundred miles of the river's course through Nebraska. In the eastern portion of the valley, warning had come in daylight so that, despite heavy property loss, nobody was drowned. But in the western two-thirds of the valley, on the average, a life was lost along every mile of the river.

An Indian legend had foretold that the Republican River would flood gigantically once in every century. Records maintained by local groups and by army engineers suggest that there is truth in this tradition.

When the flood waters subsided, tenacious Nebraskans went about the labor of cleaning up the debris, rebuilding highways and railroads, and trying to restore farmland to cultivation. For many years past, proposals for irrigation of the region had been discussed. In the 1920s, the Bureau of Reclamation and the Corps of Engineers were dominant in river development. The Roosevelt administration had created the Public Works Administration, intended to undertake projects of a more lasting character than the activities of some other New Deal agencies. If the PWA officials and the President approved a proposal for public works, the federal government usually would advance money as a subsidy for construction of the works; then the government would make a long-term, low-interest loan to some locally organized body to construct, own, and manage the project.

With this in view, groups were organized at several points along the Republican Valley, surveys were made, and applications were submitted to the Public Works Administration for flood-control and irrigation projects. The applications were earnestly endorsed by the local citizens, with few dissenters. Public officeholders supported the applications; Charles Binderup, then congressman from the Fourth District, diligently worked to advance them to the PWA. Rallies were held to gain support for the intended projects; parades occurred, with banners on which was inscribed the legend "Irrigate or Migrate!"

Yet the years 1935, 1936, 1937, and 1938 elapsed without any of the PWA applications for help to the Republican Valley being approved. When Carl Curtis was elected to the House of Representatives in 1938, he went to Washington determined to do everything he could to prevent other floods in the Republican Valley, and to see that stored water might be used for irrigating the lands of Nebraska.

Curtis was no friend to a general expansion of the activities and costs of the federal government. He did not wish a centralized political structure to assume responsibility for the wants of individuals, or to usurp the functions of state and local governments. In his first campaign for election to Congress, he had made it very clear that he opposed many of the undertakings of the New Deal.

But Curtis found no inconsistency in opposing the proliferation of what came to be called the welfare state, and, at the same time, in advocating flood control and irrigation undertaken in part at federal expense. He pointed out that flood-control works in Nebraska would furnish great protection to Kansas City in Kansas, Kansas City in Missouri, and to all cities, towns, and farmland down the Missouri and the Mississippi Rivers. This was an interstate concern, not merely a Nebraskan problem.

The first Corps of Engineers dam to be constructed on the Republican River was in Nebraska, near the town of Alma. According to the Engineers, ninety-five percent of the dam's benefits accrued to the two Kansas Cities. Curtis pointed out, moreover, that permanent public works, properly situated, contribute to the economy of a whole region or of the whole country, thus promoting general prosperity.

Genuine public works enable individuals to do more for themselves; but these works do not create dependency in the sense that many "social" programs do. Another important distinction was suggested by Curtis: "social welfare" programs almost invariably run on not merely for years but for generations, their costs increasing decade after decade. Little can be done about ceasing or reducing a "welfare" project. But a public-works program is subject to the immediate control of the Congress and the president. If the times justify it, a program of public works can be suspended for a period of years. Once proposed and authorized, most public works are completed within three to five years; then the construction cost comes to an end. Where irrigation is concerned, those benefiting from irrigation pay a substantial portion of the cost of such projects, which is not true of people benefiting from other river developments.

On being sworn into the House in January, 1939, Curtis arranged his assignment to the Committee on Flood Control. He began to acquaint the committee and the Congress with the urgent needs of the Republican Valley. In his first major address to the House (March 10, 1939), he described the dreadful flood that had ruined the Republican Valley four years earlier; nothing had been done to redeem that region. Now that the declining PWA was not granting funds to new applications, Curtis turned his attention to the Corps of Engineers and the Bureau of Reclamation.

In his first speech, he informed the House about the grand possibilities for restoring a large area to prosperity, so that not only would the inhabitants have more income but they would also be able to pay much more into federal revenues. Explaining how the PWA had failed to act on any of the Republican River Valley applications over several years, Curtis said that when the PWA's men discovered that they were to work on the Republican River, they picked up their tools and ran. Representative Curtis' House colleagues, taking this witticism good-naturedly, accepted Curtis as the spokesman for that region.

An earlier study and survey by the Army Engineers had recommended the construction of a dam for flood control in Harlan County, Nebraska, just east of the town of Alma. This proposal attracted much support in Harlan County and eastward, an area that had suffered heavy losses in the 1935 flood and that also desired development of irrigation. Curtis supported the Harlan County project, but argued as well that it could not be a solution to the whole problem. The great loss of life in that flood had been to the west of the proposed Harlan dam: the westward region, too, must be protected.

The point at which to arrest a flood is not at the mouth of a river, where the flood's force already has full momentum. To impede floods, water must be retained as far as possible upstream. Dams in Nebraska, South Dakota, Montana, and North Dakota help diminish floods in Mississippi and Louisiana.

Similarly, dams were needed at the headwaters of the Republican River to control that valley's floods. West of the Harlan County Dam, the Republican is fed by several tributaries, spreading like the fingers of a hand: the Frenchman, the South Republican, the Medicine Creek, the Red Willow Creek, and the Prairie Dog.

Soon the Harlan County Dam was authorized. Continuing his efforts, Curtis arranged construction of another on-river dam on the Republican near the town of Trenton, and a smaller dam on each of the five tributaries. These dams give protection to southwestern Nebraska from severe floods; and the water stored behind the dams is used for irrigating an area where rainfall would not suffice. (This is neither a desert nor an arid region, properly defined: it is a farming district where the annual rainfall is not quite enough for the cultivation of good crops.)

To focus the attention of the Corps of Engineers on flood control and river development west of the Harlan County Dam, Curtis offered a resolution—approved by the House's Flood-Control Committee—requiring the Corps to study the needs of the Republican Basin in that region.

With onset of the Second World War, the people of the Republican Valley put winning the war first. But they kept up their organizations, looking forward to a building program after victory. The Republican Valley Conservation Association maintained a Washington representative, M. O. Ryan; the president and driving force of the organization was Harry Strunk, a publisher.

General Lewis Pick, with his office in Omaha, was division engineer for the Corps of Engineers. He and Curtis worked together closely. Pick was often in Washington to assist at hearings and to confer with members of the House Flood-Control Committee. General Pick told Curtis that a severe flood problem existed all up and down the Missouri: Sioux City, Omaha, and the Kansas Cities were repeatedly menaced. Flood control could never be brought to this region or to the lower Mississippi until there was a program for storing water along the upper tributaries of the Missouri Basin.

Curtis asked Pick what he needed for this large undertaking. The General replied that the Corps of Engineers wanted a resolution from the House Committee on Flood Control, authorizing a re-study of the whole Missouri River Basin with a view to revised plans for flood control. Pick had such a resolution, a short one, prepared; and Curtis introduced it on May 6, 1943. In due time, the Corps of Engineers prepared a proposal calling for construction of the large dams on the main stream of the Missouri that have now been built; also it called for many tributary dams.

About this time, General Pick received orders for his transfer to the Orient, where he was to build the Ledo Road from India to Burma. He visited Washington en route to his new assignment. A half-dozen men from the Missouri River Basin arranged a dinner at the Army and Navy Club in Washington to say goodbye to General Pick.

Pick told this group that his study was completed, and that he had devised a plan that could not yet be released since it had to be cleared through the Corps of Engineers and then approved by the Secretary of War, who would transmit it to the President. In turn, the President would present the plan to Congress.

Pick could not reveal all the details, but mentioned that the plan called for dams to hold back water in the tributaries. Taking Curtis aside, the General whispered to him that the plan carried a recommendation for five dams on the Republican

River west of the Harlan County Dam. Rejoicing, Curtis could scarcely contain himself, but did keep Pick's secret until the plan was made public.

The procedure for authorizing such public works as flood control is for the appropriate committee to hold hearings, and then to report recommendations to the House of Representatives. First an authorization bill is needed, approving the plans of the Corps of Engineers and authorizing appropriation of funds to carry out the project. An authorization bill does not itself appropriate funds, but it is a necessary step before an appropriation bill can be passed later.

The Flood Control Committee of the House held hearings and proceeded to consider the Pick plan for the Missouri Basin, also known as the Army Engineers' plan. As a member of that committee, Curtis gave very full attention to the hearings and proceedings, which extended to the whole flood-control program throughout the United States.

The committee took it that it was not to authorize public works for immediate construction; that would have interfered with the war effort. Rather the committee should prepare plans for post-war projects. The committee's chairman was Representative William Whittington, of Mississippi, a man of strong intellect and a driving force. He did his homework well, knowing the geography of every river basin throughout the country. He was well informed as to what the Corps of Engineers proposed before the Corps presented its material at the hearings.

The hearings concluded, the committee undertook to write an omnibus flood-control bill, authorizing such projects in various regions of the United States. Calling Curtis to his office, William Whittington told him that the needs of the lower Mississippi could not be met unless a great expansion in the flood-control program should occur, as it had been authorized in the pre-war years. A beginning authorization for the lower Mississippi of two hundred million dollars would be required. As chairman of the committee, Whittington could not ask for such a sum without giving similar consideration to other regions that had great need. He proposed a beginning authorization of two hundred million dollars for the lower Mississippi, and another two hundred million dollars for the Missouri River Basin. This decision assured the beginning of the development of the water resources of the whole Missouri Basin. The flood-control bill, soon to become known as the Flood Control Act of 1944, was written with these sums authorized. On the committee's recommendation, it was passed by the House of Representatives.

When the flood-control bill was presented to the House, Carl Curtis went to some pains to explain to the House his distinction between make-work projects and permanent public works. "It is true that the works authorized in this bill are for the postwar period," he said. "I want to make my position clear, however, in regard to that. I am not supporting any of these projects because they will produce employment in the postwar days. The works programs of the 'Thirties were a failure, so far as bringing about re-employment. We exhausted both the alphabet and the federal treasury with works programs, but we ended up with more people hunting a real job than we started with.

"We ended up with local, state, and national governments spending more for relief than they did when the works programs were started. There were some very fine public works constructed . . . including some fine irrigation projects, but a works program for the sake of working, in a hope that it will relieve unemployment is a proven failure. I am supporting this bill because it represents needed public works. It will bring flood relief to distressed areas and save valuable land and other property. It will save human lives. It will provide additional irrigation, which will add to the productiveness of our country."

He went on to explain various features of the bill, particularly the need for a central agency—the War Department—to operate the reservoirs. The Bureau of Reclamation would have jurisdiction over the use of impounded water for irrigation.

"The Missouri River Basin," Curtis said, "represents one-sixth of the area of the United States. In that area you will find a great deal of the finest and best agricultural land in the world. The Missouri River basin includes a great portion of Missouri, Iowa, Kansas, North and South Dakota, Montana, Wyoming, and Colorado, and all of the state of Nebraska . . . This area is a great breadbasket for the entire world. In the basin can be found great industrial and manufacturing cities. It is indeed the great heart of America.''

He outlined the problems of the Republican Valley, the details of the Pick plan. The bill was passed by the House without difficulty.

ACCOMPLISHMENTS IN THE MISSOURI BASIN

While the Corps of Engineers plan, as drawn up by General Pick, was under consideration, the Bureau of Reclamation was busy with its report for the development of the Missouri River Basin. The Bureau, having general authority for such studies, did not require a special congressional resolution like the one passed for the Army Engineers. Glen Sloan was the engineer in charge for the Bureau of Reclamation. By the time the flood-control bill reached the Senate, Sloan had completed the Bureau's reclamation plan for the basin and presented it to the Senate. The two agencies had different responsibilities, but the sites they selected for the construction of dams were almost identical. Physical features of a site determine where a dam should be built; such a determination is not a political decision.

Thus the Senate had before it two plans for the Missouri River Basin. Not attempting to choose one plan over the other, the Senate proceeded to authorize both. Thus the bill became known as the Pick-Sloan Plan, or the Army Engineers-Bureau of Reclamation Plan for the Missouri River Basin.

The next legislative hurdle for this plan was the committee on conference. A conference committee is appointed to iron out differences between the version of a bill passed by the House and the version passed by the Senate. The report of a committee on conference must then be adopted by a vote of each of the two houses.

The members of the conference committee are selected from among members of the House and Senate committees that originated the legislation. This was an omnibus flood-control bill covering the entire United States. Carl Curtis, appointed a conferee, was the only member from House and Senate, and from either political party, who came from the Missouri River Basin: so there devolved upon Curtis the responsibility for the Missouri Basin portion of the bill.

This conference committee met in December, 1944. Its work was completed that month; the President signed the bill on December 22.

The Act is a landmark in river-development legislation, so far as joint work by the Bureau of Reclamation and the Corps of Engineers is concerned. Considerable rivalry between the two agencies existed, a competition extending to territory as well as to appropriated dollars. The agencies' functions overlapped. If the Engineers built a flood-control dam, they were often authorized to provide space in the reservoir for stored irrigation water. Similarly, when the Bureau built a dam, flood control was one of that dam's functions, and the Bureau was permitted to charge to flood control certain expenses of the construction.

Commonly the Corps of Engineers would build structures where ample or perhaps too much rain fell, with flood control and navigation their objectives. The Bureau of Reclamation had its domain of aridity, particularly the near-arid or very dry regions of the West.

These two regions meet in Nebraska and in the Missouri Basin generally. So the Act of 1944 became a landmark in river legislation because it was the first comprehensive plan that involved both the Corps of Engineers and the Bureau of Reclamation. The Act of 1944 became the basis for future developments of this sort elsewhere.

The Senate-House conference made significant decisions,

approved subsequently by both houses. One of these decisions was that dams to be constructed west of the ninety-seventh meridian would be built by the Bureau of Reclamation; and to the east of that meridian, running just west of Lincoln, by the Corps of Engineers. The conference report also provided that the Engineers would operate the dams they built; but when the water was released, an irrigation district under the jurisdiction of the Bureau of Reclamation would be formed. If electricity were generated at an Engineers' dam, the Army would handle the generation; but the marketing of the electricity would be handled by the Bureau of Reclamation, already set up to do that.

Another significant provision in the Act of 1944, worked out by the conferees, was that portion dealing with the power revenues. The entire Missouri Basin was treated as a unit. Power revenues produced anywhere in the Missouri Basin could be used to subsidize the building of irrigation districts anywhere in the basin. The dams built in Nebraska had little or no electrical power involved; the principal producers of power were the large dams on the main stem of the Missouri River: the Garrison Dam in North Dakota; in South Dakota, the Oahe Dam, the Gavin's Point Dam, the Fort Randall Dam, and the Big Bend Dam.

This subsidy from power revenues is what made the irrigation projects feasible. The Frenchman-Cambridge project in the Republican River Basin includes the Enders Dam, the Trenton Dam, the Medicine Creek Dam, and the Red Willow Dam; it provides Nebraska with some 56,940 acres of irrigation. The total estimated cost of the project, including all of the dams, was $86,000,000. The irrigating farmers pay $15,000,000 of that sum; $22,000,000 is charged to nonreimbursable items, principally flood control, recreation, and wildlife nurture. About $48,900,000 will be paid from power revenues for the Frenchman-Cambridge project.

In Nebraska, the Sergeant project added 13,360 irrigated acres; the Ainsworth project, 33,960 acres; the Farwell project, 47,925 acres; the North Loup project, 53,000 acres. The Bostwick project added 27,787 acres in Nebraska and about 40,000 acres in Kansas. All these projects have received subsidies from the power revenues generated in the Missouri Basin, chiefly on the main stem of the Missouri River north of Nebraska, to a total of $223,700,000.

The O'Neil project (authorized in 1972) in Nebraska, including the Norden Dam, will bring additional water to 77,000 acres; of its estimated cost of $180,000,000, some $124,000,000 will be repaid from power revenues. The Midstate project (authorized in 1965), will bring additional water to 140,000 acres; estimated cost, $172,000,000; payment from power revenues, $82,000,000. (Neither the O'Neil nor the Midstate has yet been built.)

Such are the results in Nebraska alone of the Flood Control Act of 1944. The Missouri River Basin projects, covering a sixth of the land area of the continental United States, have permanent consequences more significant than those of the Tennessee Valley Authority. (See map, p. 87)

In this vast development of flood control and irrigation, Carl Curtis, as representative and later as senator, was closely associated with other members of Congress from the Missouri Basin states. Senator George Norris, of Nebraska, was interested in the Republican Valley, but his term of office expired before construction there became effective. Senator Hugh Butler, of Nebraska, was a prominent member of the Interior Committee of the Senate, which was responsible for the authorizing legislation. Kenneth Wherry, another Nebraskan senator, served on the Senate Appropriations Committee; he was of great help, particularly in securing the appropriations. Roman Hruska and Carl Curtis worked as a Nebraska team in this development. (Hruska came to the House of Representatives in 1952; after serving one term there, he entered the Senate, cooperating with Curtis on all authorizations and appropriations occurring thereafter. In some of these Nebraska projects, Senator Hruska would present the resolution, with Curtis as co-sponsor; in other projects, their roles would be reversed.)

The increase in irrigation and the expansion of agriculture are labors congenial to a conservative. On the value of irrigation, Curtis has said, "We must not let our natural resources go to waste. We must keep in mind that when we add to the agricultural production of the country, we add to the production of new wealth. This is what generates business and jobs in our towns and our cities. All of this results in more income and more tax revenue for localities, or states, and for the national government. We have a growing population, and it is through such public improvements that we leave the good earth a little better than it was when our generation took over.''

Of course irrigation in Nebraska did not begin with the Flood Control Act of 1944. The history of such undertakings in Nebraska began with the passage of the original National Reclamation Act (1902). One of the major projects in Nebraska was built by the Public Works Administration: the Central Nebraska Public Power and Irrigation District, commonly known as the Tri-County District, which includes the Kingsley Dam, Lake McConaughy, and other features. The last extension of the Tri-County was carried out by the Bureau of Reclamation: that completing project was the building of the Carl T. Curtis Dam and Pumping Station, forming Lake Elwood.

The building of the large dam on the main stem of the Missouri River resulted in flood protection all down the river as it traversed the eastern edge of Nebraska. It met the problem of flooding at Sioux City, on down to the Omaha area. Formerly Omaha suffered many fierce floods. Storing the water upstream in the tributaries and on the main stem of the Missouri held back sufficient water to make effective the local protective works of Sioux City, Omaha, the Kansas Cities, and points beyond.

In the years since 1944, a number of protective works to meet local flood problems have been constructed throughout Nebraska. The basic authorization for these works has been the Flood Control Act of 1944. All later authorizations go back to the basic Pick-Sloan Plan.

In addition to the flood-control projects for the major rivers, Curtis obtained passage of the necessary resolutions for studies by the Corps of Engineers on the Blue River, the Nemaha, and other streams. An example of such activities is the Salt Creek Basin, draining into the Platte River, which in turn adds to the volume of water entering the Missouri River and eventually the Mississippi.

On June 21, 1944, Curtis obtained passage by the Flood Control Committee of the House of a resolution for ascertaining whether any improvements for flood control were advisable along Salt Creek and its tributaries. The Salt Creek Basin comprises an area of some 1,627 square miles in southeastern Nebraska. Floods on Salt Creek and its tributaries may occur in all the months from February to September, but are most likely to happen during the normal period of heavy precipitation in May and June. Studies developed by the Corps of Engineers in response to this resolution pointed out that during the fifty-three year period between 1900 and 1952, ninety-seven floods occurred on Salt Creek and its tributaries, exclusive of Wahoo Creek; thirty-nine occurred on the Wahoo Creek system. The most damaging flood occurred in May, 1950: nearly twenty thousand acres of land were flooded, nine lives were lost, and damages were estimated at more than $2,643,000 in the city of Lincoln. More than two hundred business establishments and more than a thousand houses were damaged.

This study and report by the Engineers set in motion a cooperative effort shared by the Corps of Engineers, the Soil Conservation Service, the Salt Valley Watershed District, and the Nebraska Game and Parks Commission. This project employed the tributary approach, building small dams rather than the huge costly dams on the main stem of a great river. Today the Salt Creek Basin is protected by twelve dams built for this purpose. Not only has it solved the problem of floods, it has brought fishing, water sports, and outdoor recreation to a region that previously had no lakes. Recent figures show that 1,871,500 people visited the reservoirs along Salt Creek during 1982. Waterfowl and other wildlife have increased significantly.

So it has come to pass that the Republican River flood in 1935 set in motion a chain of events extending to the entire Missouri Basin and the lower Mississippi. Because of the Republican Valley disaster, Carl Curtis sought a place on the Flood Control Committee of the House of Representatives. In an effort to bring flood control to the Republican Valley, Curtis sponsored the huge undertaking for the whole Missouri Basin.

Since the Pick-Sloan Plan commenced, hundreds of thousands of acres of land have obtained irrigation in the Mississippi Basin. Nebraska has received irrigation for some 200,000 acres from its network of dams and canals; Wyoming, 152,000; Montana, 71,000; Kansas, 46,000; South Dakota, 21,000; North Dakota, 7,000. Additional projects under construction will irrigate more than 800,000 additional acres; altogether, the Pick-Sloan program is expected to irrigate, when completed, as much as 1.5 million acres.

Driving across Nebraska today, one sees in town after town businesses that sell boats and fishing supplies, This is just part of the story, worth mentioning because when the flood came to the Republican Valley in 1935, there were no boats nearer than Omaha. Rescue crews could find no boats in the districts struck by the flood. The whole Missouri Basin today is very different from what it would be if the Corps of Engineers and the Bureau of Reclamation had not worked gigantic improvements in that sixth of the United States.

A WORD OF COMMENDATION
OF REAL INTERNAL IMPROVEMENTS

Much of the time of a member of Congress—especially of a conservative member—is expended in trying to prevent the doing of things that ought not to be done in this land. Other days, weeks, or months are spent in trying to ameliorate or undo policies, already in effect, that ought never to have been adopted, or else have been carried to undesirable lengths.

So a representative or a senator is mightily heartened whenever he finds himself successful in carrying through a measure calculated to work a positive general improvement of undoubted and permanent worth. The initiation of great public works that benefit the whole country, as well as helping a representative's district or a senator's state, at a cost soon repaid in general benefits, is such a positive achievement.

The old congressional term for such public works on a large scale is "internal improvements." It is true that internal improvements, public works, sometimes have been extravagantly costly in terms of benefits obtained; or that some such improvements, though paid for from national revenues, have benefited only a local district or a single state. Especially damaging to national unity have been internal improvements designed to benefit only one section of the country, chiefly at the expense of some other section.

So one understands the passionate assault of the Virginian John Randolph of Roanoke, in the House and the Senate during the first three decades of the nineteenth century, on the internal-improvement bills of his era. He believed those measures deliberately calculated to benefit the commercial and industrial North at the expense of the agricultural South. In his speech to the House of Representatives on January 30, 1824, concerning surveys for roads and canals, Congressman Randolph demanded that the Congress diminish expenditures for internal improvements, reduce the public debt, and cease to burden the agricultural interest unjustly:

"Let us, then, I repeat, Mr. Chairman, pay our debts, personal and public; let us leave the profits of labor in the pockets of the people, to rid them of that private embarrassment under which they so extensively suffer, and apply every shilling of the revenue, not indispensable to the exigencies of the Government, to the faithful discharge of the public debt, before we engage in any new schemes of lavish expenditure."

A century and a quarter later, Congressman Carl Curtis felt a strong sympathy with Randolph's sentences, finding himself in political circumstances somewhat similar. But the internal improvements of flood control and irrigation in the Missouri River Basin were of national benefit, paying for themselves through invigoration of the national economy.

Far from injuring the agricultural interest, the dams and

irrigation systems planned in 1944 aided agriculture first of all, and then commerce and industry. Nothing is more conservative than conservation; and future generations may owe their prosperity to the foresight of proponents of wise public works.

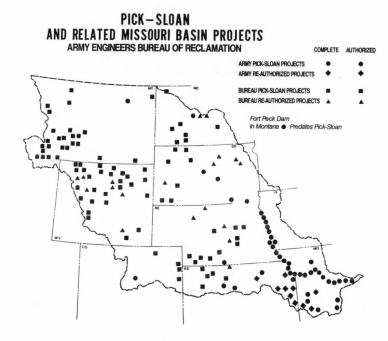

PICK–SLOAN
AND RELATED MISSOURI BASIN PROJECTS
ARMY ENGINEERS BUREAU OF RECLAMATION

Chapter 4

Our
Daily Bread
From the Government

**HISTORICAL NOTES
ON BREAD AND CIRCUSES**

By the end of the Second World War, Representative Curtis knew that this was the time to point out the danger lurking in the future for America. He rejected the notion that the role of the government of the United States was providing individuals with those things which had always been the rewards of personal effort.

The welfare state was beginning to take form in America, though not so swiftly as it grew in Europe during the same period. The war itself—with its concentration of power in Washington, its emergency controls over the economy, its increase of the federal bureaucracy—in effect had combined with the theories and measures of Roosevelt's New Deal to produce a mentality that looked to central government for direction and benefaction. Might not the central political power relieve people of many of the material burdens and responsibilities of

89

daily living? Might not Washington feed and lodge people, ensure their regular employment, school their children, pay their medical bills, and provide for their old age?

As Curtis would tell the House of Representatives in 1949, "Realizing that our post-war economy would be weighted with established obligations for the federal government, I concluded that I would not cast my vote in Congress to add to the over-burdened federal government, and that my influence would not be used to put the government into new fields of endeavor." So for more than three decades, Carl Curtis' own endeavor was to restrain the growth of the American welfare state or to modify its consequences.

Why not accept the welfare state as the inevitable wave of the future? Because that submission would alter the American character for the worse. Curtis was not ashamed to be a conservative—a word he defined later in an address to conservative members of Minnesota's legislature, in September, 1963:

"A conservative believes in the dignity, ability, intelligence, and destiny of the individual," Curtis said on that occasion. "He believes that individuals can be trusted to own property, that equitable rules should govern the economic contests among men, and that in such contests government should be the umpire and not a participant. He believes that men ought to be masters of their government and that government should be limited to the public needs of the people as a whole.

"He believes that matters which are necessarily the concern of government should be handled locally to the greatest degree possible; that those matters which cannot be handled locally should be dealt with on the state level; and that the scope of the federal government should be limited to those matters which cannot be met on any other level of government and which are in the broad national interest.

"A conservative believes in individual liberty and freedom, and in the capacity of the people to be self-governing. He rejects the need and the desirability of costly and paternalistic government. He believes that it is better to conserve than to waste, that living within income and the payment of debts are virtues for both individuals and governments. He believes that man's responsibility for true charity and a personal concern for the less fortunate cannot be met by asking the government to do it.''

On these conservative grounds, Curtis found himself a member of the opposition most of the time, until his retirement from Congress, to major legislative proposals of his era. His stand against the expansion of the welfare state did not diminish his popularity in Nebraska: in the primary of June, 1946, Curtis defeated his opponent (William Morphew, of Lincoln) by a ratio of eight votes to one; in November's election, 1946, he beat the Democratic candidate (William H. Meier, also of Minden) almost two to one. But in the nation as a whole, the sentiments of the majority of voters inclined toward the promises of the welfare state, or at least toward certain aspects of the welfare state that seemed to offer advantages to one or another bloc of citizens. (Had most voters been clearly aware that a general system called the "welfare state" gradually was supplanting the America they had known, presumably elections would have gone otherwise.) Many members of Congress, uneasily apprehensive of what might be the ultimate consequences of bills for which they cast their votes, nevertheless did not venture to resist strongly what appeared to be the Voice of the People, lest they lose office. Thus Curtis was active in what, for the time, constituted a rear-guard resistance.

What's wrong with the welfare state? Why shouldn't the central government care for the material interests of the mass of a people? The answers to these questions may now be discerned in the practical examples of the social and economic difficulties painfully encountered by such welfare states as Britain, Sweden, and Italy, at present endeavoring to turn back their political clocks. But in the years that followed the Second World War, the new political and economic order of welfare schemes in those countries seemed to not a few Americans a model for a future of equality and contentment. Curtis was one of a minority—sometimes a very small minority—in Congress that tried to explain to their congressional colleagues, and to the American electorate, the fundamental reasons why the welfare state would not function tolerably anywhere, in the long run—and why welfarism was peculiarly unsuited for the United States. Below we set down three of the principal (and grim) reasons why the welfare state cannot fulfill the promises of general happiness made by its enthusiasts.

First, the welfare state tends to create a proletariat—an ugly word for an ugly thing, popularized by the Marxists but going back as word and as reality to the early times of the Roman Republic. In the old Roman definition, a proletarian is a person who gives nothing to the commonwealth but his progeny, his children—who in turn usually become burdens upon the state. A proletariat is a mass of people without property and ordinarily without employment, citizens of the lowest order, rootless and usually discontented.

The Roman state, down to late imperial times, supported its proletariat in Rome and other cities of the Republic and Empire by doles of food—at first of grain, later of baked bread (with a special class of state-paid bakers for that public function), and presently of pork, wine, and olive oil, besides. In Rome alone, some two hundred thousand men regularly received these distributions at the height of the Empire; and most of those men had dependents. In the other cities of the Empire, similar doles were passed out, paid for chiefly from the *liturgies*, or voluntary gifts, of the more prosperous citizens. (Eventually the Roman state made those "voluntary" *liturgies* compulsory for people of means, to their ruin.)

To keep the proletariat out of mischief, the Roman state entertained them with public spectacles, the circuses and gladiatorial shows. (As yet, the American welfare state has not gone quite as far as that: major-league football and basketball make money by charging admission, remaining a part of private enterprise.) The proletariat in the great Roman cities constituted an idle and turbulent mass, producing nothing, devouring much, and eventually consuming the economic resources of the Empire, which they did not defend.

In our twentieth century, a similar proletariat—with votes—has grown up in the welfare states, living at public expense, bored, purposeless, and sometimes dangerous. America had some experience of the proletariat's destructive capacities in the urban riots of the Johnson years. So far as cost goes, Britain is the country probably worst afflicted by the burden of an increasing proletariat of several races. The winter population of Torquay, the warmest spot in England, increases annually several times beyond the town's normal number of inhabitants: people collecting unemployment insurance on false pretenses, or those managing to do well on the dole. In the welfare state, it is all too possible to exist comfortably enough, lifelong, without working, supported by public largesse, "entitlements," and dwelling in public housing.

This condition is bad for any nation; it is worse for the mass of people who form a proletariat, for they scrape along without function and without hope. Once the habit of work and the feeling of self-respect are lost, most people are unemployable and resigned to their condition. Economically, this does great damage to a country, perhaps fatal damage. Socially and morally, we see the consequences around us already. The time may come when the minority of citizens are self-supporting taxpayers, and the majority are recipients of public assistance. After that, a society rapidly falls apart, or perhaps is ruled by force and a master, or is conquered by some stronger power.

As in the case of the ADC program—aid to mothers of dependent children, out of federal funds—the creators of the plan did not foresee the swift growth of the number of households eligible for such grants; or that there would rise up second, third, and fourth generations of people who always had subsisted by ADC, forming a genuine proletariat, idle and sometimes criminal, in every American city. But it is in the very nature of massive benefactions by the centralized welfare state that a larger and larger proportion of a country's population will seek and obtain such "entitlements" and "transfer payments," and that it will grow more and more difficult for the state to support them. Proletarians always ask what the country can do for them, not what they can do for the country. A certain class of politician caters to the proletariat and is sustained in office by its organized voting-blocs in modern democracies. In later chapters of this book, we will show how the American government—perhaps with the best of intentions—has been working its own enfeeblement by encouraging, in effect, the growth of a proletarian class, fed, lodged, and generally nurtured by central political authority.

A second principal reason why the welfare state eventually

fails is that economically the demands on its generosity result in overwhelming taxation, galloping inflation of the currency, and depletion of the capital goods by which the economy had been sustained. The decline of the British economy since Lord Beveridge contrived the British welfare state is a sufficient illustration. Britain was formerly the most prosperous nation-state of Europe. Since the Second World War, capital formation in Britain has been slowed by what even a Socialist chancellor of the exchequer called "savage taxation" to pay the bills of the welfare state, and by nationalization of various industries.

At a time when many European countries (with less demanding welfare policies) were greatly increasing in productivity per capita, Britain sank behind—the quality of its goods diminishing, too. Today per capita income in Britain ranks behind that of Switzerland, Sweden, Denmark, Norway, West Germany, Belgium, the Netherlands, and France (in that order). Even tiny Luxembourg, heavily forested, enjoys a per capita income fifty per cent higher than that of Britain. Swiss per capita income is more than double that of the British, although only a few decades ago Switzerland, lacking natural resources, had very low per capita income. Switzerland is a model of private enterprise, local control of local affairs (a truly federal system), and self-reliance, with no impoverished class to support by a welfare state. Britain muddles along under the fatal benefactions of Lord Beveridge, though Mrs. Thatcher is endeavoring manfully to arrest Britain's decline. Britain has been undone by what the historian Frank Tannenbaum called "the evil benefits of the welfare state."

The architects of the welfare state bite off more than they can chew: the demand for more benefits always increases, while the resources to supply those benefits steadily diminish. The Roman distributions and *liturgies* of imperial times required taxation that extinguished the middle classes—the principal taxpayers—throughout the Empire. From the time of the Emperor Septimius Severus onward, formerly prosperous citizens often abandoned their manufactories, shops, and houses, fleeing from the tax collectors, to sink into the mass of the proletariat and subsist by public doles. During the first half of the fifth century of the Christian era, with barbarian armies marching up and down Italy, the emperors still were striving, through a host of civil servants, to supply the city of Rome with its free or cheap food. They failed. The famines of A.D. 410 and 450 appear to have carried off a great part of the Roman proletariat, people unable to shift for themselves. General "entitlements" ended in general starvation. By the middle of the sixth century, the imperial government had ceased to make any attempt to feed Rome or to exercise authority there; what charitable relief remained was distributed by the Church.

Why has it been, throughout history, that the political state's attempts to supply the material needs of a people have failed disastrously? Primarily because the government itself is not a producer of goods, or at least not an efficient producer, as we see in Communist-dominated lands today. The Roman imperial administration engaged in manufactures on a large scale during the Roman decadence, the private producers having been driven to the wall by taxation; and the imperial estates produced some foodstuffs—but all the same the Roman economy collapsed.

For government, necessarily, is force: the policeman and the soldier. Its purpose is to maintain justice and to defend the country, not to produce goods. The material goods that a welfare state distributes are produced by private firms and individuals, so long as those private producers retain some capital and are not taxed to extinction. But the triumphant welfare state kills the goose that lays the golden eggs.

It is conceivable that milk distribution in cities could be carried on by a political authority, by a city's police force, say. After all, the police have cars, and they know the city. But there is no reason to suppose that the police force could distribute milk more efficiently and more cheaply than could any commercial dairy. And the police have other things to do; in a welfare state, they have a great many other things to do, for crime rates rise rather than fall (because of boredom, for one factor) in recently-created welfare states.

So it is with the general operations of the welfare state. Economically, the state does badly when, turning away from its proper function of keeping the peace, it tries to become producer, or at least distributor, of the means of subsistence. And in the long run, almost all citizens suffer accordingly—even those, or perhaps most of all those, who are the alleged beneficiaries of "entitlements" and "transfer payments."

A third principal reason for the inefficacy of the welfare state is the corruption that it breeds. When a vast part of a nation's gross national product is funneled into the central political apparatus, all that money attracts the confidence-man, the bribe-giver, the political extortionist, the unscrupulous operator of every sort. Governmental grants and loans soon become a major source of funding for all sorts of undertakings, many of them boondoggles (to employ a word coined by Mrs. Eleanor Roosevelt). Everybody's money is nobody's money; everybody's tangible property is nobody's tangible property. Waste of resources becomes the rule, from the capital to the most remote village: "After all, it's Uncle Sam who's paying: why should you worry?" Intricate regulations oppress industry and business: to escape from these coils, the contact-man is employed and well paid. A large part of the population seeks ways to live at the expense of the rest of the population: "Why, everybody else is doing it:" Thus public and private morality spiral downward in a welfare state. The poor for whom the welfare state purportedly was brought into being find themselves badly off in this competition, for most of them are not clever enough to obtain their share of the booty and many of them are too old or infirm to stand a chance against sharp operators. All this goes on until the government is bankrupt, or until there is some popular revulsion of feeling, as occurred with the national elections of 1980. The zealots for the welfare state talk much of freedom; but the only bonds they relax are the norms of morality, public and private.

Later chapters of this book contain a great many melancholy details about corruption in the American welfare state. But let us begin with some account of the distribution of food, at prices often below the cost of production and distribution, through the agency of the federal government. Handing out subsidized foodstuffs to all who can manage to qualify for such largesse, at the expense of the general public, is an excellent way to develop a class of people dependent upon such distributions and upon political decisions made in Washington. But there is nothing else excellent about this policy—indeed nothing tolerable. O Caesar who art in Washington, give us this day our daily bread.

THE SACRED COW OF THE HOT LUNCH PROGRAM

Perhaps the most incongruous and inappropriate activity in which the federal government has engaged is the providing of funds—and of a good deal of fussy supervision—for luncheons in schools that are the responsibility of state and local governments or of voluntary associations. Let us see how this odd and costly undertaking of the welfare state came about.

Distribution of food by the federal government began the year Carl Curtis was elected to the House of Representatives, 1939. This was a New Deal food-stamp program; it lasted until 1943. In selected cities and counties, families of reduced income were entitled to buy booklets of food stamps. If they did so, they were given additional stamps to be exchanged at grocery stores for more food, the latter free, in effect. (This basic plan would be used when a food-stamp program was resurrected by the Food Stamp Act of 1964.) The primary purpose of this New Deal measure was to diminish America's "surplus" agricultural products, and so to raise agricultural prices. It was an alternative to the New Deal policy of slaughtering piglets and plowing under crops in order to reduce supply and raise farm prices proportionately, itself a dubious program at a time of unemployment and low family incomes. This original food-stamp program ceased after the United States entered the Second World War.

Programs for the direct feeding of people by the federal government began with Congress' approval of a school lunch program, as emergency legislation in time of war, to relieve mothers of domestic duties so that some of them could be employed in industrial production. On the excuse of national emergency, most of the cost of these school lunches was assumed by the federal government, although many school districts already had been conducting lunch programs for pupils, paid for by the students' parents or out of local public funds. As with most wartime legislation, little objection was raised at the time to this enlargement of the general government's responsibilities and expenses; it was assumed that the program would cease at the end of the war.

But in 1946, the chairman of the House Agricultural Committee, John W. Flannagan, a Virginia Democrat, presented a bill for school lunches as a permanent federal activity. He had broad support from many members of Congress and from a variety of influential organizations, for already cheap food (cheap for the recipients, anyway) at public expense had become a cause with entrenched interests and lobbies. Henry A. Wallace, Secretary of Commerce, earlier Secretary of Agriculture, declared that farm animals often were better fed than American children. The chief argument for this peacetime program was that it would improve the nutrition of the rising generation.

In 1985, few people remember a time in which the federal government took no part in feeding schoolchildren. Yet the pupils got along perfectly well without bread from Caesar. Many lunched in school cafeterias maintained by the local school authority, at a time when nobody thought of demanding money from Washington for the purpose, any more than they would have thought of asking Washington to pay the school janitor's wages. Other children, living within a mile or so of their school, merrily ran home for lunches provided by their mothers, something made next to impossible nowadays by the massive busing of schoolchildren that began in the 1950s (whether for racial desegregation or in conformity to a mistaken policy of building huge central schools). Yet others, probably the majority, carried their lunches prepared by their mothers to school with them, in lunchboxes or paper bags. Nobody complained; and, as a matter of fact, the home-prepared lunches were commonly more genuinely nutritious than Uncle Sam's vaunted "hot-lunch program" soon became in most school districts, for starches have predominated in the hot food of many or most school lunch menus.

Another argument, less prominent in the advocacy of the lunch program, was that the plan would result in more consumption of "surplus foods" and so help the farmers, food distributors, school cooks and caterers, and the like. But the underlying force behind the measure's success in Congress was the cry, "Don't you want to help kids?"

Nevertheless, this piece of legislation had its congressional opponents, who objected on the principle that the federal government should not become a provider of food for people not aged, disabled, or victims of some misfortune. Ultimate costs of a new governmental program can never be measured accurately by initial appropriations; governmental activities grow and grow under pressure from lobbies hired by the interests the new measure benefits.

Representative Leslie Arends, Illinois Republican, attacked the 1946 school lunch bill on the basis of its probable cost. Representative Ellsworth Buck, New York Republican, maintained that the feeding of schoolchildren was a function of states and localities, not of the federal government.

Buck yielded to Representative Curtis, who pointed out that no difference existed between the federal government's assuming responsibility for school lunches and having the federal government finance other activities of common schools. Congressman Buck concurred. Later in the debate, Curtis touched on the far-reaching effects of expansion of the federal government. Congressman George Dondero, of Michigan, having yielded to Curtis, Congressman Curtis said that food alone does not build a strong body; food must be chewed, with good teeth. Would not a federal food program be followed by proposals for a national health program? Dondero commented that such a plan had already been suggested.

In his principal speech on the subject, Curtis said, "We are all in favor of having the children of America well fed. I believe that the cost of their food should be paid now by their parents and by the local school authorities. This legislation would require these little children to pay for their own food by adding it to the national debt. Even after the federal budget is balanced, the passage of this legislation will mean passing on to our children a greater portion of our unpaid national debt . . .

"If the federal government undertakes to pay the cost when a child is born, provide him with a free school nursery, give him medical care throughout his life, give him free lunches, unemployment compensation, and old-age security, then he is going to ask, What will the federal government demand of me?" All of these so-called benefits mean additional burdens in taxes throughout the productive years of our children.

"This Congress has nothing to give to the children of America except that which it later takes away from them in taxes, plus a heavy load of interest and administrative expenses.

"We are deceiving our children when we say that the government has wealth to give away. We should stop talking about government benefits and tell the truth about the burdens of government.

"There is a further reason why this legislation is wrong. It is a false education; it is statism in its worst form. Already hundreds of little children have been instructed to write the politicians in Washington for something to eat. Shall we teach them that one must labor for his daily bread, or that he need only join a political lobby?"

Such a lobby was already at work upon Congress. Letter-writing campaigns were in full swing to affect the legislative process. It was not uncommon for a member of Congress to receive letters from children of a tender age, who had been instructed to write something like this:

"Dear Congressman, please vote for the school lunch program for our school."

As a young boy, Curtis had been taught "in the sweat of thy face shalt thou eat bread." He had been taught to pray, "Our

Father who art in Heaven . . . give us this day our daily bread."
In conscience, Curtis could not smile upon proposals to teach
the children of America to pray, in effect, "Politicians in
Washington, give us this day our daily bread." He voted against
the program.

But shortsighted sentimentality and the cheap-food lobbies carried the day. With few exceptions, those forces have
carried the day ever since 1946. To vote against enlargement
of the school lunch program requires boldness now in a member of Congress. In recent years, federal money has gone to support breakfast programs and summer-feeding programs in many
school districts.

Modest economies in the school lunch program by the
Reagan administration were received with cries of anguish by
sentimentalists, especially by those liberals who would like to
employ the public school system as a complete "child care"
apparatus, relieving mothers of domestic obligations so that
women might embark upon "careers"—in effect, to weaken
the coherence of even the nuclear family. Thus governmental
programs originally charitable in purpose gradually become
instruments for large social changes, and, as in ancient Rome,
changes for the worse. Financial responsibility for school
lunches could be returned by the federal government to states
and local school districts and families readily enough; but once
huge sums have been extracted from the federal treasury annually, for nearly four decades, it becomes very difficult
politically to effect the reform of restoring such functions to
local agencies, where they belong under our constitutional
structure. In this fashion the United States is transformed piecemeal from a federal republic into a centralized political
system—inconsonant with the Constitution.

THE FALSE CHARITY
OF FOOD STAMPS

With school lunches well entrenched, proposals for food stamps for adults were revived. In 1959, Senator Hubert Humphrey, the most influential advocate of lavish welfare programs, proposed to the Senate a food-stamp "demonstration" scheme; it was rejected forty-six votes to forty-one, nearly thirty percent of the Democratic senators opposing it. (Curtis voted against this and all later food-stamp bills.) Next Humphrey, George Aiken (Vermont Republican), and Stuart Symington (Missouri Democrat) offered a plan to authorize fifteen million dollars for a demonstration program in six cities; this was approved by the Senate, forty-four votes to thirty-eight. Agreed upon by a Senate-House conference committee in 1959, this authorization did not direct the establishment of the program.

Ezra Taft Benson, Secretary of Agriculture, opposed the plan. President Eisenhower said of it, "The plan, if implemented, would increase the already disproportionate federal share of welfare expense . . . and it is extremely doubtful that it would provide any greater benefit to needy people than the present direct method." This program never was implemented.

But in 1964, a permanent food-stamp plan was enacted. The chairman of the House Agricultural Committee, Harold D. Colley (North Carolina Democrat) called the bill "a long step forward in the nation's war on poverty." Representative Leonore Sullivan (Missouri Democrat), long an advocate of food stamps, remarked that "President Johnson put the full weight of his office and his tremendous powers of persuasion behind the legislation, and its final passage in the Congress today is largely attributed to his powerful leadership."

In 1967, the food-stamp program of 1964 was extended. At that time Senator Robert C. Byrd (West Virginia Democrat) called the program a complete success; Senator Spessard L. Holland (Florida Democrat), the bill's floor manager, said that when the program became fully operative, the cost would be about $425 million annually. Nevertheless, within four years the cost reached more than a billion dollars; fourteen years later, it was ten billion dollars for one year. (This dismaying total of 1981 resulted in part from congressional enlargement of the program's scope.)

For by 1969, pressures had mounted to liberalize the food-stamp program. The Southern Committee for Political Ethics, the American Friends Service Committee, and other organizations pushed for extension of the program to more people. In 1969, Senator George McGovern (South Dakota Democrat), chairman of the Select Committee on Nutrition and Human Needs, succeeded in obtaining passage on the Senate floor of an amendment increasing to $1.25 billion the food-stamp expenditure of $750 million approved by his committee. Fifty-four senators voted for the bill, forty against it—Curtis among the latter.

By 1975, it became evident that cost of food stamps soon would reach five billion dollars annually. In an effort to check the increase of federal expenditures, President Ford advanced a plan to reduce the program's rate of growth and to deal with abuses in the program pointed out by the Department of Agriculture. The Ford plan would have required ninety-five percent of food-stamp recipients to pay thirty percent of their monthly incomes for the stamps. Congress having rejected this reform, the Department of Agriculture attempted to carry out the Ford plan through regulations. Then Congress adopted a bill preventing such regulations from taking effect.

By 1977, this food-stamp program had become a nation-wide political issue. Everyone, it seemed, knew that the plan must be reformed; but the two groups into which the reformers were divided were poles apart. Those concerned about the spiraling cost, which by 1977 had reached five billion dollars a year, wanted the program better controlled. The other group, with the fervor of crusaders, wished to extend and enlarge the program, and to eliminate the requirement that if recipients had any income, a portion of such income should be used for food. The latter group, supported by television documentaries on hunger and by community pressure groups, won the battle.

That struggle was fought in the Senate Committee on Agriculture and Forestry, the room crowded and under the glare of television lighting. The advocates of enlarging the program moved that the purchase-price requirement for food stamps be eliminated; that is, the principle that a portion of any recipient's income should be spent for food.

If, for instance, under the Department of Agriculture's thrifty-diet plan, a family eligible for food stamps should need two hundred dollars monthly for food but should have no income, that family would be given free of charge two hundred dollars worth of food stamps. If a family should have a monthly income of three hundred dollars, that family was required to spend thirty percent of that income, or the sum of ninety dollars, on food, to secure two hundred dollars worth of stamps. Should a family enjoy a monthly income of four hundred dollars, their purchase requirement was thirty percent of that sum, or a hundred and twenty; then they would receive two hundred dollars worth of stamps. In short, a family with some income was required to use a portion of that income for food, to obtain stamps. This plan required good instruction in diet, and good discipline. When a family spends ninety dollars of its income to obtain two hundred dollars worth of food stamps, that additional two hundred dollars for food will go on the table to feed the children. But if there is no purchase requirement, a household's own income is freed for spending, prudently or imprudently, on whatever the head of the household chooses.

"Hunger marchers," lobbyists from many organizations, crowded the committee room while these matters were discussed. They wore "EPR" badges: Eliminate Purchase Requirements. Many people, watching the session on television, were led to believe that the poor could not obtain food stamps if they had no money to buy them—an error, for those with no income already got their stamps without cost.

The Committee voted to eliminate the purchase requirement. Curtis offered an amendment to limit the income eligibility for a household to receive stamps to the established poverty level, plus ten per cent.

The income test proposed by the advocates of food-stamp liberalization, led by Senator McGovern, consisted of a standard deduction plus work-related expenses, excess shelter costs, and child-care deductions. This could add up to an income level 135 to 160 per cent above the poverty level. It should be remembered that for many, food stamps are in addition to other programs of poverty relief, including Supplementary Security Income, Aid to Families with Dependent Children, Medicaid, public housing or rent subsidies, and educational loans. The food-stamp program had not been intended as an overall welfare plan to supplement the incomes of all persons of small means, but rather had been meant to deal with undernourishment, malnutrition, and hunger, assisting people with very scanty funds to obtain the first necessity, food.

Yet Curtis' motion to limit eligibility was defeated in committee, nine votes to eight. Curtis then moved to disqualify strikers from participating in the stamp program; this was defeated too, nine to seven. Third, Curtis moved to exclude college students from the program: defeated, twelve to four. Fourth, Curtis moved to require the establishment of a photographic identification system, an earnings-clearance system, all to take effect one year after the bill's enactment, so as to prevent duplication of applications, the use of stolen and counterfeited food stamps, and other fraud. This motion also was defeated, nine to seven.

Curtis' final proposed amendment dealt with an assets limitation for recipients, raising the issue of how much property a recipient might own and still remain eligible for stamps. Applicants for Supplemental Security Income (a program for aged, disabled, and blind) are subject to a limit on the value of their property, including principal residences, motor vehicles, property used in trade or business, liquid and nonliquid assets, and (with certain exceptions) household furnishings. Should not there be similar limitations upon the amount of property owned by applicants for food stamps? Yet Curtis' motion was defeated, nine to eight.

Had Curtis won his fight to retain the purchase requirement and to amend the bill as above, taxpayers would have been saved two billion dollars a year at that time—and larger savings in future years. The Curtis objections to the profligacy of the food-stamp enlargement would be grimly justified by that program's shocking abuse between 1977 and 1981.

The fight over this bill then proceeded to the Senate floor. There the agricultural bill with this food-stamp section in it came up for consideration on May 23, 1977, and Curtis made a report of what had occurred in committee.

"The hearing room was jammed with the shock troops of the hunger lobby: from USDA, from key congressional offices, and from the numerous federally funded pressure groups which use public moneys to change and expand their version of this welfare program," Curtis told the Senate. "Little yellow buttons reading 'ERP'—'Eliminate the Purchase Requirement'— were in abundance. Snickering laughter rippled through the room when a member of the committee observed the ERP would change the program into an outright giveaway . . .

"Under this bill, food stamps will be free. No longer will a recipient have to put up a portion of his income to get, in return, a much larger amount of stamps. This means the program will become nothing more than an income-transfer gimmick, not a nutrition program. A food-stamp user will not have to commit part of his income for food.

"Remember how the program was going to be simplified, and a lot of money saved, by replacing multiple deductions with a standard deduction? But Title XII of this bill allows a monthly deduction of sixty dollars for all households. That is $720 in annual income which we must pretend an applicant does not have. It also allows a monthly deduction equal to twenty percent of earned income. So we have to pretend an applicant earns only eighty per cent of his real income. It also allows a monthly deduction of up to seventy-five dollars—that is, nine hundred dollars a year—for excess-shelter costs. For anyone unacquainted with the obfuscating jargon of the welfare lobby, 'excess-shelter costs' means living beyond your means. In addition, Title XII allows a child-care deduction of up to eighty-five dollars a month. That is $1,020 a year .   .

"The true income-eligibility limit for a family of four would be—hold your breath—$10,600: almost double the poverty index.

"And that is only part of the total. It does not include the cash value of a housing subsidy or of school lunches, mealson-wheels, summer-feeding programs, or any of the other items . . .

"This bill does nothing to prohibit strikers from using food stamps to subsidize their strikes. We are not talking about lockouts, where a worker has no choice in the matter. We are talking about people who refuse to work, who sit at home or go on vacation while their union bosses negotiate higher wages . . .

"How will we justify to the American people our refusal to crack down on the use of food stamps by college students? Let no one pretend that this bill will prohibit this abuse. A student will be able to get stamps just by stating that he is not being, or cannot be, claimed as a dependent by persons who are themselves not eligible for food stamps. There will be absolutely no checking mechanism . . .

"One must wonder why this bill exempts, even from work registration, mothers with children between the ages of six and twelve. How can we justify that to the working, taxpaying mothers with children in that age bracket? Are we telling them that they are foolish to work? Why was that limit not set at age six, as is the standard in the AFDC program? Let us be candid about this. The welfare lobby wants as many loopholes in this bill as possible, and they have succeeded in making it—to borrow a phrase from our former colleague Jim Buckley—a moth-eaten fishnet . . .

"Everyone pays lip service to the need for asset limitations in the food-stamp program. The lack of meaningful limits has allowed many persons to enjoy luxuries at home while subsidizing their groceries with the taxes of their frugal neighbors. And yet, after so many years of controversy about abuses in the program, after so many documented horror stories about affluent persons getting food stamps, this bill does nothing whatsoever to stop them."

The next day, Curtis offered his amendment to restore the purchasing requirement to the bill. He lost by sixty-four votes to thirty-one. Some senators who agreed with that proposed amendment nevertheless did not vote for it: they could not get their explanations and comments heard above the din of the shouting food-stamp lobbyists. And this senatorial discussion of an immensely important proposal was supposed to be a sober legislative process in the greatest of republics!

Curtis then offered an amendment to mandate a photo-identification card, a national crosscheck of applications, and an earnings-clearance system. The emotional tempo of the groups lobbying for food stamps, and the dread of members of the Senate that they might be denounced for lack of humanity by well-meaning organizations and from some pulpits, made it impossible to have this amendment considered on its merits. It lost, fifty-seven to thirty-seven.

Curtis also offered an amendment fixing the income-limit for food-stamp recipients at 125 per cent of the poverty floor. Under the committee's bill, Curtis said to the Senate, a family's exemption might rise as high as $10,610. Even without child-care and excess-shelter costs, it might amount to more than eight thousand dollars. His amendment would save five hundred million dollars. It lost, sixty-four to twenty-seven. Senator Hayakawa of California offered an amendment that would have applied to college students applying for food stamps a work requirement; this too was defeated.

The food-stamp enlargement being but one section of a general farm bill, the vote on the bill's final passage was no indication as to how senators stood on the issue of curbing food-stamp abuses. The public, generally unaware of debates in committee and on the floor, was left with no adequate way of judging how senators and representatives had voted on food-stamp increase, a measure distinctly unpopular with the general public. The welfare lobby had triumphed.

It had become possible for a household headed by an able-bodied person to take advantage of many of these welfare programs and to become dependent on the political apparatus for all needs. Some such families become so dependent on these numerous programs that soon they lose the resolution to break out of the mold. For such a family, the future is bleak; and the cost to the public of an increasing number of these recipients of a livelihood without work may become insupportable, as at last it became in old Rome. Such a welfare household may have as neighbors a family who, by determination and force of character, thrift and self-denial, remain self-supporting on a lower income than that provided for a dependent family.

By 1981, the monthly average number of Americans receiving food stamps was nearly 22.5 million, approaching a tenth of the country's population. By 1983, this monthly average had been reduced by some eight hundred thousand persons, chiefly as a result of the Reagan administration's welfare reforms. The following table shows how costs (in round figures) of the program had increased over the years.

These figures reflect inflation of the dollar, of course; but that inflation itself was caused, in very considerable part, by extravagant expenditures on welfare programs, producing deficit budgets on a vast scale and a staggering increase in the national debt.

1965 . . . $	35,146,000
1970 . . . $	576,800,000
1971 . . . $	1,576,000,000
1972 . . . $	1,866,700,000
1973 . . . $	2,207,000,000
1974 . . . $	2,837,500,000
1975 . . . $	4,619,000,000
1976 . . . $	5,686,000,000
1977 . . . $	5,461,000,000
1978 . . . $	5,564,000,000
1979 . . . $	6,936,000,000
1980 . . . $	9,186,000,000
1981 . . . $	11,306,000,000
1982 . . . $	11,111,000,000
1983 . . . $	12,656,000,000
1984 . . . $	11,561,000,000
1985 . . . $	11,466,000,000

The Reagan administration's partial reforms of food-stamp policy, including the Food Stamp Act Amendments of 1982, were made possible by discernible public indignation at abuses of the program, and its inordinate cost. A principal improvement was the "workfare" program, requiring the performance of work in return for food-stamp benefits. Recipients otherwise unemployed must perform public service work to obtain food-stamp allotments, supposing them physically able, such work being valued at the federal or the state minimum wage.

("Workfare" was left by Congress to the discretion of state and local public authorities.) It has been the expectation of the Reagan administration that workfare will help considerably to provide food-stamp recipients with experience and skills useful in obtaining regular employment in the private sector. Doubtless the Reagan reforms, 1981 through 1983, would have achieved still larger reductions in the number of recipients of food stamps and in total costs, had not those been years of relatively high unemployment and a consequent increase in the number of applicants for food stamps.

The public's demand for the Reagan reforms, and for yet more thoroughgoing revisions of the food-stamp program, was increased somewhat by a documentary film shown over the ABC network, in September, 1981, about abuses in the program: abuses described by the commentator as "massive and overwhelming." The television audience was shown and told about organized crime in the program, more than a billion dollars' worth of food stamps stolen every year; about computer records erased and evidence destroyed by arson; about money intended for hungry people used to finance the heroin traffic. "Money stamps, that's what the crooks and cheats call these food-stamp coupons . . . tens of millions of dollars' worth of these stamps are floating around."

In San Francisco, the hidden television camera caught a crooked grocer who thought he was buying more than a hundred thousand dollars worth of stamps for twenty-three thousand dollars in cash. There had been forty-seven indictments for food-stamp fraud in Baltimore, with sixty more expected; seventy-seven indictments, to date, in Memphis. Food stamps had been used by gangsters to buy cars and jewelry and television sets—and, in South Carolina, heavy weapons.

The stamps are free, and just like money, the television viewers learned. Key documents had been stolen where printed, where processed, where mailed. Fraud and corruption in the program had occurred throughout the country. Ten thousand food-stamp authorizations were being stolen annually from the mails in New York. Investigators were told that some places were strictly off limits. "Clearly," the commentator declared, "this well-intentioned program is in critical condition.''

Near the conclusion of this TV presentation, William French Smith, Attorney General of the United States, appeared before the camera. ''The Reagan administration,'' he said, ''is determined to root out fraud and waste in government. We now have very strong indications that fraud of the worst kind has permeated the food-stamp program. And we are going to use every effort as quickly as possible to identify those responsible, to prosecute them, and to put them behind bars.''

Indeed a strong and prudent President may prevail upon Congress to achieve greater reforms of the food-stamp program, and may accomplish considerable administrative improvements. Yet enlargements of the food-stamp entitlements are still hoped for by the ''welfare lobby'' generally, and in particular by the Food Research and Action Center, lobbyists and lawyers who claim to represent the millions of food-stamp recipients.

The advocates of broader food-stamp programs, and the opponents of sweeping food-stamp reforms, declare that the controversy is merely a struggle between a group favoring greater generosity to the poor on the one hand, and a group on the other hand insensitive to suffering. But it is no favor to poor people to reduce them to a proletarian condition; nor to let public funds intended to diminish malnutrition slip into the hands of charlatans and criminals. What we require is a public sentiment calculated to bring about a sweeping reform fair to the hungry and fair to the taxpayers who pay the bills.

Also it is well to remember that Jesus of Nazareth advocated no political program, issued no political fulminations—not even against war or slavery—and led no march against Caesar demanding social changes. But He did give us the parable of the Good Samaritan.

ONE DEED FOR A PROLETARIAT LEADS TO ANOTHER

This chapter on perplexities of the welfare state, like other chapters on other aspects of the twentieth-century Leviathan, began with events and controversies of the middle 1940s, during Carl Curtis' early years in Congress; then it traced the course of such struggles over public policy to Curtis' retirement from Washington. This method of narration is intended to enable readers to perceive more clearly the continuity, for good or ill, of the growth of the American welfare state.

Similarly, the following chapter, on public housing, begins with arguments and measures of the middle 1940s, and proceeds to carry the story from the Truman administration to the Reagan administration. Some of the later chapters are on the same plan, beginning with Curtis' first participation in a congressional contest on a particular issue, and describing problems and controversies of that sort over decades of Curtis' experience.

Food is humankind's first necessity; next comes shelter. Naturally, then, we now shift from our daily bread to our domiciles. The failings of the welfare state in the provision of food are paralleled by the welfare state's unhappy intervention in the provision of shelter: that is, by the growth of a proletariat, grave economic blunders, and the decay of public and private moral habits.

Chapter 5

The Houses Built by Uncle Sam

HOUSING IS NOT NECESSARILY HOMES

Between the two World Wars, European nation-states built public housing on a tremendous scale; that process continues to the present, with results commonly lamentable. For the state can create shelter, but it has been conspicuously unsuccessful at creating homes.

Public housing came later to the United States. R. H. S. Crossman, the English socialist politician, returned from a trip to America in 1948 and wrote about it for *The New Statesman and Nation*. "Nothing is more astonishing to an English visitor than the normal American attitude to housing," he remarked. "Here the rights of private profit-making, the corruption of City and State politics, the power of the lobbyist . . . all combine to produce a deadly and growing blight . . . In Britain we have come to regard housing, like water, gas, electricity and education, as a public service. In

113

America, apart from a tiny number of Federal projects—charity buildings whose inmates must belong to the lowest income groups—public housing and town planning have scarcely begun.''

That "tiny number of Federal projects" has grown, since Crossman wrote, to huge districts of public housing, built wholly or mostly out of federal funds, in every American city and in a great many small towns. This process began very promptly after R. H. S. Crossman had traveled in America, with passage of the first major mass-housing bill by Congress in 1949. Such housing projects have become a major business of the American welfare state.

At the time of Crossman's trip to America, most Americans, for their part, would have been astonished at what had become the normal British attitude toward housing—or what Crossman took that "normal attitude" to be. Americans may have been quite as much dismayed as was Crossman by American cities with "the blight spreading round their hard sparkling centres.'' Americans were accustomed, nevertheless, to think of a home as a private domain, reflecting in some degree the personality of its possessors. The monotonous sea of drab and ill-built "council houses," owned by local political authorities, which by 1949 had lapped even at the edges of little English and Scottish villages, presented a notion of "homes" that would have been rejected by the vast majority of Americans. (Even that redoubtable Labour M. P. Aneurin Bevan soon would lament the proliferation of ugly council-houses "like goods-waggons on a railway siding.'')

To this day, the American "home" aspiration remains the detached and personalized house—though the attainment of that ambition has been made more difficult for the rising generation by heavy taxation, inflation of the dollar, vast demolitions of sound or restorable houses under "urban renewal" programs, and costs of building increased by the restrictive practices of the building-trades unions.

This American yearning has been a sound impulse. Nothing can better attach people to the preservation of a decent social order than their possession of real homes, an aspect of what Simone Weil called "the need for roots.'' Being lodged in featureless, impersonal, and often dangerous complexes of public housing tends to breed, quite understandably, a spirit of rebellion against existing political and economic dominations. We have heard much talk of the welfare state as the "democratic alternative" to communism; but when people are tenants of the mass-state, virtually under compulsion, treated as identical units in housing projects composed of identical units—why, then the communists have won in part, whatever ideology is professed by the planners. Nothing is more likely to convert people into what Edmund Burke called "the flies of a summer" than assigning them to cubicles constructed out of the charity of the state. In "homes" that are only pens for human units, people look neither backward toward their ancestors nor forward to posterity. And a society with neither reverence for the past nor hope for the future may cease to be a tolerable society.

"It will take some hammering to drive a coddling socialism into America," George Santayana had written about 1920. The swift growth of public housing after 1949 was part of that hammering.

The federal government did not involve itself in providing houses to any substantial extent before the Second World War, although there had been some federal activity in this field. In 1892, the Fifty-Second Congress had appropriated twenty thousand dollars to investigate slums, an effort limited to cities with a population of more than two hundred thousand. With the coming of the Great Depression, the federal government began to concern itself with stimulating the housing industry through extension of credit to citizens who wished to build houses, whether through direct federal loans to aspiring homeowners or by lending public funds to banks and savings-and-loan associations. In December, 1931, a conference attended by some 3,700 persons interested in house building and home ownership was held in Washington; it resulted in the adoption of a resolution endorsing President Hoover's recommendation for a system of home-loan discount banks. Other recommendations included the development of housing programs in communities (stressing single-family dwellings), improved planning and zoning, improved technology, broadened home ownership, development of systems of home credit, rehabilitation of old houses, elimination of slum and blight, decentralization of industry to prevent overcrowding, facilitation of large-scale housing operations, relief of homes from excessive taxation, and housing research.

Out of this concern grew the Home Owners' Loan Corporation, a federal agency, in effect extending credit at low rates of interest to families that could qualify on the basis of moderate income but reasonable reliability for such a privilege. Sociologically speaking, HOLC benefited the lower middle class. It did not involve federal, state, or local governments directly in the actual construction of housing. HOLC had both good and bad consequences.

It is sound social policy to encourage citizens to own their houses, giving them a stake in social order. Beginning in 1933, HOLC did that for many people, who thus came to live in domestic comfort, paid real-property taxes, and became a very stable influence in the community.

On the other hand, HOLC and similar successive programs worked an unintended mischief, encouraging the more able and thrifty people—mostly members of the lower middle class—to move from the hearts of cities to the outskirts or to suburbs. Long before the inception of the "homeowner" loan programs, the triumph of the inexpensive automobile had encouraged city dwellers of the more substantial sort to abandon the compact life of the city for the sprawling suburbs; HOLC and similar sources of capital accelerated this flight. When skilled employed people, with their families, leave what has come to be called the city core, there remain behind the elderly, the unemployable, the thriftless, impecunious "ethnic minorities"—and criminal elements. Those left behind tend to lack honest leadership and the stabilizing influence of people of property. Thus that "blight spreading round hard sparkling centres" grew; and in the fullness of time, the centers themselves would sparkle less, and great commercial streets would grow ugly from boarded-up fronts and demolition, and whole districts would become perilous for pedestrians. But during the Roosevelt administration, these unpleasant consequences were not foreseen; and although various slum-clearance projects were undertaken and complexes of low-cost housing (which today are the worst of the slums in such cities as Detroit) erected by municipalities during the Roosevelt era, no large-scale national scheme of federally-financed housing was undertaken.

Not until 1939, when Carl Curtis was a freshman congressman, did Congress consider a broad federal housing plan. Then pressure was exerted by Mayor Fiorello LaGuardia of New York, and other mayors allied with the Roosevelt administration, to have Washington assume the costs of the massive rebuilding of cities. This proposal was rejected by Congress and not revived until after the Second World War.

This housing bill's defeat was accompanied by some interesting speeches in the House of Representatives. The bill of 1939 proposed a far-reaching program for a very long term, a new departure in the United States. Some Democrats were conspicuous in rejecting the bill.

Representative Charles Faddis, a Pennsylvania Democrat, was hot against the measure: ''Mr. Speaker, this legislation is entirely too much of an adventure into socialism to suit me. My concern for the national credit and for the general welfare of this nation will not allow me to support it. It comes to us from Mayor LaGuardia and his council of mayors of the metropolitan areas of the United States, an organization which has been endeavoring for several years to have the Congress force upon the country in general the relief problem of the metropolitan centers of this nation.

''We have learned much during the past six years about relief, and we are due to learn more during the next few years. I myself have learned during the past six years that relief must be a local problem, that if we are ever to solve this problem we must solve it locally. I am confident that the housing problem of the United States is of the same character.''

The most influential speech on this question came from a young congressman from Tennessee, Albert Gore, later a liberal Democratic senator. He pointed out that this United States Housing Authority program would not be self-liquidating; that no revenue would ever be returned to the federal government. The initial cost alone, authorized by the bill, would be eight hundred million dollars; in addition, Housing Authority would be permitted to make binding contracts for sixty years, totalling

$2.7 billion. The federal government had already been committed to expend for housing twenty-eight million dollars annually for sixty years, making a grand total of $4.38 billion to be expended on public housing. He went on to criticize still more mordantly the financial provisions of the housing bill. Then he concluded:

"I am one of the youngest members of this House. Even though my people may keep me here for eighteen years, for twenty years, for thirty years, for forty years, for fifty years, this program will not then be paid for; and every year our appropriation bills will carry an item of seventy-three million dollars for this purpose, for the next sixty years. My eighteen-months-old baby will be lucky to live to see one of these contracts consummated. It is ridiculous. How many people can name an apartment house that is inhabitable at the end of sixty years?*

"The United States Housing Authority is guilty of disseminating the most reprehensible, deceptive, and misleading information.

"This program is advertised as one to rehouse the slum dwellers, and although specifically requested, not one iota of evidence has been presented that as much as one family from the abolished slum area has been rehoused in one of these projects."

After this stern opposition by Albert Gore and others, the vote came in the House, on the approval of the rule that would have permitted the House to take up this housing bill on the floor. The roll call on the rule produced 169 yeas and 191 nays, with sixty-seven members absent. Thus in effect the House rejected consideration of the housing proposal of 1939. Carl Curtis was one of the majority who voted against the bill as, indeed, did most representatives from agricultural states and predominantly rural districts; for they did not relish the prospect of paying the bills of misgoverned cities, aside from the

---

*The younger Albert Gore, the "eighteen-months-old baby" referred to here by his father, had become himself a United States senator by 1985.

socialistic and centralizing aspects of that piece of legislation.

During the Second World War, public housing programs were related to the war effort. Federal measures were authorized to provide housing for military personnel and their dependents, and also for civilians engaged in war production. Something was done to accommodate the flood of population from South to North, and from countryside to city, in the industrial and military emergency. But these programs were temporary, and most of the housing was of an impermanent sort. The prices of houses, and their rents, were controlled during the emergency by the Office of Price Administration, headed by Chester Bowles. Much doubling-up of families in houses and general crowding occurred; there was little private construction. Even former privies sometimes were converted into lodging for industrial workers in the vicinity of centers of industrial production; chicken houses, too.

So the campaign for public housing survived its defeat of 1939. Seven years later, with the war over and an accumulated need for more houses and apartments that had built up with the increase of population during the war years, sentiment for an enlarged federal housing program was stronger in Congress. It was also stronger in certain quarters that would profit from a huge-scale program—particularly with building contractors looking for work that might replace defense contracts and with the building-trades unions.

Thus there began to come to pass in the United States the high-rise slum, a grim manifestation of the welfare state. In the eyes of its British and American creators, the welfare state was the culmination of liberal democracy. Without free democratic institutions, true enough, the welfare state—as idea and as reality—would have short shrift in this age. Yet the public-housing aspect of life, whatever may be said of it, is neither liberal nor democratic.

The inhabitants of the newly built high-rise slum are wards of the state, tenants at will, permanent recipients of state charity. People in this condition have no guarantee of liberty; the freedom they continue to enjoy today may be only the dwindling political capital of nineteenth-century institutions now decaying. But more on that subject later in this chapter.

THE SOCIAL FAILURE OF
THE MASS-HOUSING PROJECTS

During the prolonged debate on public housing that began in 1945, proposals went far beyond assistance to individuals from the federal government for loans for house building. The advocates of the new legislation intended a general plan for housing millions at public expense in government-owned complexes.

In the House, the chief backers of the Truman administration's housing bills were Representatives Wright Patman of Texas, William B. Barry of New York, and A. S. Mike Monroney of Oklahoma. During the course of the debate, Carl Curtis argued that the way to meet the housing shortage was to abolish the Office of Price Administration (wartime price controls still being in effect in 1946), so ending ceiling prices on building materials.

Congressmen Robert Rich of Pennsylvania, Frederick Smith of Ohio, Carl Curtis, and others believed that the federal government should give private enterprise the opportunity to satisfy backed-up demand for housing. The expectation that prices of houses and levels of rent would continue to be set by Washington was sufficient to assure that housing would continue to be scarce, for private capital would be deterred from investing in housing. Curtis said that the passage of the new housing bill would prevent housing construction, not advance it.

In the Senate, however, the more powerful thrust for this housing program occurred. For some years, Senator Allen Ellender of Louisiana and Senator Robert Wagner of New York had advocated large-scale public housing. Now, in 1945-46, they were joined by Senator Robert Taft of Ohio, widely regarded as the Senate leader of conservative opposition to the New Deal programs of Presidents Roosevelt and Truman. Taft's reasons for supporting massive public housing deserve attention, for it was Taft who gave to American political discourse the phrase "creeping socialism."

In 1943, Taft had been appointed chairman of the Senate subcommittee on housing and urban redevelopment. It became clear to him that several million Americans were in great difficulty when they tried to find lodging—to rent or to buy—commensurate with their incomes. During his study of the problem, Taft came to reject the idea that if sufficient new housing were to be built, older dwellings would become available for people of low income. He rejected, too, a Truman administration proposal for a type of federally subsidized rent certificate to be issued to poor families, saying that it would not suffice.

He decided that the federal government must take a large part in making up for the shortage of housing that had resulted from the building dearth of the war—that is, for the sort of citizens ineligible for bank credit or government-backed loans of the HOLC type. This low-cost public housing, he reasoned, must not be luxurious, funds being limited; and if housing for the needy were superior to the accommodation of Americans above the subsistence level, incentives to self-help among working people would be greatly damaged.

One of Taft's motives in all this was to forestall the plans of liberal Democrats for embarking upon elaborately costly and impractical projects of housing. So Taft joined with the Democratic senators Wagner and Ellender in the housing bill of 1945.

This bill was founded on the estimate that some 1,250,000 housing units must be built every year for the following ten years; and of this number, about two-thirds must be intended for people who could not afford to pay more than forty dollars a month in rent. Taft proposed that ten per cent of the annual construction of housing—that is, 125,000 units a year—should be governmentally subsidized low-rent housing; the remaining nine-tenths, or 1,125,000 units a year, would be private, unsubsidized construction. (Purchase of the private housing would be made easier by an increase of funds for the federal Home Loan Bank and the federal Housing Administration, lending money at moderate interest rates, and by government guaranteed home loans to veterans.) Public housing would be provided only on the request of city councils, and would be available only for people with incomes at least twenty per cent below the level estimated, in any particular city, as sufficient to provide adequate rent money.

This bill, sponsored by Taft, Wagner, and Ellender, was approved by the Senate in April 1946. Meanwhile, the Truman administration had been promoting its own bill, which included construction, within two years, of 2.7 million low-cost and medium-cost housing units. This figure assumed a greatly expanded production of conventional and new-type building materials, through premium payments, guaranteed markets, and priorities in allocations. It planned for the recruiting and training of 1.4 million additional construction workers; and the architects of the Truman proposal expected the postponement of "nonessential" construction so that the greater part of construction materials could be channeled into houses and rental units selling for not more than six thousand dollars or renting for not more than fifty dollars a month. (What with subsequent inflation, these figures sound absurdly low today.) The Truman proposal called for price control over building materials, new and existing houses, and building lots.

The Wagner-Ellender-Taft bill was rejected by the House in 1946; nor did the administration bill make headway. Again, in 1947, much discussion of public housing did not result in an act; nor in 1948. Taft made many public addresses on the subject. At a talk in New York, early in 1949, Taft declared that he saw no alternative to public housing as a method for providing low-income rentals to people at the bottom of the income scale. "Public housing is still experimental and the experiment has been very much confused by the intervening of the Second World War and the large amount of war housing constructed directly or indirectly by the government. Many of the complaints against the public housing system relate to this war housing. Few cities have been able to give the public housing program a proper trial, and many cities require the urban redevelopment assistance provided in the Ellender bill to handle the slum question properly." He had told his senatorial colleagues in 1947 that the federal government could afford to spend a billion dollars a year for housing, public health, education, and other measures of public welfare; that billion now is only a small fraction of such annual federal expenditures. The Truman administration had made up its mind to spend far more than Taft wished.

Thirty-six years after Taft's address in New York, public housing is no longer in the experimental stage; and the slums are bigger and grimmer than they were then. Urban redevelopment—the alleged "urban renewal" of the Johnson presidency —has converted vast areas of great cities into urban deserts and jungles. This "renewal" became in many places a code word for Negro removal and Mexican-American removal from their established neighborhoods. Would the elder Robert Taft, were he still in the land of the living, regard with approbation the consequences of the public-housing statutes in which he had a large hand? That scarcely seems conceivable. The best-laid schemes of mice and men . . .

Pressure for some large-scale public housing measure was strong by 1948. In its concluding months, the Eightieth Congress passed a housing bill that incorporated some features of the Ellender-Wagner-Taft bill. Taft called this act inadequate; President Truman condemned it as parsimonious, but signed it. Carl Curtis, foreseeing that this was but the beginning of enormous expenditures on a concept of housing that could not succeed, voted against it.

Then came Harry Truman's unpredicted strong victory in the elections of November, 1948. Heads rolled that had been thought invulnerable in the Republican Party, but Carl Curtis did more than survive. He had won the Republican nomination in the First Congressional District nine to one over his opponent; in the election, he defeated William H. Meier, also of Minden, almost two to one. Returned to Washington, Curtis found the Republican minority in the House sadly chastened by the Democrats' triumph. What Truman desired for his Fair Deal, Truman got.

Thus the Eighty-First Congress passed a bill far more expensive than the one Senator Taft had drafted. The Housing Act of 1949 authorized, among many other provisions, the construction of 810,000 low-income housing units. It carried a provision requiring that prevailing union-scale wages must be paid for all construction financed or supported by the act. This regulation would increase markedly the cost to the ultimate renters and purchasers, as well as to the government; it would delay construction in many small communities where wages were always less than the union scale in great cities. For decades thereafter, this fixing of costs arbitrarily high would damage public housing projects: for the high hourly cost of labor on those buildings was generally compensated by reducing the amenities of the buildings, reducing the size of apartments, and confining the structures to ugly pseudo-utilitarian designs. It already was becoming clear that, as with various other colossal undertakings of the American welfare state, public housing afforded many opportunities for organizations and individuals to enrich themselves at the expense of the taxpayers generally and, indeed, of the intended recipients of the welfare measures. To them that hath shall be given.

Much of the Housing Act of 1949, nevertheless, was the culmination of Robert A. Taft's work over the preceding six years. Senator Taft had reservations about the act in its final form, for the Truman administration's plan (which borrowed much from Taft's labors in this field) went far beyond Taft's plan in scale and cost. Like Disraeli with the Reform Bill of 1867, Taft must have felt that his victory was badly marred by the deletion of some of his plan's better features and the addition of details and expenditures he did not relish.

Lavish though the provisions of the Housing Act of 1949 were, they did not satisfy the demands of enthusiasts for more and more construction at the expense of the United States Treasury; besides, most public housing wears out in a hurry. Powerful lobbies—the building contractors; the building-trades unions; black organizations; urban realtors' associations some times; the sentimental groups that have been called "disintegrated liberals"—pressed for larger housing appropriations, scarcely bothering to pay attention to the frequent inefficacy of existing projects. Public housing put money into the purses of many folk distinctly uninterested in the lot of the poor.

But for eight years this motley crew of zealots for bigger and taller housing complexes was impeded by the presence in the White House of Dwight Eisenhower. For sixteen years after passage of the Housing Act of 1949, Congress approved no major change or big new expenditure in the field of public housing.

COLLECTIVISM WITHOUT COMMUNITY

During that interim, the dismal and alarming results of herding millions of people into melancholy public housing complexes became obvious. They are unpleasantly familiar now to anyone who reads the newspapers, not to mention the unfortunates condemned to dwell in those prison-like high rises, or in those shabby streets of uniform two-story brick duplexes.

The people who lodge there are worse off, in several ways, than they or their counterparts were in the low-income districts from which they were transplanted. With very few exceptions, the buildings are dismal and boring, inside and out—and badly maintained. The elevators, if they function at all, are the haunts of youthful muggers, in complex after complex. Rates of violent crime are higher than they were—often far higher—in the ordinary old-fashioned districts that the public housing replaced. Not a few high-rises have been totally abandoned because of crime or of vandalism by their occupants or raiding gangs. From a certain complex in San Francisco, bands of occupants descend on passing tourists to beat and rob them. From a complex in Los Angeles, similar gangs obstruct the freeway to snatch purses from cars. Perhaps the early projects in New

York City are the worst of all. In St. Louis, the city authorities found no one who would consent to live in the huge towers of their boasted Pruitt-Igoe complex after a few years, and so demolished the ugly vast buildings with high explosives. Newspaper photographs of the fall of the apartment buildings appeared everywhere in the country, dread symbols of the failure of public-housing that the American public readily apprehended.

For what the public housing projects gave to people was collectivism, not community. Their very design usually isolated families and individuals as they had never been isolated in the old neighborhoods. Conservatives and radicals agreed on that hard truth. Everybody's property is nobody's property, besides; and many of the public housing tenants are *consumers* of housing, promptly wearing out what the state gives them by way of shelter.

Misery loving company, we remark here that conditions are no more pleasant in British public housing. Terror and destruction in Glasgow, for instance, appear to be worse in the sprawl of the council flats and council houses than in any American city; so the afflictions are not caused primarily by "ethnic minorities" that occupy much of American public housing.

For years past, policemen in certain new-housing-scheme districts of Glasgow have been instructed by their superiors, in effect, "If trouble occurs in your district, do not interfere personally. Go to the nearest telephone kiosk—you are provided with a key—lock yourself in, and call for armored cars." Such is the state of order in public-housing complexes either side of the Atlantic. What a benefit to the low-income people!

The examples mentioned above have occurred over the years; but the hideous reality of life in public housing was perfectly clear to observers by the end of the 'fifties, after a single decade of experience. Jane Jacobs, in her book *The Death and Life of Great American Cities* (1961), took it virtually for granted that everyone at all acquainted with the public housing projects knew them for a dismal failure, an aberration, "a terrible answer." Public housing simply did not fit into the American economy and the American mode of life. A good many people must be subsidized in their lodging, at least temporarily; but it did not follow, she pointed out, that the way to provide for such people of low income was to make the government their landlord.

"The notion that the fact of a subsidy required that these people be housed by someone other than private enterprise and normal landlords was an abberation in itself," Mrs. Jacobs wrote. "The government does not take over the landlordship or ownership or management of subsidized farms or of subsidized airlines. Government does not, as a rule, take over the running of museums that receive subsidies from public funds. It does not take over the ownership or management of voluntary community hospitals, whose construction is today frequently made possible by government subsidies."

What Jane Jacobs proposed as an alternative to public housing was a system of public subsidies that would encourage builders to erect suitable—and less hideous—housing; a guarantee of rents by the government on a sliding scale; a program to encourage tenants to increase their incomes and eventually acquire their dwellings for themselves; and the gradual, piecemeal restoration of cities by judicious filling in of gaps along streets and other means, rather than wholesale demolition and subsequent erection of architectural monstrosities. Her plan was intended to check the separation of citizens on the basis of income, an evil that public housing had already bestowed on nearly every large American city.

Mrs. Jacobs' book was widely and favorably reviewed. Later it exerted some influence on programs of the federal government for subsidizing rents and house-buying, though not precisely in the form that she recommended. One short paragraph of hers is a sufficient denunciation of the consequences of the Housing Act of 1949:

"From the beginning, the whole conception was irrelevant to the nature of the problem, irrelevant to the plain financial need of the people concerned, irrelevant to the needs and workings of cities, irrelevant to the rest of our economic system, and even irrelevant to the meaning of home as it has evolved otherwise in our tradition."

Such a book, had it been published fifteen years earlier,

might have dissuaded the elder Robert Taft from advocating massive "urban redevelopment" and public housing complexes; it might even have modified the views of the people around President Truman. Even should we begin to retrace our steps now, it would take many decades to undo the social harm worked by the national public housing illusions that were enacted in 1948 and 1949.

It remains to mention here another baneful effect of public housing on a mass scale: political corruption. The inhabitants of a high-rise public housing slum can form a whole political constituency at the mercy of some unscrupulous boss, whose domination is assured by his hold on these impecunious clients of his. It is in the interest of such a boss to see to it that more and more public housing is erected in his fiefdom, and that few of his clients are ever enabled to escape to normal living. The political manipulator thrives on the poverty, ignorance, and misery of his constituents.

This point may be illustrated by the grip that Congressman William Dawson had on the black wards of southside Chicago for many years. The population of Dawson's district consisted mostly of poor people living in ghastly grim newish (yet decayed) housing projects, high-rise upon high-rise. Many of the inhabitants were "ADC mothers" with dependent children but no male in the apartment. They were thoroughly uninformed about politics and isolated even from one another; in those complexes were no neighbors, properly speaking, but only other isolated and bewildered souls. A very large part of the district's population was totally dependent upon ADC payments, city welfare checks, and other forms of public assistance.

One familiar figure might flit from time to time through these cheerless buildings: a ward-heeler for the Dawson machine. Especially he appeared at apartments shortly before a primary or an election to make sure that Mrs. Jones would turn out to vote for Congressman Dawson. If for some strange reason Mrs. Jones hinted that she was thinking of giving her vote to a young reformer running in the primary, or perhaps of not voting at all, Mr. Dawson's representative would warn her that her very subsistence depended upon kind Congressman Dawson's good offices. If dear old Representative Dawson should happen to take his eye off her, unfortunate things might occur; for instance, her Social Security check might fail to arrive.

If Mrs. Jones remained a doubting Thomasina, indeed there came unhappy occurrences. On her calling at the building superintendent's office for her mail—that is, for the monthly envelope containing her Social Security check—Mrs. Jones might be aghast on being told by the super that no such check had arrived. Days might pass, and still no check; destitute, Mrs. Jones might call the genial ward-heeler, Mr. Harrison. That party agent then would lament in company with Mrs. Jones, saying that he would ask Congressman Dawson to look into this sad affair. No sooner said than done: the very next morning, the indispensable Social Security check would be handed to Dawson's lucky constituent by the building supervisor. Thereafter Mrs. Jones would not forget to vote, and to vote, of course, for Congressman Dawson.

Of course Representative Dawson and his boys possessed no direct control over either Social Security headquarters or the Postal Service. But they did possess control over the building supervisors in all that wasteland of public housing in south-side Chicago. Things go similarly in the housing complexes of Moscow and Leningrad, except that there, in every block of flats, the concierge is a spy for the secret police. Congressman Dawson never failed of re-election, nor of plums to distribute. Representative Dawson has been gathered to his fathers, but his sort goes marching on. And this occurs in the greatest republic of the twentieth century.

There is no reason therefore to lament that the Housing Act of 1949 was not enlarged for sixteen years. The Eisenhower administration resisted attempts by Democrats in Congress to increase the volume of public housing. In 1959, a housing bill was passed but was vetoed by the President; by a vote of fifty-five yeas to forty nays, the Senate sustained Eisenhower's veto. In 1960, another housing bill suffered the same fate, veto and all. During the Kennedy years, nothing of significance happened in the extravagant but depressing realm of public housing.

MISERABLE LODGING
IN THE GREAT SOCIETY

In 1965, with the overwhelming success of President Johnson and his party in the elections of 1964, the Great Society rushed into more public housing, irresistably. Four major housing acts were adopted, taking effect in 1965, 1966, and 1968.

On July 15, 1965, the Senate passed a bill entitled the Housing and Development Act of 1965, fifty-four senators voting for it, thirty against. (Three Republicans voted for the bill, eleven Democrats against it; this was not wholly a party question.) This act provided for new and enlarged urban programs, including experiments with rent supplements as a new approach, to the tune of eight billion dollars and forty-year contracts; seven hundred million dollars, over four years, to pay half the cost of extending and enlarging water and sewer facilities in anticipation of urban growth; fifty million dollars a year to develop neighborhood social and recreational facilities. It also enlarged several existing programs.

In a speech on the Senate floor on that occasion, Senator Curtis expressed his opposition to the proposed rent subsidies. "Rent subsidies should be defeated because, first, it is a new program of spending that will be most difficult to ever stop; second, it will make more of our citizens dependent upon the government; third, it will delay the day when the federal budget can be balanced; fourth, it is an unnecessary subsidy program promoted in Washington in a grasp for more power and control over our economy and over the lives of individuals; and fifth, it will discourage home ownership."

But such opposition was in vain. A second housing act in 1965 created the Department of Housing and Urban Development, with cabinet status. It carried $2.9 billion in authorization of urban-renewal capital grants; a hundred and twenty-five million dollars for urban-renewal planning grants. Besides, the bill was a tremendous delegation of power to the federal bureaucracy. Many functions long the right and responsibility of local officials were transferred to the administrators of federal programs.

Once upon a time, Senator Lyndon Johnson had proclaimed that he was a liberal where people were concerned, a conservative in financial concerns. President Lyndon Johnson became an ultra-liberal in public expenditure and "welfare" programs.

A year later, on August 19, 1966, the Senate passed another housing bill, called the Demonstration Cities and Metropolitan Development Act of 1966, fifty-three senators voting yea, twenty-two nay. Again a number of Democratic senators, some of them eminent, opposed a Johnson housing measure. Incidentally, after the fierce riots or "demonstrations" in Detroit, New York, Newark, Washington, and other cities, the title of this program was altered, with embarrassment, to "Model Cities."

This act contained nearly a billion dollars' worth of new programs. The opposition pointed out that since it was difficult to determine how to conduct programs already underway, it would be imprudent to begin new ones. Since 1949, $7.6 billion had been authorized for urban renewal and only $1.5 billion had actually been expended. The balance remained unspent chiefly because the cities were unwilling to provide the one-third of the project cost required to secure the federal government's two-thirds. In this new act, Washington's contribution was increased: as much as ninety-five per cent of the expense might come from the federal treasury.

Yet another housing act was adopted in 1967, taking effect in 1968. In the opinion of Carl Curtis, this was an unjust bill; yet Senator Curtis had been one of the sponsors of that legislation, though, in hindsight, not the only offender.

This was S 1592, introduced by the new and junior senator from Illinois, Charles Percy, on April 20, 1967. Every Republican member of the Senate joined Percy in the introduction of his bill. Many of the features of this Percy Amendment were incorporated in the bill, which the Committee on Banking and Currency reported out as S 3497 and which became the Housing Act of 1968. It was intended to promote home ownership for the poor. Carl Curtis refers to the Housing Act of 1968 as the housing program wherein he sinned.

Charles Percy, though recent to the Senate, had a long record of public service; he expressed much interest in housing programs, hoping to make home ownership attainable even for the very poor. Obviously the previous housing programs had been wretchedly unsuccessful. Many of the housing units were already badly deteriorated. The public regarded such undertakings with disfavor.

Senator Percy advocated that instead of having the federal government pour its money into housing projects run by governmental agencies, Washington should provide subsidies so that people might own their own dwellings. In various forms, one or another kind of subsidy had been recommended by people around President Truman—by Jane Jacobs and by several others—though these forms did not much resemble one another.

Percy made strong arguments, calling attention to the unpleasant fact that one might drive through the slums of any city and notice somebody in front of his domicile polishing an automobile—while the polisher's residence was in disrepair with windows broken and garbage flung into the street. Percy inquired why such low-income people care for their automobiles but not for their dwellings. The answer: they own automobiles but they don't own houses. That made sense. For the time being, Percy induced all thirty-six Republican senators to co-sponsor his proposal.

A number of stalwart conservatives in the Senate spoke on behalf of the Percy plan: Tower of Texas, Hansen of Wyoming, Thurmond of South Carolina. It appeared to Carl Curtis that Percy had hit upon something better than public housing; perhaps the Percy proposal could eliminate public housing. Percy's design might enable the poor to acquire houses, which they could not conceivably do without governmental assistance. The Republicans voted for the Housing Act of 1968 because it contained Percy's ideas.

Not long later, Curtis discovered that he had blundered. The "235 Program" created by Percy and his allies was unjust to low and moderate-income people who already owned their own homes.

Letters from Nebraska began to pour into Curtis' office. Whenever Curtis made a trip to his state, many people got in touch with him concerning the 235 Program.

One lady wrote to point out that she and her husband lived in a house that had cost $18,500—a much better dwelling than their earlier residence—and that their payments were only ninety-five dollars a month because the government provided a subsidy for the difference. Other correspondents informed Curtis that able-bodied, well-educated individuals were taking the opportunity to buy a house under the 235 Program, making monthly payments much less than their neighbors did. Those neighbors could not afford new houses.

One such informant told Curtis that a person had purchased a house for $17,000, with two hundred dollars down; this fortunate man was required to pay only a hundred dollars a month. The informant, a neighbor of the fortunate man, declared that he himself lived in a thirty-year-old residence, with monthly payments of $136. Why should the informant and his family be taxed to subsidize someone else's house— someone else, indeed, who already maintained a standard of living far beyond that of the informant's family?

These letters were not deficient in humor. One man wrote to complain that he must subsidize his neighbor's house payments, even though that neighbor's income exceeded his and so did the neighbor's living standard. This correspondent mentioned that the subsidized homeowner was in the habit of coming over to read the complainer's newspaper; but that he had taken the paper away from his visitor, saying, "I have to buy your house, and I'll be damned if I'll buy your newspaper." This correspondent concluded, "Senator, don't you realize you are tearing the country apart with such things? Don't you realize that the people who have been quietly watching such things go on and waiting patiently for them to be stopped are beginning to get filled up to their ears? Don't you realize you are destroying any reason for a man to work?"

On a trip to Nebraska, Curtis was told of a steel worker, twenty-five years old, who earned $450 a month. His debts were slight; yet the taxpayers were defraying $87.94 monthly on his house payments. He encountered another case of a salesman, twenty-eight years old, married, with one child, his income $535 monthly, possessed of a new car and modest debts; the government was paying a monthly subsidy of $83.18 on his house. These benefactions occurred while the great majority of people in the same community were meeting personally, in full, their own house payments.

Two reflections occurred to Curtis as he reviewed what had happened to Percy's well-meant design, which he had co-sponsored. First, houses were not being built for the very poor; such people did not participate in the program. Instead, finding business slow, the house-builders had promoted the use of the 235 Program to build subsidized houses. It was a boom for the construction business. But as Senator Curtis pointed out, if house builders needed a government program, it should not be the 235 Program, which produced such disparity among neighbors and extracted funds from the Treasury for unneeded subsidies, expenditures that could not be justified as charity toward the really poor.

Curtis appeared before the Banking and Currency Committee with a lengthy statement citing a number of cases of such abuse of the 235 Program. He begged the committee either to abandon this program or to make drastic changes. He appealed similarly to the Housing and Urban Development Committee and to George Romney, Secretary of Housing and Urban Development. His pleas went unheeded; the 235 Program continued for a considerable time.

Here was a plan that appealed to the charitable impulse, but it had turned out that the program did not assist the helpless. The 235 Program was employed to promote business for a particular interest in our society, discriminating against one set of citizens in favor of a minority who took advantage of an opportunity that Congress presumably had not intended. In an ironical sense, it was demonstrated that here below, too, to them that hath shall be given.

The waste and injustice of the 235 Program, however, was a minor matter compared to the ruin worked by the Johnson administration through urban renewal and its ill-considered innovating programs. So-called urban renewal demolished the very hearts of great and small cities, with tremendous destruction of good and historic buildings and the wiping out of whole neighborhoods on a colossal scale. Administered without imagination or conscience, Johnsonian "renewal" turned what had been very tolerable urban districts into howling slums by forcing people to double up in the remaining undemolished old houses or to shift into unpleasant and unsafe public housing. (Of all the money spent on urban renewal over the decades, only five per cent has gone to re-lodge people displaced by the wreckers.) "Urban renewal" made Harlem, in Manhattan, the hell on earth that it is today, by driving out the more responsible and prosperous inhabitants. During the Detroit riots, the rioters shouted "instant urban renewal!" as they threw gasoline bombs, setting whole streets ablaze. When George Romney left the governorship of Michigan to become Secretary of Housing and Urban Development, he made a final public address to the people of Michigan. He touched on those Detroit days and nights of anarchy. What had caused the uprising in the slums? Why, Romney said, urban renewal and federal highway building: the first, wiping out old ethnic neighborhoods; the second, carving the city into sectors that became almost uninhabitable. The riots were an explosion of popular wrath against misguided public policy.

We lack space here to discuss in detail the false assumptions and methods of most alleged urban renewal. The subject has been treated systematically in Dr. Martin Anderson's book *The Federal Bulldozer*. In Anderson's words, "Should government officials use taxpayers' money and the power of eminent domain to scatter residents of run-down areas of cities, demolish the buildings they once lived in, and then guide the reconstruction according to aesthetic, social, and economic standards which they feel to be more suitable? Should the individual property rights of some people be sacrificed so that their land can be appropriated and sold by the government to other private individuals who will put it to a "higher and better use?"

In urban renewal, as in various other programs, President Johnson's "war on poverty" actually was war against the poor. By 1968, even Senator Edward Kennedy was saying that the public housing program had failed. Senator Curtis remarked on the Senate floor, on March 15, that the hundreds of millions of dollars already spent for public housing had accomplished nothing worthwhile.

"For as long as I can remember," Curtis said, "we have had a Subcommittee on Housing guiding the housing policy of this country. Yet if I read the newspapers correctly, one of the most urgent needs in this country is that for housing in the slums and ghettos. One of the things that is alleged to have prompted marches upon Washington is the fact that we do not have proper housing. All of these fifty agencies or fifty housing programs—do they exist to provide government housing for the well-to-do, the middle class, the able-bodied who ought to be able to get houses for themselves? Or where do we begin?"

In 1969, Senator Edward Brooke, of Massachusetts, obtained the passage of an amendment to the housing laws that compelled local public housing authorities so to reduce rents that no tenant might pay more than twenty-five per cent of his income for rent. This measure brought dismay to many places.

Senator Curtis offered an amendment to the Brooke proposal that would have made application of this measure discretionary on the part of the local housing authorities. He mentioned having been at home in Minden for a weekend:

"A meeting was held with some individuals greatly concerned about the operation of this provision of the law which limits the amount that can be charged to twenty-five per cent of the person's income. This particular project for the elderly in my hometown has thirty apartments. The lowest rent charged is thirty dollars per month, and I believe the highest rent is forty-five dollars per month. All utilities are paid....

"One particular case was called to my attention. This lady was most happy to be permitted to occupy one of these new, well-kept apartments for thirty dollars a month. Actually, her total annual income is only seven hundred twenty dollars. She, however, felt fortunate in having this apartment for thirty dollars a month, with everything paid. Her children preferred to make a sacrifice and assist their mother in paying the rent because they wanted to. It added the feeling of well-being for both them and their mother.

"Under the terms of the Brooke amendment, this rent

would be greatly reduced. As a matter of fact, the application of this amendment to the entire thirty units would amount to an annual shortage for the local housing authority of $4,500. The housing authority is expected to reduce the rents, even though the tenants are willing to pay, and then the housing authority must make application for a federal subsidy for $4,500 from the U. S. government. This they did not want to do.

"Mr. President, here is a local unit of government that does not want to ask for $4,500 from the federal government, but we are operating under a hard-and-fast, coast-to-coast rule."

Curtis read into the record letters from other communities supporting his position. The Brooke amendment made it necessary to disclose not only the amount of rent paid by each resident, but also their incomes. This became a cause of strife among tenants of any housing authority.

Curtis' amendment was pictured as a move against the poor by the champions of the Brooke amendment; some of their speeches implied that the Curtis amendment would make it mandatory to increase rents throughout the country. When the roll was called, only nine senators voted for the Curtis amendment.

The Nixon and Ford administrations tried to hold the line with respect to public housing programs and the like, modifying some existing undertakings and methods and not authorizing expansion or new programs. Congress sometimes disagreed with those two Presidents; some controversies between Congress and the Executive Branch were taken to the courts.

The most recent major development in housing has been what is called Section VIII Housing. This measure provides in substance that direct subsidies may be paid on behalf of tenants, so that builders or owners may be rewarded for undertaking construction. This is one version of a recommendation by Jane Jacobs, mentioned earlier in this chapter. Grace Milgram, a specialist in housing for the Congressional Research Service of the Library of Congress, published an article noting that authorized expenditures for Section VIII alone (contracts under this program being made for fifteen or twenty years) stood at $110.2 billion by the end of fiscal 1980; for all "assisted housing" the total reached was $220.5 billion. (That's correct: *billion* dollars.) These figures do not include indirect assistance of various sorts from public agencies.

A grisly vignette may be a suitable ending for this chapter. By the 1970s, many big cities were afflicted, uglified, and endangered by whole districts in which the large majority of houses stood untenanted and derelict. East New York and the South Bronx were only two of the more notorious examples of this dreadful decay; bombing of various European cities during the Second World War had been less devastating than was stupid public policy in America.

Many of these houses had been desirable—sometimes very desirable and costly—residences not many years earlier. Through an expensive program of HUD, whole streets of them had been sold to poor people, on mortgages at low interest rates with small monthly payments. Unscrupulous realtors made fortunes out of selling such houses to folk obviously unable to meet monthly payments, or at least incapable of the self-discipline necessary for making even very small savings. Many of the purchasers had been women receiving various forms of welfare payments, lacking the knowledge of how to maintain the plumbing and other features of a house, let alone repair it.

Detroit was one of the cities on which this blight had fallen: Detroit, "Demonstration City" or "Model City," where many millions of federal money for renewal had gone down the drain. (Some racketeering realtors actually were prosecuted and fined or imprisoned in the Detroit scandals.) Unable to meet their monthly payments, many tenants fled from their decaying houses, or HUD mortgages had been foreclosed. Into some derelict houses moved narcotics addicts, muggers and other criminals, youth gangs, and in general the scum of the city.

The *Detroit News* ran a moving series of feature articles on this blight. Literally thousands of houses within the city's limits had become uninhabited—and mostly uninhabitable—in consequence of federal housing programs ill conceived and worse administered. One article in the *News* series began with a nocturnal scene on one of those ghostly and silent streets of dereliction.

At three in the morning, when most malefactors are asleep, a battered nondescript car drives up to a certain unlighted house. Three armed men are in it. For a time they sit in the car, looking warily about them. Then one, shotgun in hand, cautiously emerges from the automobile and makes his way round to the back door of the house. He kicks it open and shines his flashlight inside.

"O.K., fellows," he calls softly to his companions. "I guess it's all right: come on in."

Who are these men—burglars? No: they are housing inspectors.

All the governmental programs for housing have not abolished slums: they have merely shifted slums about, enlarged them, made them still worse. They have converted areas formerly liveable into slums, and people who used to take care of themselves tolerably well into slum-dwellers. American cities that never have known war now look as if they had been sacked by some ferocious enemy. And all this destruction has been accomplished at incredible expense to the general public. It is more pleasant to live in the House That Jack Built than in the House That Uncle Sam Built. Unreasonable public policy has not been the only cause of America's urban decay, but for the past thirty-five years such policy has accelerated and deepened that decline.

Chapter 6

Deficit Financing: The Need for a Constitutional Restraint

IMPOSING THE WELFARE STATE'S BILLS UPON POSTERITY

When the Second World War ended, many responsible American citizens hoped and expected that the federal government would undertake a systematic plan for paying off the national debt. They wished the world to know that Uncle Sam paid his bonds. Congressman Carl Curtis was strongly convinced that the destiny of the United States depended upon systematic reduction of the national debt and maintenance of public financial integrity. In his speeches, he frequently asked, "What are we going to do if our children look us in the eye and say, 'Does Uncle Sam ever pay his debts? Or does he just renew the bonds when they come due, and add to them?'"

In the discussion of this subject, as in several other parts of this book, we commence with events and arguments that occurred about the beginning of this controversy, and then carry the topic down to Curtis' later years in Congress.

The Truman administration followed no such course of debt-reduction; nor did the Congress. Instead, elaborate proposals were advanced for national health insurance, federal aid to public education, more public housing, additional food programs, hospitals and airports at federal expense, and federal undertakings of many types and descriptions, including massive foreign-aid programs. Growth of the welfare state would prevent reduction of the debt; indeed, it would increase the national debt to fantastic proportions.

The welfare state may be defined as a system based upon the theory that government must provide for the material wants of its citizens. Until the past half-century, the federal government was confined principally to what could be termed "general government." Its function was to administer government so that laws were enforced, the census taken, mail delivered, interstate and foreign commerce regulated, and adequate provision made for the common defense.

With the coming of the New Deal and the persuasive powers of President Franklin Roosevelt, the theory was advanced that the national debt was of small consequence because "we owe it to ourselves." The federal government began to shift from its original functions of defending the country, administering justice, and promoting the common welfare (this last in a restricted sense) to providing a large proportion of its citizens with food, lodging, medical services, cash incomes, and other "benefits" and "entitlements" of the welfare state.

All this would require gigantic sums of money. As the welfare state developed, federal taxes were increased sharply and new taxes imposed; state and local taxation for such purposes sometimes went up even more burdensomely. But a sizeable part of the federal government's money was not raised through taxation: it was obtained through issuing of long-term and short-term federal bonds and notes. Interest must be paid—presently at much higher rates—on these heavy obligations. This excessive borrowing by the federal government, both through the Federal Reserve System and the Treasury, would produce eventually severe monetary inflation, bearing most oppressively upon people with limited incomes that did not rise promptly in response to inflation—or did not rise at all. It would produce eventually a dearth of capital for productive enterprises of all sorts, with resulting stagnation in the American economy. It would impose upon future generations an immense burden of debt, with dismaying interest-charges, chiefly for the benefit of people living at the time when such federal welfare policies were adopted. (This unfairness to posterity became most conspicuous in the Social Security financing.) The deficit financing of welfare-state measures would make it increasingly difficult for national administrations to obtain sufficient appropriations for national defense, a primary function of any government. The notion that "debt doesn't matter" would encourage emulation of this illusion in the private sphere—with a resulting excessive expansion of private spending, materialism, and personal purchasing on credit.

In the beginning, deficit financing was popular as an alternative to a larger increase in taxation. And though many members of Congress might profess an uneasiness with the growth of the national debt, pressures from powerful "welfare" lobbies induced them to vote for measure after measure that would increase that debt to astronomical proportions. "After me, the deluge." By the time of reckoning, such gentlemen presumably would have retired from the Congress.

That time of reckoning is very nearly upon us, in 1986. The endeavors of Carl Curtis and other members of Congress to impose some constitutional restraint upon extravagant deficit-financing, over more than four decades, were frustrated. The Reagan administration contends against bigger deficits than ever, menacing to national productivity, the stability of the dollar and the reduction of inflation, plans to lower income taxes, the rate of interest, and the federal government's essential functions. The present overwhelming deficit results from the refusal of Congress to reduce public expenditures effectively—because of pressures from lobbies and groups, powerful at the polls, that obtain benefits from the public purse at the expense of the national economic interest, and even at the expense of national security. This chapter traces the ruinous triumph of deficit financing to support the welfare state, and efforts to curb that monstrous growth of indebtedness.

THE NOTION
OF "FULL EMPLOYMENT"

An illustration of the financial irresponsibility of the welfare-state mentality is the concept of having the federal government guarantee full employment to everybody, through federal expenditure and federal planning. Although the federal government produces no goods (as distinguished from services, in economic terminology), according to this "full employment" scheme Washington somehow would provide jobs for everybody seeking them.

In January 1944, President Franklin Roosevelt outlined what he described as "an economic bill of rights." He declared that everyone had a right to a useful and remunerative job in manufacturing, commerce, agriculture, or the extractive industries. That autumn, campaigning for re-election, Roosevelt advocated legislation to "assure to all the full realization of the right to useful and remunerative employment."

When Congress convened in January, 1945, Senator James E. Murray, Montana Democrat, introduced Senate Bill 380, which stated that all persons seeking jobs had a "right" to them, and provided for a federal policy of promoting full employment, setting up certain procedures with that objective. Murray was joined in the introduction of his bill by Senator Joseph C. O'Mahoney (Wyoming Democrat), Senator Elbert D. Thomas (Utah Democrat), and Robert F. Wagner (New York Democrat).

This bill called for a national budget for employment. There was to be an estimate of the labor force for that year and of the amount of public and private expenditure necessary to provide the jobs enumerated in the budget. Moreover, the bill provided that if this prospective spending should be less than the President thought necessary, the President was to submit recommendations for increased expenditure, monopoly control, banking policy, changes of wages and working conditions, foreign-trade policies, Social Security alterations, and development of natural resources. If, after all these measures, a deficiency of jobs should still exist, the President was to submit recommendations for additional federal spending or lending to make up the balance. In effect, this was a proposal for a "command economy" or "directed economy. "

Presently the sponsors of this bill were joined by four Republican senators: George D. Aiken of Vermont, William Langer of North Dakota, Wayne Morse of Oregon, and Charles W. Tobey of New Hampshire. "Full employment" was becoming a popular, if utopian, proposal.

The Senate's debate on this measure was thorough. Senator Joseph H. Ball, Minnesota Republican, forcefully expressed his opposition: "This insistence that complete, utter economic security must be guaranteed every individual by the federal government, regardless of what else we may have to do or what other obligations under the Constitution we would consequently have to shirk, is exactly the kind of political philosophy and attitude which, on the part of the people in Italy and Germany, led straight to fascism and naziism."

Senator Robert Taft, "Mr. Republican" from Ohio, said at one point in the debate, "There is no panacea by which we can furnish full employment unless we are prepared to adopt a totalitarian system." Nevertheless he ended by voting for the bill, and found no fault with the conference report.

Senator John L. McClellan, Arkansas Democrat, pointed out the peril of deficit expenditure that would result: "I believe that of the two, the risk of some unemployment or a program going all the way on a policy of unlimited deficit spending, the latter course would be more dangerous to this government than would the former."

The Senate passed the Murray bill on September 28, 1944, by a roll-call vote of seventy-one to ten.

The House committee changed "full employment" to read "high level of employment," and the House bill did not refer to the alleged "right" to work; instead, to "opportunity" to work. In the House Expenditures Committee the proposed national budget for jobs was changed to provide for an economic report on the extent to which the federal government's activities were, or were not, achieving the bill's policies. The

House bill also provided for a joint congressional committee on this economic report, and for creating a three-man council of economic advisors to assist the President.

Wright Patman, Texas Democrat, had introduced the administration's full-employment bill in the House. By the time the House committee had acted on its revised bill, Patman had obtained a hundred and sixteen co-sponsors. The Patman (administration) bill was offered as a substitute for the House committee bill, but the Expenditures Committee prevailed by a teller vote of 185 to 95.

While Representative Patman was speaking on behalf of the administration bill, Carl Curtis asked him a question: "I was somewhat surprised when the gentleman stated that every Fascist in America was against this bill. I would like to have him name some of them." The exchange between Patman and Curtis is of some interest, as illustrating the intemperate zeal of some of the bill's advocates.

Patman: "The Committee on Constitutional Government represents a lot of them. There is this fellow Gannett, a big chain-newspaper publisher; and his working partner, this fellow Pettingill, a renegade Democrat; and this fellow McClure, who spent two years over in Italy studying fascism under Mussolini, who is working with them, and Edward Rumley, their wheel-horse, an ex-convict who was convicted for dealing with the enemy—Germany—in World War I."

Curtis: "Which Gannett does the gentleman refer to?"

Patman: "The chain newspaperman of Rochester, New York, I believe."

Curtis: "Will the gentleman identify the other men?"

Patman: "Pettingill, who used to be a member of this House."

Curtis: "The gentleman classifies him as a Fascist?"

Patman: "Yes, I do: the Number One Fascist in America."

Curtis: "Name some more."

Patman: "This fellow McClure, who studied fascism two years under Mussolini. Get your *Who's Who* in the library and look into his biography. You will find there where he brags about it. He likes it. There is all that bunch of fellows who are with him fighting this bill.''

Actually, the people named by Patman had been opposing the bill on the ground that it would concentrate political
and economic power, as well as being impracticable. The administration bill advocated by Patman would have been con-
sonant enough with Fascist economic and political policy,
which in Italy had advocated a planned or ''command'' economy with such features, although such a scheme had been realized only partially there.

On the House floor, Curtis said, ''As I understand this bill,
it calls for a budget as to jobs, jobs in private industry and all
other kinds of jobs. How can the government budget something
it does not control, or does this bill propose to control all jobs?''
(Here Congressman Clare Hoffman, Michigan Republican,
strongly opposing the bill, interjected, ''Yes!'')

Continuing his speech against the bill, Curtis said, ''It is
predicated upon the theory that the federal government should
be a wet nurse to everything and everybody in the country. It
is predicated upon the doctrine that the government of the
United States owes every man not only a job, but the kind of
a job that he wants. . . .

''Of course the unfortunate should be taken care of. But
with the heavy load that the federal government already has,
the several states should assume greater responsibility. . . .

''We tried to cure one depression by spending and spending on government projects. Many of the projects were fine,
but the depression got worse. Unemployment continued to rise
all during that period. Now the proponents of this measure say
they love private enterprise and that if private enterprise cannot do the job, then the government will step in. Rest assured
that private enterprise will be controlled, hampered, and interfered with so that it cannot do the job if the philosophy of
this measure prevails.''

On December 14, 1946, the House of Representatives, by
roll-call vote, 255 to 126, passed its version of this full-
employment bill. A conference committee was appointed to
iron out differences between House and Senate versions; in
general, the bill agreed on in conference followed the House
bill. The bill's title was changed to the Employment Act of

1946.

Meanwhile Harry Truman had assumed the presidency; he said that the House bill was unacceptable, advocating the Senate bill. Nevertheless, the Democratic leaders of House and Senate expressed their satisfaction with the conference bill, which was accepted by the House, on a roll call of 320 to 84, on February 6, 1947. The Senate agreed to the conference bill by voice vote. Continuing to oppose the bill, Carl Curtis voted against the conference report.

The measure was enacted, but it never was fully implemented. By the early 1950s, nearly everybody, including citizens politically aware, had forgotten the Employment Act's existence. Even in the modified version that came out of the conference committee, this scheme was inoperable under the American political and economic system. For full enforcement, the Act would have required total direction of the national economy from Washington, presumably with wage and price controls, direction of labor, politically-fixed production goals, and the whole apparatus of the sort of command economy ordained (with notable lack of economic success) in totalist countries. Although the big labor unions generally had supported the full-employment concept, its actual functioning would have been inimical to their interests; union spokesmen referred to the Act infrequently after its passage.

For all that, the Employment Act did open the way for sporadic large expenditures during recessions by the federal government, "creating jobs" of dubious economic efficacy temporarily to diminish unemployment and to supply political plums to cities and states where votes would be useful to the party in power. Senator Hubert Humphrey would become the most eminent advocate of such "job creation" from time to time. Of course such lavish expenditures, which tended to retard rather than to accelerate economic recovery, were defrayed by more deficit financing.

THE STRUGGLE TO REQUIRE
A BALANCED BUDGET

Until the 1930s, the fear of having to levy higher taxes upon voters held federal spending in check. A heavy tax burden would rouse voters' resistance, and possibly result in voters' rebellion: something that officeholders view as worse than the plague.

But half a century ago presidents, senators, and representatives in Washington discovered a method for avoiding the horrid and risky task of collecting taxes to support the spending for which they had voted. Now program after program could be initiated; spending could be indulged without restraint. The way was simple: to increase the national debt. To certain politicians this discovery opened the way to heaven upon earth.

Knowledge that uncontrolled spending would lead, some day or other, to a stern reckoning—why, this did not much influence the actions either of the Executive Force or of the Congress. As the old Greeks put it, ''When I am dead, let earth be mixed with fire.'' On the occasion of a certain bill to expand the operations of the federal government, Carl Curtis, in a private conversation, called to the attention of one of his colleagues how great the cost of the proposed program would be, at the end of a decade. His colleague replied, ''I don't expect to be in Congress then.''

All of this worried Curtis. He came to the conclusion that, just as many states held their spending in check by provisions of their state constitutions, there ought to be an article in the federal constitution to limit expenditure and to require that the federal budget be balanced.

So in the first session of the Eighty-Second Congress, 1951, Curtis introduced House Joint Resolution 245, a proposal to amend the Constitution to require a balanced budget. If passed by both houses of Congress and ratified by three-fourths of the states, this amendment would be a constitutional injunction for the government to live within its means.

This first Curtis constitutional amendment provided a ceiling on the amount of taxes that might be collected by the federal government: fourteen percent of the national income. It also provided that five percent of taxes levied and collected should be applied to reduction of the national debt. And it commanded the Congress to maintain a balanced budget; appropriations that might cause an unbalancing of the budget would not be effective.

During the twenty-seven years thereafter, battling for such a constitutional provision, Curtis made changes in his approach. Finding it difficult to sell several concepts in one package, and knowing that to end deficit financing was the important thing, he concentrated on that provision which would compel the government to live within its means.

Also he came to conclude that a mere command written into the Constitution would not of itself produce a balanced budget. An amendment terminating deficit financing would have to include self-enforcing provisions: teeth. There was historical precedent for this. For instance, Section 2 of the Fourteenth Amendment provides that representation in the House shall be apportioned according to the whole nunber of persons in each state. Yet it also provides that when the right to vote at any election for state or federal office is denied to any inhabitant twenty-one years old or older (and a citizen of the United States), that state's representation in the House shall be reduced in proportion to the number of such franchise-denied male citizens, as related to the state's total population. This section of the Fourteenth Amendment long was ineffectual, for lack of enforcement provisions.

By way of illustration, five hundred thousand votes were cast in the election of 1944 for representatives in Congress from Nebraska; and fewer than 130,000 votes were cast for representatives from Mississippi. Yet Mississippi was allowed seven representatives, and Nebraska only four. (This was true until the 1960s because of the virtual exclusion of many black citizens from voting in Mississippi.)

So the need for a self-enforcing provision in a budget-balancing amendment was evident. A mere command that the total of all appropriations and spending authorizations by Congress should not exceed revenues would be insufficient. Who would decide what bills should be paid and what bills refused or reduced? What priority would be given to payments? Curtis studied these problems.

On a day in January, 1957, Curtis was driving from his house in Washington to the Capitol, listening to news on the radio. Over the air he heard that Senator Styles Bridges (New Hampshire Republican) and Senator Harry Byrd (Virginia Democrat) had introduced a constitutional amendment directing a balanced budget, and providing that Congress could not adjourn until adequate steps should be taken—either by reducing expenditures or by raising revenue—to bring the budget into balance. (In those days, Congress usually adjourned by midsummer.) This provision had strong appeal. It would require members of Congress to stay right there in Washington's summer heat until the budget should be balanced. Rushing to his office, Curtis asked to become a co-sponsor of that amendment. Here might be the sufficient procedure for enforcement.

Yet within a few years, the sponsors of this enforcing provision were to discover that it would be altogether ineffectual. For with the unceasing enlargement of the federal government, and its assumption of more and more of the responsibilities formerly allocated to state and local governments, Congress remained in session virtually the whole year. Denying a long summer recess would be a piece of archaism.

So what might bring about enforcement of any balanced-budget amendment? Curtis heard that Senator John Williams had suggested this: whenever Congress should incur a deficit, Congress must pass a statute requiring a surtax the following year to recoup that deficit. This excellent idea had but one shortcoming: the Williams proposal was for only an act of Congress. One Congress cannot bind a future Congress, so later Congresses might do as they pleased about any such surtax. Nevertheless, the Williams suggestion gave Senator Curtis an idea of how to write an effective self-enforcing constitutional amendment. Such an amendment should place responsibility upon Congress for balancing the budget. Should Congress fail to do that, a surtax would be imposed (as part of the proposed constitutional amendment) upon all corporations and individuals, automatically, the following fiscal year, of an amount sufficient to recoup the deficit.

Everybody in Congress pays lip-service to the ideal of a balanced budget. But when it comes to voting for steps to bring about this desirable consummation, members find it easy to detect flaws in any such proposal. Curtis' self-enforcing provision has been criticized over the years because Curtis advocates raising taxes, which nobody relishes. (One might use the same argument against going to a dentist.) In a speech on the Senate floor, April 19, 1977, Curtis explained his proposal to refute the charge that he relished high taxation.

"The Congress would be mandated to balance the budget every year," Curtis said. "At the end of the fiscal year, the President would be called upon to determine whether or not there was a deficit; and if so, how much. If there was a deficit, he would be required to calculate how much of a surtax would be necessary to be imposed the next year to recoup the deficit. The President would not impose a tax. No additional power would be given to him. He would merely perform a ministerial duty of working the arithmetic. The tax would go in automatically under the terms of the Constitution."

The President, Curtis continued, would be required to perform this task within twenty days after the end of the fiscal year. "I believe if Congress is faced with the decision of collecting the taxes or reducing spending, they will reduce spending. Who wants a report to go out on the twentieth of October to his state, or a House member to his district, which says we have spent too much money; everybody will have an eleven percent increase in taxes, three percent, or whatever the case might be? It will put into our system the necessary discipline to save this country from economic disaster. In other words, the people would have a remedy at the ballot box. Congress could choose between cutting expenses or raising taxes."

Gentlemen might argue, Curtis went on, that a balanced budget would produce a depression; that full employment could be attained only through budgetary deficits. But this was a foolish notion. "I feel sorry for those people of little faith in private enterprise, who have little faith in the basic principle that bills ought to be paid. I just do not believe the universe is so constituted. I think if we embarked on a program of balanced budgets, not just once in a while; if we had a general program of balanced budgets and assured the value of our American dollar, there would be a wave of optimism, enthusiasm, and confidence which would sweep this country . . . The activity, the worthwhile endeavor, and the great American dream would become a reality. . .

"We have full employment when individuals can buy more than the necessities of life. When inflation is so rampant that the paycheck goes for those bare necessities of life, there are a lot of people that go out of work."

Over the years, Curtis introduced the substance of this constitutional amendment, trying to get the Senate Judiciary Committee to report it favorably to the floor. But the Judiciary Committee was recalcitrant. Any proposal that reaches the floor lacking committee approval lies under a heavy handicap. Under the rules, Senator Curtis could not offer his amendment as an amendment to an ordinary bill. He must attach it to a proposal for a constitutional amendment. During his last year in the Senate, opportunity came to bring his constitutional amendment to the floor.

The House had passed a proposed constitutional amendment dealing with the voting rights, and certain statehood rights, for the District of Columbia. This District of Columbia bill was not voted out by the Senate's Judiciary Committee; but when sent over from the House, it was stopped at the desk and called up for immediate action. Here was a means of offering the Curtis constitutional amendment.

Should Curtis offer his amendment as a substitute, or as an addition to the District of Columbia bill? Wisely or not, he chose to offer it as a substitute.

So on August 16, 1978, Curtis sought recognition in the Senate and offered an amendment to the Columbia bill that, in effect, would substitute his own constitutional amendment. "While it is vitally necessary that we practice economy in every activity of the government," Curtis said on the floor, "it is equally important that we look at the basic cause of the great increase in the budget of the United States.

"The budget for the current fiscal year calls for spending in a total sum of $459 billion. Compare this with the amount of the budget for the last full fiscal year of the Eisenhower administration, of $92 billion. We cannot blame this on defense costs, neither is this great increase caused by expenditures for the necessary functions of government. It cannot be blamed upon the development of our natural resources. The cause of this huge budget is basically the welfare state. The cost of governing and regulating and policing it is not what is bringing about the huge expenditures. It is that role of the government which can best be described by the word 'provide.'

"Much of the legislation involving the welfare state which is now so costly was enacted in the thirties and forties. Many additional programs were enacted in the period of 1961 to 1969. Here is what these programs are costing this year: food, $8.95 billion; housing, $6.8 billion; education, $19.6 billion; assistance to local and state governments, $18.17 billion; medical and health programs, $56 billion; unemployment compensation, $10.6 billion; and retirement and disability, $122.44 billion."

Curtis went on to criticize existing and proposed welfare programs in medical care, housing, and other fields. "Reducing the size of the government is an enormous task. It calls for intelligence, hard work, establishment of priorities, and above all, men and women of courage who are deeply concerned about the future."

Then Curtis explained his constitutional amendment, which contained a provision that in time of war or of a national emergency declared by Congress, the amendment's budgetary requirement might be set aside for one year at a time.

"This constitutional amendment is a stern procedure; it does have teeth in it. If Congress spends more than the government takes in, the taxes automatically go up. If Congress is faced with the alternative of reducing spending or increasing taxes, I predict that they will reduce spending. . . . A constitutional amendment which is a mere declaration of a requirement to balance the budget and which is not self-enforcing will not do the job."

This Curtis Amendment had twenty-one senatorial co-sponsors, several of them Democrats. It did not appear that Curtis could convince the majority of the Senate; but at least here was his opportunity to bring serious discussion to the floor. He proceeded in his speech to flay the "experts" who defended budgetary deficits:

"Washington is infested with too many self-proclaimed experts who hold to economic theories that are erroneous. These individuals assume the role of 'fine tuners.' They believe that if they can add to the government spending, increase the deficits, and dissipate revenues, somehow at some future date business will pick up, and an economic utopia will be reached, and the budget will balance itself. They overlook many factors, including the results of their own self-created inflation and the record of Congress in always voting more expenditures. The 'fine tuners' have a very bad track record."

It was unfortunate that the Curtis constitutional amendment could be considered by the Senate only in connection with the District of Columbia bill. On the final vote, some senators favoring the Curtis amendment found that they could not vote for it as a substitute for the District of Columbia proposed amendment. Opposition to the Curtis amendment was led by Democratic Senators Bayh, Muskie, and Kennedy. At the end of the debate, Senator Robert C. Byrd moved to lay the Curtis proposal on the table. This carried by sixty-eight yeas; twenty-two senators voted for the Curtis amendment. The cause was lost for the time being.

Had a workable, self-enforcing, pay-as-you-go amendment been added to the Constitution a few decades ago when Curtis' was a lone voice in the wilderness, much mischief might have been averted. Instead, deficit financing became a way of life. Presidents, senators, and representatives came to love it. They could commence programs and spend money without collecting taxes. But public support for constitutional restraints on federal spending has grown stronger in recent years, as the public has become painfully aware of the burden of debt and inflation.

By the autumn of 1985, the national debt well exceeded one trillion, eight hundred million dollars. Because of rising interest rates, it appeared all too probable that for the rest of the 1980s deficits might exceed two hundred billion annually. Interest paid on the national debt, in 1985, came to about three thousand dollars per American household. The federal government was consuming through its borrowing so large a share of the gross national product that the economy faced the prospect of being starved for capital.

The following chart shows, from the Nixon administration to the Reagan administration, how the deficit has grown in proportion to America's gross national product; it also shows the increase of budget outlays (federal expenditures) as a proportion of the gross national product. It will be noted that during 1984 the Reagan administration enjoyed some success—but not enough—in reducing expenditures and the deficit, as set against the annual GNP. Yet rising interest rates threatened to wipe out these modest gains.

THE REAL CAUSE OF DEFICITS

	RECEIPTS (% of GNP)	BUDGET OUTLAYS[1] (% of GNP)	DEFICIT[1] (% of GNP)
1970	19.9	20.2	0.3
1971	18.1	20.4	2.2
1972	18.4	20.4	2.1
1973	18.4	19.6	1.2
1974	19.1	19.4	0.4
1975	18.9	22.5	3.6
1976	18.2	22.6	4.5
1977	19.1	22.0	2.9
1978	19.1	21.9	2.8
1979	19.7	21.3	1.7
1980	20.1	23.0	2.9
1981	20.9	23.6	2.8
1982	20.4	24.6	4.2
1983	18.6	25.1	6.5
1984[2]	18.7	24.3	5.6

1 Includes both off- and on-budget items.
2 Estimated.
Sources: *Budget of the United States Goverment,*
Fiscal Year 1984 and OMB Revisions, January 1984.

With strong and persuasive support from President Reagan, the Senate did pass a constitutional amendment (SJ Res 58) on August 4, 1982, intended to end deficit financing. More than the requisite two-thirds of the senators voted for the amendment, but the House did not consider it.

SJ Res 58 provided that prior to every fiscal year, Congress must adopt a statement of receipts and outlays for the year, providing that total outlays shall not be greater than total receipts. The amendment provided also that Congress may amend the statement if revised outlays are not greater than revised receipts. Whenever three-fifths of the whole number of both houses shall deem it necessary, Congress in such a statement may provide for a specific excess of outlays over receipts by a vote directed solely to that subject.

The provision requiring a three-fifths vote would doubtless exert restraint on spending. Yet is this proposed constitutional amendment anything more, really, than a mere constitutional command? It lacks self-enforcing provisions—teeth.

Several difficulties are not faced by this proposed amendment. Suppose that in a political crisis, the estimate for receipts should be high and that for outlays low; such things have occurred in the past. It should be remembered, too, that the level of expenditures for such existing programs as unemployment compensation, farm-support loans, and matching programs for the states are not determined directly by the Congress. The payment-in-kind (PIK) program for agriculture was initiated without congressional action; it increased expenditures by nine billion dollars. And what would happen if there were made in the closing days of a Congress urgent and heartrending appeals for funds to meet some crisis—and those funds were voted? This proposed amendment commands Congress to make provision for raising revenue to meet additional expenditures; but suppose that on a roll-call vote, both houses of Congress should reject the proposed increase in taxes. What then?

There is another route to a budget-balancing constitutional amendment than directly through Congress: the summoning of a constitutional convention upon request of the legislatures of three-fourths of the states. By the fall of 1985, thirty-two legislatures had adopted resolutions calling for a constitutional convention for this purpose. Resolutions from only two more states were required, and the legislatures of several other states were debating the question. The opponents of the new convention, in many state legislatures, made no strong attempt to defend deficit financing: the national debt and the deficit had become altogether too unpopular for resistance on that ground. Rather, the argument advanced by the adversaries of this constitutional reform (whether ingenuously or disingenuously) was that a new constitutional convention might decide to take up other constitutional changes than prohibition of a national deficit—and who could tell whither such an impulse might lead? A second constitutional convention might even be inclined toward authorizing public prayer in public schools; might impose restraints on abortion; might do all manner of conservative things. How horrid a prospect!

Thus some form of the Curtis Amendment might come in by the back door, to the hideous chagrin of the congressional advocates of unlimited expenditure. Nobody hates deficits but the people, really.

Yet even Democratic liberal politicians now profess dismay at the proportions of the deficit, and actually demand that taxes be increased—a far cry from their tune over the past five decades. Whether these overnight converts to the doctrine of the balanced budget possess either the courage or the desire to reduce or restrain expenditures on the welfare state is a very different matter.

However that may be, it is simply impossible to balance the budget and to increase welfare-state costs simultaneously without so adding to the tax burden that the voters would rise up in wrath and the economy would be crippled for lack of capital. (To borrow a word from Ambrose Bierce, such a conjunction is "incompossible.")

The Grace Commission, in 1984, strongly recommended drastic reductions in federal expenditure which nevertheless would not impair any of the federal government's important functions. A 1984 study by the Heritage Foundation, *How to Slash $119 Billion from the Deficit*, offered a detailed plan going still farther than the Grace recommendations, and in some cases abolishing categories of federal outlays. Theoretically, it is possible to reduce the federal deficit greatly; even to abolish it.

Only if public indignation heartens legislators to withstand the threats and blandishments of the "welfare lobby" may we bring debt and budget under tolerable control.

But the alternative to such balancing of the budget and reduction of the debt, painful though any such process must be politically, is galloping inflation, loss of faith and credit by the federal government, and virtual collapse of the nation's economy. It is later than you think.

REVENUE SHARING AND ITS CONSEQUENCES

As if the national debt had not already been hanging over Washington like the sword of Damocles, in 1971 and 1972 came to pass the program for sharing federal revenues with state and local governments—at a time when there was not one cent of surplus revenue to share but only an overwhelming federal deficit that nobody had the faintest desire to share.

This revenue-sharing plan was a design of the Nixon administration, related to concepts of a "New Federalism." President Nixon—generally conservative in his impulses but always eager for new, ingenious ideas—found governors, state legislators, county commissioners, municipal officials, and township officers throughout the land enthusiasts for this design. Why not? They would be the beneficiaries; some of them were overjoyed at their prospects.

The argument in favor of this scheme was that by receiving a portion of the federal government's revenues, state and local governments would be reinvigorated; they would be enabled to resume old functions that they gradually had abandoned to the federal government over the years, and perhaps enabled to undertake new functions—including welfare-state activities—that otherwise would be assumed by Washington. In short, it was an argument on the ground of decentralization or devolution of power, intended to promote a New Federalism that would turn away from the policy, half a century old at least, of concentrating both policy-making and administration in the federal government, to the detriment of what Orestes Brownson had called America's "territorial democracy." On the face of it, this was a plausible argument; whether such a policy would bear good fruit no one could say. It never had been tried.

States and localities could contend, with reason, that it had become very difficult for them to raise additional revenue for state and local purposes: for the increasing burden of federal taxes had closed possible avenues to state and local sources of income; and the electorate would resist increase of real-property taxation, sales taxes, and other forms of taxation as yet not usurped by the Internal Revenue Service.

Logically, if federal revenues were to be shared by state and local governments on some formula or other, what needed to be done was this: the federal government should first reduce its operations and expenditures, turning over some of its responsibilities and some sources of its revenues to state and local political units after balancing the federal budget and reducing the national debt. Then there would be revenue to share. But as matters would turn out, politically it was far easier and more expedient—in the short run, though in the short run only—merely to find "revenue" to share with state and local governments by increasing still more vastly the towering national debt.

The House's Committee on Ways and Means conducted hearings on general revenue sharing. Wilbur Mills, the Committee's chairman, opposing the concept, asked searching questions of the Secretary of the Treasury, John Connally. "What state in the Union is in more financial trouble than is the federal government?'' Mills asked Connally. To this the Secretary replied, ''I do not know that I would say that any is in more trouble.''

Before these hearings ended, Representative Mills declared himself in favor of revenue sharing if the greater proportion of the benefits would go to urban areas. Mills and several other members of the Committee introduced H. R. 11950 on November 30, 1971. This bill called for annual revenue sharing in the amount of $5.3 billion annually, with two-thirds of these funds to go to local governments and one-third to state governments. In substance, this was the bill reported out by the Ways and Means Committee.

Eighteen members of that Committee voted to report out the revenue-sharing bill, and seven voted against it. In their minority report, those seven issued a strong dissent. The bill divorced the tax-raising responsibility from the spending authority, the minority argued; they pointed out the lack of revenue to share, and the bill's failure to take into account existing programs of aid from Washington to local governments, or state assistance to localities.

A tall Texan, chairman of the House Committee on Appropriations, George Mahon (a Democratic member), made a vigorous fight against the bill when it came to the floor. This measure, he said, would spend money that the federal government did not possess; it was an authorization bill and an appropriation bill, but had not been referred to the Committee on Appropriations. He mentioned that the estimated federal deficit was $26 billion that year, and was estimated at $27 billion for the following year.

Many members of the House shared Mahon's view that revenue sharing should be subject to annual appropriations. The bill was for a five-year program, costing thirty billion dollars, brought up under a closed rule that permitted no amendments and waived all points of order. Chairman Mills stated that he had been instructed by the Ways and Means Committee to withdraw the bill from consideration if any amendments were permitted. John Byrnes (Wisconsin Republican) challenged Mills' interpretation of the Committee's instructions, calling it malarky.

The chairman of the Committee on Rules, William Colmer (Mississippi Democrat) opposed the bill. Congressman Mahon attacked the closed rule; his fight resulted in postponement of consideration of the bill on the floor twice, so allowing time to mobilize the lobbying efforts of state and local officials.

Sam Gibbons (Florida Democrat) said that despite reports of fiscal crisis in state governments, only four governors had asked their legislatures for new taxes; and the point was made by another opponent of the bill that such wealthy suburbs as Beverley Hills (California), McLean (Virginia), Shaker Heights (Ohio), Grosse Pointe (Michigan), Greenwich (Connecticut), Lake Forest (Illinois), and Palm Beach (Florida) would receive funds, despite the contention that the bill's funds were intended for decayed centers of cities. To them that hath shall be given.

The revenue-sharing bill passed the house by a vote of 275-122, much to the rejoicing of state and local officials. The Congress did not levy any taxes to pay for this thirty billion dollars distribution; the cost was added to the federal debt.

Having passed the House on June 22, 1972, the bill went to the Senate, where it was referred to the Committee on Finance. Among the Committee's witnesses supporting revenue sharing were people from Americans for Democratic Action and from the National Association of Counties. Among the opponents were witnesses from the State Chambers of Commerce, the National Association of Manufacturers, and the AFL-CIO. These union representatives argued that the measure would be a cruel disappointment to its advocates, falling far short of its goals and setting a dangerous precedent. The Committee on Finance revised the House bill by favoring states predominantly rural over urbanized states, and added a billion dollars for supplementary social services grants for the years 1973-1976.

The Senate's Finance Committee succeeded in keeping the bill out of the hands of the Senate's Appropriations Committee. To this end, the Finance Committee revised the bill's financing provisions to provide a ''permanent'' appropriation of seven per cent of personal income-tax receipts to a special revenue-sharing trust fund for the five-year life of the legislation. From the trust fund, the Secretary of the Treasury was directed to pay to state and local governments the amounts to which they were entitled under an aid formula adopted by the Finance Committee.

The Committee on Finance voted twelve to four to report the bill. Of the four senators opposed, one was Carl Curtis.

During the debate on the Senate floor, opponents of the bill made telling points but seemed to change few minds. Senator Thomas Eagleton (Missouri Democrat) said, "If we pass this bill today, we will be instituting debt sharing, not revenue sharing." Senator Len Jordan (Idaho Republican) uttered what many had on their minds when he said, "I object to revenue sharing because there is no money to share." He also remarked, "General revenue sharing promotes unsound government because it separates the responsibility for raising revenue from that of spending, thus encouraging reckless spending and discouraging thrift." Senator Harry Byrd (Virginia Independent) told the Senate, "In view of the financial condition with which our country is faced today, I think it is irresponsible to pile another spending program on top of all we have already, on top of the huge deficits that the nation has been running for several years now."

Carl Curtis spoke at some length against the bill. "There will be no federal activities discontinued or terminated," he said. "It is not revenue sharing because the federal government is going to have to borrow the money to do it. . . . I do not believe this program should be carried on with borrowed money. Therefore I cannot support it.

"According to the daily Treasury statement, the national bonded debt has increased in the last year by more than twenty-seven billion dollars. This means that in the past year, we have increased the national debt by more than seventy-four million dollars a day, or, based upon a twenty-four-hour day, this debt has risen by more than three million dollars an hour. Neither the Congress nor the Executive can escape this responsibility. There will be a day of reckoning. . . .

"The additional interest that will have to be paid if this one program is handled by borrowing the money for the five-year period will be almost four billion dollars.

"My basic reason for not supporting this legislation is that it must be done with borrowed money. However, there is one other feature of the bill which is very disturbing to me. Under the formula for distributing funds to the various states and localities, there is a factor called 'total tax effort.' This means that if by reason of economy or efficiency a state or a subdivision could reduce taxes, they would be penalized by having their federal funds reduced. If on the other hand they increased taxes, their share of federal funds would increase. This factor in the formula could well prevent any tax relief from ever being passed onto the taxpayers by reason of revenue sharing."

All such arguments notwithstanding, the Senate passed the revenue-sharing bill by a roll-call vote of sixty-four to twenty.

These thirty-nine thousand local jurisdictions receiving funds from revenue sharing included counties, cities, towns, villages, and townships. One town councilman reported that since a certain amount of revenue-sharing funds had been allocated to his county, people argued that if his town didn't seek its share, the other towns would obtain the funds. In the councilman's view, this attitude led to wasteful spending. A report from another state told of the local government's having published requests in the local press for citizens to offer suggestions as to how the available revenue-sharing funds might be used.

The pressure applied by a good many officeholders and their national associations has continued unabated since the revenue-sharing program began. Curtis was driving past the east front of the Capitol in November 1980, right after Ronald Reagan had been elected President, when he witnessed a sight that saddened him. Columns of people bearing banners and placards with slogans demanding more revenue sharing were marching on the Capitol. These people were carrying their demands into the streets to have the federal debt increased so that they might spend without having to raise the money in taxes. By their actions they were asking for more, without regard for the financial preservation of their country, without concern about the enormous burden on the shoulders of the newly elected President. Curtis later learned that this was the General Revenue-Sharing Rally, put on by the National Association of Counties.

President Johnson's simultaneous prosecution of the Vietnamese War and his colossal expansion of welfare-state measures had raised the national debt to a level previously inconceivable. In such a financial dilemma, the federal government was now handing out funds lavishly to states and localities, for functions that were no constitutional concern of Washington. In such an hour, villages installed costly systems of street lighting, far beyond their previous means, indifferent to the price: "Uncle Sam pays." Meanwhile, the lights of civilization were going out in much of the world.

By November, 1985, the national debt stood at $1.824 *trillion*, the limit of the debt previously established by the Congress; once more the debt limit had to be enlarged by statute to about $2.079 trillion. (This incomprehensible sum is represented as $2,079,000,000,000 dollars; a trillion is a million million.)

The budget deficit for 1985 was about $211.9 billion, several billion dollars less than had been estimated earlier. President Reagan estimated that this deficit would decline gradually, down to $139.3 billion in 1989—that depending on the "supply side economics" initiated by the Reagan administration, calculated to produce larger tax revenues without increasing the rates of taxation. The Congressional Budget Office, however, was more gloomy, estimating that the year's deficit by 1989 would be $263 billion.

From his first year in Congress, Carl Curtis had contended against deficit spending and the growth of the national debt. In one year of the Eisenhower administration's eight years, the budget had been balanced and there had even been a small sum applied against the debt; no more had been accomplished during forty years against the tide.

If we are to save ourselves from disaster, we need not merely to prevent waste in the federal government's programs, but also to eliminate altogether, or to reduce materially, many programs. Here are some grimly significant figures:

Fiscal Year 1981

Total outlays $687,209,000,000
National defense expenditures $159,765,000,000
Nondefense expenditures, 1981 .... $527,444,000,000

Fiscal Year 1985

Total outlays $946,800,000,000
National defense expenditures $279,400,000,000
Nondefense expenditures, 1984 .... $667,400,000,000

That is, our nondefense expenditures increased from fiscal 1981 to fiscal 1985 by almost one hundred and forty billion dollars.

Payments to individuals directly, or to state and local governments for the benefit of individuals (exclusive of the military) increased as follows.:

Fiscal year 1985 .... $422,400,000,000
Fiscal year 1981 .... $316,600,000,000
Increase in payment to individuals $105,800,000,000

Difficult although this fiscal task has become, it must not be abandoned. The alternative is the enfeebling of the American economy and the decline of the government into little better than a purveyor of favors to pressure groups that ignore the national interest.

The United States requires a workable, self-enforcing constitutional provision that will end deficit financing. "Welfare" measures themselves cannot endure long without such a reform; and such a measure lacking, government's fundamental functions cannot be carried on adequately. Great powers and dominations do decay and fall to their ruin, for lack of right reason and imagination. Like the human body, a society must renew itself from day to day, from year to year; a society incapable of diagnosing its own sickness and turning to adequate remedies is not long for this world. Deficit financing and the piling up of debt are as disastrous in political economy as in household economy. The American government and the American economy have been maintained not by political magic, but by certain virtues, among them the virtue called frugality. In matters fiscal, as in much else, we need to turn away from the magician and seek the sage.*

----

* Curtis' arduous labors on the Senate's Finance Committee were not without compensating comic moments. During the 1960s, Senator Albert Gore of Tennessee and Senator Paul Douglas of Illinois served on that powerful committee, of which Curtis was ranking Republican member. Those two senators were often at odds with the committee's other members. Gore and Douglas were antagonistic toward American business. On one occasion, when a tax bill was under consideration, first Senator Gore would offer an amendment; Senator Douglas would support him. On roll call, there would be two votes for that amendment, and fifteen against it. Next Senator Douglas would offer an amendment, and Senator Gore would support him; again, on roll call, the only votes for the amendment would be Douglas' and Gore's. This little drama having continued for some time, Senator Eugene McCarthy of Minnesota murmured to Senator Curtis, "Diogenes spent all his life looking for an honest man: Paul and Albert found each other."

CONGRESSIONAL LABORS AND INVESTIGATIONS

Had Carl Curtis been able to devote his whole four congressional decades to budgetary concerns, still he would have had his work cut out for him. The vastness and complexity of the American Republic's undertakings are beyond the full apprehension of the most industrious of economic experts. But of course members of Congress enjoy little opportunity to specialize: they must vote almost every week on immensely grave matters, and the more conscientious among them must try to acquaint themselves to some degree with hundreds of different aspects of public affairs.

Thus the issues discussed in the several chapters of this book were not faced in isolation, one by one; they were dealt with amidst the press of business, while different concerns of equal importance competed for Curtis' close attention. Simultaneously, Curtis had to busy himself, year after year, with the questions already touched on in this book: international affairs, labor disputes, food distribution, public housing, flood control, budgetary restraint; other issues, also having to be dealt with almost simultaneously, will be described in later chapters.

Curtis served on several important House committees. During his senatorial years, he was the ranking Republican member of four full committees: Rules and Administration, Aeronautical and Space Sciences, Agriculture and Forestry, and Finance. It was no life of leisure in Washington. Curtis' primary enduring concern, the thread that connects most of these chapters, was resistance to the welfare state and provision for alternatives to it; his work for budgetary reform was bound up with that endeavor. But of necessity, any member of Congress moved by some sense of duty must spend a large part of his time with matters that are secondary to his fundamental reasons for being in the Congress.

Many members of Congress hold "marginal" seats: that

is, the two major parties being about equal in strength in their states or districts, elections are won by narrow margins. Painfully aware of their political insecurity, such senators or representatives often tend to trim their sails to the winds of political expediency (though there are highly honorable exceptions to this inclination). Sometimes they vote for or against pieces of legislation on the basis of the presumed momentary popularity of a proposal, even though such a vote may go against their private judgment. They serve as delegates, rather than as legislative representatives in the sense that Edmund Burke defined that term.

It was otherwise with Carl Curtis. Although he set his course against the national tide of opinion in many matters for many years, he enjoyed unfailing popular support in Nebraska, both while he sat in the House of Representatives and later when, as a senator, he was elected repeatedly by a statewide constituency. On May 26, 1949, in a major speech on the House floor, Curtis declared his opposition to all new "welfare" programs and to expansion of the operations of the federal government. Here indeed he was opposing a tide in the affairs of men; but his congressional district stood by him.

In the First Congressional District primary of August 1950, Curtis defeated his opponent (Joseph Alexis, of Lincoln) nearly three votes to one. In the 1950 general election, Curtis obtained some 67,000 votes to about 56,000 for Clarence C. Miles, then the popular mayor of Lincoln. In 1952, unopposed in the Republican primary, Curtis won reelection over Samuel Freeman, of Fairbury, the Democrats' nominee: some 117,000 votes to some 45,000. That was a year of triumph for Republicans nationally, and Curtis entered his eighth term in the House.

It would be his last term there; for in 1954, he stood for the Senate to fill a prospective Nebraskan vacancy. A United States senator enjoys more repute and authority than does a member of the House; but also it needs to be remembered that a senator, representing a statewide constituency rather than a coherent congressional district, finds himself heavily burdened with innumerable requests. He is subjected to strong pressures from interest groups much exceeding the tribulations of members of the House. And the costs and difficulties of being elected and reelected obviously are far greater for a senator than for a member of the House. Although possessed of a safe House seat in 1954, Curtis chose to run for the Senate.

In the Republican primary of August 10, 1954, Curtis had five competitors, two of them with strong support. Robert B. Crosby, then Governor of Nebraska, came closest to Curtis, with more than 43,000 votes. But Curtis won the nomination handily enough, obtaining more than 64,000 votes.

In the general election, November 2, the Democrats ran a former governor of Nebraska, Keith Neville, against Curtis. Curtis won a thumping victory: some 255,000 votes to Neville's 163,000. Clearly Nebraskans in general heartily approved of Curtis' principles and Curtis' conduct in Washington. In the Senate Curtis would sit until the year 1978 was out, reelected in 1960, 1966, and 1972 by healthy margins. He did not turn trimmer to the winds of expediency.

Possessing a secure political base did not diminish Curtis' Washington responsibilities. A dutiful member of Congress works hard indeed, with next to no time for reflection.

Nothing is more time-consuming than work on congressional investigating committees; but some of those investigations are of high importance, achieving substantial results. Curtis served on the subcommittee of the House Ways and Means Committee that investigated malfeasance in the Bureau of Internal Revenue during the Truman administration; he was chairman, during the Eisenhower administration, of the subcommittee of Ways and Means that investigated the Social Security system; from 1957 to 1968, he served on the Senate Committee on Government Operations, and on that Committee's Permanent Investigating Subcommittee. He was a member of the Select Committee investigating labor rackets, appointed in 1957. Curtis was a principal investigator of Billie Sol Estes' machinations in connection with the Department of Agriculture, during the Kennedy administration. He was very active in the investigation of Bobby Baker and his colleagues during the Johnson years, the subject of a later chapter. He was a minority member of the Joint Committee on Internal Revenue Taxation that investigated President Nixon's tax returns during the Watergate struggle.

So investigation after investigation is woven into this book about Curtis' experience in Congress. Yet these investigations were not irrelevant to Curtis' fight against the welfare state; for corruption follows naturally upon the growth of that welfare state, with its concentration of power and revenues, its favors to bestow upon groups and whole classes, the innumerable opportunities that Leviathan offers for the contact-man and the sharp operator.

Not all of these important investigations can be described, even summarily, in this book, for lack of space. But some deserve chapters to themselves; and the first of them is the investigation of labor rackets during President Eisenhower's second term. Those rackets were made possible through immunities that the federal government had conferred on labor unions; so they too were part and parcel of the enlargement of the scope of centralized government. Thus we pass from Washington arguments about finance to the rough realm of the strike and the boycott.

Chapter 7

Investigating Labor Rackets

CRIMINALITY WITHIN ORGANIZED LABOR

After passage of the National Labor Relations Act (the Wagner Act) in 1935, labor unions had grown immensely and often in disorderly fashion. Twenty years later, it was clear to everybody that many powerful unions were abusing their privileges; that criminal acts, indeed, were being committed frequently by the officers of certain unions.

Taking his seat in the Senate in 1955, Carl Curtis was appointed to the Privileges and Elections Subcommittee of the Committee on Rules and Administration. In the course of that subcommittee's work, he became aware of violations of the voting rights of members of some labor unions—violations by union officials. He found that Barry Goldwater, of Arizona, elected to the Senate two years earlier, shared his concern for the rights of citizens as affected by the coercive tactics of certain union leaders.

In 1955, the plight of some Michigan members of the United Automobile Workers was brought to Curtis' attention. Two of them, Harry Brothers and Walter Brauninger, both Republicans, complained that they were compelled by the UAW's shop rules to pay dues to their union that were used for political purposes always to elect Democrats. They asserted that if they should not pay dues, the UAW might cause them to be discharged from employment. They cited a study completed at Wayne University, Detroit, which showed that some sixty-six per cent of union members were opposed to the use of their dues for political purposes.

Brothers and Brauninger were joined in their complaint by a member of the Steelworkers' union in Michigan, Clarence Bridgeman, a Republican candidate for public office in Marquette. His union dues, Bridgeman stated, were used to support the Democratic candidate opposing him in the election. Bridgeman had asked his union to support his candidacy; the union had refused to do so.

It was clear enough that union leaders were invading the constitutional rights of these union members; and these cases appeared to be representative of widespread union practice. Curtis supported the request of Brothers, Brauninger, and Bridgeman to testify before the Senate's Subcommittee on Constitutional Rights. But the Democratic chairman of that subcommittee found excuses for not hearing the union members, interposing delays.

So Carl Curtis approached Senator Goldwater with a novel suggestion. They two would hold an informal hearing for these union members in the Senate Caucus Room, inviting the press, television people, and others to hear these men's statements and to question them. If the Subcommittee on Constitutional Rights would not hear these men, at least two senators would.

On December 15, 1955, with Curtis in the chair, this informal hearing took place in the Caucus Room; some fifty-five people from the mass media attended, barraging the three witnesses with questions about abuse of their voting rights. The hearing was a sensation. Washington became aware that two first-term Republican senators were poking into labor questions with unconventional tactics.

For Goldwater and Curtis, this experience was a prelude to the large-scale investigation of labor-union rackets that commenced in 1957. In the middle 'fifties, the Senate's Subcommittee on Permanent Investigations of the Government Operations Committee had begun to investigate certain abuses in the field of labor and management. At the same time, a subcommittee of the Senate's Labor and Public Welfare Committee had commenced investigations of certain misuses of union funds, especially pension and welfare funds. To resolve disputes over the jurisdictions of these two committees, the Senate established a Select Committee on Improper Activities in Labor and Management, made up of members from both of the existing committees. This new Select Committee was created by Senate Resolution 74, January 30, 1957.

Four committee members from either party and from either of the existing committees were named to the Select Committee. From the Government Operations Committee came two Democrats, John McClellan of Arkansas and Sam Ervin of North Carolina; and two Republicans, Joseph McCarthy of Wisconsin and Karl Mundt of South Dakota. From the Committee on Labor and Welfare came the Democrats John F. Kennedy of Massachusetts and Pat McNamara of Michigan; and the Republicans Irving Ives of New York and Barry Goldwater of Arizona. Upon the death of Senator McCarthy, Carl Curtis was named on May 8 as replacement on the Select Committee. Senator Ives, retiring from the Senate at the end of the Eighty-Fifth Congress, was replaced by Senator Homer Capehart of Indiana. Mundt, Goldwater, and Curtis served as minority members throughout the investigation.

In the minds of many, the Senate Committee on Labor and Public Welfare was a pro-union committee. On the other hand, the Subcommittee on Permanent Investigations of the Committee on Government Operations was regarded as a hard-hitting committee vigorously opposed to union violence or corruption.

These differences of opinion persisted during the Select Committee's investigations. To what extent should unions be blamed for the troubles? How far was management responsible for the troubles that disturbed the public? The Republican members of the Select Committee were opposed to the unions' use of their money and manpower in politics. The Democratic members, in the main, found no fault with the unions' political activity.

The Democratic members held that violence, corruption, and other wrongful acts of unions should be exposed, and that all corrupt men, thugs, and embezzlers should be driven from the unions. Chairman John McClellan made such statements often. He was a fair chairman, considerate with the Republican members; he was fearless in pursuing the investigation.

The Republican members—particularly Goldwater, Mundt, and Curtis—contended that the unions held too much power: this was the basic problem. Congress, federal regulatory agencies, and the courts had conceded excessive power to the union leaders. The Republicans pointed out that working men and women, as a whole, were honest, deserving unions subject to their control. Compulsory unionism, they said, invited corruption and wrongdoing; only when union membership is voluntary can the rank and file of the workers exert such control. If a union is afflicted by bad and corrupt leadership, engaging in violence, the rank and file can work a reform if they are permitted to resign from the union: such withdrawal is their basic weapon, for bad leaders cannot proceed without dues from their members. If membership is compulsory, workers must continue to remain in a union and pay dues, without remedy. This contest between union officers and the rank and file may not be limited to financial concerns and racketeering; it may be that union money is used to support political parties and candidates with whom some or many of the union members disagree. In such circumstances, union members cannot oppose either racketeering or political involvement without forfeiting their jobs.

The pro-union partisans, within the Select Committee and outside it, favored the union shop and the closed shop. Under the union shop system, an employee does not have to belong to the union to be hired by an employer; but once employed, he must pay dues or fees to the union to hold his job. Under closed-shop arrangements, a worker must belong to a union before obtaining employment with a firm; this often involves a union "hiring hall." Union advocates contend that union shop or closed shop is necessary to advance the cause of unionism; they regard opposition to compulsory unionism as an anti-labor stand. Senators Goldwater, Mundt, and Curtis were outspoken in their opposition to compulsory unionism.

From its inception, then, the Select Committee was engaged in controversy. On December 12, 1957, the AFL-CIO, in convention, adopted a resolution declaring that the Select Committee had given a disproportionately small amount of attention to studying improper practices by management. This resolution named Senators Goldwater, Mundt, and Curtis, charging that they had demonstrated anti-labor bias and had forfeited any claim of conducting themselves fairly and objectively. "We express deep concern that the Senate Select Committee may allow itself to be used for political retaliation and as a forum for the display of anti-union propaganda." The AFL-CIO bitterly opposed the Select Committee's raising the issue of excessive power held by unions, but approved the idea of driving gangsters and racketeers out of the union movement.

Senator John F. Kennedy, with his eye on the presidency, followed the line of the AFL-CIO in his participation in the Select Committee. The Committee's chief counsel was Robert Kennedy, Senator Kennedy's brother, who also adhered to the AFL-CIO line. The Teamsters Union, guilty of many offenses, became the principal target of the AFL-CIO and the Kennedy brothers.

Speaking against an amendment to forbid secondary boycotts, Senator Kennedy said, "I would have no objection to an amendment which dealt with unfair practices of the Teamsters Union, but this amendment applies to all labor." (This on the Senate floor, April 24, 1959.) Goldwater, Mundt, and Curtis were endeavoring to attack arbitrary power possessed by unions, particularly compulsory membership and unlawful political activity. The unions were not subject to the reporting of political expenditures and receipts and limits on political activity, required of others politically active. The three Republican senators also pointed out that many of the AFL-CIO unions rose to power through coercion and violence.

Goldwater, Mundt, and Curtis maintained that the National Labor Relations Board manifested a strong pro-union bias;

that the Board's regulations and rulings increased the excessive power of the unions. These Republicans favored action to establish balance on the Board and to subject both management and the unions to anti-trust laws. Compulsory unionism, they believed, was the basic cause of unions' abuses.

During the summer of 1957, the Select Committee conducted a hearing which showed that convicts, gangsters, and racketeers were engaged in union organizing in the city of New York. These hearings revealed that some union charters had been granted not to a group of working men and women, but to individuals who wished to go out and organize the unorganized. Thus criminals might organize unions and obtain power for themselves. They created paper unions without real members, conducted no union meetings, and thrived by extortion from employers.

One example of this sort of operation involved a Max Chester, who had been president of Local 227 of the UAW-CIO, later leaving that union to work for Local 405 of the Retail Clerks. He had been found guilty of taking a two-thousand-dollar bribe, which he had obtained by threatening to organize the employees of a business establishment. The two thousand dollars having been paid, Chester had never even met with the employees in question, and they had remained unorganized.

When this case came before the Select Committee, Senator Goldwater inquired, "Is this a typical pattern that we are going to see throughout these particular hearings?" Robert Kennedy, Committee counsel, replied, "This is a pattern, not the organized pattern that is used by labor unions, but it is a pattern that is used by certain of these gangsters and hoodlums in New York City."

Senator Curtis then asked Mr. Kennedy whether Chester had represented any of the workers in the plant from which he had received the bribe. "The workers in the plant had not even been approached, Senator," Kennedy answered.

The Select Committee's investigations revealed that the Teamsters Union was the great power in such fraudulent union dealings. Robert Kennedy, summarizing such racketeering, pointed out the grip of the Teamsters on New York City:

"So the truckers have an important and integral part, a key

position in the New York area through the fact that they have control over the shipping that comes into New York City and control over the airport. If that gets into the wrong hands, of course, they can be a stranglehold over New York City.

"Now, controlling all of this, this operation, is Joint Council 16...made up of some fifty-eight locals and some 125,000 members. The Joint Council 16, Mr. Chairman, is the one that sets policy.

"Now, here are some of the matters that Joint Council controls. For instance, the meat shipments; the Joint Council 16, with one of the Teamsters locals, having control over the meat shipments, they have to look to Joint Council 16 for their policy.

"They control fruit and vegetable shipments, drugstore deliveries, garbage trucks, newspaper trucks. The control of Joint Council 16, as far as the policy of all these locals is concerned, is paramount. Its importance is not only the fact that the Joint Council 16 controls trucking done by the 58 different locals in New York City, but they have a great control over all other unions in New York City...

"As an example, if somebody wants—another union wants—to strike a particular business, they can strike the business and say, for instance, there are nonunion people in the business. Those nonunion people will continue to go into that business—in and out. The strike will not really have an effect, unless they can stop the trucking from going into that business, and stop the pickups and deliveries; if that happens the business will have to go out. It will be finished in two or three days and the strike will be a success...

"It is the Teamsters Joint Council which will decide whether the Teamsters will support a strike of another union. They are the ones that make the decision as to whether the pickup and deliveries will be made."

Direct extortion from employers was not the only consequence of such arbitrary power. There occurred cases of "sweetheart contracts," deals made between union officials and management to the detriment of rank-and-file union members. Often such union members—or alleged union members—were newly-arrived Puerto Ricans or New York blacks. Such contracts might specify a wage of seventy-five cents an hour, when the lawful minimum wage was a dollar an hour.

During the Select Committee's hearings on such extortion, sweetheart contracts, and other union racketeering, Senator Curtis asked Counsel Kennedy how many of the racketeering leaders "conducted a *bona fide* union and had meetings and transacted business."

"We have had a rather difficult time with the books and records of those unions," Robert Kennedy replied. "We find that we will come to one of these locals, for instance, and find that there was a fire the day before and the records had been destroyed. Or, again, that the janitor threw the records out, or they put the records in their car, and it happened that the district attorney was subpoenaing the records at the time, and to make sure they were turned over to the district attorney and to make sure they were down there bright and early, they took the books and records out and put them in their automobile and then some burglar broke into their automobile and stole the books and records."

Behind these New York City labor racketeers loomed the burly, sinister figure of Jimmy Hoffa, boss nationally of the Teamsters Union, who had accepted the aid of notorious gangsters in the organizing of New York unorganized workers. One of Hoffa's helpers was Johnny Dioguardi, also known as Johnny Dio, earlier described by Thomas Dewey (when district attorney) as "a young gorilla who began his career at age fifteen." Another Hoffa-assisting racketeer was Tony (Ducks) Corallo, who was given control over Local 808 of the Teamsters, made up of some air-freight drivers. In 1953, George Meany had demanded that Dioguardi and his union give up their organization of taxicab drivers. In 1954, Dioguardi's underworld connections had been publicized, so that late in the summer Johnny Dio had resigned from his union. Nevertheless, he had continued to control the union, as Counsel Kennedy brought out in testimony before the Select Committee. Called as a witness, Dioguardi took shelter a hundred and forty times under the Fifth Amendment.

Concerning such flagrant abuses of union power, the position of the AFL-CIO and its president, George Meany, was that they would endeavor to drive all the racketeers out of organized labor. In this stand they were joined by the Democratic members of the Select Committee and its Chief Counsel Kennedy.

But in the opinion of the Select Committee's minority members, the problem went much deeper. Curtis stated this position at the hearing on July 31, 1957. "I do not believe that the problem we are wrestling here with is solved when we merely drive them out of the labor-union movement," Curtis said. "Congress is responsible for having laws that grant too much power in some places and make it an invitation for bad men to seize that power. We have not given enough protection to the people who do the work, the rank and file of union members."

New York's labor racketeering was paralleled by that in Chicago. Before the Select Committee Robert Kennedy questioned extensively witnesses who testified concerning the Chicago warfare conducted by the union of restaurant workers, control of which had been seized by gangsters: harassment by large gangs of pickets, slashing of employees' tires, tacks scattered to puncture customers' tires, sugar dropped into managers' gas tanks, firecrackers thrown at employees. The Teamsters had cooperated with the hoodlums of the restaurant union so that restaurants could not obtain deliveries of food or have garbage removed; then the dump, under Teamster pressure, would not accept the restaurant garbage carried to it in a trailer. Waitresses and others had been intimidated by hoodlums who had followed them to their homes at night. The Borden Company had ceased to supply a restaurant with milk, under duress from the Teamsters. A scavenger who had agreed to carry away garbage had been threatened by hoodlums that his little boy would suffer if the scavenger did not abandon his task, which therefore he did abandon. The manager of a Cicero restaurant, Mrs. Sturdevant, was coerced into joining the union. When asked to testify before the Select Committee, she had been told by a union representative, "Not to come down to Washington, that I should get sick before coming down to Washington or be sicker when I get back."

Virgil W. Peterson, director of the Chicago Crime Commission, explained to the Select Committee the reasons why hoodlums, gamblers, murderers, and extortionists went into labor-union business. In response to a question from Senator Curtis, Peterson said, "Well, when they were able to dominate a particular union, it is—as I think will be shown in these hearings—a tremendously lucrative operation for the hoodlums themselves."

Curtis inquired whether that money came from the check-off of dues.

"The dues from the employees," Peterson answered, "and, as a matter of fact, during the period that Mr. Kennedy was inquiring about, in the 1920s, for example, in the building trades, they weren't interested in the welfare of the employees, of course, but they had these contracts with penalty clauses in them if they didn't complete a contract by a certain time.

"Well, a racketeer would go to a contractor and say in substance, 'Well, if you give me $20,000 or $30,000 or $50,000, we won't call a strike; and if you don't give me the $50,000, we will call a strike. '"

Peterson added that, "There have been instances that I don't think you are going into this morning, take in the juke-box field, where controlling a union enables monopolistic practices on the part of those with whom they may be in collusion."

At this point, Senator Curtis commented, "I think one of the most important things brought out by this committee in the months of its work has been that the laws of our land are such in reference to unions that they invited hoodlums and the wrong sort of people to come in. The law permits unions to be run from the top. We have seen that over and over again. The law does nothing about the grievances of individual union members so far as, by and large, getting any relief through court action.

"The law grants a certain cloak of respectability and immunities to unions, both as a matter of law and as a matter of practice. The unions' practice of blocking a sidewalk or street goes unnoticed, and it puts a weapon in the hand of the wrong type of people to harass, intimidate, and extort, and slow up, and do those other things. We have the helpless situation of union members and their inability to withdraw from the union without losing their jobs.

"I think that we are going to have to strive for those laws that will free the union member and no longer make it profitable for hoodlums to get in."

Money extracted from checked-off union dues, and extortion and blackmail, were only the more obvious forms of abuse of union power. Firms might be even more intimidated by the secondary boycott—an instrument by no means confined to the use of the Teamsters, though conspicuous in Teamsters operations. This became a subject of controversy in the Select Committee's investigations.

THE WEAPON OF
SECONDARY BOYCOTTS

The "secondary boycott" is a union means for applying pressure to a third party not directly involved in a labor dispute. This boycott takes many forms. The United Automobile Workers' Union employed a nationwide boycott in the Kohler strike, but the principal offender in the use of secondary boycotts had been the Teamsters.

Whoever has power to bring to a halt all transportation in America can paralyze the economy. That is too much power for any independent association. In Nebraska, the Teamsters' secondary boycott had been employed to drive small truckers out of business; the union denied merchandise to stores to compel trucking companies to sign union contracts, so increasing the powers and filling the purses of Teamsters Union bosses.

Congress thought it had forbidden all secondary boycotts

when it passed the Taft-Hartley Act; yet experience over the years, under that act, had disclosed yawning gaps. For instance, the Taft-Hartley Act prohibits labor organizations from inducing or encouraging the employees of any "third party" employer to refuse to handle goods or perform services for that employer. But the Taft-Hartley provision stops there. Taft-Hartley does not prohibit a union from threatening the third-party employer himself. A union business agent may say to a "neutral" employer, "We have a quarrel with the man down the street from whom you buy supplies. If you do not stop buying from him, we will have a picket line around your place tomorrow."

That sort of secondary boycott was employed regularly, jeopardizing every small business in America, during the time of the Select Committee's investigations.

Another type of secondary boycott, regarded by the National Labor Relations Board as beyond the restraints of Taft-Hartley, was the "hot cargo" arrangement. This amounts to a secondary boycott by contract. A strong union might insist during its negotiation of a labor-management contract that the document include a provision that the contracting firm agree to cease doing business with firms in dispute with the union.

An example of the unfairness of the secondary boycott was the case of the Coffey Transfer Company of Alma, Nebraska. This firm, one of the oldest trucking lines in Nebraska, was forced to sell its equipment and close its doors because its owner had the courage to fight demands by the Teamsters Union that he compel his employees to join the union—of which they wanted no part. Only seven of Coffey's twenty-two drivers joined the Teamsters; so to force Coffey to contract with the union, the Teamsters initiated a secondary boycott. The NLRB was ineffectual in dealing with the secondary boycott. At last the NLRB, six months after the beginning of the trouble, held a collective-bargaining election: the were four votes against the Teamsters union, not one vote for the union. But meanwhile, broken by the secondary boycott, Coffey had gone out of business. This destruction of a long-established firm required only a few months, from August, 1955, to February, 1956. The NLRB, incidentally, had taken three weeks to count the ballots of a handful of drivers.

Unions had employed secondary boycotts in every state. The Select Committee received testimony concerning the UAW boycott in the famous Kohler strike, in Wisconsin. This boycott did not fatally injure the Kohler Company, large and rich enough to withstand considerable battering, but it did hurt many other businesses. Consider the case of the Buteyn brothers.

Peter Buteyn was a small businessman who had contracted with the Kohler Company to unload a boat laden with clay. His brother, Cornelius, worked with him. Buteyn employees were unionized, and had no labor dispute pending. They were not parties to the controversy between the United Automobile Workers and the Kohler Company. Nevertheless, the UAW prevented Buteyn from fulfilling his contract to unload the clay. Despite Buteyn's plea that he had obligations to meet at the bank, and that he had a duty toward Kohler because of his twenty years of satisfactory business association with that firm, he still was not permitted to perform his contractual obligation.

This secondary boycott applied to the Buteyn Brothers was enforced by violence. In addition to losing the business of unloading the clay, the Buteyns were insulted and cursed, ten tires on their equipment were slashed, the air hoses to the brakes on their heavy equipment were cut, and their gasoline tanks were punctured. Altogether, damage to their equipment amounted to six or seven thousand dollars. Cornelius Buteyn was kicked severely. Unlawful mass picketing by the UAW completed the defeat of the Buteyns.

Dave Beck, who headed the Teamsters nationally before Hoffa's reign, stated that he favored secondary boycotts, and that in most instances such boycotts were justified, legal, and right. When Jimmy Hoffa, the arrogant head of the Teamsters, appeared before the Select Committee, Senator Curtis told him that the Teamsters Union was a powerful vested interest. One local alone had a net worth of more than $1.6 million; no one knew the total net worth of the Teamsters. Curtis charged that the Teamsters had driven little businessmen to the wall.

Hoffa's reply was sufficiently revealing: "Senator, we have driven nobody out of business, but some employers, rather than sign a labor contract, have saw fit to go out of business.''

Affording protection against people like Hoffa—and against people like Walter Reuther of the UAW, too—was the basic reason for banning secondary boycotts. Genuinely neutral employers and their employees, not engaged in a labor dispute, need to be sheltered against union coercion that is designed to give the union victory in a dispute with some other employer.

When the Senate considered labor legislation in 1959, Senator McClellan offered an amendment that would put an end to secondary boycotts and to organizational and jurisdictional picketing. Senator John F. Kennedy opposed this amendment on the ground that it would extend beyond the Teamsters to all labor unions. On the same day (April 24, 1959) Senator Curtis replied to Kennedy on this point. Curtis pointed out that the Sheet Metal Workers Union, in a jurisdictional dispute with the Steel Workers Union, had contrived a boycott of the products of the Burt Manufacturing Company of Akron all over the United States—for ten years. The Teamsters were by no means the only serious bullies of the secondary boycott. The AFL Barbers' Union, in a similar jurisdictional dispute with another union, had boycotted the Waldorf-Astoria Hotel. Assisted presently by the Teamsters, the Barbers' Union had shut down the delivery of supplies to the greatest hotel in the world. The hotel's management had then threatened to refuse to renew the barbershop's lease unless the independent barbers' union surrendered to the AFL Union.

''The intent of the law is to give to the workers the right to organize and bargain collectively,'' Curtis said on the floor of the Senate. ''That is the right we should defend today. We should not defend the right of an outsider to destroy someone's business when he does not represent any workers inside the business. As soon as we take away the unlawful and wrongful weapons of blackmail, picketing, and boycotting, which go hand in hand, we can expect honesty in unions, because evil men will not seek to get control of unions.''

This exchange on the Senate floor had its counterpart in the hearings of the Select Committee on Improper Activities in Labor and Management. Senator Kennedy and his brother

Robert, the Chief Counsel, strongly resisted investigating the UAW and Walter Reuther, eager though they were to investigate the Teamsters and Jimmy Hoffa. Reuther, described by his admirers as "the labor statesman," was a considerable power within the Democratic Party; and J. F. Kennedy hoped for the presidential nomination at the next Democratic national convention. Nevertheless, at Carl Curtis' request, Chairman McClellan authorized investigation of the UAW's actions in the Kohler strike, and presently had a subpoena issued for Reuther to testify before the Select Committee.

The Kohler strike has been described at length in several books, most notably in one by a specialist in labor law, Dr. Sylvester Petro. It was a long and fierce strike, conspicuous for deadly violence. At present, we are concerned with the secondary-boycott aspect of this attempt by the UAW to subdue the Kohler Company.

Kohler is a major manufacturer of bathroom fixtures and plumbing fittings; its principal plant is at Kohler, Wisconsin, a village of some seventeen hundred people. The United Automobile Workers called a strike at Kohler in April, 1954. The UAW's energetic activities against the Kohler Company were not limited to the area near the plant.

A nationwide boycott of Kohler products organized by the UAW was carried to all principal cities in the United States— even to the Pacific coast. Dealers, distributors, and installers of Kohler products were confronted by pickets telling them not to handle Kohler. Attempts were made to induce other unions to recognize and support the big boycott. Caravans traveled to many cities, carrying men to participate in the picketing. Billboards were plastered with anti-Kohler signs. It was a long boycott, and a costly one.

Leo J. Brierather, a Kohler striker, was brought to testify before the Select Committee. He had been chief steward of Local 833, representing the foundry group at Kohler. Questioned by Counsel Kennedy, Senator Curtis, and Senator Mundt, Brierather told the details of the well-organized boycott, of which he had been coordinator. Caravans of twenty to twenty-five cars would drive about cities and towns, displaying such legends as, "Don't buy Kohler. It is made by scabs and strike breakers." Kohler distributors were picketed in New York and Los Angeles by paid pickets. The Tribune Building in Chicago was picketed for a year. These boycott activities were not merely peaceful demonstrations to call attention to the union's claims.

Questioned by Senator Curtis, Brierather admitted that boycott representatives had been instructed to "personally contact as many people as possible among the ranks of organized labor and also in the building industry, and also owners of building projects around in their area." He believed that the UAW men's confrontations with plumbers, plumbing contractors, builders, and architects had been successful in injuring Kohler's sales.

At Duluth, Minnesota, as Senator Mundt succeeded in extracting from Brierather, the Duluth AFL-CIO Central Labor Council had demanded that St. Mary's Hospital be dropped from the list of beneficiaries of the Duluth Community Chest because that hospital had contracted to buy plumbing fixtures from Kohler. Brierather was apologetic about boycotting Community Chests. But there were worse aspects of the boycott, more intimidating.

Harold E. Kuempel, a building contractor in Niles, Illinois, questioned by Robert Kennedy, testified that when he had been installing Kohler bathtubs, he had found seven tubs badly scratched by some sharp instrument, and notes nearby reading, "Stop using Kohler fixtures." The tubs had to be replaced, at considerable expense both to Kohler and Kuempel. After that, Kuempel used American Standard fixtures on his jobs, and encountered no more trouble.

And there was the case of Joseph Schinabeck, a truck driver and a member of a Teamsters local, in Sheboygan, Wisconsin, who had made pickups and deliveries at the Kohler Company. Questioned by Counsel Kennedy, Schinabeck told how his house had been paint-bombed: one can of black paint against his front door, three cans through his picture window, spattering all over the furniture. This was done, he was convinced, because he made Kohler deliveries and pickups. (He was employed by the Scheffler Transport Company, not by Kohler.) Secondary boycott, with a vengeance!

We might offer other illustrations of the UAW's secondary-boycott tactics which, like the strike at the Kohler plant, tended toward destructive and violent actions. But now we turn to that strike itself, one of the more dismaying episodes in American labor history. The Select Committee, much to the chagrin of the Kennedys, proceeded to investigate the strike and to summon Walter Reuther.

THE UAW AT KOHLER

In 1954, the United Automobile Workers Union had attempted to establish itself as the bargaining agent for the big Kohler plumbing-fixtures firm, against the resistance of a great many of the Kohler workers—indeed, as it turned out in the subsequent NLRB election, against the wishes of the majority of employees.

The strike began with mass picketing of a kind forbidden by law. Union spokesmen reported that from 1,200 to 2,500 pickets, at one time or another, moved in a double line along the sidewalk, going in both directions for two city blocks.

The trial examiner for the National Labor Relations Board reported that when non-strikers tried to enter the plant, they were "physically blocked, pushed, shoved, and prevented from entering. In some instances the pickets refused to permit entrance despite the request of Police Chief Chappelle to let the workers into the plant...The union also put into effect and maintained during this period a pass system under which persons desirous of entering the plant, the main office, the employment office, or the medical department, housed in the same building with the employment office, were required to procure passes from the union strike headquarters at Peterson's Tavern, some miles away.''

Such were the consistent tactics of the huge industrial union headed by that eminent social democrat Walter Reuther, made possible by a tremendous UAW strike fund, against a family business in a small town. Yet months of violent intimidation did not result in the UAW's object of extracting dues from Kohler workers.

The Kohler Company charged that more than eight hundred acts of violence and vandalism were committed by the UAW. Sworn testimony before the Select Committee proved cases of terrible violence against non-strikers. William Vinson, a UAW-CIO "international representative," was found guilty of felonious assault and sentenced by Judge F. H. Schlichting; he had made an unprovoked assault on a non-striker, crushing the man's chest and inflicting injuries nearly fatal. Emil Mazey, the UAW officer second only to Walter Reuther, retaliated by an intemperate verbal denunciation of the judge, and demanded a boycott of the grocery store in which Judge Schlichting had inherited a financial interest.

William Bersch, Jr., a non-striking employee of Kohler who was working part-time in a filling station, was knocked unconscious by three assailants. The young man's father, the elder William Bersch, attempted to rescue his son; he also was assaulted and his neck was broken. He never recovered from his injuries, dying a few months later. His assailants were John Gunaca, a union "goon"; William Vrcovic, a striker; and an unidentified man. John Gunaca fled to Michigan, where Governor G. Mennen Williams, politically allied with the UAW, refused to grant Gunaca's extradition to Wisconsin for trial.

When Walter Reuther was summoned to testify before the Select Committee, Senator Curtis questioned him concerning Emil Mazey's denunciation of Judge Schlichting and cases of violence by union members; Reuther was evasive and defiant in his responses. Senator Mundt questioned Reuther about use of his union's dues-money for political purposes; again Reuther was evasive. Senator Curtis questioned Reuther about the UAW strike at Buffalo, New York, in 1949, in the course of which strikers stoned cars and buses, one of them a school bus carrying high-school students. Twenty-eight sheriff's deputies had been injured by rocks and clubs in a single day of that Bell Aircraft Corporation strike. Again Reuther was evasive.

Robert Kennedy diverted the questioning into the matter of Reuther's personal finances, though no one had suggested that Reuther was corrupt in his private affairs. At the end of the Kohler hearings, Senator J. F. Kennedy made a statement in which he called the investigation of the UAW's activities a waste of time: "I feel that the good name of this committee has been used by some in their desire to indict a union whose political philosophy differs from theirs."

Senator McClellan, the Select Committee's chairman, replied in defense of the Select Committee's inquiry into the Kohler strike and the UAW. Senator Mundt commented, "I am disturbed about the fact that the financial interests and the individual rights of dues-paying members in a great union like the UAW are held in such jeopardy that the testimony is pretty much uncontradicted that those who sought to pursue their right through union channels, instead of being given a hearing and perhaps having the charges dismissed or disproved or verified, instead of having that kind of procedure which we have been led to believe and which should become part of union democracy—in place of that they are pounced upon, and beaten up and hit by goons." Senator Goldwater said, "I agree with Senator Mundt that it is a crime in this country that we have compulsory payments into any type of fund, whether it is political, flower, or whatever you want to call it. If we don't have freedom extending into the use of money that men earn, we are in a pretty sad way in this country."

Raymond Moley, writing in *Newsweek*, summed up the Kohler hearings: "Don't believe the stories that Walter Reuther came through his examination before the McClellan committee in March with flying colors. In the persistent questioning by Senators Curtis, Goldwater, and Mundt, laboring under incredible handicaps, it was made clear that either Reuther refuses to accept responsibility for the conduct of the Kohler strike or, as he claims, he has only slight control over his own union.

He revealed a pattern of irresponsible unionism—power without responsibility...

"The union local at Kohler was the creature of the International UAW of which Reuther is the head. The International organized the local, receives dues from it, creates the rules under which it operates. In the Kohler strike it spent more than on any strike it ever had—ten million dollars. It paid relief for the strikers; it paid lawyers for defending members and officers charged with crimes; it paid their wages if they were in jail. But violence and illegal mass picketing, completely proved, were placed by Reuther at the door of the local. He visited Kohler only once, and then only to make a speech...He failed to explain why International representatives knew or were alleged to know little of the law in a state in which they had. loosed wholesale disorder."

And, after all, Reuther's UAW lost the Kohler strike and the NLRB election. Walter Reuther's reputation never wholly recovered from what had been done at Kohler, Wisconsin.

The UAW's ferocious assault on Kohler was not the most startling instance of violent, unlawful actions by the powerful union that came within the cognizance of the Committee. For earlier in its investigations, Chairman McClellan and Senators Mundt and Curtis had insisted upon looking into a glaring case of labor racketeering and violence at Toledo, Ohio. Troubles at Toledo had begun several years earlier. The Committee's investigators went to Toledo to substantiate reports of what had been done by UAW officials there; and at subsequent hearings, much interesting testimony was obtained. Next we summarize this case.

THE UAW
AT TOLEDO

In the Toledo case, Walter Reuther's involvement was more direct and demonstrable than it would be, later, in the Kohler strike. Despite the favorable press that Reuther often obtained, the UAW under his headship often was not the "clean union" on democratic principles that Reuther's admirers called it.

. A rebellion of certain UAW members in Toledo against the dictatorial rule of Richard Gosser attracted the attention of McClellan, Mundt, and Curtis. This Richard T. Gosser, an ex-convict, had become the UAW's vice-president at Toledo. Certain union members charged that Gosser had enriched himself at their expense, had maintained personal control of the union by manipulating elections, and had employed a "flying squadron" of terrorists to intimidate protesting union members. Gosser was said to have undone democratic processes within his union by holding elections at inconvenient times and in out-of-the-way spots; thus Gosser's goons could discourage the general membership from voting and ensure a majority of the poll for Gosser.

As the Toledo UAW had grown to thousands of members, the total of dues collected had become very large. This money was available for a wide range of "welfare" activities: summer camps for children of union members, recreation facilities for the membership, "retirement farms," and other expensive benefits. Additional personnel were required; and these employees—bartenders, maintenance men, camp directors, and the like—were engaged or discharged by Gosser himself. These employees reinforced Gosser's base of power, being accountable to him alone.

Indignant rank-and-file members charged, too, that Gosser had manipulated for his private profit this costly health-and-recreation program, which had burdened the Toledo UAW locals with debt for purchases of land and facilities. Gosser had set up the Colonial Hardware Store for his own advantage; in his capacity as head of the union, he had directed that purchases of the summer camp and the retirement farm be made through Colonial Hardware. Richard Gosser, ironmonger, had as his best customer Richard Gosser, UAW international vice-president.

Many charges of corruption were brought against Gosser by union members. For one thing, he had ordered that a speedboat be purchased for the union's summer camp. Promptly he had that boat removed to some other body of water; it was not beheld again at the union's camp. At length, members began to protest against such ways.

On a Friday night about the middle of October, 1949, at a UAW meeting, one courageous member, John Bolman, stood up to request formally a certified financial report. A scuffle occurred. Bolman was told that either he must state his reasons for making his motion, or else leave the room. He left.

At the Select Committee's hearings, questioning Bolman about this episode, Senator Curtis inquired whether he had left the room in the same condition as when he had entered. Bolman had not.

Curtis: "What was the difference?"

Bolman: "The side of my face was smashed in."

His principal assailant had been Walter Murphy, an assistant to Gosser, but altogether some fifteen men had assaulted him for his temerity in making a motion, some of them "goons from Detroit," Bolman believed. Charles Clarke, chief union steward at Spicer Corporation, sitting near Bolman and known to share his views, was beaten in the back with a chair; he spent six months in a cast. Bolman was carried to a hospital; there a doctor found his face so badly smashed that Bolman's sight was endangered.

On October 17, Bolman swore out a warrant for assault and battery, and demanded, publicly, certified financial reports and statements of operation of the union. Also he filed civil suit against Gosser. Only four hours after filing that suit, Bolman was discharged by Spicer Manufacturing Corporation from his job as clerk, a post he had held for nearly six years.

The pretext for his firing was that he was alleged to have been ten minutes late in returning from a lunch. Gosser was well prepared to intimidate employers as well as union members.

As the Gosser scandal entered the courts and grew in the press, a testimonial dinner was organized in Gosser's honor by his enthusiasts. To that dinner came the Mayor of Toledo, Michael DiSalle; Judge Homer Ramey; Congressman Thomas Burke, of Toledo; and some five hundred other people. Nobody held a dinner for the discharged clerk whose face had been smashed in.

But Gosser's abuses were now on the front pages of the newspapers, which was awkward for Walter Reuther and his lieutenants at Detroit, so very near Toledo. On January 16, 1950, emissaries were sent from Detroit to Toledo as a board of inquiry. These UAW officials asked Bolman to withdraw his actions at law and instead "press his grievances" through regular union channels. Bolman prudently declined. Using the excuse that now Bolman was "in violation of the union constitution," on January 17 Walter Reuther himself formally expelled Bolman from the UAW.

"I stand expelled for not going after Gosser through regular union procedure," Bolman said. "I tried this. The first thing I received was a broken jaw. Then I lost my job. And now after great formality I am expelled from the union by Mr. Reuther himself. And all this is in the 'world's most democratic union.'"

Bolman was not the man to surrender easily. On February 4, his lawyer filed a brief charging that Bolman's expulsion from the UAW was part of a deliberate scheme meant to prevent his civil suit from being decided on its merits. Outraged by the union's tactics, the editor of the *Toledo Blade* gave the case much attention. Indeed, only the *Blade* seemed willing to help Bolman with legal costs or influence.

Still riding high, Richard Gosser refused to answer questions at a deposition hearing; was arrested for contempt of court; was released on bail after appealing to his constitutional rights, declaring that his testimony "might be used in criminal prosecution" against him.

The Gosser case dragged on toward spring; and presently Bolman found allies. Union members who had been intimidated by Gosser began to take heart. On May 16, twelve women shamed the rest of the union membership when they bravely went on strike at the union's office itself, protesting against "the domination of Richard Gosser." The next day after this strike by the women at Local 12, Richard L. Lazette, president of the Toledo Industrial Union Council (ruling body of the CIO in northwestern Ohio), ventured to send a threatening message directly to Reuther at UAW headquarters, Detroit: "I request your presence here at once to try to straighten out this mess. If you don't come, I shall prefer charges against you through the National CIO Executive Board for negligence and allowing the labor movement in Toledo to be destroyed."

And on that same day, officers of five Toledo locals of the UAW issued a statement declaring that they were "strongly opposed to the dictatorial machine control which engulfs the Toledo UAW."

On May 18, two more UAW units in Toledo announced that they would join in that statement. The same evening, a group of union officers and plant stewards met at UAW headquarters to discuss tactics, while some fifty other members of various UAW locals met at the Fort Meiggs Hotel to discuss possible anti-Gosser action.

Gosser issued a defiant statement that his opponents had "a shock coming to them." Clearly he believed that Walter Reuther and the top men in UAW's Detroit headquarters would back him. But on May 19, the revolt against Gosser spread to the second-largest local (including seven plant units) in Toledo, with an official statement against Gosser: "We wish to express our sympathy and support of the honest members of our union who are struggling under difficult conditions to save Local 12 and the Toledo UAW-CIO from the evil effects caused by the dictatorial and undemocratic practices of Richard T. Gosser, international UAW vice-president."

Now alarmed, Reuther sent down from Detroit Emil Mazey, Secretary-Treasurer of the UAW, to "put out this fire." The striking girls from the union-dues office refused to meet with Mazey "until Gosser and his dominating clique are removed from their offices."

The belligerent Mazey, who had brought UAW auditors from Detroit with him, moved quickly to suppress this revolt. Among union officials who had dared to confront Gosser, fear began to grow that a whitewash of Gosser might be attempted. To make such a whitewash difficult, they issued another public statement: "Unless the International UAW-CIO takes immediate, honest, and drastic action...the continued existence of our crisis will damage the entire international union ...We know from our own experience with this man that these charges are true." They complained of "delay and ineffective activities...after five months." And they went on to declare, "We question the courage of our international president, Walter Reuther [who] slightly over a year ago when Local 14 was in disagreement with Gosser...intervened in his behalf."

Meanwhile, Randolph Gray, financial secretary of Local 12, asked for police protection, stating that Gosser had "threatened to have his ribs kicked in." Gray had been on leave for two months with a nervous breakdown caused by such threats; the twelve women employees of the local who had gone on strike against the union had worked directly for Gray, and had walked out in sympathy.

Emil Mazey called a meeting of the entire membership of Gosser's Local 12. Fifteen hundred people attended. Mazey astonished the audience of union members by giving a clean bill of health to the records of Local 12. Union members were stunned.

Gosser, defending himself before this meeting, rebutted the charge that he "had been in reform school" by alleging, "Mr. Bolman is an ex-convict, too." Later in the meeting, Gosser defied his opponents: "I tell them to go to hell."

The following morning, a group of union unit officers expressed their consternation. They charged that a whitewash had occurred: "We gave Mr. Mazey more than enough evidence to warrant an entire clean-up of the Gosser machine." Some said they would ask Walter Reuther for a hearing. But it had been Reuther who had sent Mazey to Toledo. Disillusionment was spreading among many union members who previously had believed in the "devotion to democratic practices" of Reuther and his lieutenants.

In this hour of triumph, Gosser's partisans increased their efforts to search out and beat up their union critics. Within weeks, the police made several arrests for savage beatings of Gosser's union opponents. One of those arrested was Charles (Snick) Gross, who had been arrested previously twenty-two times; he was listed as "clerk" to Gosser.

The local union paper, the *Toledo Union Journal*, wholly subservient to Gosser, continued meanwhile to press hard at ridiculing leaders of the reform group, who were represented as privy to an employers' conspiracy to defeat the UAW drive for pensions. By the end of June, the terror of Gosser's goons and pressure by the top men of UAW headquarters had begun to break the opposition to Gosser. Union critics of Gosser's dictatorship had organized the Ad Hoc Committee for Democratic Unionism. Harold Biltheimer, chairman of the Toledo Scale Company unit of the UAW, who had become chairman of this reform committee, was harassed by private detectives and presently beaten by one of Gosser's goons.

Hidden influence apparently was exerted at the highest levels in the UAW to compel the critics of Gosser to reverse their positions. Even Richard Lazette, CIO chief for northwestern Ohio, now was humiliated publicly. He found it necessary to announce his resignation from the important post of president of the Toledo Industrial Union Council. Even the Toledo Pipe Threading Unit of the UAW, whose officers had been the first union officials to defy the power of Gosser, abruptly issued a statement withdrawing their opposition.

A year earlier, Gosser had declared that his critics "were in for a shock." Gosser's confidence in the readiness and ability of the top national leadership of the UAW to protect him had been well grounded.

Such were the ways of Richard Gosser, and such was the statecraft of Walter Reuther: the one after loot, the other after power. The Select Committee took much testimony about the Toledo union troubles. Evidence obtained showed clearly that Gosser's regime had made threats, engaged in organizing through intimidation, physically beaten its opponents, and committed other offenses against law. There had existed a mysterious "flower fund" available to Gosser and his crew, for which no accounting had been made. Jess F. Motsinger, a member of the UAW who had held every local office and had belonged to the union for seventeen years, testified that he had been required to make a contribution to this "flower fund" of five dollars a week, or ten dollars every pay-period. "I was told to make the payments in cash." Randolph Gray, the financial secretary, testified that even though he had been required to pay money into the flower fund, he never had been able to discover for what purposes the fund was used. *Fleur de mal.* Walter Reuther was given to assuring the press and the public that the UAW was incorruptible.

Other grim cases of "flying squadrons" and "goon squads" and "flower funds" within UAW affiliates in other cities might have repaid investigation, had there been time. On occasion, the UAW could be tougher than the Teamsters. But the majority on the Select Committee, reluctant to give offense to the UAW, were eager to press on to the offenses of Jimmy Hoffa and the Teamsters.

TEAMSTER
CRIMINALITY

Highly though they esteemed Walter Reuther, the Kennedys detested Jimmy Hoffa. In hearings about Hoffa and the Teamsters, the majority of the Select Committee—and Counsel Robert Kennedy—displayed a zeal conspicuously lacking in the investigation of the Kohler strike.

The Committee received a vast amount of testimony concerning Hoffa's operations as president of the Teamsters: information about irregularities in his election as president, about violence, secondary boycotts, extortion, conflict of interest, and misuse of pension and welfare funds. When called to testify, many officers and members of the Teamsters refused to answer questions on the ground that they might incriminate themselves. Hoffa himself, nevertheless, did not appeal to the Fifth Amendment; rather, he would state that the matter in question had been handled by some union representative or by a union local, and that he had no knowledge of it. When the person allegedly possessed of such information was called to testify, that lesser Teamster would not answer questions on the ground of self-incrimination.

Counsel Kennedy endeavored to elicit testimony concerning cases of illegal fund-raising, dynamiting, conspiracy, bribery of a judge, income-tax evasion, and other offenses committed by Teamsters "business agents" and officers. Seventy-three past or present officials of the Teamsters refused to answer under the self-incrimination privilege. Gangsters and racketeers allied with the Teamsters also were called to testify; forty-eight of them invoked the Fifth Amendment.

Victims of the Teamsters did testify. There was the case of the Terminal Transport Company of Atlanta, Georgia. That firm's terminal manager in Nashville had been beaten by a Teamster representative, W. A. Smith, who was indicted by a grand jury for assault with intent to kill. But after the indictment, the victim and Joseph Katz (president of Terminal Transport) asked that prosecution be dropped. Katz talked with one Gene San Soucie, president of Teamsters Local 135, Nashville, and subsequently, in Chicago, with Hoffa. When Katz was asked by Robert Kennedy his reason for dropping charges against Smith, he appeared to have difficulty in replying. He did say that "apparently things were going along so well with our company," and added that his wife was very nervous about the matter.

Kennedy asked him, "Was there any discussion with Mr. Hoffa in Chicago as to the rights of your employee, Mr. Allen, in the matter?"

"Yes," Katz answered. "I told Mr. Hoffa that I was pretty aggravated about a business agent taking something like this in his hands and beating up one of my people. I told him, as far as I was concerned, it was absolutely uncalled for. Mr. Hoffa agreed with me and said, 'Well, you know how boys are some times. They will get into a hotheaded discussion.'"

Hoffa's "business agent" boys distinctly were a hotheaded breed. In several states, Teamsters business agents had been convicted of deadly assault, arson, extortion, bribery, and other offenses.

Consider the case, brought before the Select Committee, of Robert V. Whitley, Jr., owner and operator of the Woodbine Radio Cab Company, Nashville, Tennessee. Mrs. Whitley worked with him; they had some ten cabs. In 1954 the Teamsters came to "organize."

In dread, Whitley moved his cabs from Nashville to Shelbyville. For ten days or a fortnight, the Teamsters picketed Whitley's place of business, shutting it down. Then his office was wrecked. Whitley had contracted with the Davidson Board of Education to transport seventy-three handicapped children to school. Those children did not get to school at all while Whitley was shut down by the union; parents of the children asked Whitley to resume his service. He conferred with the city taxi inspector, who advised Whitley, "I had best sign up with the union if I wanted to operate, and he did not want to see anybody get hurt, and it would be best for those concerned." At this conference in Whitley's house, the Nashville inspector was accompanied by the Teamsters business agent. The inspector himself, a municipal official, was a member of the Teamsters Union; so Whitley signed a contract with the Teamsters.

But his drivers so misconducted themselves after Whitley had given way to the Teamsters that Whitley discharged the chief instigator of trouble. Then he was picketed again by the union. He hired a new crew of drivers. Union members threatened Whitley and the new drivers, and bumped his cabs in the streets to scare away passengers, and in other ways employed intimidation. The city taxi inspector rode about with the union officials. Whitley had to abandon transporting palsied, blind, and deaf children to school. One of his drivers was beaten with a motorcycle chain. Whitley appealed to the Nashville police. A policeman came to his office and "asked me why I didn't go ahead and shut down and quit bothering him." When Whitley brought charges at law against the Teamsters, they brought false counter-charges against him and his wife, and then offered to drop their charges if he would drop his. Mrs. Whitley was told by Teamsters to watch what she would say at the Select Committee's hearings: "that everybody who testified here against them would be taken care of sooner or later."

Intimidation of witnesses and juries had been another strategy employed by Teamsters officials in several states.

The Select Committee turned to consideration of Teamsters pension and welfare funds. Allies and friends of Hoffa and other national Teamsters officials had been selected as agents for the investment of such funds. The Select Committee obtained the services of experienced insurance actuaries to compare commissions charged by Teamsters agencies with customary charges made throughout the insurance business.

It was revealed in testimony about this comparison that the Central Conference of Teamsters had paid during eight years a total of $611,200 in excessive commissions; the Michigan Conference of Teamsters, over seven years, $139,400 in such excessive commissions; Local 1031 of IBEW, Electrical Workers, over nine years, $502,600 in excessive commissions. This was a conservative computation, giving the benefit of the doubt to the union-authorized agencies.

The two big Teamsters insurance policies in question had been awarded directly by Hoffa himself or through his influence. Allen Dorfman, a principal in the placing of insurance and handling of Teamsters pension and welfare funds, was called to testify. Appealing to the Fifth Amendment, Dorfman declined to answer questions about commissions granted by the Central Conference of Teamsters, the Michigan Conference of Teamsters, and his receipt of excessive payments of $1,650,000.

It was for such fraudulent handling of Teamsters funds that Jimmy Hoffa later would be sent to prison.

INTIMIDATION IN
THE BAKERS' UNION

The Select Committee made inquiry into the affairs of a third international union, the Bakers' Union, with interesting operations that extended from coast to coast. Here they found model cases of labor-racket extortion.

Joseph Kramer owned and operated a bakery on Second Avenue, New York City, with six or seven employees, members of Local 3 of the International Bakers' Union. Kramer told the Committee what had happened to him when he was solicited to give money toward a party for Max Kralstein, vice-president of the International Bakers' Union.

A union business agent named Hart asked Kramer for a donation toward Kralstein's dinner; Kramer, never having heard of Kralstein, declined. Hart then requested that Kramer buy an "advertisement" for fifty dollars; Kramer counteroffered twenty-five dollars; he was told that fifty dollars was the minimum. Four weeks later, Kramer donated a hundred dollars, in dread of a "rough time" of a sort he had experienced with the union before.

Counsel Kennedy wished to know what sort of rough time that was.

"Well, they had a picket line when I opened the new shop. I had a picket line for seven months," Kramer replied. "I figured, 'Well, that is not going to happen to me any more; I will give a hundred dollars.'" During his previous experience with pickets, he had found it necessary to make his own deliveries, and pickets had knocked cake boxes out of people's hands.

The union had extended its activities to the suppliers of Kramer's bakery. Three men had approached the Pennsylvania farmer who had delivered eggs to Kramer, declaring, "If you bring more eggs to Kramer's we will burn your farm down." The farmer told Kramer, "I can't bring you no eggs.

My wife got hysteria. I can't bring you no more eggs. I am sorry. I can't do it.''

It was not Kramer's employees, but outsiders, who had enforced the union's will upon Kramer.

Chairman McClellan summarized an audit of the amount of money collected by the Bakers' Union to give to Max Kralstein: "In accordance with the Chair's calculation, Mr. Max Kralstein and his wife received $57,818.94 in cash, and also a portrait that cost $1,477.21, and a gift to Mrs. Kralstein which cost $1,650, making a total that Mr. Kralstein and his wife received out of this affair of $61,016.15.''

The money raised by such tactics for the Kralstein "dinner,'' it turned out, was used by Kralstein to buy a house for forty thousand dollars, with some twenty-one thousand left over to buy furnishings. Even relatively minor labor racketeering paid well.

The story was similar in California. The Select Committee obtained lively testimony from Albert Barclay, of Redondo Beach, who had worked for several months for the International Bakers' Union, but had been dismissed because "I was not wholly one hundred percent going along with what they were doing.'' He had been office manager of a Bakers' Union local. Weekly, there had been an irregular financial transaction: the delivery of thirty-five dollars to one John D. Nelson, an "assistant trustee'' of the union, this sum being charged against an expense account made out to Barclay himself. The money in question was "to be used for purposes that could not be accounted for in case the district attorney came to examine the books.''

For what purpose did Nelson employ this monthly payment? "He used it,'' Barclay testified, "for various purposes, to take care of any unethical practices such as beating up of a boy, or burning of a car, or beating up of a colored gentleman, or something like that, moneys that couldn't be actually entered and accounted for.''

Senator Curtis inquired as to who was beaten. Barclay mentioned the beating of two men and one woman in San Francisco; and the beating of a "colored gentleman'' and a fourteen-year-old boy in southern California. The boy was a son of one of the owners "that was sending baked goods over to one of the plants that we had under strike." The boy had been beaten by John D. Nelson and Frank Gardon.

"The first party was Frank Gardon," Barclay related, "and he went up and he started to box. I had orders to take the picket down to the other end of the building, and then Mr. Frank Gardon went up to the boy and started pummeling him, and Mr. Nelson ran over to the car and grabbed the blackjack and went over and hit him on the head. They did not quite finish the boy, and he jumped up and saw the first three numbers of the 1954 Buick which was an International car, bearing Chicago plates, before they moved to Washington, and he recalled 177, the first three numbers of the car, which was John Nelson's car." Barclay had been told to divert the attention of the union's pickets from this rough encounter.

Senator Curtis asked who had ordered these beatings. Barclay answered that Nelson had telephoned daily to Washington, taking his orders from James Cross, president of the International Bakers' Union.

Such things were done, in the name of "collective bargaining," throughout the United States. The Select Committee had time and resources sufficient only to hold hearings on a few conspicuous and notorious cases, of course, connected with labor racketeering; but it did gather plenty of testimony to show the need for Congress to legislate in such concerns.

ROSCOE POUND ON
UNION IMMUNITIES

Why was it that criminals had been able to prosper so conspicuously within labor unions? Because they were able to take advantage of certain privileges at law.

A basic reason for violence and wrongdoing within labor unions is the fact that by court decisions, statutes, and regulations, immunities have been granted to unions which have not been granted to any other organizations or individuals. An intelligent treatment of this subject may be found in Roscoe Pound's book *Legal Immunities of Labor Unions* (1957).

"It is the general rule, applicable to everybody, that repeated and continuing trespasses upon another's land may be stopped by injunctions," Pound writes. "This is especially true where, as usually in cases of 'picketing,' the result is to prevent access to and use of the land, since the remedy of repeated and multiplied actions for damages is not adequate to protect the owner. But the remedy of injunction available to everyone against everyone else, is denied the employer as against trespassing members of labor organizations in a labor dispute." Dean Pound points out that this immunity was created by the Norris-LaGuardia Act of March 23, 1932.

"Interference by pickets with streets and highways," Pound continues, "which would be a nuisance if done by ordinary people, is an everyday matter. So are assaults on drivers, and overturning of trucks and breaking of windows and destruction of carts, and for that matter bombing of shops and houses and throwing of tear bombs, for which there is no effective legal remedy."

Pound quotes the restatement of "agency" by the American Law Institute in 1933: "The members of a union are not its agents and the union is not liable for the acts of its members in the course of a labor dispute."

As Pound puts it, "Only a labor organization is allowed

to disturb the peace and back up its claims by force and violence to the extent of creating an emergency." The Select Committee in its hearings found that one of the more flagrant abuses of power by unions was the secondary boycott. Here is what Pound says of this: "A direct and intentional prevention of shipment or delivery of goods in interstate commerce was held not in restraint of commerce. In *U. S.* v. *Hutcheson*, secondary boycotts by labor unions to keep out of the market nonunion good or goods worked on by other unions were held immune from liability under the Sherman Act, so long as the union acted in its self interest and did not combine with nonlabor groups."

Such employers as companies distributing electricity or natural gas have a responsibility to the public that is not imposed upon unions. Dean Pound remarks, "A public service company is liable in damages for failure to perform its duty of public service because of a strike of its employees. It cannot abandon its services, even if unprofitable, and it is not only liable in damages to those entitled to its services but may forfeit its charter if it does so. The propositions were well established long ago as to everyone professing a public employment. Likewise, the courts were beginning to hold that while employees of a public service company remained employees they were affected with a public character, to some extent at least, and could not be suffered to hold the employment and refuse to perform the work of the public employment.

"But the National Labor Relations Act and the Norris-LaGuardia Act, leaving the legal duties of the public service employer what they were, cut off all holding of the employees to any duty toward the public."

Perhaps the greatest immunity enjoyed by unions everywhere—except in right-to-work states—is their immunity from damage to someone who loses his job because of actions of a union. In dealing with this subject, Pound writes, "under the circumstances of employment today membership in a union may be an absolute prerequisite of obtaining or retaining employment. But unions have very wide powers of expelling members who do not follow the orders of those in control." And Pound goes on to remark, "Moreover, arbitrary exclusion from membership, exaction of exorbitant initiation or entrance fees, and the like practices have proved difficult to deal with."

Prohibitions, limitations, and restrictions on corporations in their handling of funds, and particularly in their contributing to partisan politics, are not applied to labor unions. Of this, Pound says, "Though controlling huge funds which they are coming to use for partisan political purposes, statutes regulating political contributions by utilities and corporations have not governed contributions of funds of unions. Nor have the rules of law governing the use of trust funds been applied to use by union officials of the often very large funds of those organizations. Thus they have powers with respect to such funds beyond those of other organizations and their officers."

Whenever any individual, group, or organization is not subject to the law that all other organizations and citizens must observe, abuse and wrongdoing are invited. This is one of the reasons why Senators Goldwater, Mundt, and Curtis argued that to reduce wrongdoing in labor and management, more must be done than to drive from union offices those persons guilty of wrongdoing. To deal adequately with this problem, Congress must concern itself with the power of labor unions.

EIGHT REMEDIES FOR LABOR RACKETEERING

After the Select Committee's many months of hearings and investigations, a majority in both houses of Congress perceived that there must be new legislation about labor and management; eyes having been opened by the Select Committee, the public desired reform. The Taft-Hartley Act needed to be brought up to date, and loopholes must be closed in that complex piece of legislation.

On April 9, 1958, Carl Curtis addressed the Merchants' and Manufacturers' Association of California, meeting at the Biltmore Hotel, Los Angeles. His speech, which outlined his proposals for legislative action, is printed below to summarize the investigation of labor rackets.

"My work on the Senate Labor Rackets Committee has not lessened my respect and admiration for the rank and file of men and women who work," Curtis said. "I believe them to be honest, upright citizens. The committee is dealing with a minority of union leaders who have directed a program of violence, boycotting, destruction of property, racketeering, unlawful political activities, and the misuse of funds.

"We do not seek to single out labor unions and deprive them of their just rights. We do seek equality before the law for all persons and groups.

"First, there must be legislation enacted requiring a thorough accounting of union dues and welfare funds. These funds belong to the workers. They are entitled to the same protection as if their funds were placed in a savings bank or an insurance company. Union officials must be held accountable in their trusteeship. The workers' money must not be spent and wasted at the whim of their officials or for the personal benefit of the officers of the union. The nation was shocked at the conduct of Dave Beck in his handling of workers' money for his own enrichment. They were outraged when he enriched himself out of a fund set up for the widow of his closest friend. Likewise, the members of the Bakers' Union had just reason to appeal to their government and determine what their president, James G. Cross, was doing with their money. The investigation of the United Textile Workers was another case where their two top officers, Mr. Valente and Mr. Klenert, failed to preserve and protect the funds belonging to those who paid the dues.

"More recently, our investigation of the International Union of Operating Engineers brought to light a number of glaring violations pertaining to the handling of funds. A San Francisco local purchased a tract of land for $23,000 but paid

$33,500 for it, the difference going to their own union leaders. The tract of land was broken up in parcels, sold to union leaders who resold it, and gained an advantage of some $59,000.

"A local of the Operating Engineers unit in Philadelphia lost their local autonomy about 1941. The International Union, through a system of supervision, took possession of the assets, collected dues, worker permit payments, and even a five percent kickback from the workers. When the local union regained possession of their union in 1948, they had to sign a stipulation agreeing not to demand an accounting of money that the International officers had taken from them. It may run upward of a million dollars, perhaps up to four million dollars.

"The need for regulation of these funds is self-evident. Unions are not small business. The annual income from dues amounts to over six hundred million dollars a year. The pension and welfare funds have reserves running between twenty-five and thrity billion dollars, and have an increment of five billion dollars a year.

"Secondly, there must be legislation that will insure a greater control of unions by union members. The principle of checks and balances must have a place in the self-government of labor organizations. Government should not dominate unions, but our laws should provide that voting methods, nominations, election of officers and delegates, and methods of holding conventions should be in the hands of the rank and file of members and not governed from the top down. Workers should no longer have their unions run by trustees, supervisors, goons, and guns. The president of this same Philadelphia local of Operating Engineers testified that the International seized its assets and took control at the point of guns in the hands of their goons.

"The McClellan Committee has brought to light one case where the members of a local union have had nothing to do with choosing their officers or running their union since the Local was founded in 1929.

"The San Francisco local of Operating Engineers, which I have previously mentioned, held an election at which time about two thousand men voted. Four union leaders proceeded to a cabin in the mountains to count the ballots. They counted five hundred and got tired and decided to estimate the returns. Even though only two thousand men voted, by the time they got through with their estimating the winning slate won with votes of over seventeen thousand.

"Third, the secondary boycott is economic blackmail and it should be outlawed. I have a bill on that subject, S. 76, which I introduced months before the McClellan Committee was created. I hope that it can be enacted into law.

"Secondary boycotts have been carried on in different forms. They have been applied to transportation companies and have interfered with the flow of goods through commerce, resulting in damage to consumers and to innocent and neutral businesses. Boycotts cause costs to rise, and all sorts of trouble for many people, including contractors. The wide use of the secondary boycott by Walter Reuther's UAW-CIO was fully exposed in our hearings on the Kohler strike. The products of the Burt Manufacturing Company of Akron, Ohio, have been boycotted through the land for ten years. This economic war has been carried on against the public even though the Burt Manufacturing Company has a certified union, which their own workers prefer, and there is no dispute over wages and hours.

"When individuals in business are boycotted, goods become scarcer, the consumer has a lesser choice, and he pays a greater price. How can a government that pretends to be concerned about the public welfare continue to fail to enact laws to outlaw the secondary boycott?

"Fourth, we need a more effective method for preventing the use of union funds for political purposes, such as making political contributions, providing research, furnishing manpower, and the use of publications to support candidates, parties, and issues, oftentimes contrary to the individual member's views. Two universities have conducted surveys among union members on the question of whether or not they wanted to have their union in politics. Those surveys report that sixty-six percent of the union members did not want their union engaged in politics.

"What right has a Michigan union czar to take money that workers pay in dues in that state and contribute that money to a political party operating in a far state?

"When Walter Reuther was before the Committee on Privileges and Elections of the Senate, upon which I serve, he recommended that all political contributions be limited to five dollars. I asked Mr. Reuther if he knew one Roy Reuther. He replied that that was his brother. I stated that I had the records before me where Roy Reuther had contributed five thousand dollars in a senatorial campaign in the state of Kentucky in 1954. Walter Reuther's reply was, "Oh, that wasn't his money; that was UAW money."

"Fifth, anti-trust and anti-monopoly laws have been enacted to protect the public from the abuses that come from the concentration of economic power. The public is entitled to protection from the concentration of economic power, regardless of who makes up that concentration. Therefore, legal restraint should be imposed against the concentration of union power by groups of unions when that power becomes a threat to the welfare and security of our country. What right has one group of citizens to combine and drive somebody else out of business and, at the same time, it is unlawful for other groups to do likewise?

"Sixth, the responsibilities for maintaining law and order and for the prosecution for assaults, bombings, and like offenses should remain the responsibility of local and state governments. The national government at Washington should not undertake to provide police protection for every community in the United States. Citizens in some of our states and localities need to take a look at their local government.

"Last fall, the McClellan Committee spent many days taking the testimony of the situation in Tennessee. There we received stories of beatings, shootings, overturning of trucks, the bombing of warehouses, the destruction of property generally, the blocking of highways, and all manner of offenses. In too many cases the local officials failed to do their duty.

"When we were investigating the Operating Engineers in Philadelphia, we received the sworn testimony of a Mr. Ed McCarty. He told how he was unmercifully beaten in an elevator as he left a union meeting. An attempt was made to put his eyes out. One of the blows that he received has resulted in cancer. It may mean his death. When that case was taken before a local magistrate, he refused to do anything, and said, 'Well, that is just a union brawl, and we do not go into that.'

"There are two situations where perhaps the federal government should step in, and I am inclined to believe that consideration should be given to legislation in those fields. First, in the case of the transportation of hoodlums across state lines for the purpose of committing violence in labor-union conflicts. Second, I believe that the federal government will have to step in with some laws dealing with violence and destruction of property on federally financed projects. This must be done to protect the federal taxpayers. It is necessary if we are going to hold down the costs of our public building programs such as the highway program. My bill S. 3253 will do that. Distinguished co-sponsors are Chairman McClellan and Senators Mundt and Goldwater and Ives.

"Seventh, unions should be required to adopt a form of organization that fixes responsibility on the union for their acts. Unions should be held responsible for the acts of their members and officers when they are acting for the union, just as employees and officers of businesses create a liability on that particular business.

"But there is another reason why unions should be required to incorporate or adopt some similar type of organization. The individual members would then have some rights which are defined by law and are a matter of public record. They could go into court and protect those rights, just as a stockholder in a business corporation can go into court. It would put an end to this shameful practice of union czars dominating local unions by placing them in trusteeship or under some form of supervision.

"And, eighth, *union membership should be voluntary and not compulsory.* This goes to the very heart of all of the problems involved. No American citizen should be required to join or to refrain from joining any lawful organization he chooses in order to hold his job. The right to work is a basic individual right. Our courts, including our Supreme Court, have held it so. Compulsion and compulsory membership in any organization are repugnant to our concept of liberty in this country.

"When Dave Beck was before the McClellan Committee,

I said to him, 'Suppose that your members believe these charges against you and that you have misappropriated their funds, can those members withdraw from the union and stop paying dues without losing their jobs?' He didn't want to answer. I had to keep after him for fifteen minutes. I finally got the answer from him. He very reluctantly admitted that they could not. In other words, the members of the Teamsters Union are captives. They are pawns. Even though they lose confidence in their officers, disagree with the course that the union is taking, and even though they feel that their money is being stolen, they cannot protest by withdrawing from the union without losing their jobs. That is neither just nor fair. It is not American.

"The great Samuel Gompers, the father of modern American unionism, urged upon the workers of America 'devotion to the fundamentals of human liberty—the principles of voluntarism.' He went on to warn them, 'No lasting gain has ever come from compulsion. If we seek to force, we tear apart that which, united, is invincible.' More recently, Guy L. Brown, grand chief of the Brotherhood of Locomotive Engineers, said: 'We still think that labor in the long run has a good enough product that you won't have to force men to join.'

"Compulsory union membership invites corruption and abuse of power on the part of union officers. Voluntary union membership makes for better unions and for honest, faithful trusteeship on the part of their officers. Whenever we have 'union shop' contracts or other compulsory membership contracts, the employees cannot withdraw from the union without losing their jobs, even though they know and believe that their officers are corrupt and that their union is following a course with which they totally disagree. The right to join or not to join and the right to resign from an organization are not only basic freedoms, but they are the way by which the members can effectively voice their protest against improper actions on the part of their officers. Voluntarism is the American way."

A year and a half later, some of Curtis' recommendations would be enacted.

THE LANDRUM-
GRIFFIN ACT

On January 20, 1959, Senator J. F. Kennedy and Senator Sam
J. Ervin introduced their bill S 505, which, Senator Kennedy
said, "would crack down on Mr. James Hoffa and his hood-
lum associates in the Teamsters Union and on corrupt union
leaders and employers." This bill, favored by most Democrats
and by most of the labor-union lobby, called for mild federal
intervention, joined to the sanction of public exposure of
abuses.

President Eisenhower sent the administration's labor program to Congress on January 28. This administration bill, S 748,
was introduced by Barry Goldwater, ranking Republican member of the Committee on Labor. The bill proposed to give the
Secretary of Labor wider powers to investigate suspected violations of labor law and to compel compliance. It would em-
power the Secretary to impose two strong penalties against
noncomplying unions: loss of tax exemption, and loss of access to the National Labor Relations Board, which certifies
unions as collective-bargaining agents. S 748 also forbade
organizational and recognition picketing and secondary boycotts. Calling the Eisenhower proposal dangerous to the rights
of organized labor, the labor-union leaders would have no part
of it.

It was the Kennedy bill that reached the floor of the Senate for consideration. Although numerous amendments were
offered on the Senate floor, in general Kennedy and his subcommittee prevailed, rejecting amendments to forbid secondary boycotts, organizational picketing, and recognition
picketing.

Responding to President Eisenhower's campaign to rouse
public opinion in support of labor-law reform, a badly split
House committee finally reported out a House bill, basically
much like the Senate bill. Some congressmen who desired a

stronger bill voted to bring this mild version out of committee so that some bill, at least, would be on the House floor.

Then, on July 27, Congressmen Phil M. Landrum (a Georgia Democrat) and Robert P. Griffin (a Michigan Republican), introduced a labor bill, HR 8400, proposed as a bipartisan substitute for the feeble bill that had emerged from the House committee. This Landrum-Griffin bill included the anti-corruption and union-democracy provisions of the House bill, but it also contained the strong Taft-Hartley changes favored by the President. The Landrum-Griffin proposal forbade secondary boycotts and organizational and recognition picketing. By a vote of 229 to 201, that strong bill was adopted on the floor of the House of Representatives; it replaced the original bill offered by the House committee. On a subsequent roll call, the House passed the bill as amended by Landrum-Griffin, 303 votes to 125. Eventually this bill, clearing the conference of the two houses of Congress, became the Landrum-Griffin Act.

In the House, passage of Landrum-Griffin had been considerably aided by President Eisenhower's address of August 9, 1959, over television and radio. Some have called this speech Eisenhower's most effective one.

"The issue is, shall the people govern?" Eisenhower had said in closing. "If they do not, crooks and racketeers could prevail. The business of government, including the question of labor reform, is your business. It's every citizen's business. Americans want reform legislation which will be truly effective. It is my earnest hope that Congress will be fully responsive to an overwhelming national demand."

Four days later, the House approved Landrum-Griffin. Then the legislation went to conference. Senator Kennedy and the other Democratic conferees persuaded the House conferees to soften the bill somewhat by including certain exemptions; yet the final bill agreed upon was mostly the House version. The final version of Landrum-Griffin contained these partial curbs upon organizational and recognition picketing:

1. A union was prohibited from picketing simply to "organize" a firm's workers, or to gain recognition as the bargaining agent, if another union had won an NLRB election previously, or if the employer voluntarily had recognized an-

other union even without an NLRB certification election.

2. A union was prohibited from organizational or recognition picketing if there had been an NLRB election within the preceding twelve months. This would prevent a union from picketing if it, or another union, had lost a certification election.

3. A union was prohibited from organizational or recognition picketing for more than thirty days, if by the end of that time it had not asked the NLRB to hold a certification election.

4. The bill forbade consumer-boycott picketing. Other publicity (handbills, for instance) to inform the public that a retail store was handling "struck goods" was permitted, so long as it was informational in nature and did not cause cessation of commerce.

The final version of Landrum-Griffin contained provisions for union democracy and financial reporting by unions; it took measures to restrain corruption; it amended the Taft-Hartley Act in several particulars, notably those pertaining to secondary boycott, organizational picketing, and "no-man's land" questions of court jurisdiction.

The Senate accepted the conference report, 95 votes to 2, on September 3; the House agreed on September 4, 352 to 52. Few major reform bills have been enacted by so thumping a margin.

Some union officials growled that Landrum-Griffin was worse than Taft-Hartley. But no serious attempt has been made to repeal Landrum-Griffin, and no major alteration in federal labor law has been enacted by Congress since 1959.

The fulminations of big labor unions against Senator Curtis for his conspicuous part in the investigations of the McClellan Committee did him no damage in the November elections of 1960. J. F. Kennedy was elected President by the thinnest conceivable margin; Carl Curtis (who had no opponent in the Republican primary) was re-elected senator by the greatest number of votes he received in the whole of his political career—352,748. He defeated his Democratic opponent, Robert B. Conrad, by a margin of nearly 109,000.

This was not the end of Curtis' efforts at reform of labor laws. In March, 1971, he would introduce Senate Bill 1055, meant to provide secret elections, conducted by the National

Labor Relations Board, for workers voting on whether to be represented by a union for collective bargaining. In May, 1971, he would introduce S 1903, requiring a secret ballot for all strike votes, or votes to determine whether to terminate a strike. The purpose of both bills was to protect the men and women who work; and to transfer to their hands, so far as possible, authority in such concerns. Neither bill made headway in the Senate; nor did a secret-ballot measure proposed by Senator Griffin in 1974.

Union leaders do not desire that any real power should pass from their hands to those of rank-and-file members. Nor are there enough politicians, national or state, willing to tackle the job of curbing the excessive power of labor unions.

Yet the hearings and investigations of the Select Committee on Improper Activities in Labor and Management had achieved a good deal: they had waked the American public to gross abuses of power, and in effect had produced a major reform of public policy, the Landrum-Griffin Act, which, if not perfect, was nevertheless a large gain for order in the economy and protection of working men and women.

Chapter 8

Investigating Billie Sol Estes

THE KENNEDY YEARS

The eight years of the Eisenhower administration had been an era of prosperity, stability, and, for the most part; of success in foreign affairs. This was ended by the election of John Fitzgerald Kennedy to the presidency in 1960. About to depart from office, President Eisenhower said to Senator Curtis, "Stay tough, Curtis, stay tough." That Curtis found necessary to do.

Assisted by Arthur Schlesinger, Jr., and other speechwriters, Kennedy had been persuasive on television, the first presidential candidate to make really effective use of that medium of communication. His television debates with Vice-President Nixon, indeed, had given Kennedy his tiny margin of victory in November. But television could not give him victories abroad or in the Congress.

His first television address as President was a blunder: in it he warned the people of the peril of Communist domination of remote Laos, the beginning of that American involvement in southeastern Asia which was to end with American defeat after a decade of exhausting war.

There would occur promptly the disaster of the Bay of Pigs in Cuba, botched more by United States civilian officials of the Kennedy administration than by the military or the CIA. It was Kennedy's initial major failure in office, and his reputation never wholly recovered from that defeated landing. Later, President Kennedy would boast of having browbeaten Khrushchev out of establishing missile bases in Cuba, in their confrontation of October 28, 1962; but in reality the victory was Khrushchev's, for the Soviets never agreed to an acceptable verification system to prove that indeed they had removed their missiles from Cuba, while Kennedy gave an implicit pledge that American forces would not invade Cuba. That menacing island remained a Soviet satellite.

Similarly, Kennedy was pusillanimous with respect to Germany: the Berlin Wall was built despite American protests. Here Kennedy behaved after a very different fashion from what presumably would have been Franklin Roosevelt's or Harry Truman's in such circumstances.

"Ask not what your country can do for you, but what you can do for your country." The sentence came from Kennedy's lips; but Arthur Schlesinger had purloined it for Kennedy's use from the speeches of old Orestes Brownson; it was an echo. Similarly, Kennedy's New Frontier merely was an echo of Roosevelt's New Deal and Truman's Fair Deal.

For Kennedy's was a feeble presidency, despite much propaganda at the time about the Kennedy "Camelot" in Washington, with J. F. K. as King Arthur. The lustre of those days now has vanished in public opinion; so has the notion that Jack Kennedy would found a Kennedy presidential dynasty.

One reason for Kennedy's ineffectuality, in domestic policy as in foreign, was that the election of 1960 did not confer upon him the popular "mandate" to which he had aspired. In the national popular vote, his margin over Richard Nixon was only 118,263, less than two-tenths of one per cent of the total number of votes cast. Kennedy's margin in the Electoral College was more substantial, a plurality of eighty-four. But if certain marginal states had gone for Nixon instead—and very narrowly marginal they had been—Kennedy would not have taken the presidential oath of office.

A few votes here and there would have made all the difference. Carl Curtis then was ranking Republican member on the Senate's Committee on Rules and Administration, and also on the Subcommittee on Privileges and Elections. Curtis suspected voting fraud in Illinois and Texas, where the contest between Kennedy and Nixon had been closest; so he sent watchers and investigators to Chicago. The information brought back to Curtis would have justified a full-scale senatorial investigation and a contesting of the validity of Kennedy's election.

Senator Curtis took up this grave matter with Richard Nixon. Nixon's reply, a generous one, was that it would not be well for the United States to endure a contest over the validity of the presidential election, for that would result in an interregnum of weeks, during which the country would lack leadership. Such an interim might work harm to America' s allies and well-wishers abroad. This prudence outweighed Mr. Nixon's long-cherished ambition to attain the presidency.

Curtis himself was elected in 1960 to his second term in the Senate. Unopposed in the Nebraska primary, in November he had defeated the Democratic candidate, Robert B. Conrad, of Genoa, by some 353,000 votes to 246,000. He set his face against Kennedy's ''New Frontier.'' Although Republicans remained in a minority in both houses of Congress, Kennedy had been unable to carry in with himself many new Democratic members of Congress; and his influence with members of his own party in Senate and House was limited. (Journalists who had privately polled members of the Senate during Kennedy's senatorial years as to the degree of esteem in which they held their colleagues had found that Kennedy had rated low on the roster.)

So the programs of the New Frontier, most of them vague, achieved no marked success during the three years of the Kennedy administration. No enthusiastic public supported them, and Congress enacted few of them. What increase of the welfare state occurred during the Kennedy administration was slight enough when compared with what had been done during the Roosevelt and Truman administrations; it would be trifling when compared with the sweeping and immensely costly "social" programs of the Johnson administration that was to follow.

Behind the Camelot facade of the Kennedy administration lay hesitation, self-seeking, license—and a good deal of corruption. What with the growth of the welfare state, the enormous expansion of the federal government's activities into new fields, and the seemingly limitless largesse that poured out from Washington, opportunities for looting occurred everywhere. Corruption extended to the inner circles of the people around J. F. Kennedy and Lyndon Johnson; and it enriched such fantastic figures as Billie Sol Estes.

THE FATAL ANTICS
OF BILLIE SOL

As a member of the Permanent Investigating Subcommittee of the Senate's Committee on Government Operations, Carl Curtis had taken part in senatorial investigations since 1957. Earlier, indeed, in 1951, he had been a member of an investigatory subcommittee of the House Ways and Means Committee that looked into notorious cases of corruption within the Bureau of Internal Revenue. That investigation had exposed the misdeeds of Lamar Caudle (an assistant attorney general), Joseph Nunan, Jr. (former commissioner of internal revenue), and other officials of the Truman administration. Now there came within the cials of the Truman administration. Now there came within the cognizance of Curtis and his Subcommittee colleagues the corrupt exploits of one Billie Sol Estes, of Pecos, Texas—one interesting specimen among the numerous men who had grown rich at public expense through frauds related to the federal government's multitudinous undertakings, subsidies, and outpourings of deficit-financed public profusion.

Estes was a hard-driving and ruthless young man who had amassed a fortune of thirteen million dollars or more in a very short time. In 1953, he had been named one of the nation's ten outstanding young men by the U. S. Junior Chamber of Commerce. He had developed the art of making friends with governmental officials, from clerks and other employees in the local agricultural office to members of Congress, cabinet officers, vice-presidents, and presidents. A giver of gifts, Estes contributed generously to his friends' political campaigns. In 1961, Estes founded a newspaper, the *Pecos Daily News*. On the front page of the paper's first edition were printed congratulatory messages from President Kennedy, Vice-President Johnson, House Speaker Sam Rayburn, Senator Ralph Yarborough, Dr. James Ralph (Assistant Secretary of Agriculture), and lesser luminaries. It turned out later that Estes had presented Dr. Ralph with a credit card, to employ at his discretion; and had made valuable gifts to several Department of Agriculture officials. Yet such donations were only peccadillos among Estes' doings.

Billie Sol's enterprises consisted of twenty-two corporations, partnerships, and companies. He had three main lines of business: first, in his grain-storage business, he handled huge amounts of government-owned grain for the Department of Agriculture; second, in his fertilizer business, he both retailed fertilizer and supplied farmers with a lease arrangement for fertilizer tanks, used for the storing of anhydrous ammonia fertilizer; third, Estes was a cotton farmer—a big one. This third undertaking requires some explanation.

When the federal farm-subsidy program related to cotton had been enacted, cotton production had been limited by allocating to certain farms a certain number of acres upon which cotton could be raised. This allotment went with the land: that is, any purchaser of the land also acquired the cotton allotment.

These allotments were highly valuable, for without them it was forbidden to plant and harvest cotton. Later the statute was amended to provide a form of compensation to farmers whose land was taken by the government through eminent domain— for flood control, or other purposes. Any farmer so dispossessed might have his old cotton allotment transferred from his old farm to other land that he might acquire. In no other circumstances might cotton allotments be bought, sold, or otherwise transferred.

Estes, nevertheless, perfected a plan for circumventing the law so that, in effect, he might buy cotton allotments. During 1961, he contrived to purchase more than 3,100 acres of cotton allotment.

Estes or his agents in this scheme sought out farmers whose land had been taken by eminent domain for highways, flood control, or other public purposes. These farmers were induced to transfer their cotton allotments to land that Estes owned in Texas. On paper, such farmers purchased land from Estes for the purpose of growing cotton; but no genuine sales of land by Estes actually occurred. The displaced farmer who "bought" land from Estes paid nothing down; he agreed to pay for the land in four installments, the first to be made at some future date. Then Estes would obtain a lease of this "purchased" land, paying the farmer a sum, usually fifty dollars an acre, as lease-money. The displaced farmer, theoretically the purchaser of Estes' land, never actually took possession of the land in question; he defaulted (with Estes' connivance) on his nominally promised installment payments for the new land. Upon such default, the land reverted to the seller, Estes. By this interesting scheme and device, the cotton allotment passed to Estes; and the "purchaser", the displaced farmer, received fifty dollars an acre from Estes, actually payment for his allotment's transfer to the ingenious Estes. Such was one of Estes' larger machinations, and it paid him very well indeed, for thus he became one of the bigger magnates of the cotton-growing oligopoly in Texas.

There were other Estes schemes, also highly lucrative, revealed by the Subcommittee's investigation and the course of the criminal prosecution of Estes. Take Estes' storage-tank rack-

1985 portrait of Carl T. Curtis.

Family portrait with Carl T. Curtis in center of front row surrounded by parents, five sisters and two brothers.

Kearney County, Nebraska, birthplace of Carl T. Curtis on March 15, 1905.

The Bobbie Baker Investigation. Left to right: Senator John Williams, Senator John Sherman Cooper, Senator Carl T. Curtis, Committee Counsel L. F. McLendon, Senator Everett Jordan and Senator Carl Hayden.

Senator Carl Curtis, Pres. Truman and Maurine Steyer-Biegert "June 1946, National 4-H honoree presented to Pres. Harry Truman".

Senator Carl T. Curtis with Senator Karl Mundt at news conference in reference to Billie Sol Estes.

Finance Committee chairman Russell Long and Carl T. Curtis hold a press conference.

During the Billie Sol Estes investigation. Left to right are: Senator Henry Jackson, Chairman John McClellan, Senator Karl Mundt, Senator Edmund Muskie and Senator Carl T. Curtis.

The cast for the movie based on "Advise and Consent" visiting the Senate. Left to right are: Charles Laughton, Henry Fonda, Otto Preminger, Senator Roman L. Kruska, Senator Carl T. Curtis and Allen Drury.

Wife, Lois, with children, son Carl T. Curtis, Jr., and their daughter, Claramae.

Carl T. Curtis and Mrs. Mildred Curtis.

et, which led to his arrest and indictment. This was a device for defrauding nine major finance and investment companies by selling them mortgages on nonexistent storage tanks for anhydrous ammonia. In the fullness of time it turned out that in Reeves County, Texas—Estes' stamping-ground—-the number of such mortgages far exceeded the total number of mortgaged tanks.

Estes' method here was to persuade farmers to buy these tanks on the installment plan, giving mortgages to secure the borrowed money for acquiring (theoretically) a number of tanks. But farmers secured loans on many tanks that existed nowhere, because Estes had not actually delivered those tanks to farmers. Then Estes leased the hypothetical tanks from the farmers, making rental payments to those farmers equal to the installments that the farmers had agreed to pay on their mortgage loans. Although those tank-mortgage loans originally were advanced by Estes to the farmers, Estes proceeded to sell the mortgages to finance companies. Thus Estes conjured riches out of nothing much, at no expense to the participating farmers, but eventually at great expense to the deluded finance companies.

Yet Estes having overreached himself and made discerning enemies with power to expose his storage-tank scheme, his activities were brought to the attention of the Department of Justice and of the Senate's Subcommittee on Investigations in 1962. Among the accusations made against him was the charge that he had bought favors from important officials of the Department of Agriculture and other public employees. This resulted presently in the dismissal or resignation of the men in question, among them an Assistant Secretary of Labor. It was brought to light that Estes had helped some members of Congress with money or favors: Senator Ralph Yarborough of Texas, Representative J. T. Rutherford of Texas, Representative H. Carl Andersen of Minnesota. To what other people might this trail lead?

Already it had led to the upper reaches of the Department of Agriculture; and the Secretary of Agriculture, Orville Freeman, was displeased. Out of Freeman's concern arose an ominous episode worth setting down here.

INVESTIGATORS
INVESTIGATED

In April, 1962, a federal grand jury indicted Estes and three of his associates on charges of fraud, conspiracy, and interstate transportation of fraudulent mortgages. The States Attorney of Texas commenced a vigorous investigation of Estes' activities. On May 4, at a Department of Agriculture press conference, an experienced Agriculture official, N. Battle Hales, accused his superiors of favoritism to Estes in connection with the cotton allotments of 1961. Calling a counter-conference with the press on May 7, Secretary Freeman denied that Estes had obtained favors; the Estes case, he maintained, had been "blown out of all importance." Asked why Estes had been retained as a member of the Department's cotton advisory board after having been fined for overplanting and after the Department's general counsel had found the 1961 allotments to Estes unlawful, Secretary Freeman endeavored to defend the Department's action, or lack of action. He did find it necessary to mention the strange death of Henry Marshall, the Department's official who had been in charge of Texas cotton allotments, a subject to be discussed later in this chapter.

The scandal could not be suppressed. On May 9, the Department announced that penalties of more than half a million dollars were being assessed against Estes for violating cotton-planting allotments in 1961, a rather tardy punishment. President Kennedy, who had congratulated Estes on founding his Pecos newspaper, on May 17 promised an inquiry into Estes: "The government is staying right on Mr. Estes' tail." He defended Secretary Freeman. Senator John McClellan, chairman of the Senate's Permanent Subcommittee on Investigations, announced that an Estes investigation would be undertaken; so did Congressman L. H. Fountain, chairman of the House Intergovernmental Relations Subcommittee.

As these events occurred, information came to Carl Curtis

and to Senator Karl Mundt, of South Dakota, that they were the subjects of an investigation by the Department of Agriculture. Mundt and Curtis were the only Republican members of the Subcommittee on Investigations. They seemed unlikely subjects of an investigation by a branch of the bureaucracy, having good senatorial reputations. Senator Mundt, true, had been singled out for retaliation by the South Dakota Democratic Convention, which had passed a resolution asking that the Investigating Subcommittee, the Attorney General, and the Secretary of Agriculture investigate Mundt, on the charge that a friend of his, a contributor to Mundt's campaign fund, had obtained government storage. This was a partisan red herring. On the eve of the Subcommittee's investigation of the Estes affair, apparently the Secretary of Agriculture hoped to intimidate or to discredit Mundt and Curtis.

For a cabinet officer thus to proceed against members of a senatorial investigating committee was a curiously arrogant development within the Executive Force—and harmful to the constitutional separation of powers. Mundt and Curtis promptly took action.

Calling a press conference, the two senators pointed out that they were the only Republicans on the Subcommittee; and that the Department of Agriculture's investigation was an attempt to intimidate them and to drag in material unrelated to Estes, in an effort to thwart the Senate's investigation of the Estes scandals. Mundt and Curtis obtained affidavits from employees of the Department of Agriculture to the effect that they had been ordered to make a search in federal records-centers for documents pertaining to the two senators, and had so searched. An affidavit obtained from Thomas R. Hughes, executive assistant to the Secretary of Agriculture, admitted that on instructions from Secretary Freeman, Hughes had ordered an investigation of all the correspondence of these two Republican members of the Subcommittee, on the ground that thus the Secretary could better prepare for the imminent investigation by the Subcommittee.

Rejecting this explanation, Mundt and Curtis charged that the Department of Agriculture's search was an attempt at intimidation; that the Department had intended to release bits and pieces of their correspondence to newspaper reporters, thus embarrassing the two senators. In the field of law, such tactics are referred to as "trying the prosecutor."

Moreover, Senator Curtis said, this "investigation" by the Department was insulting to the Democratic members of the Subcommittee on Investigations. Those colleagues on the Subcommittee all were honorable men, Curtis declared; Freeman's assistant's exemption of the Democratic members from investigation implied that the Department of Agriculture already had the Democratic members in its pocket.

The Subcommittee on Investigations proceeded with its hearings. Secretary Freeman having been summoned to testify, Mundt and Curtis and others questioned him. At one point, Senator Curtis said to Secretary Freeman, "You didn't remove anyone from the payroll; you didn't stop Billie Sol Estes; you didn't take any actions against Estes until after he was indicted. Is that correct?" Freeman angrily replied that this was not true; but Curtis pointed out the record in the case.

Freeman did acknowledge that breakdowns had occurred in the Department's handling of the Estes affair, but vigorously denied that Estes had received favors or that the Department had acted against Estes only under the prodding of Texas authorities and of the press.

He was questioned about the searching of files on Mundt and Curtis. Freeman replied that he had authorized the investigation as part of his effort to prepare for the Subcommittee's hearings. "I came to the conclusion that you [the senators] had prejudged, and I better be prepared to answer any questions."

The matter of a charge against Mundt was taken up in the questioning of Freeman. He was asked, "Well, how about Curtis?" How could allegations against Senator Mundt justify an investigation of Senator Curtis? Freeman replied that he figured "they sat together and probably would think alike, too." Apparently the real charge against Mundt and Curtis, in the Secretary's mind, was that they entertained thoughts awkward for the Secretary of Agriculture.

Curtis questioned Freeman about reprisals; he wished to know whether, in retaliation against Mundt and Curtis, the Department of Agriculture would discriminate in its policies against the farmers of South Dakota and Nebraska. In effect, Curtis required Freeman to go on the record as to this possibility. Of course the Secretary stated that nothing of the sort would happen.

Curtis declared that he had no objection to having newspapermen in Nebraska or from elsewhere examine all his relations and correspondence with the Department of Agriculture in past years. Darwin Olafson, a reporter from the Omaha *World-Herald*, inquired of the Department of Agriculture as to what had been discovered by searching Senator Curtis' correspondence. He was told that the Department had examined two hundred and thirty-seven Curtis letters; that all the letters examined had been routine—the sort of correspondence expected from a member of Congress from a farming state, dealing with complaints, requests, and suggestions from constituents. The Department's investigators had found nothing unethical or derogatory to Senator Curtis.

Senator Mundt pointed out that a friend of his, a contributor to Mundt campaign funds, had received government storage, in consequence of which the South Dakota Democratic Convention had demanded an investigation of Mundt. The gist of Mundt's clash with Freeman was expressed in Mundt's challenge to Freeman, "Put up or shut up." Freeman was unable to put up.

As the Lincoln *Journal* summarized this affair editorially, "Unless the Department of Agriculture comes up with a better defense of its singling out the correspondence of two Republican senators probing into its affairs, the public will be inclined to believe the charges of attempted intimidation leveled against the Department by Curtis and Mundt." The Department was unable to make any better defense.

Was Freeman's attempt at intimidation of two senators chiefly the result of bureaucratic arrogance? Or did Freeman fear that investigation of the Estes affair might proceed farther, and have more far-reaching consequences than the investigation actually did cause? That question never was resolved.

MURDEROUS
CORRUPTION

What the Subcommittee's investigation did reveal, fully substantiated charges against Estes by the federal Department of
Justice and by Texas' State Attorney. Estes illegally had acquired cotton allotments from one hundred and sixteen farmers. Testimony from an official of the Department of
Agriculture, Leonard W. Williams, program specialist in the
Agricultural Stabilization and Conservation Service (commonly
ASCS or ASC) office in Texas, showed that Williams had been
painfully aware of Estes' illegal operations. As early as October,
1960, it was revealed in other testimony, officials had ruled that
"Estes-type" transfers of cotton allotments were unlawful; yet
all of the Estes transfers had been approved at state and county levels in Texas.

Unlawful payments had been made by Estes to Agriculture's officials and employees; and Estes had endeavored to influence them by gifts. Assistant Secretary of Agriculture James
T. Ralph was accused of receiving gifts from Estes; he categor-
ically denied the charge. Later, Secretary Freeman obtained information that Dr. Ralph had used Estes' credit card, charging
long-distance calls to Billie Sol; so Ralph had been expelled
from the Department. Freeman testified that he had found out
also that Ralph had accompanied Estes to the Nieman-Marcus
department store in Dallas, where Estes had Ralph fitted for very
costly clothing, under circumstances conveying the impression
that he meant to influence Ralph.

Various Texas employees and representatives of the
Department of Agriculture were shown in testimony to have
received cash payment or gifts from Estes for help in obtaining cotton allotments. There were bigger fish: Emery E. Jacobs,
in Washington, the Department's administrator of state and
county operations of the ASC nationally, had acquired an
elaborate wardrobe at Estes' expense. (Apparently Estes had

handed the wad of cash for the purchase to Jacobs in a Nieman-Marcus dressing room.) At the devil's booth all things are sold. When the question had arisen as to whether Estes' cotton allotments should be canceled, Jacobs had told Thomas H. Miller, deputy director of the southwest area of the ASC, "I want you to send me a report containing every justification that you can find to permit the retention of these allotments."

The Subcommittee received the testimony of M. Battle Hales, an employee of the Department of Agriculture since 1941. Since 1952, his duty had been to review irregularities such as the Billie Sol Estes case. Hales had been outspoken in his conviction that Estes was receiving favors from individuals high in the Department of Agriculture. Once Hales' superiors became aware of this attitude, nothing pertaining to Estes was referred to him. Later his assignment had been changed; his office had been locked against him, and he had been denied access to his own files. His secretary had been committed to a psychopathic ward under an allegation of mental disorder.

Secretary Freeman referred to "emotional distress" suffered by this secretary, Mary Kinbrough Jones. Senator John Williams commented that she had been railroaded to an asylum because she had refused to cooperate in covering up corruption.

When the Subcommittee took up the matter of Estes' sale of mortgages on non-existent tanks for anhydrous ammonia, Senator Curtis questioned Secretary Freeman. That gentleman's reply is revealing:

"Well, first of all, Senator, I think it would be appropriate at this point that the question of the tanks was a matter of Estes' relations with private finance companies who he bilked of thirty million dollars and the federal government didn't lose a dime in doing business with him."

Apparently the Secretary saw no reason why so shrewd an operator as Estes should not sit on the federal government's National Cotton Advisory Council. Estes had been appointed to that Council after many unpleasant facts about him had been made known to the Department of Agriculture. Nor had the Secretary made any attempt to remove Estes from the Council until after Estes' arrest. So as late as May 7, 1962, Freeman had been asked at a press conference about Estes' membership on that council. Freeman had said then, "This allotment business is just a lawyers' quarrel."

Further testimony indicated that Estes had profited handsomely from unusual and highly favorable contracts for the storage of the government's grain. A certified public accountant had helped Estes in this deal by transferring to his own letterhead figures about Estes' net worth (in connection with a government-required bond) supplied by Estes himself.

Orville Freeman had been warned about Estes' character. On November 21, 1961, John E. Francis, chief of the Agriculture Department's review and judication division, had written to Joseph Robertson, Administrative Assistant to the Secretary, concerning Estes: "I recommend against subject's appointment. The service investigation made regarding subject is sufficiently derogatory in nature that I so recommend."

Yet on December 22, 1961, Joseph Robertson had signed a memorandum recommending appointment of Estes to the Cotton Advisory Council. Estes had very influential friends in Washington.

It was revealed in testimony that despite much evidence of gifts by Estes to Agriculture officials and employees, none of those happy recipients had been removed from office until April 3, 1962, by which time the Department of Justice and the Subcommittee on Investigations were stirring against Estes. Evidence of corrupt deals and use of political influence acquired by gifts to officials was too extensive to be detailed here. No employee of the Department had been suspended or expelled or asked to resign, in connection with these offenses, until the Estes scandals had been exposed in the press and had come under the scrutiny of investigators outside the Department of Agriculture.

Billie Sol Estes' generosity had been extended to other departments of the federal government. Employing much Mexican labor, Estes had obtained the fixing of a wage-rate for his region below the wage paid in other areas. The Subcommittee was informed that he had presented a check for a thousand dollars to Jerry Holleman, Assistant Secretary of Labor. Summoned before the Subcommittee, Estes was questioned about this by Senator Curtis. Appealing to the Fifth Amendment, Estes refused to answer Curtis' several questions on the grounds that he might incriminate himself. (Holleman found it necessary to resign office because of this payment.) On every question put to him by Subcommittee members or staff, Estes took the Fifth Amendment.

Although various Department of Agriculture employees cooperated readily with Estes, accepting his money, his gifts of clothing, hats, hams, lockers full of beef, hotel rooms, and air tickets, most officials and employees of the Department were honest people not to be bribed or intimidated. One such was Henry H. Marshall, who paid for his integrity with his life.

Marshall was a program specialist in the Texas state office of the Department of Agriculture, one of that department's outstanding civil servants. In the spring of 1959 he had received an award from the Department for distinguished service, at a presentation in Washington. Officials of the Department testified to the Subcommittee about his high repute. Marshall had assigned Leonard Williams (who had testified early in the Subcommittee's hearings) to look into Texan cotton allotments, with results highly unpleasant for Estes. It had been Marshall who had exposed Estes' malefactions.

Baldwin P. Davenport, of Sanford, Texas, a farmer who was chairman of the Texas ASC Committee, told the Subcommittee that at meetings in November, 1960, and January, 1961, Marshall had displayed documents related to the Estes case, and had stated that the program was being abused; he would submit the documents to Agriculture's general counsel at Washington. Marshall, doubtful about the legality of these Estes arrangements, would seek advice. Other witnesses testified concerning Marshall's efforts to prevent fraud and to carry on investigation. Marshall had conferred with Dennison and Naylor, Estes' lawyers, telling them that the Estes cotton assignments were invalid and that he could not go along with them. Cross-examination of a witness by Senator Edmund Muskie established the point that Marshall had told Estes' principal lawyer that Estes was engaged in an illegal scheme.

So if Billie Sol Estes were to succeed in his unlawful acquiring of more than three thousand acres of cotton allotment—or, more precisely, if Estes were to escape criminal indictment and Estes' associates were to escape disgrace or worse—something must be done to quiet Henry Marshall, who did not accept gifts. That something happened.

Marshall was found dead on his farm on June 2, 1961. He had been shot five times by his own .22 caliber bolt-action rifle, which measured twenty-nine inches from the trigger to the end of the muzzle. It was a seven-shot gun; for each firing, it was necessary to raise a round knob on the right side of the weapon, slide it forward, and then push it down again. Three bullets, close together, had entered near Marshall's navel; two had penetrated three or four inches to the left. It was clear that for some of these shots, the gun must have been pointed at the victim's left side.

On discovery of the corpse, the local justice of the peace, Lee Farmer, ruled that Marshall's death had been by his own hand. (In Texas, justices of the peace have functions exercised by coroners in most other states.)

Almost a year later, after inquiry into Estes' doings had commenced, Marshall's body was exhumed and a pathologist performed an autopsy saying, "It was not a suicide." The doctor reported that Marshall had a high percentage of carbon monoxide in his blood at the time of death; also a bruise on the left side of his head and a cut over the left eye. The bruise, which had occurred before death, would have been incapacitating, in the pathologist's judgment. Yet in his final report to a district judge, the doctor did not absolutely rule out the possibility of suicide, though stating that in medical probability it had been death by homicide. (On July 19, 1962, the director of the Texas Department of Public Safety sent a letter to the district judge and to Chairman McClellan, stating that Marshall's death could not have been suicide.)

In June, 1963, a grand jury was convened in Robertson County to investigate Marshall's death; it was in session for many weeks, hearing one hundred and thirty-one witnesses. Most curiously, this grand jury sustained the earlier ruling of suicide. Twenty years later, at the end of 1983, this verdict still stood, as Carl Curtis ascertained through correspondence with the district clerk of Robertson County. But another grand jury, in 1984, would alter this verdict.

After Marshall's death, Billie Sol Estes and his associates claimed that Marshall had approved the Estes cotton allotments, finding their acquisition lawful. An official assisting the general counsel of the Department of Agriculture testified to the Subcommittee that all ASC county committees in Reeves and Pecos Counties alleged that they had been instructed by Marshall—now in no position to contradict them—not to inquire about "displaced owners" of cotton allotments.

Estes had stood to lose two to three million dollars, should his cotton allotments be declared illegal. Growing alarmed, Estes had said he would take up the matter with Secretary Freeman and with the President, if necessary. He and his lawyer had met with Freeman on January 6, 1962, evidence showed; and Freeman then had made a notation to the effect that Estes and his attorney, on that occasion, had stated that they acted in the matter of cotton allotments on the advice of state and county committees, and in conformity to the advice of Henry Marshall.

Dead, Marshall could not refute this pretense that he had approved Estes' scheme and had silenced county committees. It was well for Estes that dead men never rise up.

Billie Sol Estes never was charged with the murder of Marshall, but he went to prison for other felonies. Convicted in 1965 for his fertilizer-tank fraud, he was sentenced to fifteen years' imprisonment. Emerging from prison on parole in 1971, he was convicted anew in 1979 on charges of fraud and tax-evasion. He was released again in 1983, now professing to have experienced an evangelical Christian conversion behind bars.

REVELATIONS
OF BILLIE SOL

In March, 1984, twenty-three years after Henry Marshall had been silenced, another grand jury in Robertson County looked into that mystery. Clint Peoples, a United States marshal who had been a Texas Ranger assigned to investigating Marshall's end in 1962, appeared as a witness. Peoples told the grand jury that in 1962 political pressures had been exerted on him to concur in the local verdict of suicide. By a curious coincidence, Peoples had been the federal marshal who had escorted Estes to prison at El Paso in 1979.

In a conversation during that trip to El Paso, Billie Sol had told Clint Peoples that Peoples had been "looking in the wrong direction" in suspecting Estes of Marshall's murder.

Peoples inquired, "Where should I look?"

"You ought to look to the people who have the most to lose," Estes said.

"Washington?" Peoples asked.

"Yes." And Estes had sworn to Peoples that he would clear up the Marshall case for him.

Before the new grand jury in Robertson County, in 1984, Estes professed to do precisely that. He stated that he had contributed heavily to Johnson's campaign funds; and that Johnson, in exchange, had arranged Estes' illegal transfers of cotton allotments. Clifton Carter, one of Johnson's aides, was deeply involved in this arrangement. The exposing of Estes' cotton-allotment frauds might be ruinous for Carter; it might adversely affect the interests and prospects of Vice-President Johnson—or so Billie Sol told the grand jury in 1984.

The name of Lyndon Baines Johnson had not figured in the hearings of the Subcommittee on Investigations. That name would have to wait until the Bobby Baker investigations years later. Lyndon Johnson was an ill man to cross; yet it was rumored widely during 1961 and 1962 that Johnson-Estes connections existed. Johnson long had been accomplished at dealing with courthouse gangs in Texan rural counties, the sort of people Estes courted. It was rumored in Texas, while Johnson was Vice-President, that Lady Bird Johnson was the major stockholder in Commercial Solvents, a firm manufacturing anhydrous ammonia, which had advanced to Estes nearly one million dollars; that the big finance companies lent money readily to Estes because they knew of his connections with the Johnsons; that Estes bought a plane for LBJ to use in campaigning; that various private meetings had occurred between Johnson and Estes. But none of these reports came within the cognizance of the Subcommittee on Investigations.

Certainly Estes seemed to have powerful but invisible political protectors, until he became quite indefensible. The identity of his chief protector is clear enough today. Estes' daughter, Pam, writes of Estes' fund-raising picnic for Senator Ralph Yarborough in 1961, "Hundreds of people attended that picnic and Ralph Yarborough raised a great deal of money, most of it coming from Daddy—in cash. During that time, Daddy had been supplying Lyndon Johnson with large infusions of cash, not only for his own political needs, but for people Johnson, himself, chose to help. Sometimes, he would send people like Ralph Yarborough directly to Daddy for fund raising help. On other occasions, Johnson would get bundles of cash from Daddy and distribute it himself. Since these transactions were all cash, there is no reliable way of knowing how much money went to Johnson or what became of it.'' She mentions one cash contribution, its delivery demanded by Johnson of Estes during an early-morning telephone conversation, in the amount of five hundred thousand dollars. It would be a lawyer patronized and recommended by Lyndon Johnson who would defend Billie Sol at his first trial.*

With this recently-revealed relationship between Estes and Vice-President Johnson in mind, Billie Sol Estes' testimony to the Robertson grand jury in 1984 is less astounding than once

---

* See Pam Estes, *Billie Sol: King of Texas Wheeler-Dealers* (Abilene, Texas, 1983).

it would have seemed. Here is the essence of that testimony, as reported by three newspapers.

When Estes found himself in danger of great financial loss, and perhaps worse, in consequence of Henry Marshall's inquiry into the Estes cotton allotments during 1961, a meeting had been held at Vice-President Johnson's residence in Washington. There were present Johnson, Estes, Clifton Carter, and one Malcolm Wallace.

This Wallace had been a close friend of Johnson's sister Josefa; in 1944 and 1945 he had been president of the student body of the University of Texas. In 1951, Wallace had been convicted of murder in the first degree, in Austin, but had received merely a suspended sentence. When apprehended in flight from the scene of the murder, he had told police that they must let him go—he worked for Lyndon Johnson. (These people, including Josefa, all were in their graves by 1984, except for Estes.)

On that sinister occasion at the Vice-President's residence —so Estes' account to the grand jury ran—Lyndon Johnson feared that if Estes were to fall, Carter would be involved in the ruin. And Clifton Carter knew a great deal about Johnson's confidential affairs. Everything had rested upon the knowledge and actions of Henry Marshall, who could not be corrupted. So Johnson directed that Marshall be killed; and that task was assigned to Malcolm Wallace.

That is what Billie Sol Estes told the Robertson County grand jury in 1984. And the grand jury believed him, or at least believed him enough to reject the finding of suicide that the grand jury of 1963 had accepted. This second grand jury, after testimony from Estes and from Peoples, concluded that Marshall's death had been a homicide; but no person was indicted for the crime, the grand jury's presumption being that the murderers already were dead. In the summer of 1985, a Texan judge ordered that the verdict on Marshall's death be changed officially to "homicide."

Doubtless the jury found Estes' story startling; yet they did not find it incredible. Walter Jenkins, once Johnson's chief assistant, was questioned by newspapermen concerning Estes' testimony before the grand jury. Jenkins said that Johnson and

Estes had met together only twice, and that neither of those times was the sinister gathering described by Estes. Later, questioned again by the press, Jenkins admitted that he might have lied. Jenkins' veracity will be touched upon in the following chapter of this book.

Probably the grand jurors of Robertson County had heard certain persistent rumors of Lyndon Johnson's ruthlessness; and of how certain people, who at various times might have supplied testimony very awkward for Johnson, had feared that they might come to an untimely end. There were unsubstantiated rumors that some such persons indeed *had* come to untimely ends.

Lyndon Baines Johnson was a hard man, avaricious, fiercely ambitious. If he suffered from scruples, few described them. He had accumulated wealth in labyrinthine ways.

Johnson having always an eye to the main chance, on the face of the matter it seems as if he would have sacrificed his assistant Clifton Carter rather than have involved himself in a homicide, that being a risky venture for a Vice-President. Certainly, two years later, he cast off his close associate Bobby Baker, once Baker had become too scandalous to own. Yet perhaps Carter knew too much to be cast aside: indicted, Carter might have talked, for there is plea-bargaining. And the Attorney General of the United States, In 1961, was Robert Kennedy, who had sent Jimmy Hoffa to prison; Robert Kennedy, who detested Johnson. If there is any truth in Estes' story, it was well for Lyndon Johnson that Henry Marshall should cease to be, for the Estes-Johnson connection must remain rumor merely, in 1961.

Billie Sol Estes had been a notorious confidence man, twice convicted. Yet what motive had Estes to shift the blame to Johnson, through testimony that revealed Estes' own complicity in a conspiracy to murder? True, the grand jury of 1984 had granted Estes immunity from prosecution, so far as lay in the grand jury's power; but that was no sure protection. And no man gains advantage from holding himself up to public reproach for high crimes.

More may be learned some day about this crime and the participants in it, although most of the people involved in the

Estes cotton-allotment scheme now are dead or elderly. In 1964, Estes was said by friends of his to have feared for his own life, in prison or out of it, if he should talk while Lyndon Johnson was alive and kicking. And he was said, too, to have taken the Fifth Amendment when questioned by the Subcommittee on investigations out of dread of Vice-President Johnson's efficacy at retaliation.

Also more may be learned, just possibly, about the alleged intention of President Kennedy and Attorney General Kennedy to arrange the assassination of Fidel Castro; and about the part of certain high American officials in the overthrow and murder of President Diem, in South Vietnam; and about other curious fatal events in the years of the Second Camelot. Will there be published, some day, *The Secret History of the New Frontier?* The Congress did not investigate the grim incidents mentioned above; and Chief Justice Warren's investigation of the assassination of President Kennedy was interestingly superficial. The whole truth about that murder, the Chief Justice said, might not be known for a century. How much else lies hidden?

In the case of Estes, the hearings of the Subcommittee on Investigations had limited aims and results. So it is generally with congressional investigations: they cannot possibly be comprehensive, but they may bring to light what ought not to have been hid. A piece of corrective legislation did come out of the Subcommittee's recommendations: Congress established within the Department of Agriculture the office of an inspector-general, with power to report directly to the Secretary.

Yet the muddy Estes trail was ascended no higher than an Assistant Secretary of Agriculture and an Assistant Secretary of Labor. The investigation did not disclose what pressures may have been brought to bear in Robertson County upon a justice of the peace and a grand jury so that they would insist, in defiance of reason, that Marshall had killed himself with a bolt-action rifle, even though his arm could not have extended from muzzle to trigger.

Nevertheless, the Estes investigation did suggest what splendid and frequent grand-scale opportunities for corruption exist within the intricate programs of a government that presumes to be omnicompetent. It did give notice of the trifles—

hats, hams, beef—for which some public officials may be bought. It did reveal, behind the flimsy stage-curtain of the New Frontier, a dreary vista of pestilent backwoods. And, in the light of later evidence, that investigation opened the way to an understanding of how corruption possibly may extend to the highest magistracy in the nation: to Caesar.

Chapter 9

Investigating Bobby Baker: or, The Art of The Cover-Up

THE ASCENDANCY OF THE CONTACT-MAN

Among Senator Curtis' responsibilities during the Johnson administration, one of the more interesting—but also one of the more depressing—was his part in the investigation of the Bobby Baker scandals. The notorious case of Baker demonstrates how a congressional investigation may be frustrated by the influence of executive power and partisan allegiance.

In 1943, a fourteen-year-old boy left his home at Pickens, South Carolina, to become a page in the United States Senate. He was a likable youth of considerable talents, getting along with most folks; as an employee of the Senate, he advanced rapidly.

This young man rose to be chief telephone page for the Democrats. His job was to manage the Democratic cloakrooms and direct the activity of the other pages who ran errands and answered telephone calls. Presently he became assistant secretary to the Democratic majority. In 1955, when Senator Lyndon Baines Johnson, of Texas, was chosen Senate majority leader, this young man—then twenty-six years old—became secretary to the Majority, and so a chief aide to Senator Johnson.

This young man, Robert Baker, was known to everyone as Bobby Baker. His energy seemed inexhaustible; he had the knack of working with people. As secretary to the Majority, Baker was privy to the leadership councils on legislative strategy. Standing at the door of the Senate chamber, he told the Democratic senators what measure was under consideration, and the leadership's position on that measure. He developed an ability to forecast the outcome of close votes in the Senate. A good fund-raiser, Baker served as the unpaid treasurer of the Senate Democratic Campaign Committee from 1957 to 1960.

At the close of the Senate's session in 1956, Senator Johnson had taken the floor to say that Baker's quick intelligence had kept the machinery on the Democrats' side of the aisle "working with smooth precision."

Yet it was a mistake to have as the Senate employee who stood at the door, telling Democrats how their leader would like them to vote, the very person who would play a part in raising and distributing funds to re-elect those Democratic senators. This brought the secretary of the Majority into close relations with every Democratic senator; also it put some of those senators under a feeling of obligation toward Baker. This blunder of inadequately defining the duties of Senate employees may have led to Baker's dubious business activities, achieved through influence-peddling.

When Bobby Baker began as a page in 1943, his salary was $1,460 a year. Yet he soon became a wealthy man. The minority report of the committee that investigated his activities (filed on July 8, 1964) had this to say about Baker's amassing of wealth:

"According to financial statements submitted by Baker, he had a net worth of $11,025 as of May 3, 1954. As of February 1, 1963, Baker claimed a net worth of $2,166,886. It is agreed, however, that this latter figure carried errors and exaggerations. After the known errors are taken into account, Baker's claimed net worth would be $1,664, 287. However, it may well be contended that Baker over-valued his Serv-U Corporation stock, with its very lucrative contracts in plants having huge government defense contracts, as well as his stock in the Mecklenburg enterprises and his land near Silver Springs, Maryland. If these assets are carried at their actual cost, Baker still would have a net worth of $447,849. It is obvious that these three assets were very valuable and their value had increased considerably over Baker's initial investment.''

The Committee's records show that between January, 1959, and November, 1963, Baker and his associates had borrowed $2,784,338 from lending institutions. These loans had come from twenty-four banks and other lending institutions. The Committee's investigator also reported that Baker's share in approximately six different loans was $1,704,538.

All the time that Baker was making himself a man of wealth, he continued to serve as a most important and influential employee of the United States Senate.

Fred B. Black, Jr., a management consultant whose clients included North American Aviation and Melpar, Inc., and who was associated with Baker in several business ventures, said that the late Senator Robert S. Kerr, of Oklahoma, had told him that outside of his sons and his wife, he never knew and loved a person so much as he did Bobby Baker; that there was nothing Kerr would not do for Baker if he would ask him. Later Black said that he and Baker and the Serv-U Corporation had borrowed over half a million dollars from Kerr's Oklahoma City Bank.

Baker's operations became a subject of some discussion, raising questions in the minds of several senators and Senate employees. Eventually, on September 9, 1963, a law-suit was filed by Ralph L. Hill, president of the Capitol Vending Company, which alleged wrongdoing and the use of governmental influence in Baker's business dealings.

In his suit, Hill alleged that Baker had employed political influence to obtain contracts in defense plants for his own vending-machine firm, called Serv-U Corporation. Hill also charged that Baker had accepted $5,600 for securing a vending-machine franchise for Capitol Vending with Melpar, Inc., a defense plant in Virginia. Hill stated that after Capitol had secured the contract with Melpar, Baker had tried to persuade Capitol

Vending to sell out to the Serv-U Corporation; and that when Capitol refused to sell its stock to Serv-U, Baker had conspired maliciously to interfere with Capitol's contract with Melpar. The suit contended that Baker had told Fred B. Black, Jr., that he, Baker, was in a position to help obtain contracts with the government. Hill said that in return, North American (to which Black was a consultant) entered into an agreement to permit Serv-U to install vending machines in its Californian plants.

The filing of this suit brought to light many unpleasant facts, reflecting not only on Bobby Baker but on those men about him and on the Senate generally.

At this point, Senator John Williams, of Delaware, began to take an active part. Williams was a man beyond reproach, sincere and intelligent and dedicated. During his service in the Senate he was rightly referred to as "the conscience of the Senate." He was an expert investigator, tenacious and courageous. Senator Williams became the prime mover in bringing about the investigation of Baker.

On October 3, 1963, Williams went to Senator Mike Mansfield, the majority leader, and to Senator Everett McKinley Dirksen, the minority leader, and arranged for them to call Baker before the leadership at a closed meeting on October 8. It was Senator Williams' plan to confront Baker with questions about his activities. Bobby Baker never appeared before the Senate's leadership: the day before his scheduled appearance he resigned his post with its salary of $19,600.

Senator Mansfield, announcing Bobby Baker's resignation, said that "Baker has discharged his official duties for eight years with great intelligence and understanding. His great ability and his dedication to the Majority and to the Senate will be missed." Developments during recent weeks, however, Senator Mansfield continued, had made it apparent that it would be best if Baker withdrew from office. "I deeply regret the necessity for his resignation and the necessity for its acceptance."

Senator Williams introduced a resolution calling upon the Committee on Rules and Administration to conduct an investigation of the financial and business interests and possible improprieties of any Senate employee or former employee. On October 10, 1963, the Senate adopted this resolution by voice vote.

The Committee on Rules and Administration was made up of nine members, six Democrats and three Republicans. The Committee's chairman was B. Everett Jordan, Democrat, of North Carolina. The other Democratic members were Carl Hayden, of Arizona; Claiborne Pell, of Rhode Island; Joseph Clark, of Pennsylvania; Howard W. Cannon, of Nevada; and Robert C. Byrd, of West Virginia. The Republican members were John Sherman Cooper, of Kentucky; Hugh Scott, of Pennsylvania; and Carl T. Curtis.

This Committee held its first meeting for the Baker investigation on October 29. Senator Williams, testifying in closed session, recommended that the Committee investigate the FBI files of a deported East German woman, a Mrs. Ellen Rometsch (otherwise known as Elli Rometsch), who had been identified in news stories as a "party girl" associating with lobbyists and members of Congress. He urged also that the Committee look into Baker's transactions with the Mortgage Guaranty Insurance Corporation; into the large sums of cash given by Bobby Baker to Mrs. Gertrude Novak, wife of a business partner of Baker; into the vending contract referred to in Hill's suit against Baker.

Additionally, Williams recommended that the Committee investigate circumstances surrounding the rapid growth of the Serv-U Corporation, Baker's company; charges against Baker with reference to irregularities connected with the Senate payroll of pages and other employees working under Baker; Baker's brokerage-fee from the Haitian-American Meat Provision Company. The Committee should look into the transactions between Baker and Don Reynolds connected with Reynolds' selling of insurance to Senator Lyndon B. Johnson, Williams continued. The Committee should check the performance-bond for the building of the stadium at Washington.

Having heard Senator Williams, the three Republicans on the Committee requested that the Committee hire outside counsel to conduct the investigation. This move was opposed by the six Democrats on the Committee. Chairman Jordan, presently yielding to public pressure, announced on November 13 that L. F. McLendon, a lawyer from Jordan's home state of North Carolina, was appointed outside counsel.

The Committee on Rules and Administration needed to agree on some procedures. In this the Committee received considerable help from the Subcommittee on Investigations of the Government Operations Committee, headed by Senator John McClellan, of Arkansas. McClellan had followed a procedure of first calling a witness—particularly a controversial witness—in a closed session of the Committee, to inform the Committee what to expect and how to frame their questions. Later the witness would be called in public session. In the investigation of Baker, this rule was not followed, as we shall see later in this account of the great cover-up.

Bobby Baker was a highly successful contact-man. During and after the Second World War, on either side of the Atlantic, the contact-man loomed large. Contact-men existed primarily to obtain for their clients and themselves some share of the vast pool of riches in the possession of swollen centralized political bureaucracies. The more impressive a contact-man's political connections, the better he and his clients would fare. Professor W. L. Burn, in England, well described this international phenomenon:

"One may imagine the stage festooned with forms, applications for licenses, refusals of licenses, checks that failed to command confidence and agreements that failed to produce the desired result. Music is supplied by the ringing of the telephone, the prelude to ambiguous and improbable conversations; and through the half-lit jungle, from public dinner to government department, from government department to sherry party, glides the contact-man, at once the product and the safety-valve of this grotesque civilization."

In Washington, Bobby Baker had become a principal actor in such tragi-comic dramas.

JOHNSON, BAKER, JENKINS

Baker was called as a witness early in the investigation, appearing both in a closed session and in a public session. He had received a subpoena directing him to appear and to produce certain documents. Senator Curtis requested him to submit the required records. Baker refused. The following extracts from the Committee's hearings may suffice to suggest Baker's response. (It should be remembered in this connection that a witness's refusal to answer on the ground that he might incriminate himself raises a legitimate presumption that indeed the witness has committed some act which might subject him to a criminal prosecution.)

Replying to Senator Curtis, Baker refused to produce the desired records. He declared that he had so informed the committee earlier, and therefore should not have been called back to repeat his position.

"Today's proceedings are an unconstitutional invasion by the legislative branch into the proper function of the judiciary," Baker argued. "I do not intend to participate as a defendant witness in a legislative trial of myself, when my counsel has no right to cross-examine my accusers, or summon witnesses in my defense, and when the testimony has been taken both in secret and in the open."

Baker continued that the records were not "pertinent to any *bona fide* legislative purpose." A case pending in the U. S. District Court of the District of Columbia, he mentioned, in volved some of the documents called for. "I am presently being investigated by two agencies of the executive branch, the Federal Bureau of Investigation and the Internal Revenue Service. To force production of these records against this background would be to do indirectly for these agencies what they cannot lawfully do direct." Moreover, his "privacy of communication" had been invaded by government personnel, so he was refusing to provide any additional information to government agents. Baker concluded by invoking "the protection of the first, the fourth, the fifth, and the sixth amendments of the Constitution, and I specifically invoke the privilege against self-incrimination."

So it went through the questioning of Bobby Baker. Altogether, he "took the Fifth" in response to a hundred and twenty questions.

Senator Curtis asked him, "Will you advise the committee whether or not you acquired the cash referred to by Mrs. Novak in the course of your duties as secretary to the Majority of the U. S. Senate?" Baker "stood on his previous answer"— that is, refused to answer the question.

Later, Curtis inquired, "Mr. Baker, a previous witness, Mr. Hill, testified under oath that he paid to you the sum of $250 for a number of months for the purpose of securing and keeping a contract which his company, the Capitol Vending Company, had with a government-contracting defense plant. Will you advise us whether or not Mr. Hill's testimony is true?"

Baker refused. Still later, Curtis told him: "Now, Mr. Baker, I hope that you will consider this question carefully, and the rights of all people involved. The witness, Mr. Don Reynolds, has testified that he gave to one Lyndon Johnson a hi-fi set costing something over five hundred dollars. Statements have been made elsewhere that you were the giver of the gift. Will you tell this committee whether or not you made that gift?"

Baker refused. Then came a related key question from Senator Curtis:

"Mr. Baker—Mr. Reynolds, while under oath, testified before this committee concerning this hi-fi gift. He produced certain canceled checks and invoices. He also testified that he purchased $1,200 worth of television time on a TV station in Austin, Texas. My question is: did you have any part in that transaction?"

Baker refused to answer that question, too, and many more.

It became clear in the course of the investigation that Baker's secretary, Nancy Carole Tyler, had assisted Baker in business transactions handled in his office and during his travels; and that she had handled funds involved in these transactions.

Subpoenaed, Tyler was asked by McLendon, the Committee's counsel, certain important questions. Counsel inquired about trips made by Baker to Los Angeles in connection with the business of the Serv-U Corporation; and when Tyler had resigned her position with Baker, secretary to the majority. Tyler refused to answer on the ground that she might incriminate herself.

The Committee learned no more from Carole Tyler; before the investigation ended, Tyler died suddenly and somewhat mysteriously in an airplane crash on the beach near the Carousel Motel, owned by Bobby Baker.

The key witness in the investigation was Don Reynolds, an insurance agent in the Washington area. He and Baker had been friends, and Baker was an officer in Don Reynolds, Inc., although Baker had not supplied any money for the forming of that company. Reynolds had been associated in, or was familiar with, many of Bobby Baker's transactions that were under investigation. After consulting with his wife and with Senator Williams, Reynolds decided to testify in full, under oath, whenever called upon by the Committee.

Reynolds said that he had sold insurance on the life of Lyndon Baines Johnson in the amount of two hundred thousand dollars; and that he had to make a "kickback" on the premium he received. The transaction with Johnson had been conducted through Walter Jenkins, a close aide to Johnson. (Jenkins later was disgraced by his arrest for soliciting homosexual acts in the men's room at the YMCA, late in 1964.) Baker had arranged Reynolds' appointment with Jenkins. Facing competition, Reynolds had bought $1,208 in advertising on Johnson's television station in Austin; Reynolds had re-sold this advertising contract, losing $1,100 on the deal. (This "kickback" arrangement had occurred while Lyndon Johnson still was senator from Texas.)

"Why did you purchase the television time?" Senator Curtis asked.

Mr. Reynolds: "Mr. Jenkins, in his discussion with me, showed me a letter from Mr. Huff Baines, indicating that if he had the privilege of writing...that he would purchase so much advertising time on the local·station, KTBC."

Under more questioning from Curtis, it turned out that

Station KTBC, in Austin, was owned by the LBJ Company. Reynolds went on: "And I told him that although I might not be able to do the same as far as dollar volume, that I would do the best I could, consistent with the fact that the contract I had offered him was the most favorable, if you exclude any question of advertising, sir."

Curtis proceeded to obtain from Reynolds the testimony that Walter Jenkins had informed him he was expected to buy advertising from Lyndon Johnson's television station if he wanted the insurance contract. He had sold the contracted advertising time to Albert G. Young, president of Mid-Atlantic Stainless Steel, "because I saw no use whatsoever for Don Reynolds, who was unknown in Texas, sir, to get people to listen to something they had no interest in, nor could they." Walter Jenkins had confirmed this deal by telephone to Young, whose firm sold pots and pans. After Jenkins had called him, Young went to Austin and utilized the advertising facilities of KTBC; this was corroborated by Young's canceled checks, invoices, and correspondence, shown to the Committee.

This testimony obviously alarmed the majority members of the Committee and the Committee's counsel. At the time of this investigation, Lyndon Baines Johnson was President of the United States; Walter Jenkins was one of the President's aides in the White House, handling much of Johnson's private business. Lyndon Baines Johnson had entered Congress a man of very modest means; but by the time he assumed the presidency, he was a very rich man.

A principal source of Johnson's wealth appeared to be the television station he had acquired in Austin. KTCB was the only television station licensed in Austin; and every other city in the United States, the size of Austin, had at least two television stations. Such licenses were issued by the Federal Communications Commission, upon which political influence might be exercised by persons in power not overly scrupulous. How had Johnson and his family obtained a monopoly of Austin television? To what additional awkward testimony about KTCB might the statements of Reynolds and Young lead if this subject should be pursued?

Therefore, in an effort to prevent Walter Jenkins—former

Senate employee, now a White House aide—from being called before the Committee to give sworn testimony, Counsel McLendon had Jenkins sign an affidavit: an affidavit unique in that Jenkins swore to the truth of a memorandum which was written by the Committee's chief counsel and chief investigator. This curious memorandum, referring to Jenkins, stated, "Nor does he have any knowledge of any arrangements by which Reynolds purchased advertising time on the TV station."

Unimpressed by this remarkable document, Senator Curtis further questioned Reynolds. "Well, then," he asked the witness, "do you agree or disagree with this statement of Jenkins that Mr. McLendon, our counsel, has put in the record, as a statement, not of oral testimony but sworn to before a notary public: 'Nor does he have any knowledge of any arrangements by which Reynolds purchased advertising time on the TV station.' You would disagree with that?"

Reynolds disagreed completely with the statement. In further testimony, it was learned that Huff Baines, of Austin, Reynolds' alleged competitor for the sale of insurance to Lyndon Baines Johnson, was a cousin of Johnson, and had sold a number of policies on the lives of people connected with the LBJ Company. Even though Reynolds had offered a better insurance contract than Baines had, it appeared, he had been required to provide advertising revenue to the Johnson station and the gift of a high-fidelity set as sweeteners, lest the contract be awarded to kinsman Baines. And Baker had made the deal.

Throughout these hearings, the Republican members of the Committee—Cooper, Scott, and Curtis—repeatedly endeavored to have Walter Jenkins called as a witness. Jenkins had been employed by Johnson for years. It was well established that he had handled many of Johnson's business concerns. The information given to the Committee by Reynolds clearly conflicted with the memorandum to which Jenkins had subscribed. This could be resolved only by calling Jenkins as a witness.

On March 23, 1964, occurred a roll call on the question of calling Jenkins; the vote went along party lines. Why did these six prominent Democratic senators, several of them leaders of their party, vote against hearing and cross-examining

Jenkins? After all, this elusive Jenkins had been an employee of the Senate; he enjoyed no senatorial immunity, nor was he the beneficiary of the usual "senatorial courtesy" tradition. The determined and successful fight by the Committee's majority to prevent the receiving of Jenkins' testimony may have been waged not to protect Walter Jenkins or Bobby Baker, but rather Jenkins ' principal—Lyndon B. Johnson.

The purchase of time on the LBJ broadcasting station was not the only kickback required of Don Reynolds for selling insurance on Lyndon Johnson, for Reynolds was requested to provide a hi-fi set for Senator Johnson. Reynolds, questioned by McLendon, stated that he had bought a Magnavox stereo set, costing him $584.75, and installed it in Senator Johnson's Washington residence (also paying for the installation) in 1959. But Mrs. Johnson had found the set unsatisfactory: it did not fit the space for which she had intended it. In response to questioning from two Democratic senators, Reynolds made it clear that Bobby Baker had told him to give the set to Senator Johnson, and that Johnson knew Reynolds to be the donor.

At a news conference, Johnson had told a reporter that the set was a gift from Bobby Baker. There were two witnesses who might clear up the questions as to whether the set was given by Baker or whether it was an obligation put upon Reynolds for his opportunity to sell life insurance to Johnson. Those two witnesses were Baker and Jenkins. Baker took the Fifth Amendment, refusing to testify on the ground that he might be incriminated. Walter Jenkins, protected by the Committee's majority, was not called to testify.

Later that year, in the closing days of the Johnson-Goldwater race for the presidency, television technicians in Los Angeles wore a large round button, on which was inscribed the legend, "Johnson, Baker, Jenkins. The family that plays together stays together."

MASTER BUILDERS, VENDING MACHINES, AND MOTELS

In terms of money, the affair of the hi-fi was a small matter by the side of the scandal about the construction of the stadium in the District of Columbia. Its builder was Matthew McCloskey, treasurer of the Democratic Party for a long period, and at the time of this investigation the ambassador to Ireland. Bobby Baker and Don Reynolds had been involved in the stadium scandal, as had been William McLeod, at that time clerk of the District of Columbia Committee of the House of Representatives. That Committee handled the legislation required for the building of the stadium.

Questioned by McLendon, Don Reynolds revealed that in the spring of 1960 he had participated in a meeting at Bobby Baker's office, called by Baker, attended also by McCloskey, McLeod, and Congressman John M. McMillan. McCloskey received the contract for the stadium, and Reynolds, as a broker, wrote the bond for the contract, with a premium on the bond of $73,631. Reynolds' commission on this performance bond was slightly more than ten thousand dollars. Shortly thereafter, Reynolds paid Bobby Baker the sum of four thousand dollars, "in compensation for his services in connection with the procurement of that bond." In addition, Reynolds was billed by William McLeod, clerk of the House District of Columbia Committee, for "legal services" in connection with the bond, for the sum of $1,500, which Reynolds paid. The two clerks for Senate and House did well out of the bond contract for the stadium, with the knowledge of the contractor and a member of the House.

So the minority on the investigating committee pressed for calling Ambassador McCloskey to testify. He would be asked to give his version of that meeting in Baker's Capitol office; and why the performance bond for the stadium was handled by Reynolds as broker, when the firm actually acting as agent for the bond was Hutchinson, Rivinus, and Company, with which Matthew McCloskey's son-in-law was associated. He would have been asked, too, what he knew about Reynolds' kickback of four thousand dollars to Baker, and about other kickbacks, including the payment by Reynolds to McLeod. McCloskey had erected many other costly government buildings; he would have been asked what dealings, if any, he had had with Baker or any other Senate employee, or any senator or former senator, in connection with other government contracts for construction.

Senator Curtis asked that McCloskey be called. The Committee's chairman responded, after discussion, "Well, I'm going to be forced to rule that it is not pertinent to what we are doing here and we pass to the next one and we call the roll on this." The three minority senators voted to call Matthew McCloskey; the six Democrats voted against it. McCloskey did not testify at that time.

That stadium cost the government a great deal of money; the total bill came to nearly twenty million dollars. Bobby Baker obtained his share.

Throughout the period we have been discussing, Baker, through his Senate employment and the influence it brought him, was amassing a fortune in his Capitol office. Federal departments, officers in the executive branch, senators and their staffs—all took it that Bobby Baker was speaking as agent for the majority leader of the Senate, Lyndon Johnson. Never was any notice given that Baker might not be speaking for his employer. It was obvious that he could prevail upon government offices to grant licenses and permits, or to enter into contracts, because he spoke as secretary of the Senate—not as a mere private citizen.

So great a dignitary as Bobby Baker found numerous opportunities—and varied ones—to enrich himself. Consider vending machines.

During and after the Second World War, the vending-machine business had grown a great deal. Machines were installed in factories with thousands of employees, and sold cold drinks, coffee, sandwiches, and candy; also hot chocolate. Factory management would contract with a vending company for the installation of machines. If Bobby Baker were to say a good word to a manufacturing company with government contracts, to the effect that the company would do well to place a vending contract with certain persons, his influence would be felt.

The Committee's investigation of Baker had been initiated because of the suit of one Ralph Hill, proprietor of the Capitol Vending Machine Company, against Baker. Testimony taken by the Committee—Counsel McLendon asking the questions—shows how the secretary to the Senate operated.

Hill testified that Bobby Baker, in February, 1962, had taken the initiative in this vending-machine affair by asking Hill to meet at the University Club with him and Eugene Hancock, who was involved in the vending business in Florida. At that rendezvous, Baker asked Hill to take Hancock to the firm of Melpar, Inc., near Four Corners, Virginia. Hill had not previously visited the premises of Melpar, nor did he know any of that firm's officers. Complying, Hill and Hancock were received at Melpar by a man named Bostick, Melpar's president, and Bostick's assistant, a man named Weid.

Bostick told his guests that he had promised Bobby Baker a contract; and he instructed Weid to show the visitors anything pertaining to this vending contract. This contract was with Baker himself, not with a friend of Baker. A local vending company, at the time, was serving Melpar with vending machines.

On their way back to Washington, Hancock told Hill that his own firm would not be interested in contracting with a small company like Melpar: "They were interested in big things, like North American." Hill was given to understand that the door was left wide open for Hill himself to make a proposal for a Melpar contract, perhaps without having to compete in bidding with the local vending firm, G. B. Macke.

Hill did make a proposal from his Capitol Vending to Melpar; it was accepted by Melpar on March 23, 1962. And soon Hill learned that he was required to make a cash payment to Bobby Baker, who in person told him, "if the contract was valuable to us, we were making money out of it, and he wanted a thousand dollars a month. And so we argued back and forth, and we settled for $250." This monthly tribute, in small bills, Hill delivered personally to Baker in his office, "usually having to wait for him.'' Baker regularly counted the money in Hill's presence to make sure that other people were honest.

But Hill's Capitol Vending received some compensation for this additional cost of doing business. Through Baker's intervention, Melpar found it expedient to grant to Capitol Vending what they had refused to grant before: a price increase at the plant for drinks from the machines, five to ten cents; and authorization to install hot chocolate in the machines. Thus, in effect, the employees at Melpar paid for Bobby Baker's monthly retainer. To parody a children's Sunday-school song,

"Hear the nickels dropping, listen as they fall;
Every one for Bobby's sake; he will keep them all.''

Capitol Vending's increase of net income because of this plum amounted to more than two thousand dollars a month. Baker then inquired of Hill, ''Now, do I get my thousand dollars a month?'' After bargaining, Hill agreed to pay Baker thereafter $650 monthly.

But Baker was dissatisfied with such small potatoes from Capitol Vending; there were bigger fish to fry. Baker proceeded to organize himself a new vending-machine firm, the Serv-U Company. Quite promptly, Serv-U ousted the existing machine vendor at the North American Aviation Company, in California. This was accomplished when Serv-U had no contract anywhere else, and indeed did not own a single machine or a single sandwich. But we will turn to that contract later; just now we continue with Hill's account of the Melpar contract.

In reply to McLendon's questions, Hill related that about the first week of April, 1963, Baker telephoned him that Capitol Vending was about to lose the Melpar contract; Serv-U would replace Capitol at Melpar. A meeting followed, at which Baker informed Hill ''at least ten or fifteen times,'' obdurately, ''You are going to lose Melpar. Mr. Bostick doesn't like you.'' Serv-U, supplanting Capitol, would try to pay Capitol some compensation.

The testimony was clear that Baker himself placed the Melpar contract for Hill's company, and that Baker was able to obtain price increases and other concessions for Hill after nobody else had been able to persuade Melpar to raise machine prices to its employees. (A previously-refused concession to vend hot chocolate tasted particularly sweet to Hill.) What hold Baker had on Melpar and Bostick never was made wholly clear, except that Melpar profited from government contracts.

Curtis questioned Hill: "So Mr. Baker gave and Mr. Baker took away: Is that right? He was the one you got the contract through originally?...And the first word that you were going to lose it came from Baker?"

"Correct," said Hill, in response to both inquiries.

The ingenious Baker was carrying on many activities. He was in the real-estate business, and one of the people involved in building the Carousel Motel at Ocean City, Maryland (where later Carole Tyler came to her violent end). Baker's partners in the Carousel venture were two brothers named Novak.

When funds were required for the purchase of land and for construction, often Baker would produce the money in cash. Mrs. Gertrude Novak, whose late husband had been Baker's partner, testified to the Committee that she frequently would obtain funds from Baker to pay current bills for the Carousel project. She stated that she was frightened by the large sums of money handed to her, usually in hundred-dollar bills. On one occasion, twelve thousand dollars in hundred-dollar bills was handed to her at Baker's office. Miscounting, Baker gave Mrs. Novak almost a thousand dollars too much. Carole Tyler, Baker's secretary, put the surplus back into a filing drawer.

"Music is supplied by the ringing of the telephone;...from government department to sherry party glides the contact-man, at once the product and the safety valve of this grotesque civilization."

THE INVESTIGATION REVIVED

The investigation of Bobby Baker had begun late in October, 1963. By March, 1964, the six Democrats on the Committee had determined that the investigation must end. Until that month they never had called a single witness requested by the minority members. Senator Hugh Scott, addressing the Senate on March 16, 1964, put the situation well: "The majority members of the committee have been on the brink of ending the investigation as soon as they thought they could do so without incurring the wrath of the American public."

Concerning this question, a most interesting meeting of the Committee was held on March 13. Senator Curtis offered, in the record, a letter signed by the three minority members, which he had delivered to the Committee's chairman on March 9. In this communication, the minority asked that more witnesses be called. Three of these proposed witnesses were Senate employees: Margaret Broome, Rein J. Vander Zee, and Jessop McDonnell, closely associated with Baker in his duties. Other witnesses asked for were people who had business transactions with Baker, or who were officers or partners in Baker's several enterprises: they were Matthew McCloskey, Max Kampelman, Paul Aguirre, Warren Neil, Charles Baker, Nick Popich, and two men connected with Riddle Airlines.

In connection with Reynolds' disputed testimony and the refusal of Baker to testify, the minority asked that Walter Jenkins and George Sampson also be called.

Curtis then asked that a copy of the affidavit of Milton Hauft, of March 12, 1964, be placed in the record. At this point McLendon, nominally counsel for the Committee but more realistically counsel for the majority, declared, "Mr. Chairman, I do not think that affidavit ought to go in the record."

Curtis replied, "I'll read in the record," to which McLendon responded, "Wait a minute!" There followed a lively discussion, in which Curtis challenged the right of a Senate employee to overrule a senator. Insisting, Curtis began to read. The Chairman said "Wait a minute," to which Curtis answered, "I am on the record;" and to the reporter, "You take this down." He then succeeded in reading the affidavit:

"I, Milton L. Hauft, living at 3801 Archer Place, Kensington, Maryland, do give this affidavit to Senator John J. Williams, of Delaware, of my own free will.

"On this date I was called to the Internal Revenue Service to give information relative to tax returns I had prepared for Robert G. Baker.

"During the course of presenting the information in my possession, I was questioned about some partnership tax returns prepared for the Carousel Motel. During the course of my association with Mr. Baker, I had never prepared any returns for the Carousel Motel. When presented with the return by the Internal Revenue Service, I noted that the signatures purported to be mine were forgeries.

"As a result of this, I went back to the personal returns for Mr. Baker prepared by me, and on looking at the signatures on these returns I noted that the signatures as to the person preparing those returns were also forgeries and were not my signature.

"This was reported immediately to the investigators of the Internal Revenue Service, and samples and specimens of my handwriting were also presented to them for matching purposes."

This disclosure of tax-evasion and forgery set the Committee's majority back on their heels. Some twelve hours after Counsel McLendon had received a copy of the Hauft affidavit, he delivered a report to the Committee, setting forth the plan of the majority to end the investigation. McLendon's sentences seem wondrously inappropriate:

"I think two conclusions may be drawn from this extensive investigation. First, it is highly unlikely that any additional evidence can be found materially differing from the type of evidence already placed in the record of the committee's hearings; and second, that it is a reasonable certainty that any additional evidence which can be produced will be repetitive and cumulative. If evidence differing substantially from the pattern of evidence already presented is in evidence, surely it would have been discovered in the course of the investigation." McLendon concluded by recommending that investigations into the activities of past or present Senate employees should cease, and that the Committee's staff immediately begin to prepare the Committee's report to the Senate.

A Committee meeting was to be held to consider McLendon's recommendations. It turned out that Chairman Jordan already had prepared an advance news-release, to be issued after the anticipated meeting had concluded. The six Democratic senators seemed determined to close their eyes and ears to any additional evidence, though they had called not one witness requested by the minority. That abortive news-release —as matters turned out, never issued—stated that "the committee voted 6 to 3 to follow Major McLendon's recommendations."

On the Senate floor, Senator Scott commented concerning this: "How clearly this proves that the evidence offered by minority senators over a three-hour period had been rejected before they had even been heard!"

After controversy arose in the Committee hearing on March 13, Counsel McLendon added these words to his recommendation: "...except as to the matter relating to Mr. Hauft's affidavit presented to the committee on this date...."

The investigation did not terminate quite so abruptly as Counsel McLendon desired. Curtis, leaving a closed session of the Committee's meeting, had read to the press McLendon's recommendation that the investigation be terminated and the staff disbanded. That gave the majority pause; and rather than dissolving itself, the Committee proceeded to consider whether it should receive testimony from those additional witnesses named by the minority.

In the course of this heated meeting, the question of what testimony is relevant was discussed. Rule 19 provided that if any member of the Committee should request the appearance of a particular witness, that witness should be called unless the chairman of the Committee should find the proposed testimony to be irrelevant; if he should so find, there must be a vote of the members.

It will be recalled that Bobby Baker, in his refusal to testify, argued that the investigation had no legislative purpose, and therefore he did not have to produce his records. The minority members of the Committee had pointed out repeatedly that although there are court decisions to the effect that a congressional committee does not have the power to expose for exposure's sake, and that such committees are limited to taking testimony that may serve a legislative purpose, this Baker case was different.

For whether or not the Baker investigation might lead to legislation, the purpose of the investigation was to investigate wrongdoing among senatorial employees, and possibly among senators. Congress possesses the unchallenged power to determine its own procedures and to clean its own house. The Senate had directed its Committee on Rules and Administration to look into wrongdoing within the Senate's own immediate jurisdiction. Therefore the testimony of any witness who might know about malfeasance in office would be relevant testimony. The court decisions about calling citizens to appear before congressional committees were intended as protections against general "fishing expeditions" by such committees; those decisions did not apply to congressional management of Congress' own immediate internal concerns. Investigations of that sort may have no legislative purpose in view, and yet be proper and necessary investigations.

Let us look at these witnesses whom the minority on the Committee wished to have called to testify—and whom the majority of senators on the Committee wished not to hear.

Mrs. Margaret Broome had served as Bobby Baker's secretary before that position was taken by the pretty and ill-fated Carole Tyler. The record clearly indicated that some of Baker's transactions requiring investigation had taken place while Mrs. Broome had been Baker's secretary. At its meeting on March 23, the six majority members of the Comittee voted not to hear Mrs. Broome's testimony, and the three minority members to hear her. Mrs. Broome was excluded.

The next witness-name on the list was that of Rein Vander Zee, who had been employed by the Senate in various capacities for some years. He had been assistant to Bobby Baker when

Baker had been secretary to the Majority, maintaining a desk in the outer office of Baker's Capitol suite. In his statement, Vander Zee revealed that he had seen Don Reynolds in Baker's office; that he had been in Baker's house often; that he had attended a gathering in the home of Carole Tyler, who had lived in a house provided by Bobby Baker. Vander Zee also acknowledged that he was acquainted with Ralph Hill, had lunched with him, and had discussed with Hill the vending business and the Serv-U Corporation. Members of the Committee were aware that Vander Zee had discussed with other senatorial employees problems that had arisen about their pay and alleged kickbacks; and that Vander Zee knew of many telephone calls by Baker, and had traveled with the Baker crowd to the opening of Baker's motel at Ocean City.

Nevertheless, Chairman Jordan ruled Vander Zee's testimony irrelevant; and the majority of the Committee sustained Senator Jordan. Six to three, the Vander Zee testimony was excluded.

The next witness considered was Jessop McDonnell. Senator Cooper pointed out that McDonnell had said he had disliked Baker's way of doing things, and had been fired as an assistant to Baker. McDonnell desired to appear before the Committee. Jordan ruled McDonnell's testimony irrelevant, without troubling to learn what that testimony might be, and was sustained, six votes to three. McDonnell was excluded.

Matthew McCloskey, who had built the stadium and become ambassador to Ireland, had been mentioned repeatedly in Reynolds' testimony. During discussion of whether McCloskey should be called as a witness, it was disclosed that the cost of the stadium had been fixed in 1957 at six million dollars; but that a year later Congress had passed a bill removing this cost-ceiling. The stadium contract had been awarded to McCloskey's company in August, 1960. McCloskey's low bid had been fourteen million dollars, but plan changes raised costs by three million dollars; so payments to McCloskey had brought the total cost of the stadium to nearly twenty million dollars. Regardless, McCloskey was excluded from testifying, six to three.

The next possible witness was Paul Aguirre, who had traveled with Baker. They went together to New Orleans, where they looked into the possibility of participating in a housing development. They had stopped to look at a plot of land near the Shamrock Hotel, Houston. Also they had considered together a proposal for setting up trailer parks. Information had been given to the Committee that Baker had intervened on Aguirre's behalf with reference to a matter before the Federal Housing Administration. Aguirre's statement to the investigators informed the Committee that he met Baker, Carole Tyler, and Elli Rometsch, the party girl. Chairman Jordan ruled all this not pertinent to the Committee's business. Five to four, Aguirre was excluded as a witness. Incidentally, Aguirre had declared that had he been asked anything about what had taken place in New Orleans, he would have taken all the constitutional amendments, from the First to the Twenty-Eighth. (In the case of Aguirre, Senator Byrd voted with the Republican members of the Committee.)

Then the Committee discussed the possibility of calling Warren Neil as a witness. Baker and Neil had been close friends. Neil had resided in Puerto Rico, and always had looked up Baker on trips to Washington. Neil had been Baker's host in a company apartment in Puerto Rico. Along with Aguirre, Neil had endeavored to find money from the labor unions to finance some of Baker's projects. Neil had conferred with Baker on means of reaching certain union leaders. Also Neil and Baker had talked about establishing a title-insurance company in Puerto Rico. Chairman Jordan ruled testimony by Neil irrelevant, and was sustained, six votes to three. Neil was excluded.

What about Nick Popich, of New Orleans? He and Baker had been together several times, and had made many telephone calls to each other: the Committee had such information. Popich owned, among other things, a New Orleans restaurant, and was involved in constructing a pipeline in Washington. Baker was involved in an organization called the Pansatic Corporation. Popich had sent a thousand dollars in payment for stock in that corporation. The money had been returned to Popich; Counsel McLendon said that evidence suggested that the Pansatic stockholders didn't want Popich. Senator Curtis inquired whether this was because of Popich's bad reputation;

McLendon replied that this was implied. The Committee's minority believed that Popich's testimony might bear on reports that "hot" money from gamblers and underworld characters had been funneled through Baker. Chairman Jordan held testimony by Popich irrelevant, and was sustained five to four, Senator Byrd again voting with the minority. Popich was excluded.

Walter Jenkins' testimony was more needed, in the opinion of the minority, than that of any other possible witness. Reynolds and Young had testified to Jenkins' participation in the kickback for sale of insurance policies to Lyndon Johnson. Only the testimony of Jenkins might have refuted that of Don Reynolds. Senator John Sherman Cooper, once a Kentucky judge, with much knowledge of the law and a judicial temperament, made a strong statement as to why Jenkins should be called as a witness. Nevertheless, the Committee voted six to three not to call him. Jenkins was excluded.

The next day, the Committee denied, six to three, a motion to recall Don Reynolds as witness. His testimony had been given earlier in executive session, not in public session; it was highly important testimony, worth reviewing in the light of testimony by others. Reynolds had been subjected to repeated attacks by the Committee's majority. Reynolds was excluded.

Now the minority sought to call Max Kampelman, a former Senate employee, friend to Baker. He was one of the founders and organizers of the District of Columbia National Bank. Baker had subscribed to 1,700 shares in that undertaking, and had been allocated 1,500. Baker's stock was in Baker's name, but he had purchased a third of it for Fred Black, who had been involved with Baker in several transactions, among them the Serv-U Corporation. Another third of the Baker stock was for Edward Levinson, of Las Vegas, who took the Fifth Amendment; and the remaining third was for Benjamin S. Siegelbaum, of Miami, who also pleaded that he would not testify because he might incriminate himself. From this District of Columbia National Bank, Baker had borrowed $125,000 on an unsecured note. Testimony showed that Max Kampelman knew about this loan; Kampelman was counsel to the Bank, and a director. Baker had asked Kampelman how he, Baker, might buy stock in this bank. But the Chairman ruled that Kampelman should not be called, and was sustained by a vote of five to four, Senator Byrd voting with the minority. Kampelman was excluded.

Then the name of Deane Beman was proposed as a witness. Senator Curtis said, "According to the committee counsel, the witness Hill had a conversation with Beman in which Beman was alleged to have said that he knew how Hill got the contract with Melpar. Beman refused to talk to our investigator. There was valid reason for our investigator going to see him. His testimony was both relevant and needed." Senator Cannon, acting as chairman, ruled that Beman's testimony would be irrelevant. Six to three, the chair was sustained. Beman was excluded.

Should not Paul Ferrero be called to testify? Senator Scott put the case: "We have an interview on Mr. Ferrero which I would like to see. He is the Deputy Commissioner, Federal Housing Administration, who was called by Mr. Baker on behalf of Aguirre to obtain approval of a project in which Mr. Aguirre was interested, and I believe Mr. Ferrero either ruled against it or informed Mr. Baker that there was a ruling against it. I think his testimony would be interesting and valuable as showing whether Mr. Baker sought to influence Mr. Ferrero's decision, whether Mr. Baker's approach to him was on behalf of a client or whether it was made as secretary to the majority. We are investigating, among other things here, the improper use of influence...." Counsel McLendon advised Senator Cannon, in the chair, that Ferrero's testimony would not be material. Five to three (Senator Byrd not voting), Ferrero was excluded.

Baker had been involved in Hampco (Haitian-American Meat Provision Company), a firm exporting meat from Haiti to Puerto Rico. Hampco was owned by the Murchison interest, headed by Clinton Murchison, Jr., of Dallas and New York. Strong evidence existed to the effect that Bobby Baker had negotiated with the Department of Agriculture in connection with Hampco's application for authorization to ship meat to Puerto Rico; also that Baker had received substantial sums of money through the good offices of the Murchison interest, amounting in one year to eight or nine thousand dollars. The instrument for this payment had been a kickback commission from a William E. Kentor, of the Packers Provision Company, Inc., a Chicago firm. Baker's law partner gave evidence that Baker himself got all the money from this Hampco transaction. The Committee's investigators could find no substantial services rendered by Baker to Hampco. Was the Hampco kickback to Baker payment for the use of his influence with the Department of Agriculture? Or might it have amounted to payment by Murchison to Baker for some other mysterious favor extended by Baker to the Murchison interest?

At last the Committee agreed to hear the testimony of William E. Kentor, who had purchased meat from Hampco. On all meat delivered to him by Hampco, Kentor said at the Committee hearing, Kentor had agreed to pay a half-cent per pound to a law firm known as Baker and Tucker, in Washington. This agreement had been negotiated in Haiti with a Marshall Dancy, representing Hampco.

At this testimony, the Committee's minority pressed for calling Marshall Dancy as a witness, so that they might explore this odd Baker transaction. The Chairman held that Dancy's testimony would be irrelevant. Five to three, Senator Byrd again not voting, the chair was sustained. Dancy was excluded.

Here testimony at the Committee's hearings ended. The numerous additional witnesses sought by the minority had been weighed in the balance by the majority and found irrelevant, or else not considered at all. Much evidence had been covered up.

THE ASSAULT ON
SENATOR JOHN WILLIAMS

On July 8, 1964, the Committee's majority filed a report with five recommendations. First, the adoption of new rules requiring some form of public disclosure of outside financial interests by members, officers, and employees of the Senate. Second, consideration by the two-party policy committees of the Senate of guidelines for the securities to the Majority and the minority. Third, consideration by Senate committees and senators of guidelines for committees and senatorial staff members. Fourth, consideration by the executive branch of regulations requiring accurate records of congressional intervention in matters pending before executive agencies. Fifth, immediate survey of the information assembled by the Comittee by the Justice Department, to determine whether criminal action was warranted.

The minority of the Committee supported the first of these recommendations, but found the other four vague and advisory at best. The three Republican senators declared that the investigation of Baker never had been completed. The majority had "refused to call a single witness requested by a minority member of the committee, or by all the minority members of the committee. This was in direct violation of the published rules under which the committee was operating...The full story has not been disclosed concerning Bobby Baker and those associated with him, including present and former senators and Senate employees. It has not been told because the majority prevented the investigation from proceeding."

Even though the majority members of the Committee on Rules and Administration voted to close the investigation, the Bobby Baker scandals would not go away. Senator John Williams, with dogged persistence, continued his search for the facts.

In a speech on the Senate floor, September 1, 1964, Sena-

tor Williams disclosed a statement given to him by Don
Reynolds on August 18. This document startled the Senate.

For Reynolds declared that in the affair of the performance-
bond for construction of the District of Columbia stadium—in
which the names of Bobby Baker and Matthew McCloskey had
loomed large—payment for the bond had been padded. (In the
sense that McCloskey's bill to the federal government was paid
out of public funds, the bond was padded out of taxpayers'
money.) The actual cost of the bond had been $73,631.28; yet
the check that Matthew McCloskey had given to the bonding-
agent firm was in the amount of $109,205.60, an overpayment
of $35,574.32. Senator Williams displayed on the Senate floor
a copy of McCloskey's check for the larger sum.

What had been done with this overpayment of more than
thirty-five thousand dollars? Apparently ten thousand dollars
had gone to Reynolds to compensate him for the commission
he would have received had he been the bonding agent, writing the bond himself instead of merely acting as broker; and
as a payment to him for dispensing the related kickbacks. The
bulk of the money, twenty-five thousand dollars—so Reynolds
stated—had been turned over to Bobby Baker, allegedly as a
contribution to the campaign fund of 1960, to elect the ticket
of Kennedy for President and Johnson for Vice-President.
Whether the funds actually were used for such an unlawful purpose, Reynolds could not say: he did not know what had happened to the money after it had been put into Baker's eager
hands.

Here was a pickle: the Senate could not easily ignore a
scandal involving that eminent and well-heeled Democrat
Matthew McCloskey, and the already-notorious Bobby Baker.
President Johnson and Senator Goldwater already were campaigning hotly against each other for the presidency; the national elections were less than three months distant. The Baker
affair still was like a cancer in the face, not to be hidden, despite the Rules and Administration Committee's cover-up
majority report in July.

Accordingly, Senator Mansfield, majority leader, proposed
a Senate resolution authorizing the Rules and Administration
Committee to reopen its investigation. The Senate, on Septem-

ber 10, adopted the resolution by a vote of seventy-five to three, a considerable vindication of the Committee's minority report. This new resolution included the responsibility of looking into the affairs of senators or former senators, and emphasized the business of the District of Columbia stadium.

An effort was made, during debate on the reopening of the investigation, to shift the investigation to the Senate Committee on Government Operations, of which Senator McClellan, of Arkansas, was chairman. This proposal was defeated by a vote of fifty to thirty-seven senators.

After some delay, on October 1 and 2, 1964, the Committee on Rules and Administration assembled to discuss renewal of the investigation. The chairman received the testimony of two witnesses concerning the procedures that had been followed in the letting of bids for the stadium. On the second day, Senator Cooper said that the investigation should dispense with details about such procedures and instead get to the heart of the issue: the charge that there had been a corrupt and illegal transaction by McCloskey and Baker.

Chairman Jordan departed the following day on a campaign tour. On October 12, the Committee's three minority members sent a letter to Senator Jordan, asking that Baker, McCloskey, and two other witnesses be called to testify before November 3. Jordan replied that the hearings could not be conducted fairly in the closing weeks of an election campaign, and ruled out further hearings until the November elections were past. So it came to pass that Lyndon Baines Johnson, often mentioned ominously in the earlier hearings, was elected President of the United States before the Baker scandals were aired again.

When the Committee resumed hearings on December 1, the strategy of the Committee's majority became clear: they were endeavoring to blacken both Senator John Williams and Don Reynolds in the public eye. Chairman Jordan had announced on November 24 that Reynolds could not be found to testify. But the very next day, Reynolds had appeared to accept the Committee's summons, charging that the Committee was trying to discredit him by implying that he had absconded.

At one point in the December hearings, Senator Williams walked out, saying, "This investigation is more important than any individual. It reflects upon the integrity of the whole Senate and the Congress. I have tried to be helpful to the committee. But as a result of the episode in which my veracity was challenged, I feel that I am unwanted. I shall continue to observe the committee's activities with great interest." (The chief counsel had attempted to make a point of the fact that neither Williams nor Reynolds had referred in the earlier series of hearings to the padding of the bond-payment. They had not taken up that matter because at the time they had lacked the proof: that is, McCloskey's check in payment.)

Senator Williams, not a member of the Committee, had unselfishly pursued the investigation without staff and without extra expense-money. He had laid information before the Committee that in the interest of the Senate should be followed up. But the Committee's counsel, McLendon, often went out of his way to attack Williams.

On December 3, for instance, following a statement by Senator Williams, McLendon said, "I deny every word of that as emphatically as I can. You never made such a statement to me...You ought at least to tell the truth."

At that point, Williams rejoined, "This is the first time in my life that an employee of a Senate committee at a public hearing has accused a senator of an untruth." Carl Curtis then interjected, "Mr. McLendon has no business making such a statement. I hope he withdraws it." Yet McLendon responded, "I had the same business making that statement as Senator Williams had in making his."

It appeared that McLendon was there not to investigate, but to block investigation. Senator Scott asked Bostick of the Melpar Corporation, "Do you know one Linda Morrison?" Bostick objected to replying. Intervening, McLendon asserted that the witness should not answer. McLendon often seemed to be counsel for the defense, not counsel for the investigation.

At last Matthew McCloskey was called as a witness. He flatly denied the allegations made by Reynolds. He described the overcharge in payment for the performance bond as "a goof." His company, he said, would try to recoup from Reynolds that overpayment of thirty-five thousand dollars. He denied that he had been involved in anything wrong. At one point he burst out, "I don't care what Reynolds has testified; he hasn't told the truth once." Actually, Reynolds' testimony stood up in the light of all other evidence that could be gathered.

It was well known that the McCloskey Company had erected a number of buildings for the government in Washington. Many of these buildings were under the direct control of Congress. Senator Curtis wrote to the General Accounting Office, asking for information concerning all construction projects awarded to McCloskey that had been paid for by the federal government. Instead of assembling the information themselves, the General Accounting Office people asked Matthew McCloskey to provide it. McCloskey refused.

Yet by this time the Democratic members of the Committee doubtless perceived that Baker could not be let off scot-free: the public outcry would be too great. The majority heard a witness whose testimony clearly would damage Baker badly.

This witness was Harry K. Barr, president of the Barr Shipping Company, New York. He was chairman of an *ad hoc* association, Ocean Freight Forwarders, formed for the purpose of obtaining legislation favorable to that business. On behalf of Ocean Freight Forwarders, Barr had hired one Myron Weiner as lobbyist. Weiner had been paid fifty thousand dollars. On September 21, 1961, Weiner had written a check for five thousand dollars to Ernest C. Tucker, Baker's law associate. Tucker testified that he had deposited that check at Baker's request and the next day had written a check for five thousand dollars in Baker's favor.

It would have been a conflict of interest for any congressional employee to have accepted a fee for assisting private persons in the enactment of legislation. And in this case, Baker had been operating from the office of the majority leader, with unusual power of getting bills scheduled and approved, it being assumed that Baker was acting for the majority leader. Apparently this Ocean Freight Forwarders transaction by Baker had constituted the selling of the government's favors.

The Committee's majority found it well to accept the Ocean Freight Forwarders affair as a conflict of interest on Baker's part. On this charge, but on this charge alone, the majority of the Committee eventually would suggest the possibility of indicting Bobby Baker. This charge did not involve the names of other persons high in federal office or of eminent members of the Democratic Party.

More witnesses were heard, if tardily—or rather, attempts were made to hear them. Paul F. Aguirre, previously sought as a witness, was called at last; but he refused to answer on the ground that he might be incriminated. A Committee staff report on Aguirre contained an interview with him. Aguirre had discussed with Baker the organizing of the Pansatic Corporation, to operate trailer parks. Baker had brought Carole Tyler and Elli Rometsch with him from Washington to New Orleans in May, 1963; Aguirre spent several days "partying" with them. When asked for more information about Elli Rometsch, Carole Tyler, and the "parties," Aguirre had refused, saying, "If I'm asked by the committee about this, I will deny it even if they have photographs. My wife is expecting a denial, and she will get it." Aguirre had various other connections with Bobby Baker, which could not be explored because of Paul Aguirre's refusal to testify. On December 9, the majority of the Committee voted against investigating the information provided by Senator Williams concerning Ingrid Luttert, Elli Rometsch, and other women associated with Baker. Thus the part these figures of the demi-monde played in Baker's operations, and possible security risks involved, also went unexplored.

Testimony was taken also with reference to the granting of a charter to the Redwood National Bank, San Rafael, California. The applicants employed one Wayne L. Bromley to expedite this application after some months had elapsed with no action. The charter then being granted, the Bank made out a check to Bromley for five thousand dollars. Bromley instructed the Bank to deliver the check to Baker's Capitol office. Both Bromley and Baker then endorsed the check, and Baker cashed it. Bromley refused to testify before the Committee, taking the Fifth Amendment as his defense.

Despite endeavors by the minority, here the Committee ceased to call witnesses. The majority engaged instead in an attempt to discredit Don Reynolds' testimony. The chairman obtained a report on Reynolds which he represented as prepared by the Federal Bureau of Investigation, but which was written merely by lawyers in the Department of Justice. Carl Curtis made this point on the floor of the Senate: "This report was obtained and released for the purpose of prejudicing the public mind against the testimony of witnesses who testify against the politically powerful..."

In the hope of compelling the Committee to call more witnesses desired by the minority, Senator Williams and Senator Curtis turned to the Senate floor. Williams offered a bill to expand the Committee's authority, including all sorts of business interests and any improper activity (including campaign contributions). Curtis offered an amendment to this bill providing that any three members of the Committee might request witnesses to be called, and that the Chairman must honor such requests. The Curtis amendment won by a vote of thirty-six to thirty-three. The Williams resolution, nevertheless, never came to a vote: the Senate majority leader, Mike Mansfield, contrived to table it. In these contests in the Senate, several well-known Democratic senators supported the Williams and Curtis proposals, among them Byrd of Virginia, Douglas of Illinois, Gruening of Alaska, Hart of Michigan, McClellan of Arkansas, Nelson of Wisconsin, Proxmire of Wisconsin, Russell of Georgia, Stennis of Mississippi, Williams of New Jersey, and Young of Ohio; but these reinforcements did not suffice. On other key votes related to the investigating committee, a number of other Democratic senators supported Curtis: Lausche of Ohio, McIntyre of New Hampshire, Bartlett of Alaska, Symington of Missouri. Nevertheless, the Democratic majority in the Senate prevailed, so crippling the minority on the investigating committee. The Committee's witnesses, particularly Reynolds, had named the President of the United States; so partisan loyalty persuaded the Democratic majority, in effect, to allow this investigation into unlawful and improper conduct to die.

Senator Sam Ervin, of North Carolina, was the principal advocate of restricting the investigation. If Senator John Williams was the prime mover of the Baker investigation, Senator Sam Ervin was its gravedigger. Ervin, a considerable authority on the Constitution, was in general one of the more conservative Democratic senators, later zealous in the Watergate investigation. Ervin not only voted against the power of three members of the Committee to call a witness, but he spoke several times against that proposal. On one occasion he described the purpose of the investigating committee as "to merely investigate circumstances relating to business interests of former employees or present employees of the Senate, to ascertain whether or not there was any conflict of interest between business transactions of such former or present employees and duties as employees of the Senate."

Ervin argued that the investigation had been completed now, and that the Committee should make its report. He said that the alleged forgeries of signatures on Baker's tax returns were irrelevant to the purpose of the investigation.

Back of Senator Ervin loomed the tall figure of Lyndon Baines Johnson, President of the United States, wheeler and dealer, whose right-hand man Bobby Baker had been. Like Baker, Johnson had grown rich while in public office, indeed a great deal richer than Baker. It would not do to call more witnesses, not when President Johnson's interests were in question. If Bobby Baker were indicted for crimes, who else might be indicted?

So in the spring of 1965, the Johnson forces made a desperate attempt to destroy the reputation of Senator John Williams and that of Don Reynolds. Counsel McLendon prepared a report, a secret one, denouncing Reynolds and attempting to discredit Williams. This report fell into the hands of the Washington press, with unfavorable results for the Johnson partisans.

Senator Williams, indignant, twice addressed the Senate, challenging the Democratic members of the investigating committee either to support the secret report by McLendon, or to repudiate it. No member of the Committee ventured to reply to Williams.

Why had he been so treated by the Committee's majority? Williams inquired before the Senate. "The answer is very simple. They are desperate. The decision has been made by the hierarchy of the Great Society that John Williams has got to be stopped—discredited and destroyed, if necessary—before the Baker investigation embarrasses this Great Society any more, or before the case reaches any higher...

"A reading of the report makes it clear that back of all of this controversy is a diabolically clever plan to divert the attention of the American people from the real issue of this investigation: namely, what kind of influence–peddling were Bobby Baker and his associates carrying out in his office under the dome of the Capitol?"

In this report attacking Williams, the Committee's majority emphasized that Williams had not said early in the investigations that McCloskey had padded the performance-bond in the amount of thirty-five thousand dollars. In reply, Williams had pointed out that he had urged the Committee's chairman to get the performance-bond check from McCloskey. The Committee had not done so. Williams himself at length had obtained a copy of McCloskey's check to Reynolds, obtaining it to everyone's surprise from a Philadelphia daily newspaper's published photograph of the check!

Williams' adversaries were silent in the Senate: there was no case they could make for their conduct. Allies of the Johnson administration, however, carried on a campaign against Williams in the press. A news story was published nationally declaring that Senator Williams had been seen breakfasting with a young woman at a restaurant in Delaware—presumably with the imputation that if one breakfasted with a girl, one must have spent the previous night with her. Even the gentlemen of the Fourth Estate must have been chagrined somewhat on learning, the day after the story was published, that the young person in question had been Senator Williams' granddaughter.

In the presidential election of 1964, Lyndon Johnson took the trouble to campaign twice in Delaware, a state with only three electoral votes. He spoke against Senator John Williams expressly. To President Johnson and his circle, John Williams was a highly dangerous man: too honest, too courageous. Senator Williams was re-elected.

A SCANDALOUS
MAJORITY REPORT

Still the Baker investigation proceeded. As the months elapsed, the minority members pressed that Walter Jenkins be called to testify. If necessary, the majority members could throw Bobby Baker to the wolves; but in the interest of the Johnson administration, they dared not sacrifice the President's confidential aide Jenkins. Were Walter Jenkins to testify, he would be exposed to cross-examination concerning the part of Lyndon Johnson in the entire career of Bobby Baker.

Yet at last the minority members did succeed in having a subpoena issued for Jenkins. The notorious fact of Jenkins' arrest on a morals charge in the autumn of 1964 embarrassed the majority into calling him as a witness. But on the appointed day for his testimony, Jenkins did not appear. Instead, there appeared two psychiatrists, whom the Committee interviewed and cross-examined for a day. These psychiatrists contended that Jenkins' life would be endangered, were he required to testify: not merely his health, but his *life*. Nowhere in the printed hearings of the Committee is there any reference to this pair of psychiatrists; the majority voted down Curtis' motion to make their testimony public. Cross-examination of the psychiatrists that day had shown that Jenkins had attended all the functions of President Johnson's inauguration; that he had gone on vacations; and that in other respects he was leading an ordinary life. The Committee excused Jenkins from testifying. Strange to say, the reporters' notes taken on the testimony of the psychiatrists vanished altogether.

The final report filed by the majority of the Committee on Rules and Administration bears the date of June 30, 1965. It is a whitewash, a cover-up, a disgrace to the senators who subscribed to it. It is an endeavor to protect the politically powerful and to make difficult a successful prosecution of Bobby Baker.

The report falsely represents the limitations of the Committee's responsibilities. It falsely attacks Senator Williams. It falsely declares that subpoenas were issued in several states for Don Reynolds. It falsely covers up Matthew McCloskey's padding of the performance-bond, despite McCloskey's own testimony in the record. It falsely denounces the testimony of Reynolds, the most valuable witness called, as following a "tortuous path of deception." It pretends to find nothing improper in the Redwood National Bank case of influence-peddling. The report, in short, was a sham. It ended, in its recommendations, by praising President Lyndon B. Johnson for his executive order regarding identification of outside business interests by federal employees, etc., etc. Bobby Baker's patron was almost canonized by the majority report.

The Committee's minority report, as the second and last phase of this investigation concluded, was very different. The substance of it has been the subject of this section. The minority praised highly Senator John Williams: "Without the evidence produced by Senator Williams, which evidence forced the majority to act, we doubt that the investigation of Robert Baker would ever have occurred."

Even in a section as long as this one has been, it is impossible to touch upon many details of the Baker investigation. In a phrase too often employed, the Committee saw only the tip of the iceberg of influence-peddling and use of public office for personal profit. The wheeler-dealer to whom many signs pointed was elected President of the United States, while this investigation still was in progress. "They gave unto him his heart's desire, and the iron entered into his soul withal." He would lead the United States to the country's first great military defeat and to ruinous inflation of the currency.

And what of Bobby Baker? The report of the majority of the Committee did go so far as to make a sacrificial lamb of the genial Bobby: it suggested consideration of the possibility of indicting Baker for violation of conflict-of-interest statutes in connection with his being paid five thousand dollars by a lobbyist for Ocean Freight Forwarders. Other charges against Baker apparently did not trouble the majority.

With the judicial branch of the government of these United

States, Baker did not come off quite so easily, though lightly enough. On January 5, 1966, he was indicted by a federal grand jury in Washington on nine counts, among them receiving money ($137,000) on false pretenses, evading income taxes, conspiracy to conceal income, defrauding California savings-and-loan executives of a hundred thousand dollars, and transportation of stolen money. The hundred thousand dollars feloniously extracted from the savings-and-loan people, incidentally, had been handed over by Baker to Senator Robert S. Kerr, of Oklahoma, who gave half that sum back to Baker as an unrecorded "loan."

On January 29, in the federal district court for the District of Columbia, Baker was convicted on seven counts. For all the mischief he had worked, Bobby Baker (by this time thirty-eight years old) was sentenced to one to three years in prison. Through appeals he postponed his actual jailing for four years; then he served less than seventeen months of his term, and was paroled. For the counts on which he was convicted, he could have been sentenced to forty-eight years' imprisonment and fined forty-seven thousand dollars.

Fred Black, Jr., Baker's partner in the Serv-U vending company, lobbyist for North American Aviation (fee, two hundred thousand dollars annually) and for other space-industry firms, was sentenced to imprisonment for a term of fifteen months to four years. His connections with Baker had given Black influence with Senator Kerr (then chairman of the Senate Committee on Aeronautical and Space Sciences) and with the NASA administrator. Conviction of Baker and Black was obtained by the revelations of a "bug" placed in Black's Washington hotel room in 1963 on instructions from Attorney General Robert Kennedy. After serving his sentence, Black returned to Washington for more interesting involvements.

But things did not go at all badly for some other persons associated with Baker's dealings. David Bress, counsel for Baker's and Black's Serv-U Corporation, was appointed United States attorney for the District of Columbia by President Johnson! And that influential lawyer Abe Fortas, who (at the express request of Lyndon Johnson) had represented Bobby Baker for a time during 1963, happily found himself appointed by President Johnson a justice of the Supreme Court of the United States. Later, under threat of impeachment by the House for his conflict-of-interest activities, Fortas found it necessary to resign from the Supreme Court.

The truth of many of the charges against Baker (including Johnson's involvement in various matters) is confessed with remarkable candor in Baker's memoir *Wheeling and Dealing* (1978). That book interestingly vindicates the work of the minority members of the Senate's Committee on Rules and Administration, much though Baker disliked those senators and Senator John J. Williams. Of Williams' proposed resolution that all members of the Senate be subject to investigation—a resolution shouted down by the Senate—Bobby Baker comments, "The result should have been foreseen by Senator Williams. Too many cans of worms would have been opened on both sides of the aisle had his resolution carried the day."

The mountain of a senatorial committee had labored long and produced a mouse, or perhaps a rat. Be that as it may, at least the Committee's minority, with the aid of Senator John Williams, had opened some Americans' eyes to the corruption that follows upon the concentrating of power and wealth in a central political apparatus.

Chapter 10

The Goldwater Campaign

THE CHARACTER AND RISE OF BARRY GOLDWATER

One of the more interesting political contests in the history of the United States was the struggle during 1964 to secure the Republican presidential nomination for Senator Barry Goldwater and then to elect him; Carl Curtis took a considerable part in both endeavors. In the short run, the national elections of 1964 were disastrous for the Republican Party; but in the long run, Goldwater's attempt transformed that party, giving it renewed purpose.

Curtis was drawn to Barry Goldwater not simply because they were friends and worked together, but even more because they held similar beliefs in the dignity of the individual—faith in the individual's ability to attain for himself what he could not do if shackled by a fussily paternalistic government.

Here one thinks of a passage in Alexis de Tocqueville's *Democracy in America*. Tocqueville describes "democratic despotism":

"Above this race of men stands an immense and tutelary power, which takes upon itself alone to secure their gratifications and to watch over their fate. That power is absolute, minute, regular, provident, and mild. It would be like the authority of a parent if, like that authority, its object was to prepare men for manhood; but it seeks, on the contrary, to keep them in perpetual childhood; it is well content that the people should rejoice, provided that they think of nothing but rejoicing. For their happiness such a government willingly labors, but it chooses to be the sole agent and the only arbiter of their necessities, facilitates their pleasures, manages their principal concerns, directs their industry, regulates the descent of property, and subdivides their inheritances; what remains, but to spare them all the care of thinking and all the trouble of living?"

In essence, the campaign of Barry Goldwater was manful resistance to democratic despotism.

No one found it easy to dislike Barry Goldwater. Even liberal Democrats like Senator Eugene McCarthy and liberal Republicans like Senator Clifford Case esteemed him as a person. A frontier forthrightness, hardihood, and cheerful persistence clung to Goldwater, even though Arizona is now the paradise of the retired, and the Goldwater trading post has become a fashionable department store. If Theodore Roosevelt won popularity as the exemplar of the strenuous life, Barry Goldwater retained effortlessly the atmosphere of those pioneer virtues which Americans have rated above military prowess.

Native penetration, prompt dispatch of business, realistic assessment of his fellows, readiness of decision: these are qualities that Goldwater would have brought to the presidency. He never loved committee work in the Senate, nor was he given to "agonizing reappraisals." He was willing to confess mistakes, but did not bawl over spilt milk. His dislike of cant and his almost heedless candor were remarkable among eminent politicians. Goldwater acted upon experience of the world, a healthy intuition, and the occasional advice of sensible men. Had it not been for the assassination of President Kennedy, Barry Goldwater might have been numbered among our more successful presidents.

Goldwater's rise had been swift: in five years, from 1950 to 1955, he had been metamorphosed from a Phoenix merchant to a senator of national influence. The next five years, 1955 to 1960, brought him into close association with Senator Curtis. The two of them were active in exposing Walter Reuther's abuses of union power, even making sorties into the UAW's stronghold of Detroit. Their case against Reuther's violations of the civil rights of working people influenced President Eisenhower, who, on December 5, 1956, addressing a joint meeting of the AFL and the CIO in New York City, declared that "the rights of minorities holding different social, economic, and political views must be scrupulously protected and their views accurately reflected."

Walter Reuther, put on the defensive by Goldwater's and Curtis' speeches, retaliated by arranging with Senator Albert Gore, Tennessee liberal, for the Senate's subcommittee on privileges and elections of the Committee on Rules and Administration to hold hearings that would feature favorably Reuther himself, and that would endeavor to shift public attention from union abuses to charges against business. At Gore's direction, this subcommittee's staff—members of the Committee not participating—prepared a "study" purporting to show that business and industrial corporations had contributed funds excessively to the Republican Party. In a single weekend—having been given very short notice, to put the matter mildly—Curtis prepared a stinging minority report (four pages of the Senate document of 928 pages), denouncing the Gore Report as a propaganda device released in irregular fashion as an official publication of the Senate, when in reality it was a biased production of members of the staff, dominated by Gore. On the Senate floor, February 7, 1957, Curtis exposed the unfairness and inadequacies of this "1956 General Election Campaign Report." Gore, Reuther, and their allies had expected this very lengthy (if very inaccurate) report to attract much attention in the mass media; actually, as matters turned out, the national press gave far more publicity to Curtis' rejoinder.

Goldwater's and Curtis' work together on the Select Committee on Improper Activities in Labor and Management has been described earlier in this book. With hearty approval, Curtis watched his friend Goldwater rise to a commanding position in their party.

Goldwater became chairman of the Republican Senatorial Campaign Committee. His help to liberal Republican candidates was highly effective because as a conservative he could secure votes for them that they could not have obtained for themselves. His bold stand against Reuther and other labor-union bosses, and his success as a popular campaign speaker in many states, were reinforced by publication of his blunt little book *The Conscience of a Conservative*, of which some seven hundred thousand copies were sold in little more than a year. Also his syndicated newspaper column, published in more than a hundred papers, attracted much attention. By 1960, Barry Goldwater loomed tall indeed among Republicans.

At the Republican National Convention that year, a powerful movement among the delegates developed to nominate Goldwater for the presidency—chiefly as a result of Richard Nixon's reconciliation, at the eleventh hour, with Nelson Rockefeller and the Republican liberals. But Goldwater said No, recognizing that he could not take the nomination away from Nixon and that an effort to do so might bring about Republican defeat in November. Withdrawing his name from nomination, Goldwater somewhat reluctantly endorsed Nixon on the floor of the convention. "It is our task," he said there, "as delegates to this 1960 Republican Convention to make certain the American voter is provided with an opportunity to make a meaningful choice between the two philosophies competing today for acceptance in our world, the philosophy of the stomach or the philosophy of the whole man."

After the narrow defeat of Richard Nixon by J. F. Kennedy in 1960, conservatives within the Republican Party began to press for the presidential nomination of Goldwater in 1964. Nelson Rockefeller, William Scranton, Clifford Case, Jacob Javits, and other liberal Republicans bitterly opposed Goldwater, even though he had greatly helped some of them in campaigns for re-election to office. Goldwater himself was a reluctant candidate: he would have preferred to support someone else who shared his convictions, but no well-known Republican of conservative principles likely to win election came forward. In

general, the large element in the Republican Party that had
hoped to elect the late Robert Taft to the presidency now backed
the Goldwater candidacy. And they were joined by a great many
other people, numerous conservative Democrats among them,
who were influenced by Goldwater's book *The Conscience of
a Conservative*, his success in confronting Walter Reuther and
other men of the left, and his strong personality.

The Goldwater boom swept forward like a great wave,
more among the general public than among Republican politicians. On February 14, 1964, Senator Curtis declared himself
a delegate to the Republican National Convention as a supporter
of Barry Goldwater. Senator Goldwater could win in November, Curtis said on that occasion; his nomination would make
the two-party system a reality. Goldwater had done much to
assist in the election of Republican candidates for the Senate
of varying shades of opinion; he would establish a firm foreign
policy; he would effectively resist deficit financing, enlargement of the national debt, over-concentration of power in
Washington; he would establish a sound fiscal program.

In the course of his speaking on behalf of Goldwater's can-
didacy, Curtis took part in a Goldwater rally at the armory in
Washington. F. Clifton White, in his book *Suite 3505*, describes
Curtis' part there:

·· "Senator Curtis came next, and his was one of the great
addresses of the evening. He spoke eloquently of 'the valiant—
at times, lonesome—fight that Barry Goldwater has waged for
those principles of freedom and a government of law that bring
us together tonight.' He vividly described how the New Frontier was establishing 'bureaucratic dictatorships' with 'policies
anchored in the strange philosophy that to impoverish the nation is to guarantee its strength and prosperity.' And he called
the dismal roll of recent foreign-policy failures 'from the Berlin Wall to the jungles of Vietnam.' "

The hard-fought contest for the presidential nomination,
commencing in March, 1960, was decided by the California primary late in the game. Even before that, Goldwater had held
a strong lead in pledged delegates; but had he lost to Nelson
Rockefeller in California, he might have been undone, the mass
media heavily favoring Rockefeller. To the surprise of publi-

cists and pollsters, Goldwater beat Rockefeller in California, taking all that state's delegates—though by a margin of less than one per cent of the total vote in the primary. In his autobiographical volume *With No Apologies*, Goldwater names William Knowland of California, Norris Cotton of New Hampshire, and Carl Curtis of Nebraska as his three chief senatorial backers. Along with supporters in many other quarters, those three colleagues had succeeded in bringing Goldwater to the Convention of 1964 as the leading candidate for the presidential nomination. But Curtis did not forget that there's many a slip 'twixt the cup and the lip.

CURTIS AS GOLDWATER'S FLOOR MANAGER

The Republican Convention of 1964 opened on Monday, July 13, in the Cow Palace, San Francisco. The Catholic Archbishop of San Francisco gave the invocation; ten chaplains were in attendance. Carl Curtis said that he never did find out whether the arrangement committee inviting the chaplains had in mind bringing so many eminent men of the cloth to pray so that they might be seen and heard of men, or whether that committee was unmindful of the admonition that prayers are not answered merely because they are long and verbose.

Several hundred people—delegates and their spouses—attended a breakfast meeting at the Fairmont Hotel for the Goldwater people. There Senator Goldwater dubbed Carl Curtis "the little tiger." In Curtis' remarks at the breakfast, he said that this was the first time he had attended a Republican national convention as a delegate. Stressing his inexperience, he emphasized that he would need the help of every Goldwater delegate, if the battle at the Convention was to be won. For Barry Goldwater had chosen Carl Curtis to be his floor leader at the Convention.

Indeed the floor fight was acrimonious. The day before the Convention opened, William Scranton, governor of Pennsylvania, had released to the press a letter, nominally addressed to Senator Goldwater but meant to influence the delegates. Scranton charged Goldwater with being a minority candidate and an extremist. Rarely has so intemperate a communication been sent by one party leader to the head of another faction in the same party. Scranton asked this question: would the convention choose a candidate overwhelmingly favored by Republican voters, or would it choose you, Goldwater?

Scranton told Goldwater, "You have too often casually prescribed nuclear war as a solution to a troubled world." He declared that Goldwater had been used by "radical extremists." He had stood for "irresponsibility in the serious question of racial holocaust." He had "too often read Taft and Eisenhower and Lincoln out of the Republican Party."

As Theodore White would write in his book *The Making of the President, 1964*, Scranton's letter "and the weekend seeking of confrontation ground…had made the Republican convention the stage for the destruction of the leading Republican candidate. What Rockefeller had begun in the spring, Scranton finished in June and at the convention: the painting for the American people of a half-crazed leader indifferent to the needs of American society at home and eager to plunge the nation into war abroad."

Despite such reckless accusations by Scranton and Rockefeller, information received by Carl Curtis as Goldwater floor manager indicated that not only would Goldwater receive the nomination, but that he would be nominated on the first ballot. Nevertheless, from his long experience in politics Curtis was accustomed never to take success for granted; he ran a tight ship, working as though one more delegate must be committed to Goldwater or else they would suffer defeat.

Steam had gone out of the Rockefeller effort; it seemed certain that all those opposed to Goldwater's nomination now had centered their hopes on William Scranton. But there were not enough Scranton delegates to deprive Goldwater of the nomination, unless some political accident or contrivance should upset the applecart.

The Scranton people attempted such an overturn.

In everyone's mind was present the memory of the convention contest between Dwight Eisenhower and Robert Taft in 1952. A furor had been raised on that occasion about which delegation from Texas should be seated; the Eisenhower backers had raised questions about the choosing of certain Taft delegates. No one acquainted with the men involved believed for a moment that Taft would have countenanced electoral dishonesty, or that Eisenhower himself would have so accused Taft. Nevertheless, the Eisenhower enthusiasts made much of the Texan controversy, and much of the press took up the matter. In the close contest of 1952, this business affected the convention and was a factor in Taft's defeat. The Scranton forces' only hope was that something similar might turn delegates against Goldwater.

Their move to discredit the Goldwater forces was made on the Convention's first day. Mrs. Josephine Margetts, a delegate from New Jersey, moved that until the convention's permanent organization should be settled and permanent rules adopted, the Convention should be governed by the rules adopted by the National Convention of 1960. Then Newton I. Steers, Jr., a delegate from Maryland, offered a substitute resolution providing that the rules of the Convention of 1960 should be followed— except that no one should be placed upon the permanent roll of delegates to the Convention if the Convention should determine that rules, practices, or procedures followed in the selection of such delegates or alternates had had the purpose or effect of discriminating in selection on the grounds of race, color, creed, or national origin. This substitute resolution authorized the credentials committee to investigate and report back by four o'clock the following afternoon. The Steers resolution, advanced by the Scranton people, was prompted by a question raised about one delegate, George W. Lee, a colored man from Tennessee.

Senator Curtis promptly recognized this move as the first step in an attempt to paint Barry Goldwater as a "racist" guilty of rigging the selection of delegates to deprive negroes of places in the Convention. Not unfriendly to Lee, Curtis wished Lee's case to be heard. Curtis contended that the credentials committee should interview Lee, asking questions and ascertaining facts. Curtis did not desire that the Convention should be delayed for a day, giving the Scranton forces and gentlemen of the mass media opportunity for twenty-four hours to paint Goldwater as a wrongdoer. Nor did Curtis think that the convention floor was the place to decide the issue before hearings could be held.

Steers, Bennett Webster of Iowa, and Elliot Richardson of Massachusetts spoke in favor of the Steers resolution, a total of some 1,800 words, to a courteous but unexcited audience. Curtis made the only response to these three speakers, in some two hundred and fifty words.

"There is no need for this harassing and diverting substitute," Curtis told the Convention. "An appeal has been presented in the Tennessee case relating to Mr. Lee. The Rules Committee and the Credentials Committee are just tribunals made up of men and women of integrity and fairness...Let every American have his day in court in an appropriate tribunal where he can be heard and questions can be asked in an authorized and lawful way, in accordance with our regulations."

The Convention's permanent chairman, Thruston Morton, called for a vote. A resounding response defeated the substitute resolution; the Goldwater people had won the first test.

But the forces opposing Goldwater did not give up easily. They offered a series of amendments to the party platform that had been presented for adoption—although this opposition was unsuccessful.

About this time, Mrs. Clare Boothe Luce—sometime member of Congress, sometime ambassador to Italy—remarked to Curtis that members of the Republican Eastern establishment now perceived the probability of Goldwater's nomination, and distinctly did not like it. Later, in her speech to the Convention, Mrs. Luce declared that Barry Goldwater had three cardinal virtues traditionally expected in responsible Republican leaders: "political loyalty, political courage, and political faith." She went on to say, "No audience in all America knows better than this audience that there is only one definition of courage in a politician, and that is his willingness to risk personal defeat rather than sell out his principles. If Senator Goldwater does not have political courage, then no politician has ever had it."

The time arrived for the nominating speeches. In addition to Goldwater's, seven other names were placed before the convention: Nelson Rockefeller of New York, Hiram Fong of Hawaii, Margaret Chase Smith of Maine, Henry Cabot Lodge of Massachusetts, George Romney of Michigan, Walter Judd of Minnesota, and finally William Scranton of Pennsylvania (nominated by Milton Eisenhower, President Eisenhower's brother).

When, before the Convention's opening, Curtis had been tapped to be floor leader by Senator Goldwater, he had made a study of as many past national conventions—both Republican and Democratic—as time permitted. He was well aware of what had happened at the Democratic Convention of 1912. There it had appeared that Champ Clark of Missouri was the leading candidate. William Jennings Bryan, the silver-tongued orator from the Platte, had interrupted a roll call to ask permission to explain his vote. Speaking at great length, Bryan had changed the course of that convention; Champ Clark had been rejected and Woodrow Wilson had been nominated. That episode was in Curtis' mind when the roll call at the 1964 Convention commenced.

Governor William Scranton sought recognition while the roll call was in progress. Curtis, promptly leaving his seat, mounted the platform to tell Chairman Morton privately that Governor Scranton should not be recognized. The rules of the House of Representatives governed the Convention: one could not interrupt the roll call to make a statement. Morton said to Curtis, "You have a right to stop it. What do you want to do?"

Curtis had to decide quickly. If he should insist on preventing Scranton from speaking, it might be interpreted as poor sportsmanship by the Goldwater forces. Also Curtis was convinced by this time that the Goldwater delegates were solid: there would be no substantial shift away from Goldwater, even though the delegates have the right to change their votes until the very moment the result is announced. Besides, he knew that Scranton might wish to be recognized so that he might ask for the vote for Goldwater to be unanimous, so Curtis did not press his point. On being recognized, Governor Scranton made a speech moving that the choice of Goldwater be made unanimous by the Convention.

After Congressman William E. Miller of New York had been nominated for the vice-presidency, Richard Nixon introduced Barry Goldwater. "I could introduce this man tonight as I know him—a friend, a neighbor, a good man, a man of great integrity, of courage," Nixon said. "I could introduce this man tonight as one who loves his country and will serve it well. But I present him to you tonight simply in this way: he is the man who earned and proudly carried the title of Mr. Conservative. He is the man who, by the action of this Convention, is now Mr. Republican. And he is the man who, after the greatest campaign in history, will be Mr. President—Barry Goldwater!"

Although the presidential contest of 1964 would be one of the most lively campaigns in American history, distinctly the Goldwater endeavor was not the greatest. What did happen has been related in several books, though in none of those books with entire understanding or accuracy. Here we set down merely a succinct interpretation of the events of that campaign.

A HARD ROW FOR THE
TRUTH SQUAD TO HOE

Accurately assessing his chances, Senator Goldwater never expected to win; nor that any other Republican candidate could defeat President Johnson. "At the beginning of December 1963, it was my considered opinion that no Republican could prevail against Lyndon Johnson," Goldwater writes in his memoirs. "President as a result of a great national tragedy, he could not be held accountable for the errors of his predecessor. Fate had muted all the issues I might have used in a confrontation with Jack Kennedy."

It had been otherwise before the murder of President Kennedy. Not long before that event, *Time* had published a survey indicating that had a presidential election been held in 1963, Goldwater probably would have defeated Kennedy in electoral votes. There being nothing lamblike about Barry Goldwater, it would be absurd to describe him as a Republican sacrificial lamb in the election of 1964; but he did deliberately choose, knowing that he could not be elected, to offer the public a choice between liberal ideas and policies, and conservative ideas and policies.

Before receiving the Republican nomination, Senator Goldwater scarcely possessed a staff in the sense that Kennedy and Rockefeller had surrounded themselves with speechwriters and technical advisers. "Senator Goldwater's office is run like that of the late Senator Chavez," said one friend with a smile, meaning that it was a cheerful, rather disorderly, southwestern home-town little affair. No burningly ambitious public man would have rested content for a day with so inadequate a base of operations. What intellectual assistance Goldwater required was obtained, casually, from some member of a committee staff, a conservatively-inclined professor or two of his acquaintance, a friendly newspaperman, or some old hand at Washington intricacies. Even such counsel ordinarily took the form of a brief memorandum or informal talk. What should he do for a staff in the urgent autumn of 1964?

The general direction of the campaign was placed in the hands of a friend from Arizona, Denison Kitchel, an honorable man of high principle who never before had participated in a campaign. Goldwater's inner circle for the venture was composed chiefly of Arizona friends, loyal but not conspicuously competent for the purpose. After the nomination, research and speech-writing were entrusted to William Baroody, president of the American Enterprise Institute, and the crew he assembled. The chief speech-writer was Karl Hess, an eccentric person who later converted himself into a peaceful anarchist and "junk" sculptor. There vanished from the Goldwater scene, after the nomination, Dr. Jay Gordon Hall, who previously had been Goldwater's shrewdest and best-educated immediate adviser; and Stephen Shadegg, who had managed Goldwater's senatorial campaigns. Two writers and columnists, William F. Buckley, Jr., and Russell Kirk, had advocated the Goldwater candidacy long before the Convention and occasionally had consulted with Goldwater. "Where was Buckley? Where was Kirk?" inquires Theodore White in his book about the election. The answer is that they had not abandoned ship: presumably Baroody and his people preferred to go it alone. The only occasion during the campaign itself on which Goldwater and Kirk met, as ships that pass in the night, was a chance encounter when Goldwater was entering the Beverley Wilshire Hotel in Los Angeles, and Kirk was passing out through that portal (the door being held open for them by Henry Salvatori, Goldwater's chief Californian backer).

Senator Goldwater then was about to address a rally at Chavez Ravine, in Los Angeles, organized by old Walter Knott of the Berry Farm & Ghost Town; Dr. Kirk was to speak on behalf of Goldwater at Claremont Men's College. The Chavez Ravine affair was a specimen of the inadequacy of the Goldwater campaign.

The Chavez Ravine rally consisted of thousands of Mexican-Americans, who ordinarily voted Democratic. But in 1964 those people were interested ardently in two questions of the day: the *bracero* program (for bringing migrant Mexican laborers to the United States), which had been terminated by the Johnson administration; and the urban-renewal program of the Johnson administration, which was demolishing their *barrios*. The Mexican-American voters hotly supported the first program and as hotly opposed the second. Senator Goldwater's views in these concerns coincided with their own.

Senator Goldwater might have begun with a few words of horse-trader Spanish and then launched into a vigorous endorsement of the *bracero* program and a telling indictment of urban "renewal." Instead, he read a genteel speech in praise of toleration of minorities. Mexican-Americans do not constitute a minority in the *barrios* where they dwell. The speech put into Goldwater's hands by his speech–writers did not go down well with his auditors, and no shift of Mexican-American voters to the Republican ticket occurred in November.

That was a sin of political omission. There were also sins of political commission, so far as vote-getting went. The most notorious case of the latter came right at the beginning of the campaign, in Senator Goldwater's acceptance speech at the Convention itself. This is the offending passage: "I would remind you that extremism in the defense of liberty is no vice. And let me remind you also that moderation in the pursuit of justice is no virtue."

A paraphrase of Cicero in defense of his arbitrary execution of the conspirators with Catiline (63 B.C.) against the Republic, these sentences in themselves certainly express a truth (if also they suggest an unhappy parallel, quite falsely). But during the Democratic defamation of Goldwater as an "extremist," this unlucky passage played into the hands of Goldwater's enemies; it was roundly denounced in much of the mass media. The lines in question had been approved by Karl Hess (who, however, some years later, in the course of a debate with Russell Kirk, shrugged off responsibility for them); they were the work of one of the Goldwater "intellectuals," Professor Harry Jaffe. One thinks of an aphorism of Nietzsche: "In politics, the professor always plays the comic role."

The writers of that speech failed to use the occasion to heal wounds within the Republican Party and to welcome his opponents into his camp. The ruthless and untruthful attacks on

Senator Goldwater during his fight at San Francisco for the nomination gave to Johnson's partisans and to a hostile press the foundation upon which they could build a campaign depicting Goldwater as an unbalanced, "trigger-happy" opportunist eager to lead the United States into nuclear war. That misbegotten speech also seemed to give substance to the charge that as President, Goldwater would abolish Social Security.

It had been assumed by many people close to Senator Goldwater that the acceptance-speech would be prepared under the direction of Dr. Jay Gordon Hall, a Ciceronian scholar (curious coincidence!) unlikely to have chosen that particular passage from Cicero, an able speech-writer, and one wise in practical politics. But matters went otherwise. Not long after Goldwater's defeat, Dr. Jaffe is said to have sneered at Goldwater's performance and to have expressed regret that he ever had enlisted in the contest. Such mistakes in judgment, made by men politically inexperienced and imprudent, repeatedly damaged the Goldwater campaign.

Yet even had Goldwater been aided by the more reliable strategists and advisers who had assisted him in the years and months before his nomination, the magnitude of his defeat presumably would not have been much diminished. To begin with, there existed a strong popular sympathy for the incumbent Democratic administration because of the assassination of President Kennedy—even though the murderer had been a homicidal fanatic with Cuban and Russian connections. As if this impediment were insufficient, the Lyndon Johnson campaign unscrupulously and successfully persuaded much of the public that Barry Goldwater was a public menace, intent on waging war and abolishing "social gains." The real issue on which Johnson and Goldwater principally differed—expansion or contraction of centralized government's activities—never was made clear to the voters.

The election was fought on a false issue: chiefly, military involvement, as if the United States had not already been deeply involved in Vietnam through the policies of Kennedy and Johnson. It was the Republican challenger to Democratic diplomatic and military policy, ironically, who was accused of being a warmonger!

Barry Goldwater's plan for keeping the peace was simple, though not simplistic. Goldwater was aware of the historical truth that aggressors do not initiate wars when they know that they would be defeated. Through strength is peace preserved. As Goldwater said at Pikesville, Maryland, on October 20, "If we have the strength and will, we will have peace, and the Communists will never bury us. We will instead see the day when those enslaved by communism will live under freedom."

Such sensible remarks were distorted by the managers of the Johnson campaign into "warmongering." There was shown nationwide on television the notorious Democratic spot-advertisement of a little girl picking flowers—an idyllic scene terminated by a nuclear explosion, presumably in consequence of Goldwater's alleged happiness with triggers, and presumably reducing to fractured atoms the little girl and the flowers.

The Johnson assault was not confined to questions of rashness and armaments. Goldwater's stand on Social Security and his remarks on education were grossly misrepresented by his opponents. Speaking on schooling, Goldwater declared that "the federal government has no right to educate children. The family has an obligation to educate children through local schools and local school boards and local taxation." Very promptly President Johnson charged that Goldwater had said, "The child has no right to an education."

Popular magazines published venomous anti-Goldwater editorials and articles. The worst of these smears occurred in the October number of *Fact* magazine, "a special issue on the mind of Barry Goldwater," with two sections: the first entitled "Goldwater, the Man, the Menace," by Ralph Ginzburg and Warren Boroson; the second, "What Psychiatrists Say About Goldwater." Goldwater was described therein as "mentally unbalanced," a "dangerous lunatic," a "coward"; he was said to suffer from nervous breakdowns and paranoia and to be a "compensated schizophrenic" with a "chronic psychosis."

For a candidate for public office to recover damages for language used against him, it is necessary that he prove malice. Goldwater brought suit in the federal courts. A jury returned a verdict against the three defendants, awarding Goldwater a dollar in compensatory damages against Ginzburg, Boroson, and *Fact* magazine, and punitive damages in the amount of twenty-five thousand dollars against Ginzburg and fifty thousand dollars against *Fact*. A United States Court of Appeals sustained this verdict in July, 1969.

Indeed this was a landmark case. With reference to most publications, the law grants immunity to writers and publishers during a political campaign. It requires a strong case to win; Goldwater's case was very strong.

Senator Curtis was in charge of the Republican "Truth Squad," which toured the country refuting the allegations of Johnson and Humphrey. Arriving at Cape Canaveral, in Florida, the Squad encountered a rumor (presumably inspired) that if Barry Goldwater were elected, the launching area for the space program would be shifted to another site. Knowing this rumor to be altogether unfounded, Curtis inquired of high officials in the space program concerning the matter. He was informed that the Space Center at Cape Canaveral could not be moved, being situated at a place just right for the launching; that this site had been selected because of what are called "windows to outer space."

The Truth Squad, usually made up of three or four Republican senators or representatives, found themselves often doing battle with the press. Reporters like sensational news. The doings of the Johnson administration offered plenty of such news: the Bobby Baker wheelings and dealings, the Walter Jenkins case, the misdeeds of Billie Sol Estes, Lyndon Johnson's accumulation of wealth. But many newspapermen chose rather to run with the hounds in pursuit of Goldwater, printing lengthily the fabricated charges, innuendos, and smears against him supplied by the Johnson operation.

On one occasion, Curtis, traveling with the Truth Squad, was approached by an Ohio voter, apparently a working family man, who said to him, "Well, it looks like we're faced with voting for a crook or a trigger-happy madman, and I think we'd better vote for the crook." Such was the general level of political discourse in 1964.

Few big newspapers endorsed Senator Goldwater; one that did was the *Los Angeles Times* (although in the California primary the *Times* had backed Rockefeller). Editorially, the *Times* pointed out that Johnson should share the blame for massive involvement in Vietnam, the Cuban blunders, and the Bobby Baker scandals.

Yet the wire services, conspicuously hostile toward Goldwater, necessarily are depended upon by all newspapers; and while editorial writers may lean toward one candidate, reporters and rewrite people may lean in a different direction. At a "Meet the Press" television interview, Senator Goldwater was questioned as to what might be done about the military stalemate in Vietnam. He replied, "Well, some people in the Pentagon are talking about using low-yield atomic bombs to defoliate the Ho Chi Minh Trail. I don't think we'll do that."

Within hours, in nearly all major newspapers, there appeared on front pages such banner headings as "Goldwater Says Use Atomic Bomb," or "Defoliate Vietnam, Says Goldwater." Such a heading appeared on the front page of the *Los Angeles Times*, too, even though actually Senator Goldwater had said the opposite. Put not your trust in leader-writers. No candidate can contend successfully against such a wave of prejudice and malice. It was especially shabby to do such things to Goldwater, a sincere and candid man.

In the closing weeks of the campaign, the Greater Chicago Adult Education Council sponsored a debate between Hans Morganthau (for the Democratic candidates) and Russell Kirk (for the Republicans). That mordant foreign-policy authority Morganthau told the audience that Barry Goldwater was a lovable, kindly, generous man, "a wonderful human being," but a man who "could scarcely entertain two consecutive ideas." On the other hand, Morganthau continued, Lyndon Baines Johnson was a selfish, grasping, unscrupulous man, yet keenly intelligent, "with a mind like a steel trap."

Morganthau would vote for intelligence, not for character. He must have been disappointed, to put it mildly, in Johnson's subsequent performance in Vietnam and otherwise. It was rather Goldwater, with his very considerable military knowledge, who would have tended in the presidential office to follow the general policy of "pursuing the national interest," so well expressed by Morganthau himself. Besides, Goldwater would have been restrained from imprudent action by the presumptive Democratic majority in Congress; while Johnson, with his heavy congressional majorities elected in 1964, at first encountered no such congressional restraints. As for strategy in Vietnam, the triumphant Johnson subjected North Vietnam to merciless but militarily ineffectual bombing; while doubtless Goldwater, in office, would have followed the policy of closing the port of Haiphong, with little loss of life, and so soon forcing the communist government at Hanoi to come to terms, as President Nixon did later—thus terminating the agony, in both North and South Vietnam, of the interminable civil war.

At the Morganthau-Kirk debate was present Louis Cheskin, of Cheskin Associates, scientific pollsters. The Cheskin firm was given to polling opinion selectively, in depth, with remarkably accurate predictions in consequence of their methods. Cheskin privately informed Dr. Kirk that a new poll by the Cheskin organization, taken among a good representative sample of voters in two key states (California and Illinois) was conclusive as to the result of the swiftly approaching election. Holding that the typical voter is more moved by his prejudices (often unrecognized by the voter himself) than by rational considerations, Cheskin did not ask the sampled citizens for which presidential candidate they intended to vote; rather, the Cheskin pollsters endeavored to ascertain by ingenious questioning the underlying inclinations of members of the sample.

In this subtle Johnson-Goldwater poll, Cheskin had presented his small but well-selected sample of the electorate with some one hundred questions, each with three possible responses. No question bore *directly* on what candidate the voter would support on election day. On several important counts, Goldwater scored better with the sample than did Johnson. But on one key question, Johnson scored immensely above Goldwater. It was this: "Suppose that Lyndon Johnson and Barry Goldwater were out hunting deer. Do you think that either of these candidates would fire at the first movement in the brush?"

A considerable number of respondents thought that Johnson would so fire recklessly. But approximately double that number believed Barry Goldwater liable to fire at the first movement in the brush.

"You see, Dr. Kirk," Cheskin remarked, "it's all over. The prejudice against Goldwater on the trigger-happy issue is so strong as to outweigh prejudices in his favor on some other issues." Cheskin predicted that Johnson would win by an immense margin. Actually, Goldwater did a trifle better than the Cheskin poll had predicted—but only a trifle.

On election day, Johnson-Humphrey took forty-four states and sixty-one percent of the popular vote; Goldwater-Miller, six states and 38.5 per cent of the popular vote. The Democrats greatly increased their majorities in both houses of Congress, and made similar gains in state and local offices. In plurality and in proportion of the popular vote, this was the grimmest defeat a Republican presidential ticket ever had suffered. President Johnson proceeded to turn trigger-happy, or rather bomb-happy, in Vietnam.

Reinforced by this tremendous triumph at the polls, Johnson also proceeded to enact through his congressional majorities the huge "social programs" (often anti-social in their consequences) and systems of "transfer payments" he had promised so lavishly during the campaign of 1964. Federal educational benefits (bringing federal direction of public instruction in many respects), more disastrous public housing and urban "renewal," immensely costly public medical benefits, dubious and expensive measures alleged to bring about full employment—these and other pieces of Johnsonian policy expanded the operations and the costs of the American welfare state more greatly than had the combined "social programs" of the Roosevelt, the Truman, and the Kennedy administrations. The overwhelming deficit of the federal government's budget today, and the towering national debt, are direct consequences of Johnson's simultaneous expenditures on guns and butter.

Nemesis, in the person of Senator Eugene McCarthy standing in the New Hampshire primary of 1968, four years later overtook Lyndon Baines Johnson, that "total political animal" (as Hans Morganthau called him). Disgraced in the eyes of the public that had so overwhelmingly endorsed him (or, to write more accurately, that had rejected his opponent overwhelmingly), Johnson found it necessary to withdraw from candidacy for re-election. Financially, however, nobody ever had done better out of years in the Senate and the White House. "Ah, take the cash and let the credit go," in Omar Khayyam's line.

And Barry Goldwater, who never derived from public office and political influence any cash advantage beyond his senatorial salary? Mr. Goldwater stands as high today in public opinion as he seemed low in 1964. Praised by the leaders of both parties and applauded by the very mass media that had denounced him, little more than two decades ago, as a trigger-happy fanatic, Barry Goldwater retires from the Senate the same honorable, frank, and generous man he was in 1964, a conservative with a conscience.

In the first paragraph of this chapter, we mentioned that Goldwater's ordeal opened the way, in the long run, for a revivified Republican Party. with fresh principles and purposes. The Republican "Eastern Establishment" of such "liberal" or "moderate" politicians as Nelson Rockefeller, William Scranton, and Jacob Javits (difficult to distinguish, most of the time, from liberal or moderate Democrats) never wholly recovered from defeat at the Cow Palace in 1964. The predominance of political influence, as of population and wealth, shifted from New York to California.

Thereafter, under the leadership of Richard Nixon and Ronald Reagan, the Republican Party developed into a consciously conservative power with discernible principles. Sixteen years after the Republicans' debacle of 1964, Ronald Reagan (the most effective campaigner for Goldwater in 1964) won the presidency in a victory of Johnson's proportions in 1964, carrying forty-three states and 483 electoral votes, to Jimmy Carter's six states and forty-nine electoral votes; in the popular vote, a plurality of twelve million over President Carter. The label "conservative" had become advantageous for most candidates for office, as suggested by the Republicans' capture of the Senate in 1980 and their gains in the House.

Conservatism, as Abraham Lincoln put it, is a preference for the old and tried over the new and untried. Also conservatism can be something more: the renewal of a people's hopes. Barry Goldwater lost his campaign but commenced that renewal.

Chapter 11

Welfare-State Medicine

THE ROOTS OF STATE
MEDICAL PROGRAMS

To have one's medical bills paid by somebody else: on the face
of it, that's an attractive concept. One of the difficulties in such
schemes has to do with those hard old laws of demand and supply. The demand for medical services is infinite, never to be
satisfied; and this is true especially today, when the ingenious
techniques of scientific medicine make it possible to keep alive
(if sometimes in a subhuman state) people who in any previous era would have passed naturally to eternity. Demand being unlimited, supply can never keep up with demand—not
if services are supplied free of charge, or at least well below
the cost of those services.

Yet if the welfare state supplies food below the cost of
production, and lodging below the cost of production, it seems
reasonable enough to many citizens that the welfare state
should supply medical care below its cost of production. In the

long run, nevertheless, someone has to pay the doctors' bills and the hospitals' bills, which increase vastly under systems of state medicine. Those bills tend to become insupportable, even in the most prosperous society. Two consequences come to pass: first, the quality of medical services markedly declines, supply being insufficient to meet demand; second, the burden of taxation to support state medical systems becomes a major item of national expenditure, resulting in deficit financing, inflation, and serious impairment of the fundamental functions of government.

In the United States, Medicare and Medicaid have been in effect for merely two decades; yet even older citizens tend to forget that there was a time, not very long ago, when the federal government did nothing to help with medical bills. How did people survive in such an era? Why, the vast majority of them met their own bills, without assistance from anybody; for medical costs were much lower then. (Medicare, Medicaid, and related governmental programs have greatly increased doctors' and hospitals' bills for everybody.) Those who could not pay their own medical bills were assisted by physicians who charged the needy little or nothing; by "free bed" hospitals financed from local and private benefactions; and by charitable funds and attention supplied by religious organizations, private foundations, and municipal or county governments. Few thought of the United States as deficient in medical services, and nobody argued that Americans were an unhealthy people.

Yet the wave of state intervention which swept upon the world with the coming of the Great Depression and of authoritarian political systems carried on its crest proposals for state medicine—that is, "socialized" medicine. Usually these proposals took the form of "compulsory national health insurance." (That phrase had rather an odd ring in America, though, for *voluntary* health insurance was spreading rapidly to a large part of the population.) There was far more resistance to such concepts in the United States than in Europe. Not until 1965—and then in consequence of a kind of political accident —did even a limited form of state medicine obtain adoption here.

The pressures for welfare-state medical services had begun

three decades earlier. In 1935, President Franklin Roosevelt's Committee on Economic Security had endorsed the principle of compulsory national health insurance, though the Congress did not take up bills for such purposes. High-school debaters commenced to discuss socialized medicine; so did the advance-guard liberals.

By 1943, the liberals in Congress made a gesture in favor of socialized medicine—a gesture only, for the costs of the war and the preoccupations of that struggle would have made passage of such legislation impossible then, even if the majority in Senate and House had smiled on the idea. The Wagner-Murray-Dingell Bill proposed compulsory national health insurance to cover citizens of all ages: thorough-going socialized medicine. The bill did not obtain a full-scale hearing in the House of Representatives; Representative Curtis was active in mustering opposition.

Two years later, President Truman proposed a comprehensive, prepaid medical insurance plan, to be financed by raising the Social Security tax. This plan gained no more ground in Congress than had the bill of 1943; again, Curtis worked against it.

Pressure in America for some form of government-supported medical care was increased, beginning in 1946, by the inception of the British National Health Service, a conspicuous part of the new Labour government's welfare state. For several years after the National Health Service began to operate in July, 1946, American liberals pointed to socialized medicine in Great Britain as a noble system to be emulated. But this early admiration gradually subsided. Reports of the endless queues in British doctors' consulting rooms, of the disillusionment of British physicians and surgeons, of long delays for major operations, of tremendous costs to the government— these accounts of the failures of the National Health Service, all too accurate, had their effect even on melioristic liberals in the United States.

The National Health Service was the most popular feature of Lord Beveridge's welfare state; initially at least; also it was the most costly. (In the early years of the scheme, even aspirins were supplied free of charge to all comers.) John Strachey (who was to become Minister of Health in the Attlee government) had prophesied on the eve of Labour's victory in the general elections of 1945 that the intended National Health Service would prolong indefinitely the life span of the happy residents of the British Isles: both work and death, it appeared, would be abolished by socialist planning. This did not come to pass. Instead, as the Health Service settled down into its somewhat dreary routine, British doctors began to flee to Canada, Australia, New Zealand, South Africa, the United States, practically anywhere, to escape the overwork, the low pay, and the endless form-filling that socialized medicine had imposed upon them. They were supplanted in London hospitals, and presently in a great many other places, by medical personnel from India, Pakistan, and Hong Kong, distinctly unlike the old British image of the family doctor. "Social insurance" charges, especially for the Health Service, became a major item in most British families' budgets. First-rate medical attention of a personal character, privately paid for, became almost impossible to obtain in Britain—except on Harley Street, in London, and there at high cost. Wyndham Lewis' mordant story-vignettes "The Room Without a Telephone" and "Dr. Musgrave's Rebellious Patient" sufficiently portray what happened to the medical arts in Britain under the National Health Service.

So the embarrassing performance of socialized medicine in Britain dissuaded Congress from adopting any grand measure of state medicine—aside from appropriating lavish sums to subsidize the building of hospitals—for twenty years after the Truman proposal. American advocates of a welfare state continued their propaganda for some form of socialized medicine, nevertheless—for a time gradually gaining ground in public opinion. Congresswoman Frances Bolton, of Cleveland, periodically polled her constituents on this issue, as such plans began to be presented to Congress. She found that in the earlier years of the discussion, a majority of her sample of voters in her district favored proposals for federal action in this field; yet in the House she voted consistently against such plans. As the years passed, however, the proportion of voters approving state medicine (or some modification thereof) diminished.

Meanwhile, private plans for medical insurance had come to include the majority of Americans. On the eve of passage of the Medicare plan during the Johnson administration, Representative Bolton found that the majority of voters in her sample—and hers was mainly an urban industrial district—had come to oppose bills for welfare-state medicine. The Medicare program, in short, was no response to a strong popular demand; for the most part, the need for medical insurance already had been satisfied by voluntary group-insurance plans, company and union medical policies, and private medical insurance.

But we are running ahead of our story. Carl Curtis and his colleagues were successful in bottling up the Truman proposals for state medicine. Addressing the Lancaster County Medical Association, in Lincoln, on October 10, 1946, Curtis briefly expressed his reasons for opposing the notion of state medicine, which on the face of it might seem a generous concept:

"The relation of physician and patient is a personalized, sacred relation based upon faith.

"It cannot exist under a system of state medicine; a system of state medicine means not only a humdrum life for the doctor, but the people become but cogs in the wheel. They are treated as groups and not as individuals. It is not necessary that the practice of medicine be socialized in order for the government to give due attention to public health."

Curtis said this at a time when (in the words of the British historian Arthur Marwick) "aspects of the Welfare State were matters of sharp controversy within Britain, and generally mistrusted in the United States." These cautionary remarks did not prevent the blunders of Medicare, enacted twenty years later; but they, and similar declarations by other public men, did much to prevent the American adoption of socialized medicine on the British pattern.

President Eisenhower, taking office in 1953, was no advocate of a medical program sponsored by the federal government. But he seems to have dreaded "the inevitability of gradualism"; that is, to have feared that a plan of state medicine would be adopted eventually unless some palliative measure were offered.

Therefore his administration, with Mrs. Oveta Culp Hobby as Secretary of Health, Education, and Welfare, brought forward a proposal, somewhat resembling the later "Medicare," to be implemented by and through private insurance companies. The Eisenhower plan would have established a general medical-insurance system by allowing insurers to act in concert (through an amendment to the anti-trust laws) and providing for reinsurance by the federal government. This idea was not favored either by the private insurance companies or by the advocates of state medicine on the model of the Wagner-Murray-Dingell bill; and its details were sketchy.

Replying to Mrs. Hobby's advocacy of the administration's bill, Edwin J. Faulkner, president of a Nebraska insurance company, addressed the House of Delegates of the American Medical Association on November 29, 1954. He argued that the growth of voluntary health–insurance plans made the intervention of the federal government unnecessary. He pointed out that the number of Americans insuring themselves against hospitalization costs had risen sharply from six million in 1939 to one hundred and three million in 1954; and more than three-fifths of the civilian workforce already were insured against wage-loss because of disability.

Such arguments prevailed: the Eisenhower administration's reinsurance bill made no headway in Congress.

Next, in 1957, the Democrats came forward with a bill introduced by Congressman Aime J. Forand (Rhode Island Democrat): a bill that was the forerunner of Medicare. Backed by the AFL-CIO, the Forand bill provided hospital and surgical costs for the aged, to be financed by the Social Security system. By 1960, this was a hot political issue. Senator John F. Kennedy sponsored the companion to the Forand Bill in the Senate.

Referred to the House Committee on Ways and Means, the Forand Bill was defeated, seventeen votes to eight. Representative Wilbur Mills (Arkansas Democrat), the committee chairman, was one of the bill's opponents, which showed that it would be a rough road for the Forand proposal, let alone any more comprehensive form of state medicine.

When the Kennedy administration came to power in 1961, Speaker Sam Rayburn and the administration succeeded in placing Medicare supporters on the Ways and Means Committee. By 1963, the margin of opposition had shrunk to a single vote; there it stayed until 1965. Chairman Mills remained in opposition, but in 1964 issued a statement that suggested he was inclining toward some form of prepaid medical insurance for the aged.

In 1962, Senator Clinton Anderson (New Mexico Democrat) sponsored President Kennedy's bill for Medicare. (Anderson's revised version of the Forand-Kennedy Bill had been defeated in 1960.) The Anderson-Kennedy proposal was for hospital benefits only; Representative Cecil King (California Democrat) sponsored the parallel bill in the House. King's bill died in committee, Anderson's revised bill on the Senate floor.

During the Kennedy administration, nevertheless, Congress did enact (in 1960) the Kerr-Mills program, providing for grants to the states for paying the medical bills of needy persons receiving old-age assistance. It was a relief measure, not a permanent program under the Social Security system.

The final Medicare effort of the Kennedy administration was President Kennedy's special message to Congress, in 1963, entitled "Aiding Our Senior Citizens." Neither the Committee on Ways and Means nor the Committee on Finance advanced the related bill in the House. In the Senate, Albert Gore (Tennessee Democrat) did succeed, by a narrow margin, in attaching this proposal to a Social Security bill; but the Gore amendment died in Senate-House Conference Committee.

It was clear, in the latter days of the Kennedy administration, that Congress was not inclined toward enlarging Social Security to include medical benefits for the elderly, and that no very powerful pressure from the public was behind such concepts. All this was changed by the overwhelming election of Lyndon Johnson to the presidency in 1964.

THE SHAKY CASE
FOR MEDICARE, 1965

President Lyndon Baines Johnson aspired to be remembered as a benefactor of the masses after the fashion of Franklin Roosevelt. His Great Society was intended to parallel and enlarge Roosevelt's New Deal. Roosevelt had failed to obtain adoption of any federal medical program; Johnson meant to excel his exemplar in this. With a solid Democratic majority in both houses of Congress, and the "mandate" of his huge victory over Senator Goldwater, Johnson could obtain from the legislative branch what President Kennedy could not. Passing the Medicare proposal was Johnson's first priority.

When Congress convened at the beginning of 1965, the Medicare bills were the first measures introduced: Senate bill 1, House bill 1. They provided for hospital care for the aged, but not for doctors' bills.

Opposing Medicare, the American Medical Association made this omission of the doctors part of their argument against the whole proposal. This error in strategy was one reason why Medicare, when finally enacted, carried a provision for voluntary supplemental health care, assisting in the payment of doctors' bills. Under this provision, a recipient of Social Security benefits might elect to have deducted from his Social Security check payment for that part of his Medicare program related to doctors' fees.

As an alternative to the Medicare bills, the American Medical Association backed a quite different proposal called "Eldercare." Senator Curtis was asked to sponsor Eldercare; he refused, regarding it as better than the other plans, but not wishing to endorse any medical program administered by the federal government. It would be a blunder in strategy, Curtis thought, to suggest thus that he believed there should be such legislation of some sort.

Elements of the private insurance industry advanced another substitute proposal; Curtis took the same stand with regard to their plan that he had taken with Eldercare, refusing to sponsor or co-sponsor the insurance-company alternative.

Neither the Medicare bills nor the two proposed substitutes were by any means so sweeping as the measures of state medicine advanced during the Roosevelt and Truman administrations. It was not proposed that the federal government exercise any general supervision over doctors, or pay them salaries, or own and operate hospitals, or extend medical benefits to the whole population. Even the Medicaid bills that were advanced along with the Medicare bills were limited in their scope to the indigent, and were to be administered and in part paid for by the state governments; no wholly centralized system of state medicine was advanced. Even with Johnson's domination of Congress, a sweeping system of socialized medicine could not have won enactment or obtained public approval.

For socialized medicine the other side of the Atlantic was in no healthy condition. In Europe, Belgian doctors had struck against their country's public health system, declaring that they had been converted into public servants at low pay. And now, at the very time when Congress was debating Medicare, some twenty-three thousand British doctors were threatening to quit the National Health Service, on the recommendation of the General Medical Services Committee of the British Medical Association. The total annual cost of the National Health Service had turned out to be several times higher than had been expected in 1946, even though the pay of doctors by the Service had been niggardly. British "family" doctors demanded that their pay be tolerably increased; the Health Service offered them the sterling equivalent of fourteen dollars a week more, which would bring the typical family doctor's income to $168 per week; the doctors said it ought to be brought up to $196 weekly. Besides losing income under state medicine, British doctors had lost freedom. Complaints of the cost and mismanagement of other European state medical systems reached the ears of Congress and the American public. In 1965, nobody proposed an equivalent of the Wagner-Murray-Dingell bill, with its comprehensive coverage and "socialization" of medical services.

Medicare would be confined to the elderly, and Medicaid to the indigent; and the federal government would be principal paymaster, rather than proprietor of a state monopoly of medical care. Yet even so, was the case for the Medicare bills sound?

The purpose of the Medicare plan was to provide for part of the medical wants of persons more than sixty-five years of age. In 1965, there were some eighteen or nineteen million such "senior citizens." Of these millions, it appeared that approximately one million were in real need of assistance in paying for hospitalization and doctors' bills. Yet Medicare would provide funds for all the elderly, whether or not they should be short of funds.

To be elderly is not, by definition, to be poor. In the decade preceding 1965, incomes of persons over sixty-five years of age had been increasing—and increasing more rapidly than those of other age groups. Most people over sixty-five already had subscribed to private medical-insurance plans. Men and women over sixty-five, on the average, actually were better able to pay their medical bills than were most young couples in their twenties, with childbirths and childhood diseases on the red side of their ledgers. True, the elderly had smaller earned incomes; but they had larger savings, smaller expenditures in many respects, rarely labored under mortgages, rarely supported dependents, and might receive assistance from children and grandchildren. It appeared that scarcely more than one old person in twenty required charitable help in the United States.

Those one million needy "senior citizens" would not be singled out for special help by the Medicare program. On the contrary, the richest man or woman in America would be equally eligible for the benefits of Medicare, as proposed by the Johnson administration. This conceivably might secure nineteen million votes for Lyndon Johnson & Company, at the next national election; but it would not deal adequately with the real problem. Medicare would be spread thinly over the whole elderly population, regardless of need, and regardless of cost to the general public through increased Social Security taxes to pay for Medicare.

In 1966, Social Security taxes would increase startlingly. A self-employed person with an income of six thousand dollars would have to pay $405.90 in Social Security taxes, as against the 1965 maximum of $259.20. Still greater increases would follow, year after year, as analyzed later in this chapter. Medicare and Medicaid, it would turn out, would cost several times the sums estimated in 1965.

The fact is that the large majority of the elderly in 1965 did not require federal subventions from Social Security for hospital bills and doctors' fees. Some sixty per cent of those people already had their own medical insurance. Their capital assets, on the average, were larger than those of younger age groups. In 1965, the average head of a family over sixty-five years of age was worth about thirty-one thousand dollars, (which, of course, would purchase immensely more in 1965 than the same sum would today). According to the President's Council on the Aging, between 1950 and 1961 the number of people over sixty-five increased forty per cent, but their total income increased more than a hundred and thirty per cent, contrasted with an eighty per cent increase for the entire American population during that period. Not only was income increasing, but by 1965 some seventy-eight per cent of the American population (in all age groups) possessed some form of medical insurance—private, company, union, fraternal, professional association, and the like. Medicare would impose a double burden on these do-it-yourself citizens: they would pay the vastly increased Social Security taxes, willy-nilly, although already saving to provide for their own medical needs.

Public opinion polls, in 1965, suggested that nearly eighty per cent of American citizens did not understand the provisions of the Medicare bills. President Johnson had obtained no "mandate" for Medicare; indeed, the issue did not seem to have contributed to the Democratic victory in 1964, and Democratic politicians themselves had been divided on the question.

These were some of the reasons why Carl Curtis did what he could to impede passage of the Medicare bill in the Senate.

THE MEDICARE CONTROVERSY
IN CONGRESS

No sooner was Johnsonian Medicare proposed in Senate and House than the program began to grow. Representative John Byrnes, of Wisconsin, offered the provision to add doctors' bills to the King-Anderson measure. (This is now known as Part B of Medicare.) Chairman Wilbur Mills helped to incorporate Byrnes' provision in the Medicare package.

The hospital provision of the Medicare program offered benefits to any person over sixty-five years of age: these benefits included as much as ninety days of hospital care for every spell of illness, with certain deductible amounts to be paid by the patient; up to a hundred days of post-hospital care in a nursing home, less deductibles; and as much as a hundred post-hospital, home-health-care visits by a nurse. The original Part B benefits provided that any person over sixty-five years of age might purchase for a three-dollar monthly payment a supplementary, voluntary health-insurance plan covering doctors' bills. This plan would pay eighty per cent of the cost of doctors' fees after an initial deduction of fifty dollars for the year: the services of physicians, surgeons, radiologists, pathologists, and similar services in hospitals, clinics, offices, and homes were included, as well as x-rays and laboratory tests.

Monthly payments by the recipients of services by no means would cover the full cost of these Part B benefits; the federal government was to match the amount of the payments out of general funds. The government was to collect the premiums and to administer the medical program, together with the hospital benefits. Elderly citizens not eligible for Social Security would have their medical costs defrayed by the government from general funds.

Such was the general outline of Medicare, in 1965. A basic issue was involved in the debate about the bill: is it the obligation of the political state to provide medical care for its citizens? In Carl Curtis' belief, government should provide such care for those citizens unable to provide themselves with medical necessities and for whom care is not to be obtained from another source. At that point the responsibility of general government should end. Curtis was convinced also that public responsibility in such concerns is not that of the federal government alone, but of government at every level.

Such was not the theory of the proponents of the Medicare bill. Medicare would pay benefits to every person more than sixty-five years old, regardless of the individual's assets or income. It was a plan to be run by the federal government, a subsidized program available without test of need; its rules and requirements would affect every health-care unit and every health-care provider.

Curtis could not bring himself to increase the taxes paid by working people so that the government might pay the hospital and medical bills of persons able to afford the cost of their own care. He perceived that there was a moral issue here. Some people, not regarded as wealthy or well-to-do, nevertheless have private insurance providing for their medical benefits in years of retirement; among these are civil servants and those many individuals who have worked for corporations that provide insurance as part of a fringe-benefit package. Other persons can turn to group insurance, paid for in previous years for the most part. Medicare left such people out of its reckoning, treating them as if they would be dependent on public assistance. Quite recently, Curtis had his attention called to the case of a woman of great wealth whose hospital and medical bills for a spell of illness came to seventeen thousand dollars— and were paid for by Medicare, out of the earnings of Social Security taxpayers, many of whom find it difficult to pay their Social Security contributions. Why should taxpayers assume the medical bills of persons well able to defray their own costs, any more than taxpayers should pay the grocery bills of persons perfectly competent to buy their own food?

But the majority in Congress did not appear to be troubled by such oldfangled scruples. Endorsed by the majority of the House Committee on Ways and Means (including now Chairman Mills), and heartily supported by President Johnson, Medicare passed the House on April 8, 1965, by a roll-call vote of 313 to 115. The Senate's Committee on Finance held hearings from April 29 to May 13. Anthony Celebrezze, Secretary of Health, Education, and Welfare, calling the bill a landmark, urged its enactment.

At the close of these hearings, Senator Russell Long—then the second-ranking Democrat on the Finance Committee—offered a substitute bill, which Curtis supported because it distinguished between those able to pay their medical costs and those who could not, placing deductions on a variable scale based on income. After several votes Long's substitute was defeated.

By a vote of twelve to five, on June 24, the Finance Committee reported the bill. Senator Curtis wrote the dissent of the minority, in which he was joined by the Committee's chairman, Senator Harry Byrd (Virginia Democrat) and three Republicans—Senators Williams of Delaware, Bennett of Utah, and Morton of Kentucky. The minority report emphasized the inequity of taxing the gross earnings of working people to pay the bills of the wealthy and well-to-do.

Medicare came to the Senate floor in the summer; it was obvious that this piece of legislation was going to be enacted. Some senators previously opposed to the measure were ready to acquiesce, taking Medicare to be inevitable. Medicare was not a separate measure, but part of a larger Social Security bill which carried provisions favored by most senators.

Carl Curtis' first move on the Senate floor was to move to delete the Medicare provisions from the bill. He pointed out that Medicare would increase the annual outlay for Social Security in the immediate future by another eight billion dollars, some fifty per cent more, altogether, than was paid out for Social Security benefits in 1964. Curtis' motion lost, sixty-four votes against it, twenty-six in favor. Fifteen senators, Democrats and Republicans, who had voted against Medicare in 1964 voted for it in 1965.

Thus deprived of some of his previous allies, Senator Curtis then endeavored to see if he could improve the Medicare proposal by amendment or by a substitute.

The committee's bill provided for a deduction of forty dollars for hospitalization and a deduction of fifty dollars for medical services. A destitute person would have had to pay forty dollars and fifty dollars, while a wealthy man would have been required to pay merely the same sums to receive subsidized hospital and medical services. Curtis' major proposed amendment was to establish the deduction either at the dollar levels provided in the committee's bill or at an amount equal to the recipient's income tax for the previous year, whichever was greater. Thus if an individual paid five thousand dollars in income tax in the previous year, in the benefit year a deduction of five thousand dollars would be made from his claim on Medicare benefits. Social Security benefits not being taxable, an older person would have to possess very substantial income to pay a five-thousand-dollar tax. Some eighty-five per cent of persons over sixty-five years pay no income tax. A person paying one hundred dollars in income tax would be liable to a deduction of that amount, higher than the forty-dollar deduction to be paid by a person with no income. Curtis' amendment would not have denied Medicare benefits to the person with income, but would have subjected him to a larger deduction than that required of a person without income. When this Curtis amendment was offered on the floor, Senator Long (floor manager of the bill) relinquished his position at the leader's desk to support the amendment. But the amendment lost, rather narrowly, fifty-one votes against it, forty-one for it.

Had this amendment passed, still it would have provided some Medicare benefits for the upper-middle class; it would have been insurance against the means of a well-to-do person being wiped out by catastrophic illness. The amendment would have founded Medicare benefits upon the ability to pay. There would have been no welfare workers or other inspectors determining eligibility for Medicare: income-tax records would have sufficed. Administration of the plan would have been simple enough.

Having lost this major amendment, Curtis presented another amendment to try the same plan for five years only; this motion too lost. Then Curtis turned to a substitute proposal. It is difficult to offer a complex and technical amendment to a bill on the floor: such matters should be worked out in the more quiet atmosphere of the committee room. As his final effort to improve Medicare, therefore, he did not offer another amendment but moved to recommit the bill to the Committee on Finance, with instructions to that committee to report back a bill calling for universal coverage of the aged under a plan similar to that used for governmental employees.

"We have an opportunity to save two and a half billion dollars and provide better protection at a lower cost," Curtis said in presenting this third motion. "We have an opportunity to save the country from a gigantic step into socialism, because to provide Medicare for those well able to provide it for themselves cannot be justified on any other basis."

What Curtis now advocated as a substitute for Medicare—which, unamended, would thrust the federal government into the field of medical care in a huge way—was a system modeled on the program of medical insurance already used by the federal government for the benefit of civil servants. This program is underwritten by private insurance companies. The federal employees pay a portion of the cost; the government, as employer, pays a portion. This plan works rather well. Senator Curtis proposed that this program be extended nationwide to all persons over sixty-five years of age. Universal coverage would tend to hold down the average cost of the insurance. Those unable to pay the insurance premiums would have their share paid by the government; those who could pay the entire premium, or those who could pay part of it, would be required to do so. Private insurance companies would write the insurance, collect the premiums, and pay the claims; the government would not need to intervene. The Social Security system, and Social Security taxes, would not have been involved in this program of health insurance.

Curtis' motion to recommit the bill was rejected by the Senate, twenty-six ayes, sixty-three nays. On July 9, 1965, the Senate passed the Social Security Bill, including Medicare, sixty-eight yeas to twenty-one nays. The Johnson administration had thrust upon the country an ill-designed and inequitable program, destined to be immensely costly, socialism rather than charity.

Carl Curtis had led the opposition to the Medicare bill.

President Johnson did not forget or forgive that; nor did he forget or forgive Curtis' part in the investigation of Bobby Baker. Johnson endeavored to purge Curtis from the Senate in the election of 1966, directing campaign funds and other assistance to the Democratic candidate for Nebraska's senatorial seat, Governor Frank B. Morrison. In vain: Curtis won re-election by a margin of one hundred and eight thousand votes, tremendous in Nebraska.

GLOOMY PROSPECTS FOR MEDICARE BENEFITS

By 1985, eighteen years after the Medicare program became effective, this aspect of the welfare state was in profound difficulty—worse off than the Social Security system generally. Outlays for Medicare-Medicaid benefits had risen from $4.6 billion in fiscal 1967 to $82.5 billion in 1984; these costs had become a tenth of the entire federal budget. It appeared that the Medicare Trust Fund would be totally depleted by 1991, if not sooner. The following graph and the following table illustrate this pressing problem.

For either program, outlays must be reduced by thirty-two per cent over the next quarter of a century, actuaries believe, or else income derived from Social Security taxes must be increased by forty-eight per cent—and already those taxes are a crushing burden. Or a combination of those two measures must be undertaken. By the end of 1989, if present trends continue, some $15.7 billion will remain in the Medicare Trust Fund: that

THE NEW YORK TIMES, MONDAY, MAY 20, 1985

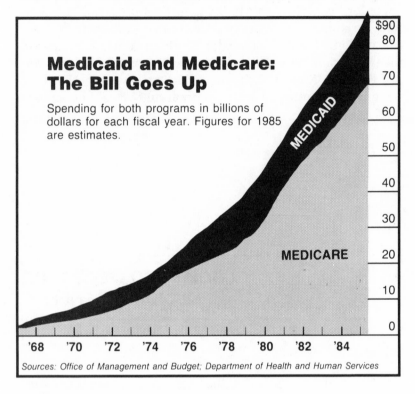

**Medicaid and Medicare:
The Bill Goes Up**

Spending for both programs in billions of
dollars for each fiscal year. Figures for 1985
are estimates.

MEDICAID

MEDICARE

$90
80
70
60
50
40
30
20
10
0

'68   '70   '72   '74   '76   '78   '80   '82   '84

Sources: Office of Management and Budget; Department of Health and Human Services

NEW YORK TIMES, APRIL, 1984

Financial Status of
The Social Security Trust Fund . . . and Medicare Trust Fund

In billions of dollars for each calendar year. The Social Security Trust Fund is a combination of Old-Age and Survivors Insurance and Disability Insurance trust funds. Figures for 1984 and later are estimates.

	Income	Payments	Fund at End of Year		Income	Payments	Fund at End of Year
1960	$ 12.4	$ 11.8	$ 22.6				
1970	37.0	33.1	38.1	1970	$26.1	$25.6	$13.7
1980	119.7	123.6	26.5	1980	26.1	25.6	13.7
1981	142.4	144.4	24.5	1981	35.7	30.7	18.7
1982	147.9	160.1	24.8	1982	38.0	36.1	8.2
1983	171.3	171.2	24.9	1983	44.5	39.9	12.9
1984	184.4	181.5	27.7	1984	46.3	46.1	13.1
1985	203.2	194.1	36.8	1985	52.5	52.7	12.9
1986	221.6	209.3	43.6	1986	60.3	58.7	20.0
1987	241.2	226.2	51.7	1987	65.1	65.5	26.6
1988	277.2	243.4	85.4	1988	69.6	73.1	23.1
1989	301.2	260.3	126.4	1989	73.7	81.1	15.7
1990	331.8	277.6	180.7	1990	77.6	89.8	3.5
1991	356.9	295.1	242.5	1991	81.2	99.4	*

Sources: Treasury Department, Department of Health and Human Services
* Fund depleted in 1991.

is *only seventeen per cent* of what Medicare is expected to spend for in-patient hospital care in 1990.

Despite numerous recommendations for reform from the Reagan administration, Congress has not acted to reduce the outlays for Medicare or to provide for additional revenue. Under Medicare, the federal government finances health-care for some thirty million people, more than three million of them disabled rather than elderly. Medicaid provides for more than twenty-three million poor. At the present rate of growth, the federal government soon will be providing total or partial medical care for a quarter of the population of the United States. Costs to the Treasury have been rising at the rate of fifteen per cent annually. Hospital costs have been rising three times faster than inflation of the dollar. What can be done?

In October, 1982, the budget office of the Reagan administration proposed to employ a means test for Medicare coverage; and the *New York Times* editorially endorsed the idea, at least in principle. "Analysts argue that runaway costs will not be checked until patients have to pay a bigger share," the *Times* remarked. "Hence the talk of linking benefits to income and wealth, so that the less-than-poor would contribute some portion of the first few thousands of dollars of their hospital bills. The poor would continue to be covered fully and all would be protected against serious and protracted illness.

"That idea is well worth exploring. The present system is already sensitive to income; those who cannot afford even $260 for hospitalization or a one-fifth share of doctors' fees are covered by Medicaid.

"Many senior citizens of middle and upper incomes could be fairly asked to pay more then $260."

The *Times* editorial went on to raise questions about how charges might be fixed and ability to pay calculated. Perhaps Carl Curtis' defeated amendment of 1965, which would have related "deductibles" directly to the amount of income tax paid by recipients of Medicare benefits, would be worth exploring by the Reagan administration and the *Times*.

The Social Security Administration still is paying hospital and medical bills running into four and five figures for persons who could well pay their own bills. Congress has not seen fit to make any change in the system with respect to the deduct-ible or co-insurance provisions of Medicare, other than to raise the charges for everyone, including the poor and the destitute.

Disagreeable side-effects result from America's venture into socialized medicine. The maze of reports and the elaborate administrative requirements greatly increase the operating costs of every hospital and every doctor's office. Thus medical costs rise for everybody—for the young and the middle-aged who pay their own medical bills, as well as for the Social Security Ad-ministration. The handling of claims, the completing of reports, and the interlacing of Medicare paperwork with old people's private insurance have become a frustrating muddle for many. Yet for lack of boldness and imagination, Medicare lumbers on toward its ruin. Something may be said in favor of Medicare, however: its failures have dissuaded Congress and the public from paying any serious attention to proposals—notably by Senator Edward Kennedy—for enacting a grandiose, compre-hensive, universal, national health-care scheme.

We have used the term "socialism" to describe the notions underlying Medicare. Of course the Medicare system is not a complete structure of socialized medical care on totalist lines, nor is it a thoroughgoing emulation of the unhappy British Na-tional Health Service. Nevertheless, as Curtis said on the Sen-ate floor in 1965, Medicare is socialism rather than charity. "It is not socialism for us to be charitable," Curtis observed then in the course of the debate. "We should provide medical care for individuals over sixty-five who have neither the income nor the resources to provide such care for themselves. In determin-ing who needs assistance to secure medical care, I want my government to be generous...Again I say that to be charitable is not socialism. However, to pay the medical bills and hospi-tal bills of individuals over sixty-five who are well able to pro-vide the same for themselves is not charity. It is not needed. It is socialism. It moves the country in a direction which is not good for anyone, whether they be young or old. It charts a course from which there will be no turning back."

The ideologues of the Kennedy and Johnson administra-tions, designing Medicare, apparently intended it to be a so-cialistic measure. They kept in mind the ends of Britain's

National Health Service, which, like other measures of Britain's welfare state, aimed at "universality." As Arthur Marwick puts it, the Labour government that took office in 1945 desired equality of condition rather than true social security. "On the principle of universality free medical treatment, family allowances, pensions, insurance benefits, and, to some extent, subsidized housing were to be available to rich and poor alike. Thus, it was hoped, the poor would feel no stigma about making use of the social services, and so a mighty blow would be struck at class distinctions; furthermore, on a more realistic plan, it was clear that only when the rich shared the services with the poor would the poor get the best available."

Later, the intellectuals of the Left in Britain, or many of them, came to regret this notion of "universality", which results in general impoverishment and dissatisfaction, rather than in harmony and security. But so late as the 'Sixties, the illusions of the British Left, already exploded in Britain, were received in certain Washington and New York circles as the rosy dawn of an egalitarian future to be emulated so soon as possible in America. The curious insistence of Medicare's architects on treating rich and poor alike—or nearly alike—in Medicare benefits and "deductibles" appears to have been inspired by the conviction that such "universality" would be a happy stride along the road to democratic socialism. It was a delusion morally contemptible: for charity is derived from love, while socialism is founded on envy. And this ideological delusion, a moving force behind the Forand Bill and Medicare, has been a principal cause of Medicare's present sorry plight.

The term "welfare state" originated in Britain during the Second World War as a pun on Germany's boasted "warfare state." The term next was employed to describe the high-flying socialist policies of Britain's Labour government headed by Clement Attlee. Blundering Medicare has been a true welfare-state scheme, intruded under false colors into American health care; it has done mischief to the medical arts and to medical costs and to the American economy. Can we disentangle ourselves from Medicare before the structure collapses entirely?

From Medicare, a late development of the American welfare state, we pass in the next chapter to the retirement program

of Social Security, an early development badly designed by the
same sort of mentality. Social Security arose before Carl Curtis entered Congress; Medicare was debated during the middle period of his Washington years. But Social Security is
discussed rather late in this book because Curtis' chief congressional success, the Individual Retirement Accounts, was
achieved late in his political career in an attempt to provide
genuine security for independent people. Like Medicare, Social Security totters today insecure.

Chapter 12

Delusory Saving
And True Saving

COMPULSORY
COLLECTIVE SAVING

America's version of compulsory collective saving, with the nation-state as banker and trustee, began when President Franklin Roosevelt signed the Social Security Act on August 14, 1935. Miss Frances Perkins, Secretary of Labor, had the guiding hand in the legislation.

The general assumption behind this plan—primarily, though not wholly, intended to assist the aged—was that Social Security payments to retired persons would *supplement* their private savings, assistance from children and other relatives, and other sources of income in retirement. Unemployment being high in the depression year of 1935, also there was some expectation—especially within labor unions—that Social Security's retirement benefits would induce people over sixty-five years of age to leave employment, so opening places for younger persons.

From 1945 until his retirement from Congress, Carl Curtis was a vigorous advocate of equity and fiscal reform in the Social Security system. His conspicuous activity in this field during the Truman and Eisenhower years has been mentioned in an earlier chapter. Here we provide more information about his endeavor to establish Social Security on a sounder basis, over the years. And we describe, in the latter part of this present section, one of his major positive achievements in national politics, accomplished near the end of his congressional service: the establishment, as a means of personal saving, of the Individual Retirement Account.

Public measures of compulsory collective saving (often called, somewhat inaccurately, "social insurance") were unknown until late in the nineteenth century. Such policies began with Bismarck's domination of a unified Germany. Various forms of state old-age pensions had been adopted in several of Europe's industrial countries before Social Security came to the United States. These systems were a response to the concentration of population in cities and in industrial occupations. Rural societies with an agricultural economy had contrived, after one fashion or another, to support their elderly and their unemployed without a centralized state apparatus of relief and benefaction. But the decay of the family as an economic unit, and the need for cash payment among populations that earned their living chiefly through factory jobs rather than from farms, led to the several measures of compulsory collective saving. Also these factors led to tremendous fiscal problems for national governments.

Forty-five years after the Social Security Act was passed, Richard Schweiker, Secretary of Health and Human Services in President Ronald Reagan's cabinet, appeared before the Senate's Committee on Finance to declare that Social Security's Old-Age and Survivors Insurance Trust Fund was on the verge of bankruptcy; unless drastic action were taken within a year, the Fund would be exhausted. The thought that no Social Security checks might be mailed to many of the accustomed recipients startled most Americans. Many were surprised who shouldn't have been.

When President Reagan presented his program for meeting the problems in Social Security, Thomas O'Neill, Speaker of the House, asserted that Reagan was trying to do away with the program that had made America great; Senator Daniel Patrick Moynihan, of New York, charged that this Reagan proposal was political terrorism. Such reckless accusations had been made for years past against any public man with sufficient hardihood to mention that the financial foundations of Social Security were becoming perilously shaky. In 1983, the administration and Congress would adopt certain changes in Social Security, chiefly an increase in taxes, to provide temporary relief: changes that seemed satisfactory to almost nobody. Let us look at Social Security's history over half a century, and at Carl Curtis' part in it.

For many years after the establishment of the Social Security system, the maximum Social Security tax paid by an individual was thirty dollars a year. By 1986, individuals wholly self-employed would pay as much as $5,166.00 in Social Security taxes alone, perhaps more than they paid in federal and state income taxes combined. Carl Curtis and other reformers did not succeed in preventing this huge increase of the burden; yet to some extent they achieved an amelioration of the consequences.

ANOMALIES AND BURDENS OF SOCIAL SECURITY

The original Social Security Act contained several titles (categories of entitlements). In addition to Titles II and VIII—which provided for the issuing of Social Security numbers, levied the Social Security tax, and authorized payment of retirement benefits—other titles provided for unemployment compensation, aid to dependent children, and assistance to the needy aged. As the years went by, other titles were added. To most people, "Social Security" signified the Title II program, now known as the Old-Age Survivors and Disability program (abridged to OASDI or OASI). In this section, the term Social Security generally is used in that limited sense.

The 1939 amendments to the Social Security Act were passed soon after Carl Curtis took his seat in the House. There were two principal changes: addition of survivors' benefits (which, should a breadwinner die, made payments to the widow if she were sixty-five years old or older, and to dependent children and their mother, regardless of the mother's age, until the children should be eighteen years old); and provision for a lump-sum payment, giving an individual or his estate somewhat more than the amount he had paid in Social Security taxes. Some lesser changes were made, among them an amendment reducing the monthly benefits of single workers in certain situations.

During the war years, 1941 to 1945, Social Security did not obtain major legislative attention. Carl Curtis became a member of the Committee on Ways and Means in 1945; he was much interested in what he observed there about Social Security. A rather sizeable percentage of the Social Security recipients, he found, were to get bargains. A corporation officer, for instance, was ruled to be an employee. If such an officer were to retire at age sixty-five, in 1950, his benefit (including his wife's benefit) would be $45.20 x 1 1/2, or $67.80 per month. His life expectancy was twelve years more, and his wife's life expectancy fourteen years more (taking her to be the same age as her husband). The officer would have paid a total of $390 in Social Security taxes, or just enough to defray the cost of his benefits for some six months. In exchange for his taxes of $390, that is, the corporation officer and his wife might receive a total reward of more than $9,763—or still more than that, should they live longer than twelve years after retirement. It is no wonder that initially Social Security was highly popular with a great many people. Of course the favorable balance of the corporation officer's benefits would be paid by people who continued to work and by their employers—and by the children and the grandchildren of those workers and employers.

A widow with several children whose husband died before the Social Security Act became effective received no benefits. Yet another widow with the same number of dependent children whose husband died after the effectiveness of the Act would obtain benefits for herself and for every child under eighteen years of age. At age sixty-five, the latter widow would receive a monthly benefit for life, if her husband had earned fifty dollars in a calendar quarter of covered employment for six quarters. In such a case, the deceased husband would have paid a grand total of three dollars in Social Security taxes.

These cases are mentioned not merely to show the unfairness of the law where individuals were concerned, but primarily to suggest that the program was not really set up as a plan for an individual to pay for his own eventual benefits. Others would pay his benefits: those who pay Social Security taxes while, and after, the fortunate recipient's benefits were being disbursed.

The Social Security law did not cover all individuals. It covered jobs by classification. For instance, a local banker was covered, but not a janitor at the school house.

In 1949, Congressman Curtis called attention to the case of a man then forty years old, who had worked in covered employment since Social Security began, and would continue to work until reaching the age of sixty-five. Supposing his wife to be the same age, the couple would be entitled to a benefit of $106.70 a month. The total taxes for Social Security paid by this man would have been $1,440; a like amount would have been paid by his employer, for a total of $2,880. In two years and four months, the benefits payable would have exhausted all the money that the man and his employer had deposited in Social Security, but the recipient's life expectancy was twelve more years and his wife's fourteen years.

At that time, Curtis cited also figures for a man who had reached sixty-five years of age on January 1, 1949, with an average monthly wage of one hundred dollars. This man had paid $144 in taxes, and his employer an equal sum. If the man and his wife were the same age, the two of them would draw a benefit of little less than seventy-five dollars a month. In less than six months, they would draw out as much as the man and his employer had paid in; yet these benefits would continue for their lives.

In 1950, Curtis called to the attention of the House another anomalous case: if a husband should earn fifty dollars in a calendar quarter, paying for six quarters in covered employment, his total Social Security taxes would be three dollars; should he die, his widow and children would be entitled to survivors' benefits. If, however, he had worked only five quarters but had earned three hundred dollars in each quarter, he would have paid fifteen dollars in Social Security taxes; yet his widow and children would not be entitled, under the Act, to any benefits.

It was evident that someone should take a close look at the workings of Social Security, particularly at its financing. When, in 1953, the Republicans gained control of both Senate and House and the Eisenhower administration began, Curtis succeeded in convincing Congressman Dan Reed, chairman of the Ways and Means Committee, that the House should pass an appropriate resolution to this effect and provide funds for a study. This was done; Curtis was appointed chairman of the subcommittee for the study. He selected a staff to do the work and prepare the report. The early sponsors and architects of the Social Security system regarded any criticism of the program as an attack on Social Security and all the elderly: so the subcommittee's chairman and its staff were not conspicuously popular.

The subcommittee's report showed that as of December 31, 1952, there was a balance in the OASDI trust–fund of $17,441,719,000 available for payment of future benefits. But as of the same date, there were 2,644,000 aged persons currently drawing primary old-age benefits, and another 2,382,000 persons currently drawing secondary benefits in awards to wives, husbands, children, widows, widowers, mothers, and parents.

These 5,026,000 obtaining OASDI benefits, at the end of

1952, already had received a total of $6,010,700,000 in benefits; and, according to estimates by actuaries of the Bureau of Old-Age and Survivors' Insurance, these same persons would draw an additional $21,826,000,000 in future benefits before their entitlements would end.

So against a balance in the trust fund of more than seventeen billion dollars, there existed a liability for future benefits payable to persons already on OASDI rolls of nearly twenty-two billion dollars. This liability did not take into account any of the benefits to be payable to Social Security taxpayers who would become recipients of benefits after December 31, 1952.

In the subcommittee's hearings, Robert J. Myers, chief actuary of the Social Security Administration, stated that "The present trust fund is not quite large enough to pay off the benefits of the existing beneficiaries. Therefore, you may say that under that basis or conception there is nothing left in the fund for other contributors."

Thus thirty-two years ago no deposits lay in the trust fund to pay benefits to people who would reach retirement age after that time. The subcommittee's report further illustrated the precariousness of Social–Security financing, as in the following passages:

"As of December 31, 1952, there were 2,644,000 persons currently drawing OASI primary benefits. They themselves had paid $356,470,000 in OASI taxes. They already had drawn $3,665,400,000 in benefits—or more then ten times the amount of their own tax contributions."

According to actuarial estimates of the Bureau of Old-Age and Survivors' Insurance, these same 2,644,000 primary beneficiaries at that time could expect to receive, under existing law, an additional $13,500,000,000 in benefits before their names were removed from the rolls. Thus the total of past and future benefits for this group was approximately $17,165,000,000—or a ratio of benefits to taxes of forty-eight to one.

"If OASI taxes previously paid by employers on the past wages and salaries of the 2,644,000 primary beneficiaries at the end of 1952 are taken into account," the subcommittee's report continued, "the total OASI benefits ultimately payable to them will be equal to approximately twenty-four times the amount of taxes paid by and for them.''

Just so! From the beginning of Social Security, the public had been misinformed and misled about the plan. The major delusion was that Social Security constituted an insurance system. On this point, we quote below from a memorandum addressed to Chairman Curtis by the subcommittee's staff director, Dr. Karl T. Schlotterbeck—a memorandum subsequently made part of the subcommittee's report.

"The original Social Security Act of 1935 at no place contained the word 'insurance.' In none of the publicity in the year or so immediately subsequent to the passage of this act was the word 'insurance' employed. The reverse side of the social security card, distributed to millions of workers, referred to the program under Title II (now known as OASI) as 'Federal old-age retirement benefits.'''

In the Supreme Court's decision (May 24, 1937) upholding the constitutionality of Title II and Title VIII of the Act, Dr.Schlotterbeck continued, the decision did not mention insurance. Indeed, the government, defendant in this case, stated that "The act cannot be said to constitute a plan for compulsory insurance within the accepted meaning of the term 'insurance.'" Yet thereafter, beginning the very day following the Supreme Court's decision, the government began to employ the word "insurance" in connection with Social Security. By August 7, 1939, a federal spokesman was telling the press, "Think of it! It is just as if you had written a group insurance policy, covering 45 million people, and it is because it is like trying to read the fine print in that insurance policy that it is hard to understand." By 1952, an official pamphlet stated: "Your card is the symbol of your insurance policy under the Federal Social Security law."

But, as Dr. Schlotterbeck pointed out, courts have held that insurance, properly defined, requires a contract. There have existed several other federal programs which generally constitute insurance—federal crop insurance, federal mortgage insurance, war-risk insurance, and the like. In each of these programs, the insured person has a contract guaranteeing indemnification in the event of a specified loss. It is otherwise with Social Security payments and benefits.

Yet members of Congress, labor leaders, publicists, and the general public often mistakenly thought that Social Security benefits were derived from a contractual relationship. Dr. Schlotterbeck concluded, "Testimony in the hearings brought out the fact that the rights of individuals to Title II benefits are statutory, and are neither natural, constitutional, nor contractual rights. In this, the rights are like those existing under veterans' benefit programs and under public assistance." In short, what Social Security benefits are to be paid, and on what terms, depend on the will of the federal government, not on any contract between the payer of Social Security taxes and the Social Security Administration.

This fact was admitted by the Commissioner for Social Security in his testimony of 1953 to the subcommittee studying Social Security. Here is the pertinent dialogue.

Chairman Curtis: "The individual who perhaps was twenty-one years of age in 1937 and who has been in covered employment since then, since 1937, and will have to continue to pay these taxes until he is sixty-five, has no contract? Is that your position?"

Commissioner Altmeyer: "That is right."

Curtis: "And he has no insurance contract?"

Altmeyer: "That is right."

Curtis: "It is a statutory right?"

Altmeyer: "It is a statutory right enforceable by law. . . .Now, the question of whether it is a contractual or a noncontractual right is immaterial and unimportant, so long as it is statutory right, enforceable by law, and not subject to the whim and caprice of any political body or administrative official."

Curtis: "Now, a statutory right can be changed by the duly constituted elected body, can it not?"

Altmeyer: "It certainly can."

Now from the original enactment of the Social Security Act, Congress has retained the power to alter, amend, or repeal any provision of the Act. Thus a statutory right exists only until the Congress changes it. Benefits for Social Security have been reduced in the past. As the subcommittee's 1954 report put it,

"For instance, a single worker with 40 years in covered employment at a wage of $250 a month would have received on retirement under the 1937 Act a primary benefit of $81.25 a month. Under the 1939 amendment his retirement benefit amounted to only $56 per month."

Congress and the public, in the early years of Social Security, did not understand how great the cost of the Social Security program would become. In 1950, fourteen years after the system began, only one individual out of every five persons more than sixty-five years old was eligible for benefits. Few asked what the cost would be when the system matured and virtually all aged persons should become eligible for benefits.

This general misconception about future costs gave opportunity for politicians and others to promote increases in benefits, and to refrain from collecting taxes adequate for the full costs of the retirement and survivor benefits—let alone the costs of expanding the program to include educational benefits, disability benefits, and Medicare benefits. Social Security taxpayers did not feel the full cost until many years after such enlargements of Social Security were enacted. No checks and balances existed to reconcile the disparate interests of those who pay and those who receive.

Social Security taxpayers were misled concerning costs in three ways: first, by the government's failure to collect the full cost of the benefits being paid or promised to those already on the benefit rolls; second, by the fact that early in the program only a small proportion of people over sixty-five, or their survivors, were eligible for benefits—as late as 1952, 13,305,000 persons were aged sixty-five or more, while only 3,824,000 were drawing Social Security benefits; third, the public was told that Social Security was insurance and that their taxes, plus interest, were being laid by to pay their benefits when they attained retirement age.

Some of the more thoughtful members of Congress, informed about the workings of the Social Security system, saw that short of a total revision of old-age benefits, the only way to diminish future costs and to prevent the unwise expansion of Social Security into such new fields as disability, education, and Medicare, was to mature the system immediately by paying benefits to *all* retired aged. Thus everybody would become aware of the real cost of what had been enacted. Collecting taxes from the many and paying benefits to a few gave the public a false picture of the financial problem.

Investigation showed that the line between those who received Social Security benefits and those who did not receive—why, it was a very thin line. Testimony taken in 1953 made it clear that many inequities existed. At the end of 1952, a person might have contributed to Social Security as little as $4.50, with another $4.50 from employers, and yet on retirement be eligible for minimum benefits of $25 monthly. A person who had contributed to OASI only a few cents less than $4.50 would have been ineligible for any benefits. On the other hand, a person who had contributed $131, plus an equal contribution from his employer, could have been eligible after retirement (having worked the required full six quarters), for maximum OASI benefits for the rest of his life—then $85 per month.

It may be argued that at the beginning of Social Security payments, because of actuarial requirements, some persons necessarily received much more than they had contributed. But certainly it was not necessary during those early years that the Social Security bureaucracy should circulate pamphlets declaring that "your Social Scurity is a matter of right; you have paid for it."

OBSTACLES TO REFORM,
INDUCEMENTS TO PROFLIGACY

To alter the structure of the Social Security system is perilous politically, and has been virtually impossible in past years. Yet the thing must be done. Carl Curtis essayed the task in 1954.

The future fiscal difficulties of Social Security were perceived by the Social Security committee of the United States Chamber of Commerce, which had an able staff headed by William Baroody, who later founded the American Enterprise Institute. The Chamber recommended that the system be matured, and that all the aged and all the orphans be made eligible for the system's benefits.

At the end of the work of the House subcommittee investigating Social Security in 1954, Representative Curtis introduced H. R. 6812. Among other things, H. R. 6812 would have extended OASI benefits to five million more of the aged and to all fatherless children and their mothers in cases of fathers who had died without having established eligibility for benefits for their survivors. This was a large expansion of benefits, but its intent was to make the program more equitable and to "mature" it on sound fiscal principles.

When the press published reports of Curtis' bill, it was as if the heavens had fallen. Liberals declared that Curtis was destroying Social Security; union leaders joined in their protests. Conservatives said that Curtis was irresponsible. In part, the blame for this deluge of hostile criticism must lie upon the shoulders of Curtis' staff and of Curtis himself: they had failed properly to inform the public of the facts which had led to Curtis' conviction that Social Security must be "matured" promptly if it were to become financially reliable, and if imprudent expansion of the system into new fields were to be averted.

Curtis' bill contained a number of worthwhile improvements. In addition to extending Social Security to practically all occupations, it raised the amount of money an individual might earn per month without reducing his Social Security benefits; it removed the Social Security tax on earnings above the work-test limit for all persons after they should attain the age of sixty-five, provided they should have forty quarters of coverage; it raised the minimum benefit from twenty-five dollars per month to forty-five dollars; it provided that a widow or a widower would not receive less than the minimum primary benefit. The bill eliminated many of the abuses in the payment of benefits to individuals living in foreign countries; it provided for survivors' benefits in cases where the father had died before becoming eligible for benefits. It extended the minimum Social Security benefits to substantially all persons over sixty-five years who were not receiving benefits; that is, to five million aged people, some of them in their eighties and nineties, over half of them widows.

Opponents of the Curtis bill objected to paying benefits when no Social Security tax had been paid. They forgot that in 1950 the Congress had raised the benefits of all those already retired (at a cost of $5.46 billion), though no taxes had been paid to provide for this increase in benefits; and similar action had been taken in the Social Security amendments of 1952. They forgot, too, that since the inception of Social Security, a substantial number of beneficiaries had paid only nominal taxes.

Senator Robert Taft, Sr., had recognized the true nature of the Social Security system. On June 14, 1950, Taft had said, "It is not insurance; and, at least to date, this system has not been very social either, because it has covered only a very small portion of the total number of people who are over sixty-five years of age . . . Under the new-start principle, a man who pays in practically nothing will get seventy dollars a month. Why should we not give the man who does not pay in anything seventy dollars a month, or at least sixty-five dollars a month? As I see it, we have practically destroyed the theory of social insurance. All I regret is that we still use the name 'insurance' when as a matter of fact there is no insurance about it."

Curtis' proposal to extend benefits to all the aged was not enacted. Curtis lost the propaganda battle. American businessmen never were adequately informed about the real basis for the position of the United States Chamber of Commerce; while the liberals, the union leaders, and the bureaucracy condemned Curtis' bill. He ended with little or no public support.

The Social Security amendments of 1954 contained several of Curtis' proposals, but they did not mature the system by making all the aged eligible for benefits. At one point in the consideration of the measure, Curtis appeared before President Eisenhower and several members of his cabinet to explain his proposal. He was equipped with an easel and a number of charts on large cards. The easel fell down; the cards, scattered, fell out of sequence. So, frustrated and embarrassed, Curtis had to proceed without visual aids. President Eisenhower was gracious. Had not Curtis been battling against public sentiment and the bureaucracy, he might have convinced the President.

Congress always has provided that increases in Social Security taxes would become effective at future dates. The act of 1950, for instance, called for the following schedule of tax rates:

Rate of Social Security Tax on Wages
Earned in Covered Employment

1 per cent	1950-53
1½ per cent	1954-59
2 per cent	1960-64
2½ per cent	1965-67
3¼ per cent	1970 and after

The actuaries always were asked if a proposed tax-rate schedule would assure sufficient funds to pay the benefits for the future. (There are many honest actuaries and technicians who have rendered competent service in connection with Social Security financing, but their task has become well-nigh impossible. One of the abler is Robert J. Myers, long chief actuary and for a time deputy commissioner of Social Security.) Such a question, totally unfair, was impossible to answer because no one knew how many times, in the years ahead, Congress might expand the program, increasing its benefits. Congress has increased benefits in each of the following years: 1940, 1950, 1952, 1954, 1958, 1965, 1969, 1970, 1972, and 1974. In addition, during the following years, increases based on the Consumer Price Index were provided automatically.

Here they are:

1975	8.0%
1976	6.4%
1977	5.9%
1978	6.5%
1979	9.9%
1980	14.3%
1981	11.2%
1982	7.4%
1983	3.5%
1984	3.5%
1985	3.5%
1986	3.1%

These increases have been cumulative. The percentage increases in benefits voted in 1972, for instance, were on top of the percentage increases voted in 1970 and prior years. The percentage increase automatically paid, beginning in July, 1981, was on top of the prior percentage increases. With the high inflation of the 1970s and early 1980s, many beneficiaries deserved to receive an increase; but this multiplier effect may produce surprising results over future decades. If an individual was on the benefit rolls at the beginning of 1974, his Social Security monthly benefit payment had been doubled as of June, 1981, because of the eleven per cent increase voted by the Congress in 1974 and the automatic percentage increases that began in 1975.

During consideration of the 1950 Social Security amendments, Curtis predicted that the benefits being approved would cost, by the time his ten-year-old son had attained fifty years of age, twelve billion dollars a year for old-age and survivor benefits. His son is now only six years short of being fifty years old; yet OASDI costs for the fiscal year ending September 30, 1981, already had reached one hundred and sixty-eight billion dollars!

Many of the increases in benefits voted by Congress have been scheduled to take effect just before an election. One such raise, Curtis never will forget. In 1972, the House of Representatives passed and sent to the Senate a bill raising benefits by five per cent. Then the chairman of the Ways and Means Committee, Representative Wilbur Mills, began to aspire to the Democratic presidential nomination. Around any candidate for the presidency there can be found unwise and zealous backers urging him to make most generous promises to the public. Chairman Mills was credited with a statement that he had decided that benefits could be raised by twenty per cent— without increasing the tax rates beyond what was specified in the pending Social Security bill, which called for a five per cent raise. The chairman of the Senate Finance Committee, Russell Long, who had an uncanny skill at predicting what the Senate as a body would do, took the position that the Senate would raise benefits by twenty per cent, and that the Committee on Finance should raise them by twenty per cent in the bill that would be sent to the Senate floor. Senator Curtis opposed this move to raise benefits without providing for adequate tax revenues. The Committee agreed with Curtis, but Chairman Long was correct in his expectation.

A motion was made on the Senate floor to raise the benefits by twenty per cent. This amendment was offered by Senator Frank Church, of Idaho, who four years later sought the Democratic presidential nomination. The Church amendment also contained the provision for automatic cost-of-living raises that now is in the law. When the Church amendment came to a vote on June 30, 1972, only four senators ventured to oppose it: Fannin of Arizona, Jordan of Idaho, Buckley of New York, and Curtis. Of these, Curtis was the only senator then standing for re-election, and that election was but four months distant. His opposition to the Church amendment did cost Curtis votes in Nebraska. This handicap increased the task of the Nebraskan committee working to return Curtis to the Senate: some of his friends and supporters dependent on their Social Security checks couldn't see why Curtis had opposed the big raise. The populace does not strew garlands along the path of financial responsibility. That trail is a tough uphill pull, but a public man may sleep soundly after he has walked that way.

The vote on the Church amendment having been taken, Senator Harry Byrd, of Virginia, came to Curtis' desk on the Senate floor with some kind words. "Carl, you have cast one of the most courageous votes I have ever seen in the United

States Senate," he said.

Curtis had won the senatorial election of 1966 over an incumbent Democratic governor by a huge margin, and had been unopposed in the primary. It was somewhat different in 1972, four months after the senatorial vote on Church's Social Security benefactions. Three opponents popped up in the Republican primary, though Curtis overwhelmed them. In the senatorial election of November 7, 1972, Curtis defeated Terry Carpenter, the Democrats' nominee, by some 36,000 votes (about 302,000 to 266,000), a healthy victory but by a margin far smaller than in any of Curtis' previous senatorial contests. This price in votes was what Curtis paid for withstanding financial irresponsibility in Social Security.

During the 1972 Senate debate over Social Security, an exhaustive study of what was involved in the principle of automatic increases should have been made; this was not done. Facts could have been presented by competent witnesses to show what the long-term effect would be, should all benefits increase annually by an automatic formula. Such an effort would not have changed either the position of the Committee on Finance or the vote on the Church amendment; but it would have left a better record for the opposition.

Today the Reagan administration faces Social Security problems that result from actions, or failures to act, during the past four decades. The misguided legislation of 1972 has been the direct cause of the present crisis.

One of the difficulties has been Congress' tendency to raise the wage-base for computing Social Security taxes rather than raising the tax rate. If the wage-base is twenty thousand dollars and then is raised to twenty-five thousand dollars, the increased tax falls only on those who are paid more than twenty thousand dollars and on their employers. Thus politicians may make benefit increases without raising the taxes paid by four-fifths of the workers.

By 1977, Congress faced the need for more money to keep the Social Security fund from defaulting. The Carter administration recommended the use of general revenues and a tax on a higher wage-base, to be paid by employers but not by employees. The Finance Committee of the Senate approved a proposal, later reversed, that would have fixed the taxable wage-base for the employer at one hundred thousand dollars. Senator Gaylord Nelson offered a floor amendment that would have set the wage-base for the employer at seventy-five thousand dollars.

Curtis then offered an amendment to keep the wage-base the same for employers and employees, but to raise the tax rate by one-half of one per cent. This was defeated in committee by a vote of nine to eight. Curtis offered a similar amendment on the Senate floor; it survived by a single vote. Later, the Carter administration's forces having been mustered, the Curtis amendment was rejected, fifty to forty votes.

Next Curtis modified his amendment, but kept the wage-base for employers and employees the same. On a motion by Senator Nelson, the Curtis amendment was tabled, forty-one votes to forty-one. On a tie vote to table, the amendment would have survived; but Vice-President Mondale, presiding over the Senate, cast the deciding vote against the amendment and it lost, even though Nelson had said that the Curtis amendment would make the fund solvent. This was the first occasion on which a vice-president had cast a deciding vote on legislation since Vice-President Agnew's vote, July 17, 1973, on the construction of the Trans-Alaska pipeline.

Social Security was intended primarily to be a program for retirement; then it was extended by providing for survivors. Later it was extended to provide benefits for the disabled; presently educational benefits were added. A child of a deceased covered worker was paid a benefit until he should reach the age of eighteen years. If, however, the child should continue in a school, the benefit was continued until age twenty-one, regardless of the family's wealth or income. Eligibility hinged merely on going to school or college. Clearly this was an educational benefit paid in addition to all other available educational programs supported by the federal government. The Omnibus Reconciliation Act of 1981 phases out the college benefits, and allows high-school benefits only until a child's nineteenth birthday. In 1965, hospital benefits were added to the Social Security program for all covered persons sixty-five years of age and older, regardless of need, wealth, or income. Many of these recipients never have paid a cent in taxes for this benefit. Working people have had their Social Security taxes increased to pay for hospital benefits for the well-to-do. Individuals who already had retired when hospital benefits were added to the program were made eligible for those benefits, without paying taxes.

Let us consider who the Social Security taxpayers are. Nearly everybody who works pays Social Security taxes. They begin paying them on their very first dollar of earned income. The handicapped worker, who with great effort pulls himself up to a bench and struggles to perform a needed task, has Social Security taxes deducted from his pay. The blind person, walking along with his dog or his white cane to some work that he can manage to perform, pays the Social Security tax. Old men and women, who must work to supplement their Social Security benefits, must pay Social Security taxes. It is not surprising that in 1972 there|were| some twenty-two million persons paying Social Security taxes who did not enjoy enough income to pay any income taxes. In addition, there were more than nine million people who paid more in Social Security taxes than they did in income taxes. Yet in 1972, Congress increased Social Security benefits by twenty per cent—at the expense of such people, and as a fresh burden upon their employers.

The Social Security tax is a sizeable item for the young and the middle-aged, even though they may be neither handicapped nor disadvantaged. These are people rearing families, educating children, buying houses and life insurance, paying their families' medical expenses, supporting worthwhile causes in their communities. Precisely these people pay the taxes to provide Social Security hospital benefits to the aged, many of whom may have the means to pay their own medical bills and who may have insurance covering those bills. These Social Security taxpayers are the people who provide educational funds for the rising generation in college (now numbering about a million). These Social Security taxpayers are those who pay all the other benefit-costs of the system, including the multiplier effect of the automatic percentage increases that operate after the fashion of compound interest.

The actuaries in the Social Security Administration inform us that if an individual began working at the age of twenty-one, in 1937; and if that individual earned the maximum covered wages and paid the maximum tax, and retired at age sixty-five on January 1, 1981, he would have paid in taxes the total sum of $11,698.98. His employer would have paid an identical amount. This individual would receive monthly benefits of $752.90. If this person had a spouse who was sixty-five years of age, her monthly benefit would be $367.50. (For persons retiring in 1986, monthly benefits would be larger, and prospective longevity greater.) Thus the monthly benefits for the two of them total $1,129.40. In eleven months, the couple draw out more than the husband has paid in twenty-two months, and more than the total paid by both employee and employer. The average remaining life expectancy for a man aged sixty-five is more than thirteen years; for a woman, more than fifteen years. The Social Security Administration advises us that if future increases (including the Consumer Price Index increases) for this couple are projected, the estimated total of their future benefits will be $447,000. (The amount of Social Security taxes shown above as paid by the hypothetical taxpayer-worker is computed without interest.)

One need not be an actuary to understand that some important changes must be made in the Social Security system if the federal government is to keep faith with the American people. Neither the people now elderly nor the present Social Security taxpayers are responsible for the mistakes that have been made, nor for the lack of prudence and of courage that is obvious.

What should we do about this large difficulty? The federal government's commitment to its citizens should be maintained. Certain reforms in Social Security, therefore, must be brought about.

First, the Social Security program should be reduced to a retirement program over a period of years, with the other features eliminated. Second, the automatic and cumulative increases in benefits must be discontinued. (This is not to forbid all future increases, but the automatic and cumulative processes are getting out of control.) Third, we should work out a plan by which benefits paid have some relation to the amount of Social Security taxes that have been paid in; and then make available more benefits through the supplementary-security income system for those aged who truly need more money for their maintenance. Proposals to tax the Social Security benefits of people in the higher-income brackets are sound. If we can restore responsibility and restraint in our spending for social purposes, taxpayers will feel increased confidence in that system and will be willing to pay benefits which are needed by their fellow–citizens.

The true friends of Social Security are not people who would temporize by borrowing money or using general revenues or employing other dubious schemes to relieve present necessities. The real friends are those who will display the wisdom and the courage to devise and support those just and fair reforms necessary for the Social Security system to carry out its original objective of providing retirement income supplementary to the individual's own effort when old age comes.

CURTIS' INDIVIDUAL RETIREMENT ACCOUNTS

All of us grow older. Scientific medicine, improved diet, and the disseminating of knowledge about health have extended the common life span. Many of the aches and pains formerly the lot of the human race have been diminished. But even if one escapes a degenerative disease, there comes a time for every man and woman when it is possible no longer to produce economically.

Old age is upon us, and we must retire. Where does one find the funds, then, to provide the necessities of life and a tolerable standard of living?

In rural economies, farmers and their wives might lease or sell their land upon retirement, or pass on a farm to children, retaining some income from the land. It is otherwise for most people in industrial societies near the close of the twentieth century. Heavy taxation—including Social Security taxes—have made it difficult for most people to save any substantial sum from a lifetime's earnings. Before passage of the Social Security Act in 1935, those who had not accumulated money and property for themselves often faced a bleak future upon retirement. Some folk had no savings at all. Passage of the Social Security Act brought hope to millions. They were told that this plan would pay benefits to them; that their Social Security entitlements, plus what they might do for themselves, would make their retirement years golden.

Half a century has elapsed since Social Security was enacted. Meanwhile, payments of Social Security money for retirement years have increased manyfold. Thirty-six million people now receive monthly cash benefits under Social Security; payments during 1986 will total more than one hundred and seventy-nine *billion* dollars.

Yet despite increased benefits, the individual who has laid by for himself no funds or property, who must depend wholly on Social Security payments, confronts a future as bleak as it was for many before Social Security's enactment. The vision of golden years free from worry has not taken on flesh for many people.

Why has not this multi-billion-dollar Social Security program of ours provided what people expected for their years of retirement? The answer is complex. First, despite what Social Security promoters have proclaimed, the system never was intended to accomplish more than to furnish a "floor of protection." Second, the same planners who devised Social Security also gave us the welfare state and government programs without number that have resulted in colossal government. The dollars paid from Social Security no longer will buy much, chiefly because of deficits caused by excessive public expenditure.

It is not the purpose of this chapter to dwell on what gigantic enlargement of governmental functions has done to the American people. Rather, we return to the question, "What can we do for ourselves before old age comes?"

It is necessary to make it possible for the individual to earn and save for himself so that when he has reached retirement age, he may possess funds and property of his own. But that is no facile task.

What with the ever-increasing cost of all that a family must buy; with the ever-rising real-property taxes; with Social Security taxes, federal income taxes, state income taxes, sales taxes, tax upon tax; with all the costs of our complex general life-style—well, how on earth can one save for his own old age? True, people who work for a large company that has established a pension plan generally manage well upon retirement. Added to Social Security benefits, their pension-income plus their other savings gives them a competence or something better. But not everyone can work for large well-paying companies with generous pensions.

Carl Curtis, reflecting on all this, began to examine the operation of pension plans. They are not difficult to understand.

The funds placed in a pension plan by a corporation are tax-sheltered. If General Motors, or the American Telephone and Telegraph Company, or some other large employer puts sizeable sums into a qualified pension fund to provide for the retirement of officers and employees, not only are the company contributions to the fund a business expense deductible from taxable income, but the earnings of the pension fund accumulate tax-free. The fund earns interest and dividends, and may enjoy capital gains; but such earnings are not taxed as they accrue. By removing the tax–burden, employers are able to provide significant pensions for their workers.

But how about the individual? How may he save for his old age? If from his earnings he sets aside a monthly sum toward retirement, what happens to that money? For one thing, the sum so reserved is saved only in "after-tax dollars." Then, if he places his after-tax savings at interest or invests them in some enterprise paying dividends, he has to pay federal (and perhaps state) income taxes on those earnings.

Yet the answer as to what to do in prospect of old age is rather simple. It is this: to give the individual the same tax-advantages in providing for his own old age as is given to corporations when they provide retirement benefits for employees. Allow the individual to set aside certain amounts from his earned income, free from taxation; let him put such sums into a retirement fund, and let it be provided that the earnings on such investments may not be taxed.

During the 1950s, doctors, lawyers, and self-employed businessmen became aware that they lay at a disadvantage. They saw corporate employees reach retirement and draw handsome retirement benefits. The professional people and men of business said, in effect, "We want the opportunity to establish our own pension plans, even if we are not incorporated." They were seeking equal opportunities to save.

The self-employed started a movement to secure for themselves the right to accumulate funds for retirement in the fashion already enjoyed by corporate employers and employees. It took time for such a program to assume form. Eventually this plan entered congressional discussion as "H. R. 10 Plans" or the "Keogh Plan." Congressman Eugene Keogh served with Carl Curtis on the Ways and Means Committee. Curtis sponsored the first hearing held by Ways and Means, at which advocates of what later became H. R. 10 Plans were presented to the Congress. The H. R. 10 Plans did for unincorporated business entities what corporations were doing for their employees. Those who took advantage of H. R. 10, or Keogh, to secure qualified pension benefits for themselves, were required to provide pensions for their employees as well. In this respect, the new plan resembled corporation plans.

Even after the passage of H. R. 10, about half of the American population was not protected by a private pension program. Many small employers, millions of farmers, other self-employed persons, and employees working for employers who could not or did not establish a pension plan, still had to earn their money, pay a tax on every dollar earned, and try to save.

There were those in the Treasury Department and the Bureau of the Budget who looked with favor on proposals for giving everybody opportunity to provide for retirement out of their own incomes; but the men in power at the Treasury and the Bureau of the Budget opposed the concept. They set their faces against it because they feared the loss of federal revenue. They pronounced it a good idea, in the abstract—"but not right now."

When the Keogh Plan was adopted by Congress in 1962, Carl Curtis attempted on the Senate floor to extend Keogh's tax relief to all persons who had earned income. This was the beginning of what became known as the Individual Retirement Account, now popularly called an IRA.

Curtis knew that to establish the principle, he must make a modest start. Also he knew that some critics would say that the people Curtis was trying to serve were incapable of setting up complicated, trustee-governed plans like those of corporations or of Keogh. Therefore he offered an amendment to Keogh, providing that any person not covered by any other public or private pension plan might set aside twenty-five dollars a month or three hundred dollars a year, before taxes; and that earnings on such funds would be free from taxation.

Curtis knew that the amount in question was very small, but he was fighting for a principle. For the sake of simplicity, he provided in his first amendment that such funds must be invested in special government savings bonds, which could be bought at a discount dependent on the purchaser's age; and which would be payable when the possessor should reach the age of sixty-five. Curtis had offered previously such an amendment in the Finance Committee, where it had lost by a close vote. His amendment failed in the Senate in 1962. More public education and more promotion were required. The sponsors of the Keogh Plan, to which Curtis sought to attach an amendment, resisted it—not because they opposed it in principle but because as a matter of strategy they wished to have their proposal unencumbered by any amendments.

Later Curtis introduced a bill, S. 1361, which was referred to the Committee on Finance (March 4, 1965). At that time he raised the amount of income to be exempted from tax from three hundred dollars a year to six hundred dollars. Had he been able to get the proposal enacted then, the following illustration might have become more than hypothetical—and of wide benefit.

Suppose we take an individual who does not enjoy the benefits of a company pension plan. Assume that he could save fifty dollars monthly, and that he stands in the nineteen per cent tax bracket. Income tax would reduce his fifty dollars, saved out of current earnings, to $40.50. Assume that his savings earn five per cent interest, and that this earned interest also is taxed. If such an individual were to save fifty dollars monthly, and to keep it up for thirty years, he would accumulate $27,498 from the age of thirty-five to the age of sixty-five. This would pay him a lifetime annuity, at age sixty-five, of an estimated $221 per month. Now if the same person were to save fifty dollars per month and to have the benefit of Curtis' 1965 proposal, the fifty dollars would not be taxed; so the full amount would go into this person's retirement fund. Earnings from his fifty dollars-a-month savings likewise would be tax-free. This person with the more equitable tax treatment, over the same thirty-year period, would accumulate $39,864—or enough to pay him a lifetime annuity, at age sixty-five, to an estimated amount of $319 per month.

On larger savings, invested at higher interest, of course the retirement–funds would have been much greater. But this did not come to pass in 1965.

Undismayed by congressional rebuffs, Curtis continued to advocate an individual–retirement bill; he knew that it was practical and just, the only way to bring tax equality to persons seeking to provide for their own retirement. It would have been foolish and contrary to the public interest to reduce the favorable tax treatment of corporate pensions. The only way to achieve equality was to give everyone who earned income a chance to save for retirement years without paying federal income tax on the savings, and without having taxes take a dismaying chunk of interest earned on those savings.

The hour did come. During the Nixon administration, a gentleman from the White House asked to converse with the Republican members of the Senate's Finance Committee. At that meeting, he told them that revisions in pension laws were needed. He went on to say that the administration had incorporated in its proposal language providing for individual retirement benefits for all taxpayers not already covered. Curtis, overjoyed, interrupted the gentleman to say that he wished to introduce the bill. Now Curtis had the backing of the Treasury Department and of the administration generally. On February 14, 1971, Curtis introduced S. 3012, with distinguished co-sponsors: Senators Bennett of Utah, Fannin of Arizona, Hansen of Wyoming, Jordan of Idaho, Scott of Virginia, and Dominick of Colorado.

"The measure I am introducing," Carl Curtis told the Senate, "is the proposal referred to by the President in his message of December 8, 1970. It would bring about equality before the law. It would enable the other half to do what one-half of our people are now doing. It would enable an individual to save twenty per cent of his earned income, not to exceed $1,500, to put it in a fund for his retirement, and it would be tax free. He would take that out before he figures his tax. Also, the earnings on those savings likewise would be free . . . This bill is certainly in the public interest. It will promote savings; it will promote self-reliance; and it will lessen the pressures on the government for many programs. This, of course, is a supplement to our existing Social Security program."

By the time this bill was introduced, the plan had been developed so that no longer was it necessary to restrict the investment of the savings by statute. The individual was given a wide choice of how he might manage his retirement fund. Under Curtis' bill, the individual would be permitted to invest in a broad range of assets, including stocks, bonds, mutual-fund shares, annuity and other life-insurance contracts, face-amount certificates, and savings accounts with financial institutions. Although these assets could not be commingled with other property, they could be held in custodial accounts, and a taxpayer would not be required to establish a trust for this purpose.

The Ninety-First Congress ended without taking action on pension legislation. So, soon after the convening of the Ninety-Second Congress in January 1973, Curtis reintroduced his bill. It was now S. 374, identical to the bill introduced two years earlier. This time Bennett of Utah, Dominick of Colorado, Fannin of Arizona, and Hansen of Wyoming joined him as co-sponsors—all of them senators from spacious states with considerable farming and ranching populations.

In the Ninety-Second Congress, pension legislation became involved in complexities. Previously, the only senatorial committee with jurisdiction over pension legislation had been the Committee on Finance, and the only House committee with such jurisdiction the Ways and Means. Now, upon urging from labor unions, the committees in Senate and House with jurisdiction over labor legislation involved themselves in pension questions. The bill finally enacted by the Ninety-Second Congress had to run the gantlet of four committees rather than merely two. Wide differences existed in the provisions of the House and the Senate versions of the pension bill (quite aside from Curtis' Individual Retirement Account proposal), and these differences had to be ironed out in conference. This conference did not consist of a small group from one committee in the House and one committee in the Senate, but instead a somewhat large delegation from the two committees in each house. And this was the bill to which Curtis had attached his individual-retirement provision.

The version of the bill sent over by the House and referred to the Senate Finance Committee said nothing about IRA plans. Curtis thought that this was his last chance, all too possibly, to secure a right for the individual to provide for his own retirement; surely this was a golden opportunity. He missed no occasion during pension–bill discussions to extol the virtues of the individual retirement account. When the Committee on Finance considers the make-up of a bill, the staff of the Joint Committee on Taxation, as well as the staff of the Senate Finance Committee, are present at the deliberations. Dr. Lawrence Woodward was then chief of the Joint Committee staff. Woodward vigorously opposed Curtis' argument in favor of individual retirement accounts; but seeing that Curtis was making progress with the chairman and with Finance Committee members, Curtis persevered. Woodward raised all manner of objections to the proposal: it was complicated, difficult to administer, hard for the Treasury to enforce. At one exchange in the discussions, Curtis said to Woodward, "Larry, would you please confine your muddying of the waters to one point at a time, so that I can answer them?''

Thereafter Curtis encountered slight opposition from the staff; many staff members were in sympathy with what he was trying to accomplish. The man Curtis had to convince was his friend Senator Russell Long. A chairman has a good many responsibilities; he relies on staff for materials upon which he makes decisions. At a Committee meeting one morning, Chairman Long announced to Curtis, ''We've decided to let you have your individual-retirement-account proposal for a maximum yearly amount of a thousand dollars.'' The Nixon administration had recommended twenty per cent of earned income, or not to exceed $1,500, as the maximum. Curtis now knew that he and his IRA colleagues were on their way. He had won the battle in the Committee on Finance, and later the IRA provision was sustained on the Senate floor.

The general bill for pensions, to which Curtis' IRA proposal had been attached, went too far in its attempt to regulate company pensions—a result of pressure by the labor unions. Curtis' main objective, however, was to see that the individual-retirement proposal remained in the bill. It did; and now it is the law of the land. The year 1973 was almost ended before work on that legislation was completed by Congress.

For some time after enactment, the individual retirement account received little attention. Only gradually did individuals, savings-and-loan associations, banks, and insurance companies perceive how beneficial the program might be. Meanwhile, soaring inflation pushed up earnings and made the pinch of taxes more painful. Today the IRA plan, expanded by the 1981 Tax Act, has come into its own.

The Economic Recovery Tax Act of 1981 enlarged the IRA program so that the individual might avail himself of its benefits even if already covered by a company pension. Also the amount of savings now has been increased from $1,500 allowed annually to $2,000 for every participant—and for his spouse an equal amount, if both have earned income.

Earlier in this chapter, we suggested figures as to what benefits would accrue with the saving of a mere fifty dollars a month and an interest rate of only five per cent—this example drawn up in 1965. None of us knows what the rate of interest may be five, ten, or thirty years from now. For a plan to be projected with a hypothetical rate of twelve per cent or more in interest on an IRA plan might be speculative indeed. Therefore the following figures are based on a rate of interest of ten per cent, and monthly savings of a hundred dollars from earned income, with a tax rate of twenty-two per cent.

Were an individual to save a hundred dollars a month from his earnings, starting his plan at age thirty-five, and continuing it for thirty years, his total accumulated for retirement at age sixty-five, without the benefit of the Individual Retirement Accounts law, would be less than half of what it would amount to with IRA advantages. Assuming that this person is in the twenty-two per cent federal-income-tax bracket, and that the interest paid on his savings during this period is ten per cent, without IRA he would accumulate $111,508. This sum would purchase a lifetime annuity for him, at age sixty-five, with an estimated value of $1,215.84 a month.

Now take the same case with the same figures but with the tax benefits provided in the Individual Retirement Account Plan: this person would accumulate during the same period the pleasing sum of $236,268. This amount would purchase for him a lifetime annuity at age sixty-five with an estimated value of $2,576.18 per month.

In addition to this gain of more than one hundred per cent in his accumulation for retirement, this individual saver would have reduced his federal income taxes every year over three decades. The amount of money he places in a retirement fund is a deduction from annual income. Of course this payment into an IRA must be from earned income. The IRA plan benefits the individual currently by reducing taxes and permits him to build up a significant amount for retirement years without the burden of taxes on interest generated by the saved money.

Unlike the Keogh Plan, the Individual Retirement Account Plan was not named after its originator. But that omission does not diminish Carl Curtis' satisfaction when he thinks of the benefits that IRA has brought, and will bring, to millions of citizens.

As Curtis was about to retire from the Senate, Senator Russell B. Long wrote him a letter dated December 12, 1978. ''I will always remember the successful fight that you put up that led to the enactment of the Individual Retirement Account provisions of law," Long told Senator Curtis. "You were the originator of the idea, and you started offering amendments in the Committee and on the floor of the Senate back in the early 1960s. You kept at it with dogged persistence. And the bill you introduced in the Ninety-Second Congress, and which you were successful in getting enacted in the Ninety-Third Congress, set forth the plan that is now the law."

As the act providing flood control and irrigation for the Missouri Basin had been Carl Curtis' first large success in Congress, so his Individual Retirement Account Plan was his final large success of his Washington years. The early success benefited directly a sixth of the United States, and indirectly the whole of the country; the late success benefited all those independent people who are the backbone of America's social order and America's economy. Both measures were works of conservation, in the larger sense of that word. Despite all defeats and disappointments as a member of the minority in Congress most of his forty years there, Carl Curtis had these two enduring accomplishments to cherish.

The Social Security Act, well intended and indeed necessary although it was, had brought on delusions about saving and finance, and the end of those troubles is not in sight. The IRA Plan, in part an antidote to the burdens imposed by Social Security and other taxation, promises to shelter and nurture the sort of people by whom this Republic was founded. In the "mass-age" when it seems as if Things are in the saddle and ride mankind, a campaign had been won in defense of honest independence.*

---

* What with Curtis' special work on Social Security, he developed a habit of asking searching questions of the Secretary of Health, Education, and Welfare. Sometimes these inquiries made the Secretary uneasy. After Curtis had announced his intention to retire from the Senate, Secretary Joseph Califano ap-

peared before the Finance Committee. When Curtis' time to question came, he remarked, "Mr. Secretary, you are of all secretaries of your department the most fortunate." Califano asked, "Why do you say that?" To this Curtis answered, "Every Secretary of HEW always has longed for the time when Senator Curtis would be defeated, retire, or die. You are about to see that come to pass: I am retiring." Committee members and the audience laughed; the Secretary was noncommittal.

Chapter 13

The Harassing of a President

THE EVENTS OF WATERGATE

The fall of President Richard Nixon was unparalleled in the history of the United States. Until the winter of 1973, the Nixon administration had enjoyed high popularity and a series of successes in diplomacy, military operations, and most domestic policies. Then, in the space of ten months, the administration reeled downward to its dissolution. Mr. Nixon's resignation on August 9, 1974, was his only alternative to impeachment, trial by the Senate, and possible criminal conviction.

Few men have fallen more swiftly and terribly from public favor. Recall Mr. Nixon's tremendous triumph of his reelection to the presidency in November, 1972. He had defeated George McGovern in the popular vote as badly as Lyndon Johnson had beaten Barry Goldwater, eight years earlier. As for the electoral vote, it stood at 521 for Nixon, 17 for McGovern, more crushing than Johnson's electoral margin over Goldwater. Senator Goldwater had carried six states; Senator McGovern, only Massachusetts and the District of Columbia. (Even Massachusetts might have given Nixon a majority, had it not been for the early lamentations about the Watergate burglary.) Mr. Nixon's margin in the popular vote over Senator Humphrey in the presidential contest of 1968 had been narrow, although less narrow than J. F. Kennedy's margin over Richard Nixon in 1960. (Indeed, it is doubtful whether an honest count in certain states, in 1960, would have given Kennedy a popular majority.) But clearly the American public, in forty-nine out of the fifty states, by 1972, heartily backed President Nixon. A year and nine months after the election of 1972, Richard Nixon was undone.

Senator Curtis' political fortunes had not been dependent upon presidential elections. Against the Kennedy tide, he had carried Nebraska by a large majority in 1960. In 1966, conspicuous though he had been in the disastrous Goldwater presidential campaign two years before, Curtis had been re-elected over a strong Democratic opponent by a resounding margin. In 1972 (Curtis' last campaign), Senator Curtis had three opponents in the primary: he had won more than 141,000 votes to his three competitors' total of less than 50,000. Despite Curtis' outspoken resistance to the Church amendment to Social Security legislation in 1972, Curtis had been sustained by Nebraska's voters in November's general election, still winning re-election by a margin of some 36,000 votes. Obviously the Nebraskans who sent Curtis to his fourth term in the United States Senate approved of their senior senator's obdurate frugality and of his diligence in senatorial investigations.

The Republican Party had been riding high in 1972, but from this pinnacle of success the party tumbled swiftly to disrepute. Presently Curtis would find himself involved in the last of his senatorial investigations—that of President Nixon's tax returns. And Curtis would become an advocate of the rule of law and just procedure in the passionate Watergate controversy, a cause intensely unpopular.

Here we do not mean to go into all the complexities of the dismaying Watergate affair. Rather, this chapter is confined to the endeavor, wholly successful, to bring down an incumbent president. While the House of Representatives discussed impeachment, in the Senate Carl Curtis tried to withstand the tide of passion and partisan eagerness. Here are his observations, founded on his own knowledge and findings.

First, we will look at the effort, when the vice-presidency fell vacant, to transfer to the Congress—with Democratic majorities in both houses—that power of choosing a new vice-president assigned by the Constitution of the United States to the president. This design would have brought about, in effect, the accession of a Democratic president despite the public's overwhelming rejection of the Democratic presidential candidate in 1972.

Second, we will examine the intensive, well-organized campaign to arouse public support for the impeachment of President Nixon.

Third, we will discuss the plan of the Democratic majority in the Senate to change the standing rules of the Senate that provide for trial of an impeachment.

Fourth, we will analyze the treatment that the President endured with respect to his taxes.

The sequence of events from September, 1972, to September, 1974, needs to be recalled.

A federal grand jury, on September 10, 1972, indicted several men for the Watergate conspiracy and burglary.

Richard Nixon was re-elected president, by a huge majority, on November 7, 1972.

The Watergate criminal trial of the burglars began on January 10, 1973.

The Senate appointed a select committee to investigate the Watergate affair on February 7, 1973.

Provisional maximum sentences were imposed on the Watergate burglars on March 23, 1973.

Federal investigators stated on May 1, 1973, that evidence existed of an attempt by White House officials to obstruct investigation of the Watergate burglary.

The Senate's Watergate Committee, on May 17, 1973, opened hearings concerning the Watergate affair.

President Nixon, at a news conference on August 22, 1973, acknowledged the difficulties created by the Watergate controversy, but said that he never had thought of resigning.

U. S. District Court Judge John J. Sirica, on August 29, ordered President Nixon to make available to the Court tapes relevant to the Watergate investigation.

Vice-President Agnew resigned on October 10, 1973, in the face of criminal charges unconnected with the Watergate affair. It became necessary to choose a new vice-president.

Archibald Cox, the Watergate special prosecutor, was removed from office by President Nixon on October 20 in a controversy over the Watergate tapes; and Attorney-General Elliot Richardson resigned.

The House Judiciary Committee decided on October 24 to proceed with an inquiry into the possibility of impeachment.

President Nixon appointed a new special prosecutor, Leon Jaworski, on November 1, 1973; on the same day, Congress opened hearings on the nomination of Gerald Ford to the vice-presidency.

President Nixon, on December 8, made public much of his financial files. Nevertheless, on December 10, 1973, the congressional Joint Committee on Internal Revenue announced its intention of investigating all of the President's tax returns since he had taken office.

The General Accounting Office, on December 18, reporting on President Nixon's expenditures at his private residence, found some governmental expenditures there questionable, suggesting that a portion of the expenses should have been paid for by the President personally.

Nixon on January 4, 1974, refused to comply with a subpoena from the Senate Watergate Committee, on the ground of the confidentiality of presidential correspondence; more than five hundred tapes were in question.

The House voted on February 6, 1974, to authorize its Judiciary Committee to pursue its inquiry into impeachment— with broad powers of investigation. On February 7, the Senate Watergate Committee decided to turn over all its investigative files to the House Judiciary Committee.

President Nixon, at a news conference on February 25, stated that the House could not impeach him unless it presented evidence that he had violated criminal law.

Nixon, on April 3, 1974, agreed to pay nearly $433,000 in additional income taxes and interest thereon.

The Supreme Court, on July 8, ruled that President Nixon must surrender to the Special Prosecutor some sixty-four White House tapes and documents.

The House Judiciary Committee, on July 27 and 30, recommended three articles of impeachment to the full House.

President Nixon released transcripts of three subpoenaed tapes, conversations with his former chief aide, H. R. Haldeman, together with an explanatory statement, on August 5, 1974. Republicans in House and Senate were shaken in their defense of the President.

President Nixon announced his resignation on August 8, 1974.

Gerald Ford was sworn in as President on August 9.

President Ford pardoned Richard Nixon on September 8, 1974, for any offense with which he might be charged.

These are only some of the principal events in the complex Watergate scandal and struggle. They are set down here to supply a framework for the discussion that occupies the remainder of this chapter. Thus the first president ever to resign his office was not impeached, let alone tried and convicted on an impeachment. Amidst a thousand immensely important cares of office—among them the later stages of the Vietnamese misfortune—President Nixon was harassed out of office by his political opponents and by the mass media. Here follows some account of this harassment.

A PRESIDENT TO BE CHOSEN BY CONGRESS?

First we take up the question of the appointment of a new vice-president of the United States; or rather, the question of whether the Democratic majority in the Congress might determine the choice of a new president to succeed Richard Nixon, who had been elected less than two years earlier by tremendous electoral and popular majorities. This was a threat unfulfilled, but a brief ominous possibility endangering the constitutional separation of powers.

By October, 1973, presumably everybody in America had read or heard a good deal about the Watergate affair. The forced resignation of Vice-President Agnew (October 10), on quite different charges, offered the enemies of the Nixon administration an opportunity to drive the Nixon people out of the White House altogether. Democrats held majorities in both houses of Congress. In these circumstances, might the Democrats take control of the White House by a clever tactic, choosing both president and vice-president without any national election? Nothing of that sort had occurred before in American politics, although the Radical Republicans had aspired to a similar deposing of President Andrew Johnson at the beginning of Reconstruction. But the thing might be attempted.

This scheme was advanced publicly by Clark Clifford in an article, "A Government of National Unity," published first in the New York *Times* on June 4, 1973, and reprinted in the New York *Times* on October 29, after Agnew's resignation of the vice-presidency. Clifford, a leader of the left wing of the Democratic party, had been White House counsel for four years during the Truman administration, and Secretary of Defense in the Lyndon Johnson administration. He began his *Times* article by declaring that the damage done to the repute of the Nixon administration by the Watergate scandal and the Agnew scandal was irreparable. He blamed Nixon for inflation and the war in Indochina. Then came his innovating proposal:

"The 25th Amendment provides in Section 1 that the President of the United States can resign, and, if so, he shall be succeeded by the Vice-President. Section 2 provides that when there is a vacancy in the office of the Vice-President, the President shall nominate a Vice-President who shall take office upon confirmation by a majority vote of both houses of Congress.

"Under authority of this Amendment, Mr. Nixon could announce that he and Vice-President Agnew had decided to resign. Mr. Agnew would then resign immediately. Mr. Nixon would then ask the Congress to present him with a list of three qualified individuals from whom he would select a new Vice-President . . . Mr. Nixon would then select the person he preferred and appoint him Vice-President. After the new Vice-President was confirmed by the Congress, Mr. Nixon would resign and the new Vice-President would become President."

Before the *Times* put Clifford's piece into print a second time, Agnew already had resigned; but of course this curious opportunity still lay open to the President. Could Clifford's proposal (the second paragraph of which is altogether unsuggested in the Constitution) have been seriously intended? In 1973, with the Democrats holding safe margins in Senate and House, any list of "three qualified individuals," candidates for the presidency, presumably would have consisted of names of eminent Democrats, though Clifford did mention the possibility of a bipartisan committee to select those names. Mr. Nixon could have been required to choose as his successor the gentleman least obnoxious among his adversaries. The Clifford plan, in effect, was a design for Nixon's opponents to gain the White House overnight. Asking Richard Nixon to submit to this scheme was a demand for the surrender of the Republican Party.

The Twenty-Fifth Amendment to the Constitution, ratified in 1967, does not mention any possibility of asking Congress to commend three candidates for the vice-presidency in the event of a vacancy: clearly the Amendment makes this nomination a presidential prerogative. No president could request Congress to give him a list of "three qualified individuals" without seriously impairing the constitutional separation of powers—at least if he should bind himself to choosing one of the three.

So what could Clifford and the radical wing of the Democrats have meant by this proposal? Perhaps they assumed that Nixon might accept it lest worse befall him. By consenting to make some Democrat the new president, Nixon might escape impeachment, conviction, and conceivable punishment. There lay behind the Clifford proposal this implication, "Surrender the presidency to us, and you might spare yourself a prison sentence." It was a grim, unconstitutional maneuver. Nixon replied to it by choosing Gerald Ford, Republican leader in the House, as his successor.

Clifford's scheme suggests the unscrupulous zeal with which some Democrats sought to drag down President Nixon, well before the President's ruinous tape recordings came to light. Yet Clifford's denunciation of Nixon was moderate, if compared with the language employed by more reckless partisan enemies of the President.

HOW TO DESTROY
THE CHIEF EXECUTIVE

There had commenced a ferocious, concerted campaign to blacken Nixon in the eyes of the public. The strategists of this operation paid especial attention to college campuses, so fertile a field for radical agitation in the 1960s and early 1970s.

Here is one specimen. At the University of Wisconsin, on November 7, Arlie Schardt, associate director of the American Civil Liberties Union, addressed a hundred students on the subject of impeachment, which, he said, ". . . does not require that the President has violated some law, but can merely consist of serious abuses of public trust." This statement was false: Article II, Section 4, of the Constitution speaks only of "Treason, Bribery, and other High Crimes and Misdemeanors," not of vague and indefinable "abuses of public trust." What an argument from an officer of an organization professing its ardent concern for civil liberties! But people like Schardt were little concerned for the rule of law: what they sought was vengeance on their adversary Richard Nixon.

A wondrous ignorance of law often was revealed by Nixon's enemies in the heat of their wrath. Considerably after Nixon's resignation, Frank Mankiewicz—who had been George McGovern's political director in the presidential campaign of 1972—and Russell Kirk were debating before a large audience on a Texan campus. A professor rose to inquire why Nixon had not been impeached for slaughter in Indochina. Masters are responsible at law for the acts of their servants, the professor declared; and American troops in southeastern Asia had been the President's servants. Mankiewicz correctly replied that the professor was thinking of the law of commercial contracts, not applicable to public magistrates; Kirk added that if any president were held responsible for every act committed by the millions of people employed by the federal government, no one ever would be persuaded to stand for the presidency. At the time, most universities seemed given over to the Reign of Unreason.

But demonstrating students and absurd professors were not President Nixon's more formidable adversaries. In December, 1973, a meeting attended by representatives of groups publicly committed to impeachment was held in Ralph Nader's office on Capitol Hill. Among them were men from the AFL-CIO, the American Civil Liberties Union, the United Automobile Workers, and Americans for Democratic Action—along with leaders of various pacifist and New Left organizations.

Ever since October, 1973, indeed, weekly meetings of the

Washington lobbyists for such labor, liberal, and radical groups had been taking place for the exchange of information and to work out some coordinated policy to bring about impeachment of the President. The American Civil Liberties Union had prepared a handbook listing seventeen actions that citizens might take to advance the cause of impeachment, among them making speeches, talking to editors and clergymen, and writing to members of Congress. Many of the reasons advanced for impeaching Nixon at such gatherings or in such publications were quite unrelated to Watergate. The war in Indochina was a principal cause of accusation against Nixon in such circles—even though the war had commenced during the Kennedy administration and had grown to tremendous proportions during the Johnson administration, while Nixon and Henry Kissinger were endeavoring to terminate the struggle and withdraw.

In January, 1974, Powell Lindsay, a writer for the Scripps-Howard newspapers, remarked accurately of the pro-impeachment forces, "By and large, the groups seeking to remove Nixon from the presidency are a mélange of old-line or *ad hoc* liberals, leftist organizations, and remnants of the anti-war movement, with one huge exception—organized labor."

This was as true in Nebraska as in Washington. In December, 1973, a printed circular was distributed in Lincoln by a "Coalition for Impeachment"; the circular included contributions from organizations so diverse as the American Civil Liberties Union, the Student Bar Association Council at the University of Nebraska, the Lincoln Gay Action Group, and the AFL-CIO. Most of the reasons alleged by the several authors of this pamphlet for impeaching President Nixon had nothing to do with the Watergate affair. For that matter, the charges had little enough to do with the Constitution or with law.

A Mr. Thomas Manig, of the department of philosophy of the University of Nebraska at Lincoln, for instance, declared that Nixon should be impeached for violations of "moral law," rather than of any positive law. A Philip W. Dver listed twelve reasons for impeachment, among them for "vetoing bills like the day-care bill that would alleviate many children's and parents' suffering in this country" and "for generally being insensitive to the plight of millions of suffering oppressed people in this country and around the world, for putting corrupt privileges ahead of the equality and the liberty of the masses of the people.''

Still more interesting were the reasons for impeachment advanced by the Lincoln Gay Action Group. These persons were incensed because ''During Nixon's five years in office, he has failed to implement even a single recommendation of the 1969 Report of the National Institute of Mental Health's Task Force on Homosexuality.'' Worse still, Nixon had continued to fight a war in Asia. ''Human interaction based on sexual roles conditions boys to be aggressive, competitive, and to fight others, while it conditions females to submit to a passive role and to support decisions made by men . . . War, American-style, is conceived and fought by men who are reared to play a dominant, aggressive role and to feel guilty if this sexual role is not fulfilled.'' Nixon should have withdrawn immediately from Asia; because he did not, he must be impeached.

The AFL-CIO, in this pamphlet, listed twenty reasons for impeachment, only four of which were directly related to Watergate. The great labor unions generally had supported military intervention in Asia, through the Kennedy, Johnson, and Nixon administrations; and the labor leaders emphatically were masculine. One wonders how comfortable the union officials felt in company with the eccentric professors and self-proclaimed homosexuals of this coalition. But the drive for impeachment could not have gone far without the unions' endorsement.

Such intemperate and often frantic denunciations of President Nixon were part of a well-directed campaign for impeachment in every state of the Union. Nixon never had been popular with newspapermen; now was their opportunity to have their sport with the politician who once had told them in his anger (very prematurely, as matters had turned out), ''You won't have Dick Nixon to kick around any more!'' The television pundits, notoriously less informed and more unfair than the journalists of print, were harsher still upon the President. David Susskind charitably observed over a television network that Watergate was worse than the Holocaust (rather a curious assessing of iniquity).

Nixon was overwhelmed daily by abuse from the molders of public opinion. Every charge against him was repeated over and over, so that a large part of the public, perhaps three-quarters of the American people, had come to believe in his guilt even before proceedings toward impeachment had commenced in the House of Representatives.

John Adams, writing to Thomas Jefferson near the end of their lives, mentioned "that immense unpopularity which fell like the tower of Siloam upon me . . . *Sic transit gloria mundi.*" So it came to pass with Richard Nixon, undone by the mass media. At his re-election in 1972, Nixon had carried everything but Massachusetts and the District of Columbia; two years later, he was so generally condemned that even Republican stalwarts in the Congress, cowering before this storm, hesitated to make any defense of the President against even the most unjust or exaggerated charges. Senator Sam Ervin, North Carolina Democrat, proclaimed that the scandal of Nixon's tape recordings was a greater tragedy than the Civil War had been—so suggesting, as with Susskind, an interesting indifference to the destruction of human life.

Carl Curtis, in the Senate, was astounded by the prompt success of this campaign of defamation intended to bring about impeachment—all this well before any testimony about the Watergate affair had been taken. Nobody had demanded impeachment of Lyndon Johnson because of the Estes and Baker cases of corruption; earlier, nobody had aspired to impeach Harry Truman because of the numerous governmental scandals during his administration. Many of the politicians and journalists most extravagant in their denunciations of Nixon were perfectly aware of "cover-ups" in national politics since the Second World War, more reprehensible though more successful than the Watergate cover-up. A latitudinarian standard had been applied to earlier presidents; while Nixon, like Caesar's wife, was expected to conduct himself beyond reproach.

The House's three articles of impeachment, as drawn up by the Committee on the Judiciary but never put to a vote of the House, accused President Nixon of obstruction of justice, abuse of power, and contempt of Congress. Supposing the specifications in these articles to be substantiated, did Nixon's alleged actions constitute high crimes and misdemeanors within the meaning of Article II of the Constitution? Crimes or misdemeanors so grave as the treason and the bribery specified in that article? Little precedent existed to guide Congress here: there had been but one impeachment trial of a president, that of Andrew Johnson—who was acquitted.

However that may be, Richard Nixon was lynched in public opinion long before the majority and minority reports of the House Judiciary Committee were issued on August 22, 1974. The public was not at all sure of what offenses President Nixon had been guilty; but most people had been convinced by the zealots for impeachment that Nixon must have been guilty of something or other. Fearful of this wave of public disapproval, the large majority of members of the Senate were ready to convict the President of whatever the House might charge him with, regardless of what defense the President's lawyers might have offered. Richard Nixon was convicted by the press, television, "Coalitions for Impeachment", and his partisan enemies—not by due process of law. This was a sore blow to the separation of powers and the reign of law.

Despite his several great successes in election campaigns, Mr. Nixon always had been uneasily aware that the political ground might shift beneath his feet. In an hour-long conversation with Russell Kirk at the White House, a few days after American troops entered Cambodia in 1971, President Nixon touched on this disquiet.

"Where does a president get his support when he has to make hard and unpopular decisions?" he asked Dr. Kirk. "I mean any president, not necessarily myself. I know people think I have the backing of big business; but when I have to make hard decisions, I find those people absent. Sometimes I have support from George Meany and his unions. I have some friends in the Academy. And I still have Main Street . . ."

"As you know, Mr. President, Main Street means less than it did once," Kirk remarked. The President nodded. He knew too well the fickleness of great interests and volatile electorates. At the time of this conversation, Watergate was a cloud no greater than a man's hand.

Three years later, when Richard Nixon would need support more than at any previous time in his life, that reinforcement would be wanting: men of his inner White House circle, on whom he had relied most, would serve him ill or turn their testimony against him. The tower of Siloam fell upon Nixon.

The Constitution makes no provision for impeachment of a president on the ground that he has grown unpopular; or that his policies are imprudent; or that he has lost the confidence of Congress; or that he has exercised authority considered by some to exceed the powers delegated to the president. Yet it was on such charges that President Nixon found himself compelled to resign, rather than for proven "high crimes and misdemeanors." The courts have held that high crimes and misdemeanors signify very serious or aggravated offenses— those nearly allied and equal in enormity to treason and bribery. Such offenses, according to the Constitution, must be of a magnitude sufficient to justify, by presidential impeachment, the toppling of a government of the United States.

Had an impeachment trial come to pass, the Senate would have had to decide whether the alleged offenses of President Nixon had been all that reprehensible. But perhaps most senators already had made up their minds, or else their minds had been made up for them by public-opinion polls. They had decided to vote for the President's conviction, tide what might betide during the expected trial. A principal concern of the Democratic leadership of the Senate appeared to be to make certain that by no conceivable means might Richard Nixon be acquitted. For the concerted campaign to cover Nixon with opprobrium had swept the Senate along in its strong current.

STAR CHAMBER
RULES

"The Senate shall have the sole Power to try all Impeachments." So runs the first sentence of the sixth paragraph of Section 3, Article I, of the Constitution. "When sitting for that Purpose, they shall be on Oath or Affirmation. When the President of the United States is tried, the Chief Justice shall Preside: And no Person shall be convicted without the concurrence of two thirds of the Members present."

Standing rules of the Senate provide for impeachment trials. Would those standing rules stand firm in 1974?

While the House held hearings on the possible impeachment of the President, and people throughout the country began to assume that impeachment would occur, the Senate's Rules Committee considered a re-writing of the Senate's standing rules on impeachment. At that time the members of the Senate Committee on Rules and Administration, for the Democratic majority, were Howard Cannon (chairman) of Nevada; Claiborne Pell of Rhode Island; Robert Byrd of West Virginia; James Allen of Alabama; and Harrison Williams of New Jersey. The Republican minority members were Marlow Cook of Kentucky; Hugh Scott of Pennsylvania; Robert Griffin of Michigan; and Mark Hatfield of Oregon.

Talk that the rules might be rewritten for the trial of Richard Nixon disturbed several members of this committee—and not the minority members only. Would new rules be an attempt to deny to President Nixon the civil rights guaranteed to all citizens of the Republic?

On July 31, 1974, Senator Mansfield of Montana, the majority leader, deposited with the Rules Committee a resolution proposing a complete revision of the Senate rules for impeachment trials. Senator Scott, Republican leader, sent a formal letter to all Republican senators, notifying them of this resolution.

This Mansfield resolution proposed that the chief judges of the court of impeachment be the majority leader and the minority leader of the Senate, with the assistant majority leader and the assistant minority leader as deputy chief judges. The provision in effect contravened Section 3, Article I, of the Constitution, cited above, which specifies that the Chief Justice of the United States shall preside at a presidential impeachment trial.

The wisdom of the framers of the Constitution in this provision is sufficiently evident. The chief justice is not an elected officer who must stand for re-election. He is trained and experienced in the law, and particularly in the rules of evidence; he is qualified to direct an impeachment trial when the Senate sits as a court of impeachment. The Mansfield resolution did not propose to exclude the chief justice from participation, but certainly it would have diminished his prerogative and authority.

Were the majority leader and the minority leader in the Senate to supplant the chief justice, effectually, in presiding over the possible impeachment trial, that change of rules would give to the chief judges and their deputies broad power over the conduct of the trial. They would control the scheduling of proceedings and the power to call for yeas and nays, which under the old standing rules could be called only with the assent of one-fifth of the judges (senators) present. Such a change would give the chief judges power to invite attorneys, other than counsel for the parties; to make statements on questions of law; to permit them to submit briefs; to recommend to the court (the senators) that such outside lawyers might offer oral arguments on any legal question or issue; and to determine how much time should be allowed for such arguments.

Mansfield's proposed new rules also would have authorized the chief judges, with the approval of the court, to appoint panels of judges for such purposes as the court might prescribe. Full exercise of these powers by the proposed chief judges could have taken away substantially the constitutional authority assigned to the Chief Justice of the Supreme Court—an invasion of the powers of the judicial branch by the legislative branch.

A highly significant additional change in the standing rules for impeachment trials, included in the Mansfield resolution, was the authorizing of discovery: a procedure whereby one party can compel the adverse party to make disclosures of evidence. In an impeachment trial, the discovery procedure would enable the judges—that is, the senators—to shift the burden of proof in some degree to the respondent (President Nixon), and might lead to a question verging on violation of the protections against self-incrimination. In effect, "discovery" would have been a license to hunt for admissible evidence on the basis of evidence known to be inadmissible.

As if "discovery" might be insufficient to catch President Nixon, another new rule proposed for the impeachment trial was a provision permitting hearsay evidence. This was proposed Rule 8: hearsay would not be admissible in an impeachment trial, *except* in accordance with subdivision (a) of this new rule. Among other things, it was provided in subdivision (a) that hearsay evidence should be admitted if the court, upon the recommendation of the chief judges and the deputy chief judges, should decide to admit such evidence. In other words, the Senate—made up in 1974 of fifty-nine Democrats and forty-three Republicans—could have admitted hearsay evidence whenever the Democratic majority might so have desired.

Mansfield's proposed new rules never were acted on by the whole Senate; for only nine days after the Mansfield proposal had been circulated, President Nixon resigned from office. Had the Mansfield rules been approved by the Senate and had Nixon been brought to trial by that body, the President could have entertained no hope of acquittal. With such rules, discriminating monstrously against a defendant, the Senate would have converted itself into a kind of twentieth-century Star Chamber; or, to draw another analogy, Richard Nixon would have been in the plight of Charles I tried by a committee of the Roundhead House of Commons. Mr. Nixon's resignation saved the Senate of the United States from disgracing itself by adopting the rules of a kangaroo court—all for the sake of partisan advantage. *

---

* Curtis did not believe that Senator Mansfield was the originator of this resolution, which did not accord with Mansfield's concept of justice. The resolution probably was thrust upon the majority leader by others who managed the plan of impeachment.

RICHARD NIXON, TAXPAYER

Finally, some pages about President Nixon's tax returns. The accusation that Richard Nixon had evaded payment of income tax was a death blow to his standing with a great many American citizens, painfully aware that they had found it necessary to pay their own taxes.

President Nixon's tax returns had been unlawfully released to the press—and to his enemies—by a civil servant in the Internal Revenue Service. Late in 1973, various journalists and politicians were alleging that the President had paid too little tax on too large an income.

Aware of the mischief that might be done to him by such rumors at this period of his fortunes, President Nixon took steps to refute the rumors that somehow he had amassed and concealed great sums during his presidency. He endeavored to explain to the Congress and the public his actual financial condition; but in doing so, Nixon became still more entwined in the net that his enemies had cast about him.

Intending to make it clear that he had not been evading payment of income taxes, Nixon sent a letter to Senator Russell Long, of the Joint Committee on Internal Revenue Taxation, on December 8, 1973. Questions had been raised about two items in Mr. Nixon's tax return. Nixon asked the Joint Committee to determine whether or not these items had been correctly reported by him to the Internal Revenue Service.

"In the event that the committee determines that the items were incorrectly reported," President Nixon wrote, "I will pay whatever tax may be due. I also want to assure you that the committee will have full access to all relevant documents pertaining to these matters and will have the full cooperation of my office."

Thus Mr. Nixon waived the established right of all taxpayers to challenge an adverse interpretation of a return. Nixon's own tax lawyers, believing firmly that the President's case was sound, wished to take the matter to court. Would Nixon have asked the Joint Committee—dominated by Democratic senators and representatives—to examine his tax returns if he had knowingly endeavored to evade payment of part of his taxes or to misrepresent his exemptions?

The Joint Committee did take cognizance of the President's request; but, holding no hearings nor making any investigation of their own, the Committee turned over the inquiry to the Committee's staff.

The staffs of congressional committees provide background material for a committee's members; the staff of this Joint Committee was accustomed to undertake research on tax questions, make reports on tax proposals, work with Treasury officials and staffs, and provide technical assistance in writing tax legislation. The chief of this Joint Committee staff was Dr. Lawrence Woodward, who persistently had endeavored to obstruct the Finance Committee's deliberations, in 1973, on Senator Curtis' proposal for Individual Retirement Accounts. A writer for the Philadelphia *Bulletin* later ascertained that of the twenty-five members of the Joint Committee staff in 1974, not one appeared to be a Republican.

This staff proceeded to examine the President's tax returns. Early in their work they reported that it would be necessary for them to examine all the Nixon income-tax returns, from 1969 to 1972. The members of the Joint Committee authorized this enlargement of responsibilities.

On April 3, 1974, the staff filed a report of 994 pages on these Nixon returns. This report was similar in character to the initial bargaining position of an Internal Revenue agent at an audit of a tax return, and was sharply unfavorable to the President. It differed in a number of important particulars from the usual reports of congressional investigations.

The Committee and its staff had called no witnesses to be sworn and placed under oath for testimony.

There had been no cross-examination of any witness.

At no time did President Nixon's lawyers participate in the deliberations of the staff.

At no time was any member of the Joint Committee, from

either Senate or House, or any other senator or representative, present at the staff investigation.

Except for Carl Curtis, a minority member of this Joint Committee, no member of the Committee read any part of the staff's report before that report was accepted by the Committee and released to the public; nor did any other senator or representative, not a member of the Joint Committee, read any part of the report before its release to the public.

In short, a request from the President of the United States was consigned to congressional staff personnel merely— without any supervision from chairman, vice-chairman, or any member of the Joint Committee. This unusual procedure saved members of the Joint Committee from having to sit in judgment on the questions raised by Nixon.

What with the overwhelming political pressures under which he labored at that hour, President Nixon accepted the staff report, as approved by the Joint Committee, without protest, volunteering to pay in consequence more than four hundred thousand dollars, plus interest, in additional income taxes. But was that staff report just?

The Joint Committee's staff found the Nixon tax returns faulty in several particulars. Two major items were in dispute. First, was the President entitled to a tax deduction for the gift of his pre-presidential papers in 1969? Second, when the Nixons sold their New York apartment and purchased their house in San Clemente, was their gain on the sale of the apartment subject to capital-gains tax?

Let us look at these concerns: first, the gift of the Nixon Papers. For many years, federal-income-tax statutes had provided that deductions from income tax might be taken by taxpayers who had made contributions of valuable papers and documents to public or institutional libraries or archives. Writers, leading men and women in many fields, and members of Congress or of other political bodies frequently had made such donations, and ordinarily had been permitted substantial deductions accordingly, provided that the claimed value of such "other than cash" contributions could be certified by valuators or assessors.

This provision of the Internal Revenue code was intended to encourage citizens to preserve and donate important papers, particularly those of historical interest. But abuse of such deductions aroused protest. Some members of Congress had claimed excessive deductions for having donated long runs of *The Congressional Record* and other public documents. Some congressional reformers were especially disturbed by reports of the sum that President Johnson had deducted from his taxable income for the donation of his papers to the Johnson Presidential Library.

Precisely how much Johnson claimed and obtained as a tax deduction for his donation has been kept secret by the Johnson family, but it was widely asserted in 1969 that the deduction had come to nearly thirty million dollars. Two years later, a writer in *The Nation* of June 5, 1971, reported that President Johnson, before his contribution of papers, had obtained the appraisal that they were worth between fifty and sixty million. The Johnson collection consisted of some thirty-one million items, including five hundred thousand photographs of the Johnson family. ("One wonders whether the law of diminishing returns has been suspended for this gallery," commented N. C. Chriss, author of the *Nation* article.) The Johnson Library building itself was "a sixty million dollar enterprise"; and the cost to taxpayers of operating the library, by 1971, was some eight hundred thousand dollars annually—quadruple the estimate of such cost given to Congress in 1965.

This IRS provision for income-tax deductions for the gift of papers, so lucratively employed by President Johnson, remained unaltered when Richard Nixon was elected to the presidency in November, 1968—and unaltered throughout the early months of his administration. Soon after taking office, the new President made arrangements to donate to a Richard M. Nixon Presidential Library his papers as Congressman, Senator, and Vice-President.

But in the course of Nixon's first administration, Congress amended the statute concerning income-tax deductions for such gifts to libraries and archives. No longer could any donors of their own papers obtain tax deductions, once this amendment should become effective. Public men no longer could claim deductions for having contributed documents and papers produced in a public office at public expense. This change became effective on July 25, 1969.

This restriction on such tax deductions has been a cause of sorrow, ever since, to scholarly libraries: its practical effect has been to reduce to a trickle what once was a flood of contributions. Well-publicized accounts of abuse of this deduction had led to Congress' reforming action.

More than three years after this reform, when in 1973 the Senate's Committee on Finance was discussing charitable contributions, Senator John Williams, on November 21, sent to the National Archives and Records Service of the General Services Administration a letter requesting a list of all papers presented to presidential libraries (which are under the jurisdiction of the Archives) for the preceding ten years. President Nixon's papers, already donated, had been a gift to the National Archives, intended for a Nixon Presidential Library.

James O'Neill, acting archivist of the United States, replied to Senator Williams on December 7, 1973, providing lists of the names of persons who had made donations to the several presidential libraries during the decade in question. The archivist mentioned that the National Archives does not appraise the value of papers being donated, nor has it available information as to appraisals of value made for the donors.

As for the intended Nixon Presidential Library, the archivist listed a large gift of papers by Richard Nixon in 1968 and another large donation in 1969; other gifts by three friends of Nixon, in 1973.

For the year 1969, the archivist's list gave the month and day of all contributions, so that it might be ascertained whether or not these donations had been made before July 25, 1969, the date when Congress' alteration of the statute concerning such gifts to libraries became effective. The Nixon gift of 1968 clearly had entitled the President to a deduction from income tax. Only concerning the donation of 1969 did any question arise.

The contribution of 1969 had been a major gift of some six hundred thousand documents, appraised at a value of $576,000, a modest sum by the side of President Johnson's appraisal of his papers. The Nixon deduction was to be spread over four years of tax returns. James O'Neill's response to the inquiry of Senator Williams fixed the date of the gift of the Nixon papers at March 27, 1969.

This donation had occurred not only before the effective change in the statute concerning such contributions, but also before either the House Ways and Means Committee or the Senate Finance Committee had acted on proposed reforms of that law. Nixon's papers had been delivered to the Archives in March; but, as is frequent enough with such donations of papers, the paperwork connected with the gift had not been wholly completed until some time later.

Soon after the Joint Committee's staff had commenced work on the Nixon tax returns, Senator Curtis delivered in person to Lawrence Woodward, chief of that staff, a copy of the archivist's letter and list of contributions to presidential libraries. Nowhere in the staff's report of 994 pages—as Curtis would point out later in a speech to the Senate—can be found any reference to the archivist's letter and list, although that list showed clearly that Nixon's donation of 1969 had been made months before the legislative change concerning *tax-deductible* gifts of papers took effect.

When public men or private citizens donate their papers to libraries or museums, often they attach conditions to the use of those materials or even specify temporary retention of some of those papers. Lyndon Baines Johnson, for instance, provided in his donation that whenever he, his wife, or his daughters might decide that some document included in the Johnson Presidential Library was personal rather than public, they could obtain the return of that document. Similarly, Richard Nixon attached some reasonable conditions for the delivery, use, and safeguarding of his papers. Yet the Joint Committee's staff proceeded to question whether these conditions affected the time of completion of his gift; and eventually the staff disallowed his whole tax deduction for the donation of 1969.

The report of the staff discussed various aspects of the Nixon gift, among them questions about a deed of gift. Now the principle is well established in law that a gift of personal property does not require a deed: the gift is complete when the property itself passes from donor to recipient. Although a formal deed *may* be employed, it serves more as a memorandum of the understanding of the parties than as a formal conveyance. A deed is not itself a validation of a gift, nor does it indicate the time of the gift.

The logic of the staff in denying that Nixon's gift had been made before the change in the law was effective seemed flimsy to Carl Curtis. Although admitting that a deed is not necessary for a gift of personal property, the staff held that it has been necessary in President Nixon's case. Mr. Nixon's intention as a donor had been shown in connection with the gift of papers he had made in 1968. The staff broke with the legal principle that actual passage of the gift suffices to complete the transaction.

Consider the gift of the Franklin Roosevelt papers. Some of those documents had remained in Roosevelt's possession when he stated at a small gathering that he would give his papers to the Roosevelt Presidential Library. Some of those papers still were held by Roosevelt at the time of his death. In a case at law, a New York court in 1947 determined that the retaining of some of Roosevelt's papers in the White House (still being needed there) had not defeated the entire gift; Roosevelt's previous announcement that he had intended to contribute all his documents sufficed to validate the whole of his benefaction.

So the staff's investigation of the Nixon donation of papers seemed to Carl Curtis inadequate and unjust. He pointed out then that the members of the staff who had conducted the investigation were persons without any experience as lawyers; also without experience in evaluating evidence; and that none of them was a Republican. On dubious technical grounds, the staff report denied to President Nixon the tax deduction readily extended to previous presidents.

Now we turn to the controversy about another aspect of the Nixon tax returns: whether the Nixons had failed to pay in full capital-gains tax owing from the sale of their New York apartment, at the time when they moved to San Clemente, California.

Federal tax law provides that if a taxpayer sells his principal residence, and within the requisite time limit reinvests the proceeds in a new principal residence, he will not be required to pay a capital-gains levy on whatever may have been his gain from the sale of the first residence. (Under some circumstances, the taxpayer may be wholly exempt from taxation on such a transaction; under other circumstances, he is authorized to defer payment of any sum of taxes eventually due because of gain on the sale of the first residence.)

But the staff of the Joint Committee held in their report that the Nixons' gain on the sale of their New York apartment was subject to taxation, fully, as capital gain. For the statute specified sale of one "principal residence" and purchase of a new "principal residence." Mr. Nixon's second principal residence was not San Clemente, the staff report contended, but rather the White House.

This finding bordered on the absurd. The White House is a public building; its occupant does not own even its furniture. It contains the offices of public officials, as well as the President's private rooms. Daily thousands of tourists visit the building. No president's tenure of the White House exceeds eight years.*

A president has as much right as does any citizen to choose his place of residence and to establish his house or apartment at that place. This situation is not altered by the necessity of being away from home on business for extended periods. San Clemente had become President Nixon's principal residence— home to him. Whenever opportunity arose, the President and his wife returned to San Clemente. The staff's own report conceded that Mr. and Mrs. Nixon spent thirty-five days at San Clemente in 1969, fifty days in 1970, fifty days in 1971, thirty-four days in 1972, and forty-two days in 1973.

In their 1969 tax return, the sum set down as a gain by the sale of their New York apartment by the Nixons was $142,912. Ruling that the San Clemente house was not the Nixons' prin-

---

* During the Coolidge administration, Calvin Coolidge happened to pass by, on a stroll, while a visitor from abroad was inquiring at a White House gate, "Who lives there?" President Coolidge interjected, "Nobody: they just come and go."

cipal residence, the Joint Committee's staff declared that the Nixons should have paid full capital-gains tax on that sum.

This staff report was discussed by the Joint Committee on April 3, 1974. No member of that committee except Senator Curtis had read the report; no member of the committee had participated in its preparation. Yet the Joint Committee voted to accept the report and to release it to the public. This decision was made with but one dissent: that of Carl Curtis. Before approval of the report, Senator Curtis argued that the whole matter of the Nixon tax returns should be referred back to the Internal Revenue Service, there to be dealt with as all tax cases are handled, with possible recourse to courts of law.

On the Senate floor, April 11, 1974, Curtis summarized the business of the President's tax returns. He pointed out that after accepting Nixon's request for examination of his returns, the Joint Committee had held no meetings at all from early December to April 3. On the latter date, the Joint Committee had been presented with the huge staff report. That same day, the report had been filed in Congress and presented to the press.

"For weeks I made repeated requests of the staff for a copy of its statement of facts concerning the President's tax matter," Curtis told the Senate. "I was always told it was not ready. On Friday, March 31, 1974, I appealed to Chairman Russell Long for assistance in getting this material from the staff. On Saturday morning, April 1, 1974, there was delivered to me one hundred and fifty pages of typewritten material, and I was informed that it was substantially the full and complete statement of the staff in reference to the gift of the President's papers. Over the weekend I read this material line by line and studied it thoroughly.

"The staff report is not based on statements taken under oath subject to cross-examination. The President's lawyers were not present when the witnesses were interviewed, nor was any member of the Joint Committee on Internal Revenue Taxation.

"Not only is the staff report made up of material not taken under oath, but considerable space is given to statements which are mere conclusions. As I reviewed the staff report, certain items of testimony literally cried out for cross-examination under oath. It does not contain all of the facts that are available . . .

"The point has been made that the Internal Revenue Service agreed in substance with the staff report. This calls for some clarification. The usual practice of the IRS in proceeding to assess additional taxes is to include in their notice all items remaining in question. Then there follows the usual opportunity for the taxpayer to present his facts and legal analysis. Conferences can be held, and there are certain appeal procedures within the IRS. In the case of the President's taxes, he announced his intention to pay as soon as the staff report was released, and the above-mentioned procedures of the IRS were not used.

"Two key points emerge from the aftermath of the lengthy and complex examination of President Nixon's tax returns.

"First, Richard Nixon will pay every cent the congressional committee and the Internal Revenue Service say he owes.

"Second, the President of the United States has been singled out for harsher treatment than any other taxpayer.

"At the same time, President Nixon turned aside the advice of his tax counsel to appeal the IRS decision and, in doing so, denied himself the legal remedy afforded any other taxpayer in the country.

"The real crunch in the tax story is how President Nixon received treatment on his taxes that is wholly different from that given any other taxpayer. Whenever there was a question—and there were many real issues of tax-law interpretation—the committee decision came down on the high side.

"The major point of contention between the President's tax counsel and the committee auditors was over his donation of the vice-presidential papers. This alone accounted for the largest portion of the new tax bill.

"Appraised at nearly two million dollars, these papers had been given to the National Archives. But the joint committee said this was not a valid gift, because he placed access restrictions on them and because he failed to give sufficient evidence in 1969 of his intent to donate them.

"Every president who has donated his papers to the Archives has placed restrictions on their access—such as dates and times when the papers are open to scholars and the public . . .

"President Nixon's gift stands on much firmer footing than F. D. R.'s—yet Nixon was denied the tax deduction.

"The Internal Revenue Code permits every taxpayer to sell his home and invest the proceeds in another principal residence within a year. And no tax is assessed on capital gains. This applies in every case, except Richard Nixon's . . .

"Another point on which the President was assessed taxes was on the use of government aircraft.

"As a result of the wave of aircraft hijacking, the Secret Service advised the members of the Nixon family to travel by government air service, rather than on commercial flights; and the Nixons prudently complied. The President responded, in 1971, by becoming the first president in history to absorb some of the cost; and he has been paying a share of the bill ever since.

"No previous president—Truman, Eisenhower, Kennedy, or Johnson—paid for any government flights taken by their family members. Richard Nixon did; yet he is now told he must pay full fare retroactively.

"There are other points on which President Nixon was singled out for heavyhanded treatment. His tax counsel, for example, were never given an opportunity to see, much less contest, more than ninety per cent of the committee staff report—despite committee promises that they would have such a right.

"But the President has said he will pay; and pay in full he will.

"It comes not only at great personal cost, but it comes in a manner which should outrage every American taxpayer who now knows the President of the United States was treated unfairly."

At that late hour, Senator Curtis' words could not much affect either senatorial action or public opinion. The nation had been sharply divided concerning the charges brought against President Nixon and about his possible impeachment. But when newspapers and broadcasters told everybody in the country about the Joint Committee's report, Nixon's remaining support began to wane. People who had viewed the Watergate burglary as a stupid wrongdoing in the heat of a national political

campaign, and as an act unauthorized by the President—
why, many such citizens now turned against Nixon. If President Nixon had been cheating on his taxes, if he hadn't paid
his fair share, who would stand him up?

Actually, the Nixon tax deductions of 1969 were as well
justified and substantiated by evidence and precedent as are
most returns of honest and substantial citizens. But so much
mud already had been thrown at Richard Nixon that the mud-
pie of "tax evasion" clung to him fatally.

THE NAME
OF RICHARD NIXON

Not long after President Gerald Ford took charge of the Executive Force, he was asked in the Oval Office of the White House
how Richard Nixon had contrived to bear his misfortunes without going mad. "He was strong," Ford said, with something
like a sob.

Contrary to the opinion of most journalists, Richard Nixon by nature is idealistic, rather than ruthlessly practical; given
to long views; somewhat lacking in imaginative power, but desirous of attracting to himself men of imagination; conservative in basic inclinations, yet eager to make improving
innovations. What Nixon has most desired is a high reputation
with posterity.

So the saddest thing about Nixon's fall from popular favor,
after a vigorous presidency of considerable achievements, is
not the scorn with which he was treated by people whose own

lives might not bear close examination. The frustration of his yearning after a good name that might endure down the centuries: this deprivation was the cruelest blow to him. In that sense, Richard Nixon's overturn was a tragedy.

Yet the judgment of history not infrequently rejects the hasty judgment of the leaders of today's crowd. It was so with President John Adams, who murmured *sic transit gloria mundi*. It was so, in some degree, with President Andrew Johnson, not nearly so much harassed in 1868 as President Nixon was in 1974.

In a time not far distant there may emerge "revisionist" historians who find that Nixon was more sinned against than sinning. No president ever has been eager to proclaim misdeeds by his subordinates; what brought Nixon down were sins of omission, not of commission. Had he not been harassed out of office by a political strategy less scrupulous than any political ploy ever devised by the resourceful Nixon himself, he might have achieved a decent peace in southeastern Asia, a strong improvement of the American economy, and an enduring reputation for practical statecraft. We have not yet heard the last of him.

Chapter 14

Political Party and Political Principle

NOW IS THE TIME FOR ALL GOOD MEN TO COME TO THE AID OF THEIR PARTY

When Gerald Ford succeeded to the presidency in August, 1974, Carl Curtis was an Elder Statesman; although, unlike Lord Claverton in T. S. Eliot's play *The Elder Statesman*, Curtis lay under no compulsion to retire from public life unregretted. His influence in the Republican Party now stood at its height. The remaining years of his fourth term in the United States Senate would be spent principally in renewing that party, so battered by the Watergate troubles and the fall of President Nixon. Then he would retire from the Congress.

When January 3, 1979, came round, he would have served precisely forty years in the Congress. From 1789 to 1979, some 10,739 persons had been senators or representatives. Of all those, only twenty-one had been on Capitol Hill longer than Curtis had. At the time of his re-election in 1972, Curtis had resolved not to seek a fifth senatorial term: he regretted that some of his senatorial colleagues, at an advanced age, had endeavored to serve too long. Curtis had enjoyed his congressional years mightily—the lively debates on the floor, the examining and cross-examining of witnesses in committee rooms.* For four decades he had done what he wished to do, and what he could do best. Yet forty years would have been enough by 1979: it would not be well to run the risk of waning powers. In his remaining six years in the Capitol, Senator Curtis meant to strengthen his party.

Badly shaken by Watergate, the Republican Party needed to regain confidence in itself. President Gerald Ford, true, had

---

* If he had fought hard fights on the floor of House and Senate, Curtis had known also many amusing moments. One of them had to do with a "private bill" he had introduced in the Senate. A private bill is of no great importance to the Congress as a whole, but of high importance to the particular individuals or communities that need such helpful legislation. Congress always having large measures before it, it is not often easy to obtain swift passage of a private bill.

On this particular occasion, Curtis had pending in the Senate a private bill important to him; he did not expect it to be called up promptly. On the Senate floor, however, was a senator of the majority party, in good standing with the majority leader. This senator who held the floor now and again took too much strong drink; such was his condition at the moment. Addressing the chair, this tipsy senator called up a bill by number. He gave the wrong number—not at all the number of the bill he meant to call up.

Actually, the number cried out by the tipsy senator was the number of Carl Curtis' pet private bill. Senator Hruska, hurrying to Curtis' desk, told him, "That's your bill: you better do something about it." Curtis answered, referring to the tipsy senator on the floor, "Let him go; he's doing fine." Indeed he was, this unwitting ally on the floor: out of deference to him, the Curtis private bill was passed promptly, perhaps to the tipsy senator's later chagrin.

a steady hand, in part because of his long successful leading position in the House of Representatives. A president less intimate with the ways of the Congress would have found himself in very serious trouble with the exultant Democrats in Congress after President Nixon's fall.

Ford's principal instrument of control over Congress was the presidential prerogative of the veto. He employed the veto more frequently and successfully than had any president before him; and he employed it with a conservative purpose. Counting pocket vetoes, Ford turned to the veto power forty-two times during his two years and five months in the White House, the bills he thus undid ranging from agricultural conservation to duties on zinc ore. He prudently impeded a mass of legislation that would have enlarged the welfare state and yet more tremendously increased the national debt. Never before had he held any executive office, and until the calamity of Watergate he had entertained no expectation of obtaining the presidency of the United States. In his circumstances, he conducted himself with remarkable strength. Ford, like Curtis, had spent most of his adult life in Congress and throughout had been a pillar of the Republican Party. Although conservative in inclination, Ford was not so conspicuously conservative as Curtis; but then, who else was?*

According to the usual indices, Curtis had been the most

---

* The good-natured Gerald Ford tells a story about himself. While in the House, he rendered a service to a lady constituent for which she was mightily grateful; she insisted that when next he was in Michigan, he must speak at a meeting she would arrange. This came to pass. Introducing Congressman Ford, the lady constituent referred to him "as a great, great man." After the meeting ended, Ford and his wife, Betty, getting into their car, had the following exchange:

Gerald Ford: "I wonder how many great, great men there are in the country."

Betty Ford: "I don't know how many there are, but there is one less than you think."

consistently conservative Republican on Capitol Hill. During the latter portion of Curtis' years in office, two conservative political organizations had ranked members of Congress on the basis of their voting record: Americans for Constitutional Action and the American Conservative Union. Two organizations of the left had rated members of Congress from an opposed point of view: Americans for Democratic Action and the AFL-CIO Committee on Political Education. Carl Curtis' cumulative score, when he was ready to retire from the Congress, stood conservatively approved at ninety-six per cent with ACA and at ninety-five percent with ACU. He had been distinctly unpopular with the left-liberal ADA, which cumulatively accorded him a rating of merely 2.3 percent; COPE was slightly more generous with its five percent rating. His had been a conservatism of honest principle, Curtis trusted, and not merely the conservatism of those who growl, "Let me rest; I lie in possession."

Curtis had aspired to make his party one of intelligent and vigorous conservatism. In 1974, he found himself so situated that he could help to lead in this endeavor. Ten years earlier, the Goldwater campaign had inclined Republican preponderance toward conservative policies; neither the triumph of Lyndon Johnson nor the fall of Richard Nixon has reversed this Republican inclination. Curtis' influence in the Senate was substantial: during 1973 and 1974, he was the ranking Republican member of the Committee on Agriculture, and from 1975 to 1979 he would be the ranking Republican member of the Senate's Committee on Finance. Not meaning to stand for re-election in 1978, he would not have to expend his energies in that homestate campaigning which is necessary for senior incumbents who hope for yet another term. He was free during those remaining years to continue his vigorous fight against the welfare state and to energize the Republican party in the Senate.

Recent years had brought tribulations to Curtis—and not political disappointments only. In 1967, there had occurred the painful death of his lovely and talented daughter, Clara Mae Curtis Hopkins.* In 1970, Lois, his devoted wife and helpmate for nearly forty years, died. Solitary in Washington, and often struggling in what seemed a desperate resistance to the tide of events, Curtis was disheartened frequently, if unyielding. But in December, 1972, he married Mildred Genier Baker, strong and kind, sharing his interests, lending encouragement and assistance; it was as if providence had sent her. With Mildred beside him, Curtis was prepared in 1973 to do what he still might for party and for Republic.

It is honest loyalty to party that makes possible sound representative government. Edmund Burke enunciated that truth in the year 1770, in his *Thoughts on the Present Discontents*.

"When bad men combine," Burke tells us, "the good must associate; else they will fall, one by one, in an unpitied sacrifice in a contemptible struggle . . . Party is a body of men united for promoting by their joint endeavors the national interest upon some particular principle in which they are all agreed. For my part, I find it impossible to conceive that anyone believes in his own politics, or thinks them to be of any weight, who refuses to adopt the means of having them reduced into practice. It is the business of the speculative philosopher to mark the proper ends of government. It is the business of the politician, who is the philosopher in action, to find out proper means towards those ends, and to employ them with effect."

Being no speculative philosopher, Curtis at least could aspire to be a philosopher in action: an honest politician endeavoring to take long views. He subscribed to Burke's argument that an honest party must be attached to certain principles; and that it is better for a party to lose office than to retain office by abandoning those principles for the sake of "place." Burke's Rockingham Whigs had formed the first genuine party of well-defined principle in the modern era of representative government. Early in his career, Burke had taught the Rockinghams their principles. Might Curtis, late in his political life, remind the Republicans of their principles?

---

* Carl Curtis has a son, Carl T. (Tom) Curtis, Jr., and a granddaughter, the daughter of Clara Mae Hopkins, Denise Hopkins Kuhlman.

"Now is the time for all good men to come to the aid of their party," Cicero had declared, rallying the Optimates against demagogues and military commanders. (That Ciceronian line was better-omened than the 1964 paraphrase of Cicero, "Extremism in the defense of liberty . . .") Indeed the Grand Old Party of the Republicans distinctly required rallying, and there was no better place to begin than in the Senate. Though he had not the gifts of Cicero or of Burke, Carl Curtis of Nebraska would urge the good to associate.

On what principles should they associate? Primarily the principle of the preservation of the United States as the land of freedom, and of opportunity for the generations that were yet to come. There were other Republican senators who adhered to that principle. They must be brought together.

THE SENATE STEERING COMMITTEE

Ever since Carl Curtis first had taken his oath of office on Capitol Hill in 1939, there had been many occasions when it had seemed to him as if he had been a lonely combatant contending against a legion. This had been so especially when he had been endeavoring to withstand some bill calculated to enlarge what has been called, with sad perceptivity, "the evil benefits of the welfare state."

Sometimes, going to the Senate floor, Curtis had found one of his colleagues delivering an admirable speech, the result of much thought and research; yet not one of that senator's friendly colleagues would have received advance notice of the speech, nor would they be prepared to support the speaker. Speaking himself, now and again, on the budget, or excessive governmental regulation, or a tax bill illustrating John Marshall's dictum that the power to tax is the power to destroy, Curtis would find that not one other senator was present who would support his position. For want of collaboration, battles were being lost that might have been won. Clearly there existed, in 1974, an urgent need for an organization of conservative senators to plan together and to work together.

Already the House of Representatives possessed such an organization. Besides the staffs of the congressmen involved, the House group, called the House Republican Study Group, relied on their own group-staff of researchers and experts. This Group, a conservative league, had for its staff director Edwin J. Feulner, Jr., able and energetic, later the head of the Heritage Foundation in Washington.

Apart from the House Republican Study Group and its staff, a ferment was occurring among members of the staffs of conservatively-inclined senators. These Senate staffers, heartened by the House conservative staffers, developed parallel activities on the Senate side. The Senate staff-members met to listen to speakers and to discuss legislative programs. Most of them were young men and women opposed to the radical left (so noisy and violent during the previous decade); they were in accord with the legislative stands of conservative senators. Among them were people on the staffs of James Allen (Alabama Democrat), Dewey Bartlett (Oklahoma Republican), James Buckley (New York Republican), Robert Dole (Kansas Republican), James McClure (Idaho Republican), John Tower (Texas Republican), and Carl Curtis.

These staffers were eager for an organization corresponding to the House Study Group. Edwin Feulner offered them guidance. It was decided that Paul Weyrich of Curtis' staff and Richard Thompson of McClure's staff should confer with Senators Curtis and McClure to see what might be arranged. This meeting was to be held in Curtis' office.

Individually, the two staff aides had briefed their senators; Weyrich later remarked that the meeting "went like clockwork." Senator McClure was willing to organize the operation; but being a junior member of the Senate, McClure thought it inappropriate for him to assume the group's chairmanship. Curtis, though believing that someone should be involved who might be closer to the younger members, agreed to serve as chairman. Thus Curtis became chairman and McClure vice-chairman.

They agreed to invite several other senators to a private luncheon in Senator Curtis' suite to tell them about the idea. The first members of the group were Senators Buckley of New York, Cotton of New Hampshire, Dole of Kansas, Dominick of Colorado, Fannin of Arizona, Goldwater of Arizona, Hansen of Wyoming, Helms of North Carolina, Hruska of Nebraska, McClure of Idaho, Thurmond of South Carolina, and Curtis. Their first formal meeting was held on April 30, 1974, with Buckley, Cotton, Curtis, Fannin, Hansen, Helms, Hruska, McClure, and Thurmond present: all Republicans.

This group adopted the designation "Senate Steering Committee" rather than "Republican Study Committee", hoping that a few Democratic senators occasionally might participate in its activities. It was arranged to meet weekly, every senator bringing one staff aide; Curtis and McClure were confirmed as chairman and vice-chairman. The group agreed not to publicize its formation, preferring to let people gradually discover what had been formed. (The House Republican Study Group had been similarly reticent.)

Thereafter the Senate Steering Committee met every week at Senator Curtis' private room in the Capitol. Usually their agenda was limited to an announced subject and to an hour, so encouraging regular attendance of senators, each accompanied by one staff member.

The Steering Committee developed into a well-informed and effective group. Curtis and McClure engaged Tom Cantrell, from Senator Bartlett's staff, as the Committee's first executive director; he was succeeded by Margo Carlisle. The Steering Committee promptly became active in legislative contests on such subjects as the Consumer Protection Agency, the Cargo Preference Act, energy bills, budget measures, election statutes, appropriations bills. Often the Steering Committee would coordinate its activities closely with those of the House Republican Study people: a bicameral relationship new in conservative efforts.

The Steering Committee soon found that it could influence the course of legislation in the Senate. On particular proposals they were able to enlist on the Senate floor a good many senators of both parties, not members of the Steering Committee but on one or another issue favorable to the Steering Committee's position. The Senate Steering Committee began to win some important battles, ''promoting by their joint endeavors the national interest.''

THE REPUBLICAN CONFERENCE

Carl Curtis desired to become chairman of the Republican Conference, which is made up of all Republican senators; the chairman is its presiding officer. In the Conference, Republicans as a group take official action. The Conference's chairman possesses authority to appoint the standing committees of the Conference, of which two very important ones are the Committee on Policy and the Committee on Committees. The composition of these two committees can have strong effect on the direction which Republican senators take as a group. The Conference's chairman is elected by secret ballot.

In the Ninety-Third Congress, Senator Norris Cotton had been chairman of the Conference. Cotton had made it known that he might retire from the Senate at the end of the Ninety-Third Congress. Election of the Republican leader in the Senate, the Conference chairman, and other Republican officers would not occur until the Ninety-Fourth Congress should be convened in January, 1975.

But in seeking the Conference's chairmanship, Curtis applied the tactics he had learned in his Nebraska campaigns, uniformly successful. He asked Senator Cotton to let him know when and if he should make up his mind to retire. Having obtained that information, Curtis made personal calls on every one of the other thirty-six Republican senators, at their offices, not being satisfied with mentioning his aspiration casually in the Senate restaurant, or on the floor, or in the corridors. In these private meetings with his colleagues, Curtis first discussed Republican programs generally, and then said that he would like very much to serve as Conference chairman: he did not hint but plainly stated that he wished to be chairman. He thanked his colleagues for considering him, yet never sought a pledge for support, knowing that whoever his opponents might be, they would be fellow Republicans. He did not ask his colleagues to take public positions against some Republican friend who might be Curtis' competitor for the chairmanship.

When the new Congress was convened in January, 1975, the Republican senators met to organize. Curtis' name was placed in nomination for the Conference chairmanship by Senator Howard Baker, of Tennessee. Baker said that the Senate's Republican leadership should be composed of individuals representing the broad base of Republican opinion; he believed that the post of chairman of the Conference should go to a conservative, and that man should be Carl Curtis.

Senator Lowell Weicker, of Connecticut, spoke against Curtis' candidacy on the ground that Curtis had taken a strong and well-known position in defense of President Nixon. Ballots were distributed, and the senators voted. Curtis was elected chairman of the Repulican conference, twenty-three votes to fourteen.

Assuming the chairmanship, Curtis believed that he should serve all the Republican senators. He made sure that the views of every senator desiring to express himelf should be heard, though presiding with dispatch. He found high talent among the new senators and did everything possible to assign them to important activities.

Before his election as chairman, Curtis had lent his support to the movement for providing staff expertise for all new senators and for all senators who were not ranking members of a committee. He had sponsored also a rule in the Republican Conference that no senator could have his choice of a second committee until the place had been offered to each of the senators who had not secured a committee post of his first choice.

Curtis, with the staff director, made the Conference office a center for providing background material to Republican senators who confronted difficult issues. The Conference's staff analyzed and organized for the senators' use the great amount of valuable research that was available—chiefly from nongovernmental sources. Among the more important research projects undertaken were studies of the military balance of the United States and the Soviet Union; prospective energy supplies through the year 2000; how to double coal production by 1985, including problems of transportation and production; atomic energy production, including the plutonium breeder; gasohol; excessive governmental regulation of business; the fiscal impact of President Carter's major legislative proposals; the Hansen-Steiger and Roth-Kemp tax proposals. The Conference's staff drew up two reports of concern to black Americans, "Management and Affirmative Action in the Late '70s" and "Black Americans" (a handbook of social research); also a study of the impact of minimum-wage legislation upon young blacks.

When the Ninety-Fifth Congress was convened in January, 1977, Curtis was re-elected chairman of the Conference; no other candidate for that post was proposed. Long seasoned in opposition to Democratic presidents, Carl Curtis would spend the concluding two years of his congressional career in concerting an intelligent resistance to the administration of President Jimmy Carter.*

----

* In some matters, Mr. Carter has been too harshly blamed. He had campaigned for the presidency as an outsider who meant to change things in Washington. Much of the electorate had fancied that great problems might be resolved by putting such a professed adversary of the Washington Establishment into the Oval Office. But nothing is accomplished by a mere change of faces in the White House. Millions of voters soon regarded Carter as a failure. They forgot that the obesity from which the federal government suffers has been accumulated over half a century.

Of Senate Republicans in the Ninety-Fifth Congress, Howard Baker became minority leader; Ted Stevens, assistant leader; John Tower, chairman of the policy committee; Clifford Hansen, secretary; and Robert Packwood, chairman of the Republican senatorial campaign committee. Holders of these offices constitute the Republican leadership of the Senate.

During the Ninety-Fourth Congress, President Ford had held frequent meetings in the White House with this party leadership. Sometimes these gatherings had included the Democratic leadership of the Senate, and sometimes both Senate and House leadership. During the Ninety-Fifth Congress, when Mr. Carter was President, he sometimes included the Republican leadership from Senate and House in his White House meetings.

At such conferences, the President would discuss his programs and give his reasons for the positions he took. During the discussions, the President would be informed concerning the mood and inclination of the Congress, the prospects for his programs, and much else. At such consultations it is highly important what persons make up the leadership of either party. The general desire of the leaders participating is to give the President honest responses and objective answers; Curtis noticed, nevertheless, that a president tends to give much weight to the *personal* views of the individual senators and representatives present, knowing that where they lead, many of their colleagues will follow. Thus such conferring in the White House may exert strong effect upon such issues as defense, enlargement of governmental activities, labor policy, fiscal policy, taxation, and social-welfare measures.

Sometimes even a seasoned politician marvels that the government of the United States can be carried on at all: the American population is so vast, the extent of territory so great, the conflicts of interest often so powerful, the activities of the general government so multitudinous and multifarious. One source of order amidst this political confusion is the party Conferences—the function of which is little known to the general public—in the two houses of Congress.

TASKS FOR CONSERVATIVES: DOMESTIC CONCERNS

Curtis' long-run purpose in his work with the Senate Steering Committee and the Republican Conference was to establish within the Congress a body of opinion, conservatively inclined, that might take long views and plan for the restoration and the improvement of the American Republic. The two great American political parties usually have been vague in their principles and amorphous in their organization; their platforms are improvised hastily at national conventions concerned principally with the nomination of presidential candidates; neither party provides adequately for continuity of policy or for that research which is essential to the forming of sound policy. It was Curtis' hope that the congressional leadership, within the Republican Party at least (but sometimes transcending party), might come to remedy, in part, this lack of political forethought. The need of the nation by the later 'Seventies, after decades of foreign wars and domestic disturbances, was to settle down: to learn anew how to maintain the peace and to prosper under the Constitution. The American public yearned for stability and harmonious order. This undertaking is a conservative task. Curtis trusted that his successors in the Steering Committee and the Conference would carry on the labor of conservative reconstruction which Curtis and his colleagues had commenced in 1974 and 1975; and that for a good while to come Congress would be much influenced by these two groups, moved by a reflective and imaginative conservatism.

Curtis' short-run purpose with Steering Committee and Republican Conference was to prepare the way, especially in the Senate, for the coming of a conservative presidential administration, with which congressional conservatives could cooperate effectively. He foresaw that the popular movement toward conservative policies, which had been frustrated temporarily by Goldwater's defeat and had been expressed only partially in the Nixon administration, probably would be realized soon in large-scale electoral victories, carrying a conservative president to office. The Congress ought to be made ready, so far as possible, for able response to a conservative Executive Force. Two years after Curtis' retirement from Congress, as matters would turn out, his expectation of a national conservative resurgence would be fulfilled by the popular triumph of Ronald Reagan, carrying forty-three states and every region of the United States, and bringing with him a Republican majority in the Senate for the first time since 1954. In 1981, it became possible for Senate Steering Committee and Republican Conference in the Senate to exercise a dominant influence. But for the preparations made by Curtis and his colleagues in 1974 and 1975, Senate Republicans might have been quite unprepared for their abruptly-conferred responsibility of leading a senatorial majority.

And what a responsibility they confronted! The national debt had doubled since 1972, by the time Mr. Reagan entered upon the presidential office. Inflation had caused the costs of housing and of education to soar, and threatened the American standard of living. Interest on the national debt had reached a hundred billion dollars. Deficits were higher than had been predicted. Social Security disbursements were greater than receipts; the Trust Fund approached exhaustion. Medicare was in worse condition than was Social Security proper. Public finance had been Carl Curtis' principal field of committee work in both House and Senate, and Curtis knew that the American Republic could not continue longer to live extravagantly beyond its means. Nor was this financial conundrum the only domestic perplexity.

By the time of the conservative political victory that Curtis had expected, America confronted problems of such magnitude that they could not be alleviated by small economies here and there. The operations and scope of the federal government must be reduced to diminish the quantity of governmental regulation and to chart a course promoting initiative and opportunity. Like the general public, the Reagan administration underestimated the upward thrust in the cost of carrying on those features of the welfare state already entrenched. No longer was the problem simply one of resisting the growth of government and its increased costs; and the Reagan administration was not properly prepared to undertake a drastic retrenchment.

The laws of cause and effect have existed since the beginning of time: man did not invent them but discovered them. Wars have causes; inflation has causes; excessive political regulation has causes; so do oppressive taxation, the burden of interest on the national debt, the insolvency of financial institutions, devaluation of the currency, virtual bankruptcy of the Social Security system, and the ever-increasing dependence of much of the population on federal largesse. Centralization of power has causes. As Scripture puts it, "Whatsoever ye sow, that shall ye also reap."

Knowing the causes of our present discontents, American conservatives must address themselves to those causes, not to palliatives merely. A root cause of our troubles has been the appetite, encouraged by a certain breed of politicians, for voting huge "social benefits" to be paid for by future generations. "Democracy in the United States will endure until those in power learn that they can perpetuate themselves through taxation," Alexis de Tocqueville wrote a century and a half ago. Politicians of the past half-century were able to perpetuate themselves by a method still easier: the piling up of national debt.

In domestic concerns, the most urgent necessity for conservatives is to restrain and reduce "the evil benefits of the welfare state." A major stride toward this end would be the constitutional amendment, repeatedly proposed by Carl Curtis, to require—and enforce—balancing of the federal government's budget. It now appears conceivable that the several states will call a new constitutional convention for that express purpose, doing what the Congress has lacked the resolution to accomplish. Battles that had seemed lost sometimes clear the ground for ultimate victory.

"A 'welfare State' is one which accepts a responsibility to ensure the social well-being of all its citizens," Arthur Marwick writes: "the commanding heights, so to speak, of social well-being are income security (which ideally, as well as insurance or assistance to cover interruption of earnings, includes an economic policy directed towards the maintenance of a high level of employment), health, housing and environment, and education. Beyond the commanding heights a sophisticated welfare state may try to extend its domain to the romantic mist-capped peaks of culture, entertainment, morals and the manifold lesser problems of social relations and social welfare.''

In fine, the welfare state aspires to be all in all: either it grows into Leviathan, the totalist state, or else the monstrous creation collapses under its own weight. As Tocqueville knew, the total state is wholly inconsonant with the American democracy; should the welfare state be fully realized, the old American Republic would be transformed into a servile society. Political government of the constitutional pattern we have known in America is no adequate instrument to supply a whole nation with income security, health, housing and environment, and education—let alone culture, entertainment, and morals. For a welfare state to maintain itself, it must become a despotism, bureaucratically and harshly directing the whole of existence for everybody.

It is not impossible to extricate the American nation from the errors of the welfare state, which have been described in some detail in the preceding chapters of this book. Careful studies have been made of the means for redeeming ourselves, among them Martin Anderson's *Welfare: The Political Economy of Welfare Reform in the United States* (1978) and Roger Freeman's *The Wayward Welfare State* (1981). President Reagan, though much hampered by the powerful ''social welfare'' lobbies and by the timorousness or self-interest of many in the Congress, has made a beginning at such sweeping renewal of sound public policy; in his second term of office he may accomplish much more. Either conservatives must muster resolution and practical talents sufficient to lead us out of welfare-state bogs, or else the Republic will decay swiftly in its political virtues, its economy, and its morals.

TASKS FOR CONSERVATIVES:
DIPLOMATIC AND MILITARY CONCERNS

Despite its military power and its tremendous economic resources (tremendous, that is, except that a great part of those resources is pre-empted by the welfare state), the United States has been curiously feeble since the end of the Second World War, both in diplomacy and in military undertakings. Richard Nixon and others have referred to our age as "The American Century": if there is truth in that tag, American influence has grown despite our policies in foreign affairs, not because of those policies.

Carl Curtis, during those early years in the House when he endeavored to preserve America's neutrality in the contest of the European powers, was labelled an "isolationist." But it was not isolation for the United States that he sought, then or later: it was the preservation of peace. War comes when diplomacy has failed. Since World War II, or at least since the war in southeastern Asia, a great many liberals have become far more "isolationist" than Curtis ever was. Conservatives need to avoid both the extreme of frequent and grandiose intervention by force of arms, and the opposite extreme of a sentimental, left-leaning pacifism that neglects the national interest and would leave the United States naked before enemies.

During his forty congressional years, Curtis did not serve on the principal committees concerned with foreign affairs, but he was not silent on such questions. He was distressed by the frequent ineptness of American diplomacy. In 1943 and 1945 he introduced House bills for the founding of a United States Academy of Foreign Service. Addressing the House on July 7, 1943, Curtis inquired, "For many years, we have had a Military Academy and a Naval Academy. Why not have a West Point of Diplomacy? . . . We need a permanent and constructive foreign policy based on justice. We need an institution where such a policy will be evolved and where the young men and young women will receive the practical and technical training necessary to carry out that policy.''

The proposed Academy of Foreign Service, though endorsed by a number of newspapers and magazines during the Second World War, never was close to congressional approval: the outspoken opposition of Cordell Hull, Secretary of State, sufficed to give the quietus to Curtis' "West Point of Diplomacy." In no important respect has America's diplomatic service been improved during the past four decades. Its chief alteration, indeed, all that time, was Henry Wriston's "democratizing" of the State Department, so that practically all personnel above the clerical and janitorial levels were created Foreign Service Officers—virtually irremovable from office, however much they might blunder and whatever sympathies they might display for unpleasing ideologies.

George Kennan, in 1958, pointed out that the State Department was heavily overstaffed; that deadwood on the upper levels impeded the rise of more able young personnel; that Wriston's "reforms" had rewarded mediocrity of performance. When asked what might be done to improve the State Department, Kennan answered, "Only some form of catastrophe— natural disaster, financial collapse, or the atomic bomb— [could] dismantle it or reduce it to healthier dimensions." Possibly an Academy of Foreign Service, if founded in 1943, might have had beneficial results fifteen years later.

Yes, the failure of diplomacy brings on war, or the menace of war. During his congressional years, Curtis thought often about the Americans who died or were crippled in wars—in conflicts that a more astute diplomacy, backed by strength, might have averted. Some 292,000 American military men were killed in World War II, and more than 670,000 were seriously wounded; in the Korean War, 33,000 dead and 103,000 critically wounded; in the Vietnamese War, 47,000 slain, 155,000 badly wounded. From the eighteenth century through the twentieth, no American conflict was inevitable or irrepressible. The arts of diplomacy, properly exercised and timely applied, could have made the American War of Independence unnecessary (along the lines recommended by Burke in his great Speech on Conciliation); those arts could have prevented the War of 1812, the Mexican War, and even the Civil War. America entered World War I and World War II primarily because Presidents Wilson and Roosevelt so desired; the Korean and Vietnamese Wars came about, in considerable part, because of American illusions in diplomacy early in the game (particularly the notion that peace and stability might be secured in Asiatic countries by drawing arbitrary lines of partition between North and South, and making the North a Soviet sphere of influence). There come times when a nation must fight on a grand scale; but very commonly such crises occur, where major powers are concerned, in consequence of diplomatic and political miscalculations by one belligerent or the other—or, in most cases, miscalculations by both principal belligerents. A diplomatic stitch in time saves nine.

The repeated failures of American policy with respect to Cuba and Fidel Castro seemed to Curtis melancholy instances of the illusions that often pervaded the foreign policies of the United States. On August 24, 1961, recommending to the Senate a "pacific blockade" of Castro's Cuba, Carl Curtis said that "the people of Cuba are now under a tyranny more despotic and destructive of their freedom than they have ever before known—and the people of Cuba have known many. They truly are the victims of Communist aggression . . . Is the Monroe Doctrine still the doctrine of the United States? Is that doctrine still an instrument to keep the people of the Western Hemisphere free of foreign conquest?"

Sagacious diplomacy, backed by American strength, might have averted the triumph of Castro, or brought about his fall before he was thoroughly entrenched. For lack of stern, prudent action in time, a Cuban Marxist empire has arisen, with garrisons in Ethiopia and Angola and "advisers" to the guerrillas of Central America. Similarly, injudicious meddling with the affairs of El Salvador, by personnel of the State Department during the Carter administration, unhappily succeeded only in bringing on the civil war that the Carter people intended to prevent. And the foolish diplomacy of the Kennedy administration in Vietnam, culminating in the overthrow and murder of President Diem, led to the most humiliating defeat that the United States ever has experienced. It was the considered judgment of Carl Curtis that America required fewer Henry Cabot Lodges in high diplomatic posts, and more people who had been schooled in the curriculum and the internship Curtis specified in his bill for the Academy of Foreign Service.

Yet it will not do to blame the State Department or certain presidents wholly for American diplomatic and military reverses. Much of the fault has lain with members of Congress.

At the end of the Second World War, it became fashionable for senators and representatives to involve themselves in foreign affairs, whether or not they knew anything of foreign parts. This involvement justified their travel abroad at public expense. It gave them, and it continues to give their kind, material to use in speeches back home, delivered to Rotary or the Women's Literary Club. For some members of Congress, such "official" travel is a diversion from legislative duties—and a relief from half-suppressed worries about the financial consequences of certain measures for which they have voted recently.

After a few junkets abroad and after making the rounds of Washington's embassy parties, some of these senators and representatives constitute themselves experts in foreign policy. They second-guess the president and the secretary of state. They produce plans to solve all the internal problems of many countries. They may win favor with ethnic groups in the United States by backing American policies presumably beneficial to this or that client-state, but not at all beneficial to the American national interest. Such travel also gives such gentlemen media coverage not often accorded to a mere hard-working member of Congress who sticks to his last.

Carl Curtis refrained from such congressional peregrinations. Only in the closing years of his senatorship did he go abroad on political business; and then only when President Ford designated him, as a senior senator, to represent the President at presidential inaugurations in Nicaragua and Argentina. Also President Ford appointed Curtis head of a presidential mission to the People's Republic of China in the autumn of 1976. Unlike certain eminent politicians and publicists who returned from their first expedition to Communist China professing that they understood China even though they did not understand Chinese, Carl Curtis came back to Washington unenthusiastic for Chairman Mao's Cultural Revolution.

Conservatives, in Congress and out of it, need to turn their attention to the forming of diplomatic policies which will advance the national interest without entertaining the illusion that all the world should, or could, promptly model itself on American manners and institutions. America should not embark upon crusades "to make the world safe for democracy"; neither should America fancy that some miraculous SALT treaty would make the Soviet Union lamblike. American conservatives should bear in mind certain aphorisms of foreign policy, among them Theodore Roosevelt's admonition, "Never first shake your fist and then shake your finger." (At Vienna, during the Hungarian rising against the Communist government, when Henry Cabot Lodge met with Russian representatives to diminish the danger of a general outbreak of hostilities in central Europe, Lodge did precisely what Roosevelt cautioned against: in effect, first he shook his fist at the hard-bitten Soviet delegates, and then, intimidated, shook his finger at them.)

Over the past two centuries, conservative statesmen have been pre-eminently successful in many a crisis. Think of John Adams and John Quincy Adams, or of Disraeli and Salisbury in England. Sometimes, as in the instance of Winston Churchill, a nation turns to a man of conservative principles only at the eleventh hour, after disasters brought on by liberals' or socialists' or trimmers' presumption or negligence. One hopes that a prudently conservative foreign policy will take form soon in the United States; it is foolhardy to count on rescue at the last moment by some heroic genius previously rejected.

An intelligent and courageous diplomatic policy is more urgently required at this writing than ever before in the international concerns of the United States. A truly effective system of military defense—which need not mean a financially profligate system of defense—we dare not postpone for the sake of more federal aid to education, or to spend more money on housing projects. If defense is inadequate in the Atomic Age, soon there may be no welfare state—which might be quite endurable, were it not that neither would there survive any welfare or any state.

PROSPECTS
FOR THE REPUBLIC

Yet these great concerns, domestic and foreign, must be left to the rising generation of conservatives. On January 3, 1979, Carl Curtis departed from the Senate of the United States, undefeated, still in good health, nearly seventy-four years of age, having been a member of the Congress longer than had anyone else elected from the state of Nebraska.

As he descended the steps of the Capitol, he saw about him a Washington very different from the city he had entered first in 1938. Pennsylvania Avenue had become a place of dereliction; restoration had not commenced. Only a few minutes' stroll from Capitol Hill, one could enter the "Demilitarized Zone" of muggers and worse; not much farther were the streets devastated during the great riots of the sixties.

On either side of the Potomac rose huge office buildings to accommodate the chairborne command of federal civil servants, multiplied manyfold during Curtis' Washington decades. Old quarters like Foggy Bottom and the Watergate area were swept away for apartment complexes, the Kennedy Center, flashy hotels, and office space—always more office space. The traffic swirled endlessly round the Capitol. Some downtown churches were derelict; a massive classical public library, too. The old commercial district was down at heel; a good many of the little parks created by L'Enfant had sunk into scruffiness. Such was the legacy of the Johnsonian "Great Society," for Washington had suffered worst during those years. An uninformed traveler from Iceland or Burundi might have fancied that the city had been rather badly bombed not many years before.

Yet this urban decay had occurred gradually, like the decay of the old pattern of constitutional government and the old pattern of the American economy; and one grows accustomed to such decline and begins to think that nothing can be done to arrest it. "Change and decay in all around I see . . ."

And Washington, for all that, still retained charms. Curtis would practice law in the capital from 1979 through 1982, before going home to Nebraska. Washington! Curtis thought now and again of General Washington's words at the Constitutional Convention of 1787: "Perhaps no plan that we propose here will be approved by the people, but if to please the people we offer that which we ourselves disapprove, how can we afterwards defend our work? Let us raise a standard to which the wise and honest can repair; the event is in the hand of God." The city that bore George Washington's name might suffer the mutations to which nearly all great cities are exposed in our time; but George Washington's words at the Convention endured untarnished, uncorrupted, at the intersection of time and the timeless.

Those forty years in the capital had swept by swiftly for Carl Curtis, immersed as he had been in the pressing duties of office—not the least of which had been the labor of responding annually to many thousands of letters from his Nebraska constituents. As best he could, he had repaired to President Washington's standard; and now, as then, the event lay in the hand of God. Like Burke, Curtis might attest the rising generation.

What had he accomplished, those four decades? Chiefly, he had helped to hold the line against political and economic follies—a function distinctly conservative. Often Curtis had been beaten down, horse, foot, and dragoons, by the legislative hosts of the welfare state. But he had not skulked from the stricken field; and toward the end reinforcements had joined his little stalwart Republican band.

Then, too, there had been the consoling positive achievements, necessarily limited in number for a man who almost always had sat with the minority in the halls of Congress. The Individual Retirement Accounts were his legislative creation; he had succeeded in doing much toward the economic improvement of all the lands drained by the broad Missouri; and he had heartened and shored up his party in his closing years on the Hill. He had not voted against his informed conscience, nor done any political act of which he need be ashamed. Now let thy servant depart in peace.

The faces of presidents flickered before his mind's eye: Herbert Hoover, Franklin Roosevelt, Harry Truman, Dwight Eisenhower, Jack Kennedy, Lyndon Johnson, Richard Nixon, Gerald Ford, Jimmy Carter . . . And there came the faces of those many colleagues in House and Senate, most of them departed before him. He was grateful to them all: to his friends in Congress for their comradeship, to his adversaries in Congress for giving him a good enjoyable fight.

Carl Curtis, the courthouse janitor's son, had come a long way. He was grateful to the Nebraskans who had given him this long opportunity to fight the good fight in politics, the fight for honest party, the fight for enduring principle. Most Nebraskans had thought politically as Curtis had thought: he had been their genuine representative, with no need to trim his sails for political survival—not even on the touchy issues of Social Security. Curtis had entered the House, forty years earlier, a man of modest means; now he emerged from the Senate, that "rich men's club," a man of modest means. Presumably his effigy never would be erected in the Hall of Fame; but he had something better than that—men's knowledge, and his own, that Curtis never had been bought with a price. He thought of a Roman senator, a pillar of the high old Roman Republican virtue, old Cato—not that Carl Curtis was any Cato, or that he had in mind any Carthage to destroy. "I would rather have them ask, 'Why is there no monument to Cato?'" the stern Censor had said, "than to ask, 'Why is there one?'"

All in all, Curtis' years on the Hill had been happy years, because purposeful. Someone had written, "We must find our happiness in work, or not at all." Curtis had worked hard, and he thanked his constituents for having permitted him to labor hard and long, and especially he thanked God for having granted him that high opportunity to serve.

Now Carl Curtis, the courthouse janitor's son from Minden, was on his way out. He supposed he had done, his limited talents considered, what he had been put into the world to do; "marshalled by a divine tactic," he had made his little contribution to the civil social order here below. But what of the

Republic?

In the procession of nations, the United States is young—only two centuries old, or, if one reaches back to the very beginnings in this continent, three and a half centuries. Most great civilizations endure a thousand years at least; so presumably, barring accidents, the American Republic will live for centuries more.

But what sort of life will this be? Will America last as a republic in name merely? Will it sink into what Tocqueville called "democratic despotism"? Will an American proletariat grow in numbers, and the number of independent Americans as steadily shrink? Will the country impoverish itself through ruinous taxation and crushing public debt? Will the morals of most Americans be the morals of Bobby Baker's Carousel Motel? Will American voluntary community be supplanted by involuntary collectivism? Will America continue to resist effectually the "armed doctrine" of the Soviet Union? Will life in this land be worth living? Will Americans, most of them, be permitted to retain even the consolations of religion?

Nobody can answer those questions, the event being in the hand of God. It is forbidden to Christians to endeavor to pry into futurity—to "describe the horoscope, haruspicate or scry . . . riddle the inevitable with playing cards, fiddle with pentagrams or barbituric acids." "Ye unborn ages, crowd not on my soul." For what we call history is no impersonal, inexorable, ineluctable force: history is merely the written record of what has been done in the past. You and we make history. What is to come, you and we will create, or at least we will fulfill unwittingly whatever providence means us to accomplish, our intentions being good. It is not well that we should know the whole future of the Republic, any more than we could endure, any one of us, full knowledge of one's own future. If any man were given certain knowledge of precisely how and where and when he were destined to die, years in advance of that fatal event, either he would give himself up to despair as the time approached, or he would engage in futile struggles to break the chain of fate. Such a prophecy might work its own fulfillment.

So it is with nations. More than once, Carl Curtis had pointed out that the gravest disservice to the American people which a responsible man or woman might perform would be to magnify our public problems so that we should give up the struggle in despair. If most people come to believe that the American Republic must fall—why, fall it will.

But if most people, or even a sizeable saving remnant of the people, continue to believe that personal and public renewal remain possible, and may be achieved through intelligent activity, then the Republic is restored. The dull domination of the welfare state is not inevitable; not if we bestir ourselves against its failings. The corruption of American politics is not inevitable, nor of American morals generally—not if we begin afresh to think of virtue, and to teach it. The triumph of fanatic ideology, in its Communist form or in some other aspect, is not inevitable—not if, keeping our wits about us, we remind ourselves that politics is the art of the possible.

Carl Curtis entered the Congress with such oldfangled notions in his head, and departed from the Congress with those notions still in his head. Perhaps, as was said of the restored Bourbons, he had learned nothing and forgotten nothing. But also it is quite possible that some truths endure so long as human nature endures; and that if you contrive to get hold of such a truth, by all means keep it safe and do not open your ears to every wind of doctrine. The open mind, in the sense of the mind without principles, is the empty and uncertain mind.

The Republic, friends, will be what you make it. Its form and direction will be determined in part by the character of the men and women whom you send to the Congress of the United States; have an eye to them, but choose them as your genuine representatives, not as mere bound delegates. And have an eye to your own moral habits: for Tocqueville discerned that the relative success of the American democracy is produced not by circumstances, not by laws, but by *mores*: that is, by good moral habits, customs, beliefs.

If you embark in your small boat upon the turbulent waters of the civil social order, soon you may find yourself contending against the running tide of corruption, triviality, and indifference. Yet life is for action: were there no tide to oppose, the voyage would be boring. And after hours of rowing against an ebb tide, presently you may find the tide's resistance diminished; and in time you may be able to take the tide at its flood, which will bear you triumphantly into harbor. It may be so with those who would repair to General Washington's standard.

A CURTIS CHRONOLOGY

March 15, 1905: Carl T. Curtis is born on a farm in Kearney County, Nebraska.

1911—1923: Curtis attends rural School District No. 48 and the Minden public schools.

1923: Curtis graduates from Minden High School and for the following year teaches in the Danbury, Nebraska, public schools.

1924—1930: Curtis attends Nebraska Wesleyan University at Lincoln, Nebraska, and teaches grades nine and ten in a rural Kearney County school; later he is made principal of the Minden elementary school. Studies law in the office of Charles A. Chappel.

1930: Curtis is admitted to the Nebraska bar, and in the same year is elected county attorney of Kearney County.

1931: Curtis marries Lois Wylie-Atwater, of Minden.

1936: Curtis' adopted daughter Claramae is born.

1938: While practicing law, Curtis files as a candidate for the U.S. House of Representatives; in August, he obtains the Republican nomination; in November, he is elected.

1939: Curtis is sworn in as member of the House of Representatives, 76th Congress, from the Fourth Congressional District of Nebraska. His maiden speech deplores America's drift toward war; his second speech laments the loss of life in the Republican River flood, and asks for flood-control assistance for Nebraska.

Autumn, 1939: The European War begins; Curtis opposes amendment of the Neutrality Act.

December, 1939: The Curtis' second adopted child, Carl T. Curtis, Jr., is born.

Summer, 1940: France falls, and Churchill appeals to the United States for aid; Curtis continues to oppose intervention.

November, 1940: Curtis is elected to his second term in the House; Roosevelt defeats Willkie in the presidential contest.

March, 1941: "Lend-Lease," opposed by Curtis, is enacted by Congress.

August, 1941: On Columbia radio network, Curtis speaks against involvement in the European conflict; Selective Service is extended.

December, 1941: The United States enters World War II.

April, 1942: Curtis introduces a bill prohibiting the requirement that workers must be union members to be employed in defense plants.

November, 1942: Curtis is elected to his third term in the House, this time from Nebraska's First Congressional District.

May, 1943: Curtis introduces the resolution that results in the Pick-Sloan plan for flood control and irrigation in the Missouri Basin.

April, 1944: The federal government seizes Montgomery Ward's Chicago property; Curtis opposes the action, and later participates in the House Select Committee's investigation of that action.

June, 1944: The Allied invasion of German-dominated Europe begins.

November, 1944: Curtis is re-elected, for the fourth time, to the House of Representatives; Franklin Roosevelt is elected to his final presidential term.

December, 1944: Pick-Sloan bill is signed by the president; Curtis continues promotion of Missouri Basin development.

January, 1945: Curtis is appointed to the House's Committee on Ways and Means.

April, 1945: Franklin Roosevelt dies; Harry S. Truman succeeds to the presidency.

May, 1945: Germany surrenders.

August, 1945: Japan capitulates.

1946: Congress passes the first major public-housing bill and the Full Employment bill, both opposed by Curtis. The Cold War begins. In November, Curtis is re-elected to his fifth term in the House.

1947: Congress passes the Taft-Hartley Act. Curtis is active in the Committee on Ways and Means; he becomes a member of the Budget Committee.

1948: The Berlin airlift begins in June. Curtis introduces a bill, later enacted, permitting farmers to deduct from income taxes the costs of soil and water conservation. In November, he is elected to his sixth term in the House; Truman is elected president.

1949: NATO is established. Curtis expresses his opposition to the growth of the welfare state; he opposes the Housing Act of 1949.

1950: The Korean War begins in June. Curtis proposes to Congress restraint upon expansion of federal activities, a policy of returning functions to state governments, and a constitutional limitation upon federal expenditures. He is elected to his seventh term in the House.

1951: In the 82nd Congress, Curtis introduces a constitutional amendment requiring a balanced budget. Investigation of Internal Revenue scandals begins; Curtis is a member of the Subcommittee of the Ways and Means Committee, charged with this task.

1952: The Korean War is at its height; Curtis advocates investigation of Communist subversion. Curtis is elected to his eighth term in the House; Roman Hruska, later to work closely with Curtis, also is elected to the House from Nebraska; Eisenhower is elected president.

1953: The Korean War ends. Curtis serves as chairman of the Ways and Means Committee's Subcommittee investigating the Social Security system, and recommends large changes.

1954: Curtis' Subcommittee releases its staff report exposing failures in the Social Security system. Eisenhower recommends that Social Security be extended to the self-employed and to state and local governmental employees. Curtis is elected senator from Nebraska.

1955: Curtis is appointed to the Senate Committee on Rules and Administration, and to the Committee on the Post Office and Civil Service. He introduces a bill to consolidate into one bill all general appropriation bills; also introduces a bill to establish a commission on industrial uses of agricultural products, eventually adopted.

1956: Hungarian and Suez crises. Dwight Eisenhower is reelected president.

1957: Curtis is appointed to the Senate's Committee on Government Operations, and to that committee's Permanent Subcommittee on Investigations. (This Subcommittee was to investigate labor racketeering, and its members were to serve on the Select Committee on the Investigation of Labor and Management Relations.) Also he is appointed to the Joint Committee on Libraries. He becomes the ranking minority member of the Committee on Rules and Administration.

1958: The Select Committee on the Investigation of Labor and Management Relations investigate the Kohler strike improper practices of the Teamsters and the UAW, and other labor disputes and abuses; Curtis is very active on the Select Committee's investigations.

1959: Curtis is appointed to the Senate's Committee on Finance. During the year, he introduces a constitutional amendment for balancing the budget, a proposal to permit the president to reduce or eliminate items from appropriation bills; an amendment to the Keogh Bill to provide for individual retirement savings; a bill to ban the secondary boycott (incorporated in the Landrum-Griffin Act, a piece of legislation resulting in large part from the Select Committee's work); and other legislative proposals of importance.

1960: Curtis is elected to a second term in the Senate; J. F. Kennedy is elected president.

1961: Curtis again introduces a proposal for a budget-balancing constitutional amendment. The Bay of Pigs expedition fails, and problems with Communist states increase.

1962: The Permanent Investigating Subcommittee investigates the Billie Sol Estes scandals; Curtis is active in this. He continues to advocate income-tax provisions of the sort that later become the Individual Retirement Act.

1963: President Kennedy is murdered; Lyndon Johnson succeeds to the presidency. The Senate's investigation of the Bobby Baker scandals begins; Curtis is active on that committee. He is appointed to the Senate Committee on Aeronautical and Space Sciences, and the Joint Committee on Atomic Energy; he continues to serve on committees to which he had been appointed earlier.

1964: Barry Goldwater obtains the Republican presidential nomination; Curtis is Goldwater's floor manager at the Republican National Convention. Lyndon Johnson defeats Goldwater in November.

1965: Elementary and Secondary Educational Act passed by Congress; Medicare and Medicaid added to Social Security system; Curtis opposes and speaks against these "Great Society" undertakings. Curtis denounces the majority report of the Senate's investigation of Bobby Baker. More American Troops enter the conflict in Vietnam.

1966: Curtis opposes the Johnson administration's housing bills. He is elected to the Senate for the third time.

1967: Curtis supports the Percy amendment to the housing programs. His daughter Claramae Curtis Hopkins dies.

1968: Richard Nixon is elected president.

1969: Curtis is appointed to the Senate's Committee on Agriculture and Forestry; he continues to serve on Space, Finance, Rules, and Atomic Energy Committees.

1970: Curtis becomes ranking Republican member of the Senate's Committee on Space. His wife Lois dies.

1971: Curtis introduces an Individual Retirement proposal in the form finally adopted. He is appointed to the Joint Committee on Internal Revenue Taxation.

1972: Congress adopts sharing of federal revenues. The Watergate burglary occurs. Curtis is elected to the Senate for the fourth time; President Nixon is re-elected. Curtis marries Mildred Genier Baker.

1973: Curtis is appointed to the Senate's Select Committee on Standards and Conduct; he becomes the ranking Republican member of the Committee on Agriculture. Congress passes a bill regulating private pensions, which includes the Curtis IRA plan, helping the self-employed and small-business people to save.

1974: The Senate Steering Committee is organized; Curtis is made chairman. On the floor of the Senate, he attacks the report of the Joint Committee on Internal Revenue Taxation concerning President Nixon's income-tax returns. In August, Richard Nixon resigns the presidency.

1975: Curtis is elected chairman of the Senate's Republican Conference. He becomes ranking Republican member of the Committee on Finance.

1976: President Ford appoints Curtis to head the presidential mission to the People's Republic of China.

1977: Curtis is re-elected chairman of the Republican Conference. He writes his devotional book *To Remind*.

1978: Inflation and fiscal difficulties increase during the Carter administration.

1979: Carl Curtis retires from the Senate on January 3, having served twenty-four years in that house and sixteen in the House of Representatives. He engages in practice of the law in Washington.

1980: Ronald Reagan is elected president in a resurgence of conservatism.

1981: The United States is increasingly involved in the struggle against Marxist guerrillas in El Salvador.

1982: *To Remind* is published.

1983: In January, Carl and Mildred Curtis leave Washington to settle in Lincoln, Nebraska.

BIBLIOGRAPHICAL NOTES

Personal Papers

The Carl T. Curtis collection has been given to the Historical Society of the State of Nebraska, at Lincoln. This collection contains more than one hundred and sixty cartons of correspondence, papers, and files accumulated over the forty-year period during which Curtis was first a member of the House of Representatives and then a United States senator. Marvin F. Kivett, director of the Historical Society, and his staff have made all of these documents available to scholars. Among the papers are the following—

1. A complete collection of scrapbooks for the Curtis years, compiled by Curtis' staff;

2. Legislative files which give the legislative history of every proposal introduced by Curtis. The progress or lack of action on a bill is traced; this is a valuable source for persons interested in the workings of Congress;

3. Hundreds of photographs of presidents, members of Congress, important and ephemeral events: a cross-section of America over four decades;

4. Separate files containing information of peculiar interest, such as the Bobby Baker case, Social Security, IRA, the Watergate affair, Missouri Basin flood control, Curtis's speeches. The largest single political file is that concerning Goldwater's presidential campaign in 1964.

Memorabilia

Harold Warp's evocative Pioneer Village is situated at Minden, Nebraska, Curtis's home town. Among the exhibits of Nebraska's heritage—a railroad station, a sod house, and an early church are included—is one dedicated to Carl Curtis. There are several glass cases containing Curtis artifacts: election posters, buttons, campaign publications, and a full-size replica of his Washington office.

Publications Cited

There are listed below merely books and periodical articles mentioned in the text, with a few additional references; no attempt is made to offer a general bibliography of forty years of political history.

BIBLIOGRAPHY

Abbazia, Patrick. *Mr. Roosevelt's Navy: the Private War of the U.S. Atlantic Fleet, 1939-1942.* Annapolis: Naval Institute Press, 1975.

Anderson, Martin. *The Federal Bulldozer: a Cultural Analysis of Urban Renewal, 1940-1962.* Cambridge, Mass.: MIT Press, 1964.

Anderson, Martin. *Welfare: the Political Economy of Welfare Reform in the United States.* Stanford, Cal.: Hoover Institution, 1978.

Aucoin, James. *Water in Nebraska: Use, Politics, Policies.* Lincoln: University of Nebraska Press, 1984.

Baker, Robert, with King, Larry L. *Wheeling and Dealing.* New York: Norton, 1978.

Barnard, Roy, and Smith, James. "Carl Curtis: Some Memories of Seven Presidents," *Platte Valley Review,* Spring, 1982.

Benton, Thomas H. *Thirty Years' View.* 2 vols. New York: D. Appleton, 1854-55.

Blaine, James G. *Twenty Years of Congress.* 2 vols. Norwich, Conn.: Henry Bill Company, 1884-86.

Brooks, Warren T. *The Economy in Mind.* New York: University Books, 1982.

Budget of the U.S. Government, Fiscal Year 1984, OBM Revision, January, 1984. Washington: U.S. Government Printing Office, 1984.

Burns, James MacGregor. *Roosevelt: the Lion and the Fox.* New York: Harcourt, Brace, 1956.

Burns, James MacGregor. *Roosevelt: the Soldier of Fortune.* New York: Harcourt Brace Jovanovich, 1970.

Caro, Robert A. *The Years of Lyndon Johnson: the Path to Power.* New York: Alfred Knopf, 1982.

Chriss, N.C. "Lyndon Johnson Gets His Library," *The Nation,* June 7, 1971.

Cole, Wayne S. *Senator Gerald P. Nye and American Foreign Relations.* Minneapolis: University of Minnesota Press, 1962.

Curtis, Carl T. *To Remind.* Henderson, Nebraska, 1982.

Divine, Robert A. *The Illusion of Neutrality.* Chicago: Quadrangle Books, 1962.

Doenecke, Justus D. *Not to the Swift: the Old Isolationists in the Cold War.* Lewisburg, Pa.: Bucknell University Press, 1979.

Estes, Pam. *Billie Sol: King of Texas Wheeler-Dealers*. Abilene, Texas: Noble Craft Books, 1983.

Federal Writers' Project. *Nebraska: a Guide to the Cornhusker State*. Lincoln: University of Nebraska Press, 1979.

Feulner, Edwin J., Jr. *Conservatives Stalk the House: The Republican Study Committee, 1970-1983*. Ottawa, Ill.: Green Hill Publishers, 1983.

Freeman, Roger A. *The Wayward Welfare State*. Stanford, Cal.: Hoover Institution, 1981.

Goldwater, Barry M. *The Conscience of a Conservative*. New York: Hillman Books, 1960.

Goldwater, Barry M. *With No Apologies: the Personal and Political Memoirs of United States Senator Barry. M. Goldwater*. New York: Alfred Knopf, 1979.

Hoffman, Ross J.S., and Levack, Paul. *Burke's Politics*. New York: Alfred Knopf, 1949.

Ickes, Harold L. *The Secret Diary of Harold L. Ickes*. 3 vols. New York: Simon and Schuster, 1953-54.

Jacobs, Jane. *The Death and Life of Great American Cities*. New York: Random House, 1961.

Johnson, Lyndon. *The Vantage Point: Perspectives of the Presidency, 1963-69*. New York: Holt, Rinehart, and Winston, 1971.

Johnson, Paul. *Modern Times: the World from the Twenties to the Eighties*. New York: Harper and Row, 1983.

Kirk, Russell. *The Conservative Mind, from Burke to Eliot*. Sixth revised edition. Chicago: Regnery Gateway, 1978.

Kirk, Russell. *John Randolph of Roanoke*. Third edition. Indianapolis: Liberty Press, 1978.

Kirk, Russell, and McClellan, James. *The Political Principles of Robert A. Taft*. New York: Fleet, 1967.

Kissinger, Henry. *White House Years*. Boston: Little, Brown, 1979.

Kissinger, Henry. *Years of Upheaval*. Boston: Little Brown, 1982.

Lewis, Wyndham. *Rotting Hill*. Chicago: Henry Regnery, 1952.

Marwick, Arthur. *Britain in the Century of Total War: War, Peace, and Social Change, 1900-1967*. Boston: Little, Brown, 1968.

Meadows, Edward. "Peter Grace Knows 2,478 Ways to Cut the Deficit," *National Review*, March 9, 1984.

Moley, Raymond, with Rosen, Elliot A. *The First New Deal*. New York: Harcourt, Brace & World, 1966.

Moley, Raymond. "Irresponsible Power," *Newsweek*, April 28, 1958.

Morris, Charles R. *A Time of Passion: America, 1960-1980*. New York: Harper and Row, 1984.

Neutrality Act of 1939, House Report 1475, 76th Congress, 2d Session. Washington: U.S. Government Printing Office, 1939.

Neutrality Act of 1939, Senate Report No. 1155, 76th Congress, 2d Session. Washington: U.S. Government Printing Office, 1939.

Nicoll, Bruce H., and Savery, Gilbert M. *Nebraska: a Pictorial History*. Lincoln: University of Nebraska Press, 1975.

Nixon, Richard M. *The Memoirs of Richard Nixon*. 2 vols. New York: Warren, 1979.

Olson, James C. *History of Nebraska*. Lincoln: University of Nebraska Press, 1966.

Osborne, John. "With Cheops in Texas," *The New Republic*, June, 1971.

Palffy, John (ed.). *How to Slash $119 Billion from the Deficit*. Washington: The Heritage Foundation, 1984.

Patterson, J.T. *Congressional Conservatives and the New Deal*. Lexington, Ky.: University of Kentucky Press, 1967.

Patterson, J.T. *Mr. Republican: a Biography of Robert A. Taft*. Boston: Houghton Mifflin, 1972.

Petro, Sylvester. *The Kohler Strike*. Chicago: Henry Regnery, 1961.

Petro, Sylvester. *Power Unlimited: the Corruption of Union Leadership*. New York: Ronald Press, 1959.

Pound, Roscoe. "Legal Immunities of Labor Unions," reprinted in *Labor Unions and Public Policy*. Washington: American Enterprise Institute, 1958.

Schlesinger, Arthur M., Jr. *The Imperial Presidency*. Boston: Houghton Mifflin, 1973.

Smith, James. "Carl Curtis: Some Early Memories," *Platte Valley Review*, April, 1980.

Stans, Maurice. *The Terrors of Justice*. New York: Everest House, 1978.

Stromer, Marvin E. *The Making of a Political Leader: Kenneth S. Wherry and the U.S. Senate*. Lincoln: University of Nebraska Press, 1969.

Taylor, A.J.P. *English History, 1914-1945*. Oxford: Oxford University Press, 1965.

Tocqueville, Alexis de. *Democracy in America*. Edited by J.P. Mayer. Garden City, New York: Doubleday, 1969.

White, F. Clifton. *Suite 3505: the Story of the Draft-Goldwater Movement*. New Rochelle, N.Y.: Arlington House, 1967.

White, Graham, and Maze, John. *Harold Ickes of the New Deal: His Private Life and Public Career*. Cambridge, Mass.: Harvard University Press, 1985.

White, Theodore H. *The Making of the President*. Volumes for the years 1960, 1964, 1968, and 1972. New York: Atheneum, 1961, 1965, 1969, 1973.

INDEX